Praise for *So you want to b*

‘Those wanting to be leaders of our key in ... and in this collection the stories and critiques of those who speak from long, hard experience as well as those with a bold new vision for a free and confident nation making its contribution in a troubled but scintillating world. These are grounded accounts of refreshing hope which will inspire the next generation of Australia’s leaders.’
Fr Frank Brennan SJ AO: human rights lawyer

‘Philip Crisp’s *So you want to be a leader* is a valuable tool for any aspiring leader who has a thirst for discovery and a preparedness to refine leadership skills by drawing on the wisdom of their peers.’
The Hon. Sussan Ley MP: Commonwealth Minister for Health

‘Experience is a brilliant teacher and *So you want to be a leader* is a very fine collection of 36 essays from distinguished Australians generously offering us the benefit of their wide experience. There is much to learn from this treasure trove of wisdom. I highly recommend it for all aspiring leaders.’
Andrew Catsaras: independent political analyst

‘Against the bleak backdrop of today’s public discourse, *So you want to be a leader* comes as welcome relief … [It] is an invaluable guide and source of deep nourishment for young leaders “before”, as Philip Crisp puts it, “they become too busy or battle-scarred”. Ultimately, it holds a promise – a great promise – of who we could be if led by our better angels; and how you, dear reader, might help us get there. And soon.’
Akram Azimi: Young Australian of the Year 2013

‘Philip Crisp’s *So you want to be a leader* is a most timely and comprehensive analysis of leadership and the making of good leaders – an issue that bedevils our age of individualism and doubt. The breadth of experience in the contributors alone makes it compulsory reading.’
Anne Henderson AM: political historian

‘Leadership cannot be taught, but it can be learned. *So you want to be a leader* adds substantially to the most important aspect of learning leadership – reflection on the story of others. This book is a journey of discovery for young readers and aspiring leaders. We don’t realise we are learning leadership when we are, but the power is in the story. These stories of leadership are informed by personal qualities, character and experience. But at its heart is *vision* which more than anything else differentiates leadership from management. We can all be better and we can all choose to be leaders – striving to be so enriches all of us, as will these essays.'

The Hon. Dr Brendan Nelson: Director, Australian War Memorial; federal Opposition leader 2007-08

'Young or old, experienced or otherwise in public life, Philip Crisp's book is a "must read" for any aspiring leader. It provides a treasure trove of invaluable insights into effective leadership. In fact, at a time of increasing disenchantment with Australia's political elite, some of our own so-called "leaders" could do worse than pick up a copy. Open the book at any chapter and you'll find something worthwhile.'

Laurie Wilson: freelance journalist and consultant; President, National Press Club of Australia

'Whilst there appears to be no shortage of people aspiring to be leaders, we never appear to have enough who are generally considered to be "good". Philip Crisp has done us all an enormous favour by assembling not only a first class and diverse group of leaders, but ones who are willing to be frank, confronting and not merely offering the usual "leadership" platitudes. None of us are too young (or "green") let alone too old (or "past it"!) to take up the calling of leadership. All that is required is the right motivation and a desire to keep learning, especially through the experiences of others.'

Simon McKeon AO: Chairman, CSIRO; Australian of the Year 2011

'There is no magic formula for successful leadership. It is true that some people are born leaders while others acquire leadership skills along the way, but every aspiring leader needs to learn from the experience, successes, mistakes and wisdom of others. These are the life lessons you will find in this book.'

Prof. Kerryn Phelps AM: writer on health issues; President, Australian Medical Association 2000-03

'In the maelstrom of a public life that can be dogged by short-termism and a culture of tribal opposition, this inspirational and wise collection of essays will help leaders remain centred, reflective and nimble.'

Prof. Penny Sackett: astronomer and science educator; Chief Scientist of Australia 2008-11

More reviews at: www.soyouwanttobealeader.com.au

SO YOU WANT TO BE A LEADER

PHILIP CRISP

HYBRID
PUBLISHERS

Published by Hybrid Publishers

Melbourne Victoria Australia

First published 2015

National Library of Australia Cataloguing-in-Publication entry
Creator: Crisp, Philip, editor.
Title: So you want to be a leader : influential people reveal how to succeed in public life / Philip Crisp.

ISBN: 9781925000986 (paperback)

Subjects: Leadership.
Civic leaders – Australia.

Dewey Number: 303.34

Typeset in Baskerville 11.5/14

Cover design: Gittus Graphics ©

Printed in Australia by McPherson's Printing Group

FOREWORD

Dr John Hewson AM

The term 'leadership' defies specific definition and complete explanation, yet most know leadership when they see, or experience it.

The academic literature abounds with competing theories and attempts at explanation. The popular media is saturated with leadership anecdotes and examples. There are a myriad of academic and vocational courses offering to instruct/educate on leadership.

In my view there are a number of elements that are important to any understanding of leadership.

Leadership obviously depends on the individual(s) and their circumstances and, essentially, how they respond. Sometimes leadership is planned. At other times it's just accidental. Some are elected or appointed to lead, which they may or may not do successfully. Others simply emerge as leaders by responding effectively to circumstances and challenges as they unfold.

Leadership is defined by outcomes, not attributes; it's about influence, not power or authority; it's about passion, not position; it may be driven by fear or opportunity; it is a potent combination of strategy and character. As Geoff Gallop says in his essay, 'leadership is personal'.

Leaders can be incremental or disruptive; some are extroverts, and some are introverts. The clear majority of leaders (put as high as 90 per cent) are incremental, focused on maintaining the stability of the organisation while attempting to develop and grow over time. A disruptive leader works to break down the fundamental structure of things, to create major, noticeable change.

While the extroverts are easy to pick, some of the greatest leaders are introverts – the likes of Abraham Lincoln, Warren Buffet, Bill Gates, Rosa Parks, Larry Page, Steven Spielberg and Steve Wozniak.

Much of the literature about *business* leadership has emphasised a distinction between qualities traditionally associated with leadership – such as technical skills, intelligence, toughness, determination, and vision – and what is referred to as 'emotional intelligence', claimed as the sine qua non of leadership, which includes self-awareness, self-regulation, motivation, empathy and social skill. I would add integrity, humour, the empowering of others, and probably even more.

Two quite influential views on business leadership are from Jack Welch, ex-CEO of General Electric:

> Before you are a leader, success is all about growing yourself. When you become a leader, success is all about growing others

and Bill Gates, ex-CEO of Microsoft:

> As we look ahead into the next century, leaders will be those who empower others.

There are similar assessments of the ingredients for successful *political* leadership. In my experience, skills and experience pre-politics don't translate easily into a successful political career. So much depends on how you adapt and handle yourself in what are difficult, dynamic and, mostly, unaccustomed, evolving circumstances.

With the recent death of ex-Prime Minister Gough Whitlam I was reminded of an occasion shortly after his appointment as ambassador to UNESCO when he was asked by a journalist what qualifications he had for the job; he replied, with a withering look, 'Young lady, neither you nor I have the time for that long an interview'.

However, I would draw your attention to two assessments of political leadership that I believe are instructive. First, Harvard Professor J K Galbraith who said:

> All of the great leaders have had one characteristic in common: it was the willingness to confront unequivocally the major anxiety of their people in their time. This, and not much else, is the essence of leadership.

And Harry S Truman:

> Men [read people] make history and not the other way around. In periods where there is no leadership, society stands still. Progress occurs when courageous, skillful leaders seize the opportunity to change things for the better.

However, there is no magic mix of personal characteristics that will make one a leader; there is no cookbook by which leaders can be manufactured, although it is possible to learn from the relevant experiences of others, to hopefully improve one's capacity to lead.

All this is precisely why a volume such as this is so valuable, documenting a broad cross-section of leadership experiences, and of opinions about leadership – views from all levels and strata of our society.

The book includes the reflections of leaders from politics, the public service, business (both for and not-for-profit, public and private), and a range of commentators, thinkers, advisers and activists. It spans experiences from many fields, from science, through business, human rights, to politics, and many in between.

Clearly, with leadership, one size does not fit all. Indeed, it may be that the differences are at least as important as the similarities.

The book has prompted me to reflect anew on my own experiences as a political leader. It is suggested widely that virtually every politician aspires to lead – the so-called 'baton in the knapsack'. I certainly didn't enter politics with that aspiration. My objective was a more modest one, namely to become Treasurer – I thought it would be a good thing to have a professional economist in that role. This is where, and how, I thought that I could make a difference.

However, after stints as Shadow Finance Minister under Howard and Shadow Treasurer under Peacock, and in the aftermath of Peacock's election loss in 1990, I reluctantly stood for the leadership of the Liberal Party and the Federal Opposition, simply because I couldn't contemplate yet another round of Howard/Peacock leadership wrangles.

I announced to the first Joint Party Meeting that I believed that we faced three key challenges. First, to re-establish unity within, and between, the Liberal and National Parties, especially as Hawke had campaigned quite successfully on the slogan, 'If you can't govern yourselves, you can't govern the country'.

Second, to rebuild policy credibility which I put at zero, following the Howard policy debacle of 1987 where his tax/fiscal policy didn't add up, and Peacock's inability to recall the Health Policy in the 1990 campaign.

Third, to restructure and reinvigorate the Liberal Party organisation, which I saw to be anachronistic, still back in the 1940s, especially as an effective campaigning force against an ascendant, and effective, ALP.

These were the three principal objectives of my leadership. There were two other fundamental dimensions. First, all policy development was to be measured against the longer-term, national, strategic objective that Australia should aspire to play a significant leadership role(s) in the Asia Pacific region by 2000, and second, everybody, both front and backbench, should be assigned a specific role, with specific tasks, in working to meet these three objectives.

I hoped that in time we would be accepted as the alternative government, clearly ready to govern. In these terms, our parliamentary and media strategy was to be constructive and basically positive, to hopefully get out in front of the government on issues and in policy terms, essentially to attempt to set the agenda, of course while holding the government to account.

I aimed to have a detailed policy in every major policy area. While the result of this process, *Fightback*, which added up to some thousands of pages, was soon dismissed after the election loss in 1993 as the 'longest political suicide note in our history', I still look back on this as a very constructive process. From the time I entered politics I had sought to frame a positive policy agenda, and this made it much easier for Hawke/Keating to govern although they did not always take the opportunities presented. For example, as now evidenced by the release of cabinet documents for 1988–89, I argued that the government should be putting up interest rates sooner and faster, otherwise they would ultimately have to put them up higher than would otherwise be the case. This gave the government some policy room to move, and their failure to do so led to the 'recession we didn't need to have'. I also advocated zero tariffs, which made it easier for the government to reduce them; I led the micro-reform and privatisation agenda; I called on Hawke to make a commitment to the first Gulf War; when Hawke fell out with China over Tiananmen Square, I led a delegation to sustain dialogue on trade and investment, while condemning their performance on human rights – the first Western leader to do so; I led the first trade mission to Taiwan, initially opposed by the Hawke government but soon opened up for ministerial visits.

However, the downside of *Fightback* was clearly that it also made it all too easy for the government to run a scare campaign with an electorate that mistrusted politicians generally, an electorate that, therefore, was easily persuaded that I was lying, or could not, or would not, deliver.

Others, enjoying the benefit of hindsight, have tagged me as politically naïve. Certainly I misjudged Keating who, for example, having been rolled by Hawke on his 1985 tax package which had included a broad-based consumption tax, gave a most passionate speech to the parliament stating essentially that he would die fighting for it!

I was surprised, indeed, when Keating said to me on the first day back to the parliament, after the 1993 election, that I needed to understand that to him politics was just a game, where he would say or do whatever he had to, to win.

He had got away with the lie that the 'LAW Tax Cuts' that he promised and had legislated for could be delivered without a GST. In this, he was aided by a media fascinated with the colour and movement of the political theatre he created, and at the same time prepared to ignore (or ignorant of) his incapacity to deliver the tax cuts. Once he subsequently admitted that he couldn't deliver these tax cuts, his poll standing collapsed, pretty much by the extent to which he lost to Howard in 1996.

The shock to me was that he referred to politics as a game. I had always believed that politics was mostly about government and policy, a contest of ideas and alternative solutions, a very serious business, genuinely concerned with the wellbeing of all Australians. In policy terms. I had always believed that good policy would be good politics, with a relatively short lag.

If politics was a game in 1993, that game has been progressively elevated to an art form today. Politics today is very short-term, opportunistic, populist, sometimes alarmingly personal and mostly negative; it is increasingly dominated by political apparatchiks who essentially see the game as the end in itself. The focus is to do whatever it takes win the daily media cycle, generally moving on the next day to another issue, another location, with other people, and so on.

So, as we saw in the last election, policies have been reduced to mere dot points or sound bites – 'stop the boats', 'fix the budget', 'create 2 million jobs', etc. Today it is a political imperative to be a small target, and certainly not to 'do a Hewson'!

The result – good government is the casualty. While political games are played, issues and problems are left to drift, and the longer-term wellbeing of Australians is put at risk.

While much of opposition can be about politics, government is about policy and governing. While I give credit to Rudd for taking some policy detail to the 2007 election, both Gillard and Abbott have failed to appreciate the significance and challenge of this transition, and we are poorer as a nation for it.

The need for national leadership has probably never been greater than it is now. While it is no easy matter to say what that leadership should look like, in my experience, one thing is for sure. As the 6th President of the US, John Quincy Adams, once remarked:

> If your actions inspire others to dream more, learn more, do more, and become more, you are a leader.

Hopefully this volume will help you do just that!

John Hewson
January 2015

Dr John Hewson AM is the former Federal Opposition and Liberal Party leader and is a Professor and Chair in the Tax and Transfer Policy Institute at the Australian National University's Crawford School of Public Policy.

CONTENTS

INTRODUCTION

Philip Crisp

There is a hunger for more inspirational leadership in our society, especially among young people.

If you are reading these words it is likely that you share a concern over the condition of our civic dialogue, and are sufficiently engaged that – when your leadership moment comes – you hope to do better. Perhaps you are 40 years old and have newly embarked on a career in federal or local politics. Perhaps you are 35 and a sporting administrator, or the driving force behind an NGO, or the leader of a union or professional association. Perhaps you are 30 and have just been appointed to a minister's office or the electorate office of your local member of parliament. Perhaps you are 25, practising a trade or profession, and plan to run for your local council. Perhaps you are 20 or younger, studying 'civics' (however described) at school or university, starting to form views about the quality of our democracy, and hope one day to make a positive difference in the world. If you answer to any of these descriptions, then this book is written for you.

So you want to be a leader comprises 36 essays by successful Australians addressed to our next generation of leaders. Contributors include two former premiers, the former most senior Commonwealth public servant, two currently serving federal politicians, a number of people who have held CEO positions in the public, non-profit and private sectors, and other leaders, role models, thinkers, advisers, advocates and observers from diverse backgrounds. Their combined expertise embraces politics, the electoral system, social activism, economics, finance, law, small business, public administration, the classics, history, philosophy, education, psychology, personal development, crisis leadership, conflict resolution, human rights, effective communication, science and technology, change management and futurology. Most contributors have distinguished themselves in more than one role. By their accomplishments they are eminently qualified to share their thoughts about what you can expect from public life, and how you might go about it.

The contributors are primarily doers rather than commentators, and almost all have significant achievements to their credit outside party politics. Indeed, many of them would not have thought to write such an essay, had I not asked them to do so. As a result you will find fresh voices here. While a few contributors are recognisably of the left or of the right, in most cases I have little idea of their politics. They range in age from those who are semi-retired to those who are in their twenties. All of them are in some sense Australian (two are expatriates), and they come from all states as well as the ACT.

Contributors were given a simple brief:

> 'What could you say to an audience of potential new leaders that would most enhance their capacity to engage in public life?'

The book brings together their ideas about what you – as a potential future leader – should know, do, say and be to achieve success in public life.

In addition, the contributors were asked to consider some even larger purposes:

- to promote trust, friendship and ethical interaction between people from all places on the political landscape
- to help stimulate, over time, an improved civic dialogue in this country.

Occasionally I suggested to a contributor a theme they might explore, but I was scrupulous about not insisting. Each contributor wrote on a topic of their own choosing, and the book is better for that.

I think you will find, as I have, that the essays get better with each reading. Although some passages make reference to Australian institutions, characters and events, the essential messages are universal. Those messages will have equal relevance in two, five or ten years' time.

I sought to exclude discussion of substantive policy issues for their own sake, especially issues that are contentious in a party political way. Indeed, my insistence on that point led some potential contributors to withdraw. If you expect to find fodder for your political views here you will be disappointed; there are plenty of other places for that. *So you want to be a leader* is more concerned with how policy debate is conducted. It describes the challenges, processes and institutions of public life and explains how you might succeed with dignity – improving the quality of dialogue – regardless of your political values. In that respect the book differs from some other political literature which promotes a predictable and well-ventilated narrative, or which preaches only to the converted.

Of course it is human nature to prefer the company of people with similar values and allegiances. But we should be careful not to confine ourselves to forums that are agreeable in that sense. We should be careful, as well, never to assume that our viewpoint is so self-evidently right that everyone in our audience must surely agree with it. Indeed, that assumption underpins the political correctness we see occasionally from one or other camp on the political landscape. It marginalises the minority in our audience who would disagree, and could be seen as a form of bullying. As Tania Sourdin says, quoting Maya Angelou:

> People will forget what you said, they will forget what you did, but they will never forget how you made them feel.

Arguably a well-adjusted person cannot be made to feel anything, but not everyone is perfectly adjusted and so ultimately you will be more successful in public life if you can avoid being opinionated. Relax! You may in the end discover there is not so much that divides us, and the battles that seem so important at the time are rarely about the fate of civilisation as we know it.

What do I mean by 'public life'? In this book the term relates to any form of service or work that entails engagement on issues of shared concern with a wide range of groups, communities and interests – that is, a wider range than if you were merely involved in private or semi-private transactions or relationships.

Politics is perhaps the most obvious form of public life, but it is not the only one.* You may be in public life as an advocate or interest group representative, NGO leader or philanthropist. Public life also extends to community engagement by volunteers, and to some activities described as 'social activism'. Journalism may amount to engagement in public life, even extending to blogging and the smart use of social media.

---

* There is an alternative way of making the same point. One might say that although the book is about 'politics', that term should be understood broadly. As Craig Wallace says: 'Politics, in its broadest sense, is happening all around us and in every … retail district, body corporate, office, school and community'. As the cliché goes 'politics is ubiquitous'.

Engagement in a profession or business – to the extent that you merely serve clients or customers – is not per se public life. But you are in public life if you have a leadership role in your profession or industry: setting standards, defining ethical practice or engaging with government; and whenever you accept a 'corporate social responsibility' that entails acting for the benefit, not just of partners or shareholders, but of a broader class of interested parties.

Sport and the arts are not public life per se, but again they can be – if you have a leadership role, or prominence of the kind that attracts endorsement, makes you a role model and subjects you to higher standards for your peccadilloes than the average person.

What are the implications of being in public life? First, you are likely to be in the public gaze. You might relish that, but remember, you may be vilified more frequently than you are thanked. You will be subject to comment and criticism, not all of it fair, and for that you will need a thick skin. As Geoff Gallop says:

> … when someone becomes a leader they enter a completely new space. They are now looked to when decisions have to be made and judged when the decision is made.

You will be servant, not master, of the people you represent and the situations you are presented with. Ian Harper puts it well:

> If you are called to public life, you are there to serve the people without fear or favour. You do not have the luxury of choosing whom you serve, unlike your private sector counterparts.

You may be held accountable for the failings of others that happened on your watch. You may be called upon to do or say something that you do not wholly support. You may find that your options are fewer – and your ability to solve 'wicked problems' is far more limited – than you anticipated.

You may find yourself constantly on duty, and you may not enjoy the luxury to be forthright in the expression of private views. You may also find that your privacy, and that of your family, is compromised to a greater or lesser extent. 'There will be temptations. Resist them', says Ray Groom. People will gossip anyway. More seriously, accusations or insinuations of impropriety may be made against you that will stick sufficiently to compromise your standing. While you are entitled to a presumption of innocence in any criminal matter, that privilege will not necessarily protect your position in public life.

Depending on the circumstances, you may be required to resign, or stand down temporarily, from whatever public office you hold.

And if all that is not enough to think about, ponder the fact that you will probably earn much less than you might in the private sector.

With all those drawbacks, why would you enter public life? Perhaps your motivation is concern for a cause, or a group that you seek to promote or protect. Perhaps it is, in part, publicity. Perhaps it is partly prestige; as Richard Cogswell says, public life is 'great fodder for the ego'. Perhaps some part of you is drawn to the power of public office. And perhaps you are attracted to public service as a noble calling; and despite the fact that (or maybe *because*) it requires sacrifices.

Arguably it does not matter what mixture of motivations you have, provided that you have some insight into yourself, and provided, of course, that you do the job well.

Although this book is about public life generally, the circumstances that caused me to embark on the project in 2012 were political. At that stage there had already been widespread expressions of dismay over the poor state of federal politics. As evidence, the Lowy Institute poll of 5 June 2012 reported a significant level of disenchantment with democracy, especially amongst young people (18- to 29-year olds).* The thinking of some could be summed up by the question, channelling Monty Python, 'what has democracy ever done for me?'

The more immediate catalyst occurred unexpectedly. One night at about the time of the Lowy poll I found myself watching a live feed of the Leveson inquiry into the British press. You may be aware of the inquiry, and the political fault lines upon which it was conducted. I watched lead counsel Robert Jay QC questioning the British Prime Minister, David Cameron. Notwithstanding the latently adversarial nature of their exchanges, each protagonist displayed courtesy and grace. I saw two men, each with their own purposes, and each in command of his brief. I saw mutual respect, a willingness not to assume ill will in the other, and a mindfulness of shared values.

---

* See http://www.lowyinstitute.org/publications/lowy-institute-poll-2012-public-opinion-and-foreign-policy. Similar results were obtained in the 2013 and 2014 polls.

The incident impressed upon me that civic dialogue can indeed be done well – something we in Australia have evidently forgotten. By comparison with the British example, I thought, Australia's leaders too seldom exemplify the virtues I have mentioned. Our politics sometimes seems like civil war, rather than civic dialogue.

I wondered, could something be done about that? The idea for a book was formed then, combining voices reaching across the political divide to promote an improved civic dialogue. It took some six months to fully develop the idea. In this period I benefited from discussions with a number of people who helped me to refine my ideas into a coherent set of propositions about what the book should – and should not – seek to do.

In my view Australia has suffered from instances of poor policy-making by governments of both major persuasions in the last decade – and we have sustained prosperity and wellbeing largely through luck. There is continued disenchantment with the quality of our national conversation, evidenced from many sources, and a widespread feeling that we could do better.

Yet I would rather be constructive than negative. I am often dismayed to hear politicians described as by nature venal, untrustworthy, self-serving, and so on. My experience has been that one person's examples of bad politicians just happen to be all on the conservative side, while another person's examples just happen to be on the progressive side of politics, but this bias is not acknowledged. Thus we avoid the discomfort of conflict by the device of making politicians the common enemy. There is a creative tension in conflict that can be better used if we own it; or as Nadja Alexander puts it, there are:

> … opportunities in conflict to make choices which will transform … destructive conflict energy into realistic, constructive outcomes.

Too often we project our unresolved conflicts onto politicians as 'a class apart'* and then complain that they have failed us, and are overpaid to boot.

I come now to the premises on which this book rests:

- Many Australians are disenchanted with our political processes and leaders, and are inclined to disparage the political

* I owe this phrase to Craig Wallace.

classes as 'them'. This is especially true of young people, who are casual about the merits of democracy and disinclined to enter conventional public life.

- Australia has been a lucky country for a long time, but some of the conditions that underpin this luck may not last. We face new challenges that our political leaders seem poorly prepared to meet, and our children may one day condemn us for helping ourselves to an unsustainable lifestyle at their expense.
- There is much unbalanced, ill-informed opinion, particularly in online media, expressed in vitriolic, even poisonous, language. In facing future challenges, we would benefit from a national conversation that is more rational and competent, kinder and gentler.
- There are great examples of leadership in public life. In particular, (as documented by Lucas Walsh and Jan Owen), young people are finding new ways to engage with social issues and new models of entrepreneurship. We could learn much from those examples.

All contributors broadly agree with these premises, although some would express them in different language. At any rate, all of the contributors demonstrate, through their willingness to be a part of this project, optimism that it is possible to effect an improvement in the standards of public life, and that this book might help.

How might this happen? Probably not by reaching our existing leaders. Cynics will no doubt say they are a lost cause. While I cannot agree with that, I think it unlikely they would have the time; if they do that would be a bonus. In any event, the book does not presume to reform current leaders. Rather it seeks to inform and inspire a newer generation of leaders, before they become too busy and battle-scarred.

There are also secondary audiences for the book. I hope, first, that *So you want to be a leader* will provide useful material for teachers of civics, government, politics or leadership at various levels. Second, that it will be of value to the public servants, political advisers and lobbyists who interact behind the scenes with our more visible leaders. And finally, that it will reach thoughtful voters – on the premise that any project that aims to improve leadership should also focus on the people who elect our leaders. If I may resort to a cliché: we get the politicians we deserve.

For you personally, my hope is that this book will help you to see clearly, to understand what is true for you, for others and for the world, and to apply that understanding to bring clarity, integrity and good will to human affairs.

Philip Crisp
January 2015

ACKNOWLEDGEMENTS

So you want to be a leader has been an undertaking of almost three years, and those who helped along the way number in the hundreds. I cannot possibly list them all, but I must mention some.

I owe my greatest debt to each of the authors of essays making up this collection – and to John Hewson AM, who wrote the foreword – busy people, all of them. I thank them for their commitment to the cause of a better civic dialogue, and the trust that they placed in me, putting aside valuable time to write when they must have known there was a risk I might never bring the project to fruition. Among the authors, Ray Groom and Jeremy Shearmur were particularly valuable in the early stages in helping me refine a vague concept for the book into something more coherent.

One of the better decisions I made was to engage *Wilton Hanford Hanover* to advise on the manuscript. I thank Virginia Wilton for her strategic advice, Helen Portillo-Castro and Eleanor Garran who edited the entire manuscript and picked up many infelicities that I had missed.

I owe a vote of thanks to *Hybrid Publishers*, in particular director Louis de Vries for his flexible business approach, and managing editor Anna Blay who was meticulous and invariably responsive. Also to Suzanne Kiraly (*Creative Knowhow*), whose wise strategic advice about book marketing and social media, extending to all aspects of creation and communication, continues to be invaluable.

My thanks go also to the sub-committee of authors – Peter Acton, Margaret Halsmith and Lucas Walsh – whom I consulted regularly at different stages of the project, and who will decide how any profits will be applied to serve the purpose of an improved civic dialogue.

There are numerous others that I thank for their general support, for their assistance in recommending suitable contributors or in opening doors for me, for their comments on various drafts, for sharing their knowledge of the publishing world, for their feedback on cover designs and for their offers of help in launching the book. At the risk of omitting someone, I list them in alphabetical order: Leah Armstrong, Jimi Bostock, Chris Clark, John Groom, Margaret Halsmith (again), Charmine Härtel, Anita Heiss, Tom Howe QC,

Marlene Kanga AM, Ben Macklin (BWM Books), Maria Maley, Matthew Rimmer, Greg Rudd, Peter Shergold AC, Loma Snooks, Andrew Stojanovski, Peter Strong, John Uhr, Craig Wallace and Cassandra Wilkinson. Some may be surprised to see their name here, but they helped me more than they know.

I am grateful to all those who were kind enough to review the book. Not all their reviews are printed in the book, but they are reproduced in full on the book's website:

www.soyouwanttobealeader.com.au

Finally for their encouragement and support I am indebted to my three wonderful sisters, Gillian, Elisabeth and Mary, and my partner Elizabeth who has been by my side throughout.

OUTLINE

So you want to be a leader is arranged in four parts, each containing eight to ten essays. You might decide to read the book in sequence from cover to cover; or you might prefer to keep it as a bedside book, and dip into it according to your mood and interests. Each of the essays is a self-contained work.

Part 1: Leadership concerns the most visible form of leadership, exercised by those who are front and centre in public life – the archetypal leaders. They cannot pass the buck, for the buck stops with them. Essays in this part are written by those who are or have been leaders in this sense, and those who have closely observed them. The essays consider the deepest question about leadership: what leaders should be.

For Nick Jans, the most inspiring leader–follower relationships involve a magic element, and while it may seem practically indefinable – like great art or falling in love – we know it when we feel it and we can be moved by it without knowing exactly why. Among the qualities of a leader, self-awareness, integrity and empathy are important, Geoff Gallop says, not merely technical knowledge and understanding of institutions and the levers of power. Andrew Hughes maintains that a great leader is defined, not by actions but by what he or she embodies, nurtures in others and authentically lives. Real leadership doesn't wait for permission, and it doesn't need an audience, says Cassandra Wilkinson; leaders can be found throughout the community, not always in the obvious places, and they can emerge unexpectedly in times of crisis. In an insightful essay Nadja Alexander explores the melodramatic nature of the tales we tell when we find ourselves in conflict, and shows how discovering our own inner hero – the tragic hero – leads to understanding.

The remaining essays in this part take a closer look at some of the themes developed in the Introduction: to what extent Australia's present prosperity rests on luck or good decisions, whether our luck has run out, whether youth will take up the call to public life, and whether wise choices are possible in a world of rapid change and short news cycles. Countering the usual complaints of poor policy making, Daryl Dixon gives an insider's account of some farsighted and courageous decisions in the past – decisions which have shaped Australia. He argues that future leaders – though faced with difficult economic choices – can emulate those examples. Ray Groom contends that on objective measures Australia is one of the most advanced and civilised nations in human history, and this is surely evidence of wise leadership in the past. He encourages young Australians to consider a career in politics and offers practical advice for political aspirants.

If there could be said to be any concluding message from this part, it is a hopeful one of cautious optimism that future leaders can make the most of the advantages and opportunities we enjoy. With logic, common sense, maturity, manners and willpower, Greg Rudd argues, we can improve the way our democracy works, and build a remarkable Australia.

Part 2: Influence concerns the exercise of persuasion. Essays deal with topics such as the management of organisations, the language of dialogue, engagement as a lobbyist or adviser in reform processes, and speaking truth to power. Influencers are themselves leaders. Indeed, the form of leadership they practise is arguably more complex than the more visible form of leadership discussed in Part 1. Influencers lead, and at the same time serve a leader or constituency. They may operate at any level in a hierarchy, and sometimes they work in the background rather than in the public gaze. Part 2 has a more practical orientation than Part 1, focusing less on what leaders should be, and more on what they should do and say.

Each of the first three essays contains reflections from writers with an outstanding career in public service. Peter Shergold argues that a willingness to acknowledge personal responsibility for failures – rather than blaming systemic factors – is the key to developing leadership qualities. Tom Sherman delivers lessons for each stage of a career in public service: first for those starting out, second for those in middle-management positions, and finally for those at the top. Sue Vardon discusses the importance of creating a positive work environment in the public sector, rewarding initiative so that public service is the best it can be.

Four essays concern the way we relate to people whom we seek to influence, and the language we use in doing so. Tania Sourdin explains various negotiation styles and argues that a sophisticated, rather than a primitive, approach is a marker of wise leadership. Margaret Halsmith throws fresh light on the term 'civic dialogue' which she describes as 'constructive conversation between leaders and stakeholders that takes place prior to leaders' decision making ... the kind, gentle and potentially robust exchange of ideas about public issues among people, including leaders, who attribute value to their own and to others' perspectives'. Charmine Härtel discusses psychopathic behaviours that can do enormous damage within organisations, and suggests strategies to combat them that will help you along your path to leadership and enlighten you as a steward of the wellbeing of those affected by your decisions. Tim Mendham shows how we can respond sensitively when confronted by strongly held beliefs that are based on emotion rather than evidence.

The last three essays in this part are written by people who have exercised influence in a particular sector or constituency, although their purpose here goes beyond advocacy. Peter Strong describes the challenges faced by small business people who make up the majority of employers; he also argues that local people, with the right resources, are best placed to manage change affecting a community. Craig Wallace speaks of third sector organisations as a real engine for democracy, noting their powerful role in achieving political consensus for the National Disability Insurance Scheme. Bruce Chapman, who describes himself as a naive academic rather than a lobbyist, relates his experiences in two major reforms in the higher education sector. His essay is an illuminating case study of influence in action.

Part 3: Commitment is directed especially to young, emerging leaders. Before arriving at the pinnacle of leadership, and even before acquiring a degree of influence, comes commitment. If you are a potential leader intent on public life then you may prefer to begin with this part. It examines the issues, choices and challenges you will face as you start out in public life, and different ways in which you might make a contribution to society. There are some threshold issues: when should you enter public life (perhaps after you have established yourself in a career), and what form of public life should you choose (conventional politics is not the only option). Most of the essays here are written by people who are themselves young role models or who, while now older, distinguished themselves at an early age.

The essay co-authored by Lucas Walsh and Jan Owen addresses one premise of the book: that young people are disengaged from their democracy. It paints a more complex picture of the attitudes of young people, and reports that they are finding innovative ways to make an impact in public life.

Ian Harper asks: what does it mean to be in public life, and are you qualified to take this path? There are several sound motives for entering public life, as long as you understand your motives and the implications: for example, you will be scrutinised by the public, and not as well rewarded as if you pursued a career in the private sector. In contrast, Melanie Irons speaks of her experiences in entering public life 'by accident' in the wake of a bushfire emergency. For her, the critical factor in choosing to enter public life is simply that you are doing something you love so well that people look to you for leadership.

A skill that you must acquire early, if you are to acquire it at all, is how to communicate a message effectively to your audience. Christopher Balmford discusses communication style, the importance of plain language and the need to take responsibility for how your message is received.

There are careers other than party politics that may lead you to public life. An obvious example is the law – not only because many politicians receive their grounding in the practice of law, but because courtrooms are public places and advocacy is a form of public life. Richard Cogswell notes that courtrooms involve occasional confrontation and high emotion, but discourse can be managed to ensure that the adjudicative process takes place in the most effective way. Marlene Kanga deals with a less obvious choice of career. The work of engineers has saved more lives than the work of doctors, she says; in fact, most of the problems we face today will be solved by engineers. So if you want to change the world then consider becoming an engineer. Ashlee Uren describes the disenchantment of young people with politics – which is seen as something other people do. Yet young people can be powerful if they are prepared to engage. Volunteering is an excellent way to start, and can lead to engagement in other areas of public life. Fiona Jose describes the important work of the Cape York Institute for

Policy and Leadership, established by Noel Pearson. At the heart of the Cape York Agenda is a simple assertion: maximum participation in economic life is key to overcoming disadvantage. Fiona stresses the need for prospective leaders to hold a clear sense of purpose.

What of conventional politics? Andrew Leigh describes his transition from academe to parliament, and distils from that some advice for young leaders of the future: do what you love, expect a measure of bad and good luck, and be a bit unreasonable! He says that a life of service to others is a life well lived. Finally in this part, Anya Poukchanski's essay 'To the lady in the Lodge' is a thoughtful open letter to Australia's next female prime minister. It will repay reading and re-reading by any young woman who aspires, however faintly, to that high office.

Part 4: Knowledge is concerned with what you need to know to succeed in public life. It contains the most eclectic mix of essays. It does not claim to be comprehensive, but includes a selection of topics that contributors and this editor judged would be helpful to your career. Some of the essays ask you to step back a little from politics; to widen your gaze so that it takes in a broader range of subject matter. This serves in part to reinforce a message from Part 3 – that public life includes not just the obvious choice of politics, but many other possibilities. But in the main, the intention is to equip you, a potential new leader, with a broader knowledge that will deepen your understanding of your role in public life.

Peter Acton's essay explains the benefits of a broad education for those in public life. By studying history, literature and philosophy we can learn much about how to respond to current challenges. Learning the classics enables us to make more interesting conversation on a wide range of topics, and an added benefit is never being bored – or boring. Peter Ellyard, by contrast, looks to the future, distinguishing reactive management of the future we take and proactive leadership in the future we make. He argues that we need more of the latter skill.

Malcolm Mackerras critically appraises the language that we use when discussing Australia's electoral and political systems, and exposes some myths and faulty ideas in the public's understanding of these systems.

Two essays examine the relationship between government and markets, from complementary perspectives. Frank Milne shows how clumsy intervention in marketplace may go awry – even producing effects that are the opposite of what is intended – and supports his argument by giving some classic examples of failed policy. Flavio Menezes, on the other hand, shows how designed markets can improve the business of government, offering effective solutions for key problems of our time such as the ageing population, climate change and securing the wellbeing of all Australians in an increasingly complex and interconnected world.

Jeremy Shearmur's essay considers Plato's idea of the 'guardians', or ruler-philosophers, who would live in seclusion, developing superior knowledge, and use it to make the important decisions for society. He sees traces of that doctrine in our public institutions and argues that, if the country is to prosper, leaders cannot make decisions in isolation but should make better use of the knowledge that is dispersed in the community.

The last two essays deal with policy agendas. Tim McCormack discusses a topic lately neglected by governments of both persuasions – the possible presence of war criminals in Australia. He argues for proactive investigations leading, where appropriate, to criminal prosecutions. At the same time he acknowledges counter-arguments. His essay is a useful case study in how to explore a complex policy argument. In contrast, Mark Butler discusses two policy areas that are inevitably at the top of the agenda for any government. On the ageing of the population, he says we should avoid characterising the baby boomers as a 'burden' to be borne, but rather rediscover our cultural respect for older people and the contribution they make to society. As for climate change, he sees hope that the next few years will bring bipartisan consensus and a fresh global commitment to policies which discharge our obligation to future generations.

Part 1: LEADERSHIP

Leadership in a time of disaster – lessons from Black Saturday

Nick Jans

Dr Nick Jans OAM is a principal of Sigma Consultancy, specialising in military leadership and strategic human resource management as key mechanisms for organisational change. A graduate of the Royal Military College, Duntroon, he served in the Australian Regular Army in field artillery, training and personnel policy development, and is currently a brigadier in the Army Reserve. Nick is on the editorial board of the journal *Armed Forces & Society* and holds visiting fellowships at the Australian Defence College's Centre for Defence Leadership and Ethics and the School of Business, UNSW@ADFA, Canberra. He is the lead author of *The chiefs – a study of strategic leadership* (2013).

Good leadership often seems like magic; the most inspiring leader–follower relationships involve an almost indefinable spark between the leader and the led. But while it may be almost indefinable – like great art or falling in love – we know it when we feel it and we can be moved by it without knowing exactly why.

Nick Jans' essay concerns leadership in a time of disaster. Following the Black Saturday firestorm of 7 February 2009, the Marysville Triangle district of Victoria faced a bleak future. In the following weeks and months, Nick worked alongside three outstanding individuals who exemplified that 'magic spark'. These three people inspired a group of ordinary citizens to work to rebuild a stunned, fractured and dispersed community – a goal they achieved with remarkable success.

Leadership is one of the most observed and least understood phenomena on earth.
—James McGregor Burns

My wife and I live in Marysville, in a beautiful mountain valley in the Victorian Central Highlands. However, the things that make it an icon of the Victorian tourist scene also make it a bushfire risk. In the period leading up to 9 February 2009, we had worked hard to minimise the risk for our household by siting our home in a defensible place and building it of fireproof materials. We had equipped and trained ourselves for bushfire defence. My wife had spent the week before Black Saturday making arrangements for a weekend of extreme fire danger which, after an unprecedented three days of temperatures in the mid 40s (Celsius), was tipped to be potentially horrendous. After spending the previous week on professional duties in Sydney, I returned on the first plane that Saturday morning to help her with the final preparations.

By the evening we found ourselves literally fighting for our lives, in the face of perhaps the most extreme bushfire conditions ever recorded. Our part of the village was the first hit, and we were immediately engulfed in flames. It was like being in a cage that was being lowered into the depths of hell. Through luck and good management our house survived, but the houses on each side burned to the ground in less than 30 minutes. By midnight, the lovely mountain village that had been our home had been devastated, with 34 of its citizens dead and only 32 buildings out of 600-odd still standing.

If any community needed good leadership, it was the Marysville Triangle district immediately after Black Saturday. The survivors were shell-shocked, emotionally gutted. Most had to be relocated, often some distance from where their homes used to be. And as if the experience during the fire itself weren't bad enough, most of Marysville's citizens were excluded from the town for another 10 weeks while the coroner and her team sifted through the wreckage for further bodies. Moreover, when people were allowed to return and begin to piece their lives back together, they had to look on as dozens of rubble-filled truckloads rumbled out every day with most of what remained of the village and its houses. Meanwhile, there were already worrying signs of the thickets of red tape that would soon entangle us. Many of Marysville's citizens wondered whether the town would ever be restored to its former glory, let alone when.

In the aftermath of a disaster, some communities fracture under the strain of fear and anger. But others become more united and cohesive, and emerge from the experience stronger and more supportive than they were before. Marysville was to become an example of the latter.

On Anzac Day 2009, just a few weeks after the fire, the community celebrated its biggest Anzac Day ever. While the major focus was on the celebration of the Anzac spirit as it was revealed on Black Saturday and afterwards by citizens and emergency services, we wanted also to use the occasion to lift the spirits and the optimism of the community. So, in the Anzac Day address that day, I stressed that the community's very ability to mount such a big event so soon after coming through the fire was a demonstration of its resilience – to the world, and to itself.

And to prove the point, exactly one week later the community engaged in a huge collective brainstorming activity, where we began thinking constructively and creatively about what we wanted from a new township. More than 300 of us gathered together in a huge marquee on the practice fairway of the golf course to spend the day engaged in small group and plenary sessions. This activity was rounded off in July by a smaller, more intensive workshop over a long weekend, when a blueprint for the new Marysville and Triangle area was developed.

By mid June, with the help of philanthropists, notably the Fox and Forrest families, the community had established a temporary village that was housing dozens of displaced residents. The government had played only a minor role in this particular project. It was essentially the work of the community and its leadership group.

By mid May, the golf club had restored its front nine holes to playability, and by November the whole layout was back in business and running its first ever pro-am tournament. And by the end of the year, Marysville again had a viable retail facility, a facility that also served as a social hub.

I had two main roles in all of this. I was one of half a dozen citizens who formed a community leadership group in the weeks immediately following the fires. And, from mid March onwards, I served as president of the Marysville Community Golf and Bowls Club, one of the few viable local businesses still running for most of that year.

As I 'did' leadership and observed examples of leaders and leadership – some great, some not so great – I relearnt a number of fundamental lessons about the practice of leadership in circumstances of uncertainty and volatility.

Three leaders

Imagine yourself there in Marysville, on the Sunday evening of the second weekend after the firestorm. The town has been all but destroyed. A public meeting has been called, at very short notice, but you're not quite sure what its purpose is. Despite the short notice and the damage to the communication systems in the district, word of mouth has drawn a crowd of more than 300 anxious people. You and the rest of them are packed into the main room of the Marysville golf club, virtually the only public building of any size left in the vicinity. It is very hot. The evidence of bushfire devastation can be observed at all sides through the long windows; the smell of smoke is still thick in the air. People are stressed and worried; you can see tired, strained faces all around you. Virtually all have lost friends and material possessions. Uncertainty is rife. Rumour has it that it might be weeks, maybe months, before the coroner's investigation will be complete and the survivors allowed back. Attention is at its maximum, with people hanging hope on every word.

The meeting lasted for about three hours. Its effect on community morale was profound and widespread among those who attended. For example, a local resident spoke the following day of how she had come to the meeting in very low spirits but had left it feeling as though she was walking on air.

Much of this morale-lifting effect was due to the words of two men who addressed the meeting that night.

One was a fellow soldier, Major General John Cantwell. In the weeks immediately following Black Saturday, General Cantwell was appointed deputy head of the Victorian Bushfire Reconstruction and Recovery Authority. He had spent the weekend touring the district, accompanied by Andrew Forrest, the mining magnate and philanthropist, and one of Australia's richest men. They had arrived in a helicopter (belonging to another billionaire, Lindsay Fox) mid-morning on Saturday, 21 February, and had conducted a number of debriefing sessions with grassroots representative members of the community – chosen as 'ordinary citizens' rather than as local government or police officials – in various parts of the Marysville Triangle area. At the end of that Saturday, impressed by what they had seen and heard, they requested that a public meeting be called in Marysville for the Sunday evening. Now here they were to address it.

John Cantwell was the first speaker. He was the very image of the modern major general: fit, slim, dressed as a simple soldier in baggy camouflage suit and slouch hat. He took off his hat and waved away the proffered microphone, with the jovial remark that he was used to talking to soldiers in a loud voice and that microphones often 'got in the way'. He began by telling us a bit about himself. He told of how he had come from 'humble origins' – had in fact risen from the ranks (unlike me and the vast majority of his contemporaries, who had gone straight to the Royal Military College or the Defence Academy soon after school).

John then related how he too had been in war zones, had been shell-shocked, and, like many men, had initially declined the opportunity for counselling – and how he soon came to realise how dumb he was being. He urged all of us to take advantage of the counselling services which would be provided – 'don't be too proud'. And it was advice that would resonate deeply within the community in the months that followed.*

Having won over the crowd by his fair dinkum demeanour, John simply and calmly outlined what he saw as the immediate function of the Reconstruction and Recovery Authority: the emergency provision of food, supplies and shelter, and cleaning up of debris. After that he took questions. For more than an hour. The majority of these questions, coming as they did from people still traumatised by the events of the previous fortnight, were on mundane local domestic topics. When can we return to the village? Where and how will we be housed? When will the store and petrol station reopen? When will Black Spur Drive be open? How will the lord mayor's fund be used? Will part-time residents be treated differently to full-time residents? What say will the community have in what happens? When can we expect our fences to be restored? When can we expect to hear from insurance companies? And so on.

Some of these questions John referred to other people present that evening. Some he asked his staff officer to note, with the promise that he would get back shortly with the answer. But most he dealt with himself. And the way that he did so was masterful. John

* After his assignment to bushfire recovery, General Cantwell was deployed as Australian commander in the Middle East. An account of his military career is contained in his book: Cantwell, J, 2012, *Exit wounds: one Australian's war on terror*, Melbourne University Press, Melbourne.

treated every question and every questioner with equal seriousness, even though some of them were a bit bizarre or obviously based on wild rumour. He projected empathy, composure, confidence and competence. In doing so, he left the audience with the conviction that the right person was in charge; that although the situation was dire, there was a plan for dealing with it, and that everybody's needs would be attended to at the appropriate time.

I was so proud of him and of the Australian military that evening.

The next speaker was Andrew Forrest. He was in the district because of his passion for helping Australian communities, and his intention was to help the relief effort through his charitable foundation, the Australian Children's Trust. Despite a huge business workload, he and his family had visited the bushfire-affected areas in the preceding days, gaining a very good understanding of what was required, and what was, and was not, being done by the authorities.

Andrew Forrest had a fairly simple message, and he made it with emphasis and clarity. He told us that he had some time previously researched the question of how and why certain communities bounce back from a disaster, such as Hurricane Katrina, while others just fade away. And the answer was fairly simple. Communities that bounced back took responsibility for their own recovery and rebuilding. They didn't wait for governments or other agencies to help them. They went about helping themselves, but they didn't hesitate to ask for any help they needed. Forrest's research showed that these communities recover faster and become stronger and better than they were before the disaster. And they begin by setting themselves what Forrest called 'big, hairy aggressive goals'. But even if, as often happens, they didn't quite achieve those goals, they still advanced themselves by much more than they ever thought possible.

'You in the Marysville Triangle,' Andrew Forrest told us, 'you must do the same.'

I'll give you an example of the power of his words. At that time, I was president-elect of the Marysville Community Golf and Bowls Club. The committee had already decided that, since the club was one of the few viable businesses left in the district, we had to do our part to help with local economic development. Even though our fairways and bowling green were unplayable, we had a reasonable chance of reopening for business within a few months. We needed a big splash event to tell the world that we were ready and willing. So, at that meeting, on that night, emboldened by Forrest's advice, I announced to the assembly that the club was setting itself a big hairy aggressive goal, to conduct a pro-am tournament before the end of the year. To many citizens at the meeting such a goal may have seemed absurd. But we set the goal because we realised we needed to set it: for ourselves, for the district, and for the effect on morale of the assembly that night.

And, by the way, before the end of the year we didn't run just one pro-am; we ran two.

My two examples so far have been of very senior, high-profile executives: people who expect and receive respect and obedience if only because of their status. My third example is a Marysville resident who exercised her influence without these advantages. In fact, you could say that this leader had influence precisely because she didn't have these advantages: because the people with whom she dealt appreciated that what she was trying to do would have little personal payoff to her.

Her name is Judy, and in the months following Black Saturday she created a community enterprise that became known as Plant Aid. Its mission was to connect the gardeners of the Marysville Triangle district with those who wanted to support the rebuilding initiatives following the bushfires. This enterprise was born just six days after the fires, on the day telephone communications were first restored. Judy telephoned the Jon Faine morning talkback program on ABC 774 and proposed a way of helping out the people of our district that might appeal to those of modest means, or those gardeners of Victoria who wanted to do something to help us but could not think of a way to do it. She suggested that these gardeners propagate plants and seedlings, and hold them in reserve for the gardeners of Marysville – for the day when they returned to establish their homes and gardens.

Let me put this into context. When almost all other local people were still totally focused on their own personal tragedies – and despite her own traumas from the bushfire – Judy saw the symbolic importance of getting people gardening again, and of giving people hope for the future. And she set out to do something then, in the early stages when a boost to morale was sorely needed. The benefits in restoring the community's identity seem obvious now, but many people shook their heads when the idea was first raised and the notion of regrowing gardens seemed impossibly distant and secondary.

Before she had finished talking to the ABC, its switchboard had received six telephone calls of support. And the momentum continued. In the days and weeks that followed, Judy got a commitment from agencies all over Australia, ranging from corporations, through community garden clubs, to ordinary citizens. One of the more touching contributions was a $20 note from an 86-year-old lady, which came in an envelope addressed simply to 'Judy, The plant lady, Marysville'. (The postmistress knew who it was for.) She worked tirelessly, and inspired others to do likewise. She negotiated and soothed and organised local citizens and big donors alike, and left them all feeling that their needs had been satisfied.

Enlisting the aid of celebrity gardener Don Burke and other media sources, Judy raised more than $35,000 and she continued to receive calls of support from businesses and groups for many months afterwards. Plant Aid became the employer of two permanent part-time staff and the operator of a large nursery, and its plants, shrubs and seedlings continue to be distributed to Marysville gardeners.

However fascinating we might find these examples of outstanding individual leadership, the smart leader never loses sight of the fundamental fact that leadership will only be effective and sustainable if it is exercised as a collaborative process. And what I'm talking about is much, much more than the simple process of delegating effectively in a team setting (if indeed the process of delegation can be called simple). I'm talking about active engagement; and this can only be achieved if the nominated leaders relate to group members in ways that make those members feel respected, feel important, feel that they are not a group but part of a team, and feel that as part of this team they are making a valuable contribution to a worthwhile goal. This feeling of inclusion and self-esteem is a powerful force.

Let me mention some examples.

The first concerns the committee and senior staff of the Marysville Community Golf and Bowls Club, mentioned earlier. I'm quite sure that at least part of the basis for the extraordinary effort of all these people was that the committee framed its vision very much in community terms. Every time one of us spoke in public, whether it was to the members or in public speeches or media presentations, we spoke of the key role of the golf club in community recovery. We stressed that we were working for a more important outcome than simply the restoration of our playing facilities; that the club's future and the community's future were inextricably linked. We sought to articulate the goal, as well as a logical path to its fulfilment.

The second example relates to the Marysville and Triangle Development Group. Its nucleus was a half dozen or so local citizens who initially took it on themselves to provide a conduit between the community and the authorities, a process that somewhat naturally morphed into the broader activity of taking the initiative for energising the community as part of the recovery process. The community leadership group took Andrew Forrest's words – that recovering communities not only *can* but *must* do it for themselves – to heart. We established a charter. We set operational and strategic goals. We consulted intensively with the community. And we ensured legitimacy by conducting elections in the middle of the year. At all stages – sometimes consciously and sometimes unconsciously – we did things to engage the spirits of the community.

Such a philosophy was all the more important because it was the direct antithesis of the approach that the authorities wanted us to follow. They wanted us to wait for a phased program of reconstruction to unfold, and to take advantage of the multitude of services that were increasingly provided. Their assumption was that communities that have just been subjected to a disaster would be still dazed by the experience, and therefore would not be capable of managing their own destiny.

Perhaps this philosophy makes sense to a politician or a senior bureaucrat. But it ignores two vital truths about social activity: that the very process of engagement stimulates and lifts the human spirit; and that the recovery of the *spirit* after a disaster is just as important as the recovery of the *physical environment* in which people live.

This aspect, the importance of the spirit, is something that is fundamental to the concept of leadership, but it is not well understood. It illustrates the essence of 'followership', the neglected other side of the leadership coin. 'Spirit' denotes the emotional or psychological side of engagement, in respect to the effect of leadership on optimism, morale, psychic energy and the like. 'Followership' is very far from being a passive process, and entails the process of actively engaging and collaborating with the plan and the program that someone else is proposing, not just because doing so furthers one's own material interest, but because of the intrinsic satisfaction we derive from participating in a collective process aimed at the greater good.

The magic spark effect

If there were a recipe for what I call the 'magic spark effect', it would involve six significant ingredients.

Most fundamentally, effective leaders require **competence**. You'll never get people to collaborate with you if they don't trust that you have the necessary know-how. All our examples show competence in spades, derived from the professional and personal backgrounds of the individuals, from having a good brain and an understanding of 'how the world wags', and by collaborating to maximise individual strengths and compensate for individual vulnerabilities. In situations of uncertainty, when most people have no idea what to do next, let alone what to do after that, they respond strongly to a person who seems to know what they are doing and where they are going. Like John Cantwell on that Sunday evening so soon after the disaster.

The second ingredient is **character**. I use this word in the sense of being moral and principled, trustworthy and reliable, without an agenda, and prepared to put the needs of the team and the institution ahead of your own needs. (An old-fashioned term for this is 'honour'.) There are many parts to character. As well as *honour and ethics*, character involves the sense of *courage* and *self-confidence* that leads to the exercise of *initiative*. Like Andrew Forrest, one of Australia's richest people, putting aside pressing business concerns to work alongside the people in the bushfire-affected areas; getting on with things without first asking somebody's permission, and particularly without having to work a proposal through the bureaucracy. Character includes the qualities of *resilience* and *doggedness*. And character includes the *generosity of spirit* to allow others to take the credit for the accomplishment of a team effort.

The third and fourth ingredients relate to what's involved in working with people. I call these **collaboration** and **consideration**.

As a leader, you don't necessarily 'lead from the front', organising and managing processes. Leadership is a team sport. This especially applies when those in the team are well qualified and keen to achieve the goals. Leaders lead best when they elicit active engagement and purposeful decision making by others. As head of the community golf and bowls club, I saw my main task as simply to make it easier for the members of my team to do what they needed to do. I left most of the day-to-day activities to the excellent citizens who were my colleagues in this enterprise, managing the process as necessary so that everybody was pulling in the same direction and their total effect was greater than the sum of the parts. I sought to 'stay in the crow's nest' so that I could look ahead to the next challenge in the recovery process.

I also saw it as my role to provide the support that all the members of these teams needed, support that ranged from ensuring that they had the resources and technical advice when it was needed, through to continual reassurance that they were on the right track and that they were doing a great job. And this is where the ingredient of consideration comes in. People won't trust you if they don't feel that you are fair dinkum about respecting them as individuals and that you hold their individual and collective interests as the priority.

Leaders are not micromanagers. Leaders get people aligned and working together to achieve shared goals, and support them with resources and advice so they can get on with the job.

And leaders hold the strategic vision, which brings me to the fifth ingredient: strategic **consciousness**. The consistently effective leader can see the bigger picture; can see where the goals and direction of the group fit in with those of the broader constituency. And more than this: such a leader is able to simultaneously consider and cope with a number of different levels of thought and activity. While they are dealing with the immediate crisis, they are thinking about its implications for the broader plan and how it might affect the team's ability to tackle both its short- and medium-term objectives. Like Marysville citizen Judy, who recognised the strategic importance of getting people gardening again, and of giving people hope that things could be done in the foreseeable future – even while she was still dealing with her own wounds.

Not all effective leaders have a sense of strategic consciousness. This especially applies to those who are operating simply at the tactical level: responsible for getting jobs done on a day-to-day basis. But I have rarely seen a leader operating successfully at the higher levels of an organisation without this ability.

The final ingredient that I will mention is **communication**. Getting the message across – like John Cantwell with his down-to-earth, sympathetic and unruffled dealings with a diverse crowd of shell-shocked people; like Andrew Forrest with his articulate challenge to reach beyond ourselves; like Judy with her ability to persuade others of her vision for the re-gardening of Marysville, striking just the right balance of confidence, empathy and moral authority.

Of course, all leaders have to communicate. But the best ones do so in ways that have an impact *on the heart* as well as on the head. They communicate to influence and inspire, not just to inform. In part, they do this through their choice of words and by having a sincere and compelling delivery style, and by ensuring that what they say and how they say it is congruent with what they do.

You will communicate best if you have the courage to 'get away from the lectern'; to speak, like John Cantwell did, from the cuff using plain and vivid language and in the right tone of voice. Some people seem blessed with an innate ability to do this. But my own experience tells me that effective oral communication and top-notch public speaking skills are generally learned and honed by dint of hard work and continual practice.

Skill in communication is derived from strengths in all the other five factors. Showing that you know what you're talking about (competence), plainly being a person who can be trusted (character), being enthusiastic about working through others (collaboration), patently going beyond self-interest for the good of the team (consideration), and maintaining awareness of the whole picture (consciousness). All these ingredients help to make that impact on the heart as well as on the head, and the combination of all these is greater than the sum of the parts. The effect is magical and profound, and usually inexplicable through the objective analysis of normal business processes.

The six ingredients combine to make a powerful leadership brew that mainstream literature describes as 'transformational' – the kind of leadership that gives people hope in tough times, and that appeals to their hearts as well as their heads and hip pockets. This is because action that comes from the heart tends to spark performance – and even sacrifice – beyond the ordinary.

Leadership when only the best will do

Only the best kind of leadership can take a community or an organisation towards a brighter, more sustainable future.

Why don't we see such leadership more often? Some might say that it's because the ability to lead 'transformationally' is a natural talent; you've either got it or you haven't. But I don't subscribe to this. Each of the six qualities – with the possible exception of consciousness – can be developed by the right teaching, coaching and practice. But if you want to be a leader for the tough times you need to work hard on your game and take every opportunity to build your skills.

It is all too tempting to use a less demanding leadership approach when things are stable. The kind of leadership that works best is neither easy to acquire nor easy to practise. And it will come at a cost. You will have to spend time on many activities that you could be devoting to 'your in-tray' and to administration and immediate priorities, time you could be spending on tasks that meet the short-term needs of your stakeholders. A more mundane carrot-and-stick style takes less effort. No wonder so many of us choose this easier short-term option.

But you are likely to find that your choice of the lazy option becomes a handicap in the times when you do need to be this kind of leader. This is not just because such a style must become habitual in order for you to be resilient but because being a tough-times leader in the easy times helps you to establish 'moral capital': a store of credit and faith in you as the leader that you can draw on in the tough times. This particularly applies to character, which is not something that you can turn on and off.

Conclusion

First, aspiring leaders will benefit from the habit of reflecting on what they do as leaders and why certain behaviours have certain effects. Leadership is a science as well as an art. Understanding the science sharpens your appreciation of its artistic application. (My professional motto for a number of years has been that 'there is nothing as practical as a good theory'.) My position in the Marysville community after Black Saturday gave me an insider's view of all this and more during 2009. And as I watched and I listened and I 'did' leadership, I learned a lot. Just as importantly, as I practised leadership myself in 2009, I was able to perform my own running self-critique. I was able to learn from my own successes and mistakes, and adapt both my own style and my deepening understanding of leadership in general.

Second, subconsciously at least, many of us tend to associate 'leadership' with something done by those in positions of power within the community: the captains and the kings, the CEOs and the bigwigs, that is, not by 'everyday Australians' like us. Management books and articles from business magazines unknowingly reinforce this by focusing all their examples on CEOs and celebrities. But we shouldn't look for examples and direction only from 'them' rather than from 'us', because in so doing we deprive ourselves of 'ordinary' opportunities for leadership and the 'beyond ordinary' learning that comes with it. Judy – the extraordinary 'ordinary citizen' – could be regarded as the most effective of our examples. Because she had no institutional status or power to provide initial status and credibility, all of her leadership success was down to her intrinsic ability and character.

Third, you don't become a leader overnight. And you will certainly be handicapped in exercising leadership if you delay starting to develop yourself as a leader until after early adulthood. It's a process you have to grow into, and it's a role that takes some getting used to. Taking responsibility when things are tough and promoting yourself as someone who can be trusted to take charge in such situations requires a lot of self-confidence and comfort with one's ability. I'm not talking about cockiness and ego here: I'm talking simply about being comfortable with what, for most people, is the toughest task they will ever undertake.

My fourth point is a recommendation, particularly aimed at aspiring young leaders who may read *So you want to be a leader*. Start as early as you can. Put yourself forward to help out when you can, and take the lead when this is necessary (naturally, without being too ambitious initially). Build experience at working with and through people. Team sport is a common way in which this is done, but joining community teams and committees and the like will also be beneficial. And if it sometimes seems a drudge – as it almost inevitably will from time to time – stick with it, because no life learning experience is wasted for the aspiring leader. Try to choose the broadest educational experiences you can. Travel is another useful area from which you can learn. The more you learn about society, economics, politics and the way things work in the world, the better leader you will be.

You are going to make mistakes – all leaders do. However, those leaders who emerge as people we trust and respect are those for whom a mistake is never wasted, but is instead seen as an opportunity to learn.

My very last revelation is the one about which I am most proud. It is only fair that I tell you that Judy, the exemplary local leader, is my wife. I have learned more about leadership from watching her, especially in the context of my refreshed understanding of the true process of leadership, than I have from any book.*

I can only wish that you, the reader, will be as lucky as I have been in choosing partners in your life and endeavours.

---

* A fascinating account of Judy's story is contained in her 2009 witness statement. See Victorian Bushfires Royal Commission, Witness statement: Judith Margaret Frazer-Jans, http://vol4.royalcommission.vic.gov.au/index.php?pid=100 (ed.)

Leadership – it's all about you

Geoff Gallop

Professor Geoff Gallop AC is a former Labor premier of Western Australia. After studying economics at the University of Western Australia, he was awarded a Rhodes Scholarship and studied politics, philosophy and economics at Oxford University. His doctorate was awarded in 1983. From 1986 to 2006 he was a member of the Western Australian Legislative Assembly. He was a minister in the Lawrence Labor government in Western Australia from 1990 to 1993 and the Leader of the Opposition from 1996 to 2001. He was the Premier of Western Australia from 2001 to 2006.

Professor Gallop is currently director of the Graduate School of Government at the University of Sydney, initiating public sector executive education programs, some of which have been delivered in Africa and South-East Asia. He is currently chair of the Australian Republican Movement. He has published three books – Pigs' meat: selected writings of Thomas Spence (1982), A state of reform: essays for a better future (1998), and Politics, society, self: occasional writings (2012). In 2008 Professor Gallop was made a Companion of the Order of Australia.

At its core, leadership is personal – it's all about you! It's true, of course, that leaders need technical, managerial and political capacities and skills – they are necessary for leadership, but not sufficient. Leadership in an accountable society needs not only personality and presence but also self-awareness, integrity and empathy. Egos, emotions and morality are involved and cannot be ignored.

Nosce te ipsum (Know thyself).

—Delphic maxim

When we speak of leadership we may be thinking of those who become – or wish to become – leaders in their field of endeavour. On the other hand, we may be thinking of the exercise of leadership in particular circumstances, sometimes by those who we wouldn't normally think of as leaders. In the case of the latter, leadership may be shown in an act of compassion by a member of an otherwise unforgiving community, an act of courage in the face of danger, an inspiring speech when all seems lost or a display of honesty in a world corrupted by deceit. The list is as long as the beliefs we have about what makes humans distinctive in the world of nature.

Such acts of compassion, courage, inspiration and honesty remind us of what really matters, and none of us, no matter what our circumstances in life, can contract out our personal responsibility in instances like these without a loss of self-respect and dignity.

There is, however, another way of looking at leadership. Organisations, whether they are public, private or community-based, have layers of power and authority, both formal and informal, and it's hard to know with precision why some people become leaders and others don't. In some cases it's a question of personal ambition, or sometimes individuals are literally drafted into the position by colleagues who respect ability and recognise potential. There's not one reason nor is there one process.

What we do know is that when someone becomes a leader they enter a completely new space. They are now looked to when decisions have to be made and then judged on their decisions. In a democratic and accountable society like ours, the second factor, judging, is as important as the first, and it applies not just to the decision itself, but to the way it is made.

Leadership capacities and skills

It's clear for all to see that certain capacities and skills are needed for the task of leadership. The necessary skills may be technical, managerial or political.

In respect of technical skills, it may be that the organisation being led requires them as a matter of course. For example, understanding parliamentary procedure would be needed for a political leader, as would being able to 'read the books' for a business leader and knowing all about research methodology for an academic leader. Should an organisation be heavily dependent on sophisticated technology – as so many are today – skills in that area would also be necessary in respect of both procurement and day-to-day operations. In some circumstances, expertise in a particular area rather than general knowledge may be the key. Leadership when fighting fires or handling floods comes to mind.

In and of themselves, intellect and knowledge are also important. Leaders need to be hungry for information about everything that's pertinent to the organisation they lead. They need to ask, what is happening in the world that is relevant to them, what new ideas have been tried, and of those, which have worked and which haven't.

It's not surprising to me, then, that good leaders are usually well versed in the range of scanning and anticipating methodologies such as SWOT (strengths, weaknesses, opportunities, and threats) analysis and scenario planning. Such approaches allow a leader to move beyond thinking of the future in terms of the past – a habit that can be highly dangerous in an ever-changing world. Such methods also require us to consider the all-important 'what if?' questions and prepare for contingencies.

In the worlds of politics, community service and business today, the capacity of leaders to engage important stakeholders and the general public has become central. Engaging people may be a simple case of information provision and communication or it might mean an exercise in consultation or democratic engagement. Such activities won't be effective if they're undertaken on the basis of instinct, nor if they're performed in an unprofessional way. It follows that knowing how to engage people is a prerequisite for modern leadership – indeed, it is a science that needs to be fully understood and embraced in good faith. Not doing it well can be as bad as not doing it at all. How often do we hear communities say of governments and businesses, 'you were never really serious about consulting us about your work or engaging us in your plans'? All too often this result is a case of good intentions being undermined by bad practice, but whatever the reason, it can seriously undermine the trust needed for organisations to succeed.

It's not just important for leaders to understand their organisations, the context in which they operate and the technologies they use and need – they also need to understand the people they have been given the responsibility to lead. Leadership will involve management, and management requires people and political skills.

Leaders may inherit well-functioning organisations and their task then is to keep them that way. On the other hand, they may inherit dysfunctional organisations struggling for survival in the political or commercial marketplace. They may have to consolidate a nearly completed change management exercise or start a new one.

However, they will only rarely be given a blank sheet of paper on which to map the future, and there will always be some things they can't change as well as some they can. Recognising the difference between the two requires a deep knowledge – not just of what can and can't be done but also of people and how they respond when challenged.

There will be a political element in the functioning of most organisations. There will be team players and those for whom self-interest is paramount; perception may matter as much as reality; customs may be as important – or more important – than rules and regulations; and just as is the case in the wider community, there will be different interests within any organisation vying for power and influence. The level of political give and take may be minimal or it may be defining but it has to be acknowledged – and managed.

In such a world, leadership can't come down to one person, even though responsibility does. At the top, a good team of advisers will be crucial and down-the-line functions will need to be properly aligned with capacities. Behind all of this there must be a narrative about the past, present and future of the organisation that can be translated into meaningful job descriptions for all involved. Communicating such a story to a range of different people with different tasks will be as important as developing it in the first place. All of us need meaning in our work, and leaders can inspire us to that end.

The legal requirements attached to management will vary from sector to sector and organisation to organisation, but should never be underestimated or ignored. We live in an era of judicial review and due process, and many leaders have fallen on the sword they have created for themselves by cutting corners in the interests of a quick decision. Labour relations, financial disclosure, environmental reporting, work health and safety, equity and access are all part of the modern managerial equation.

Remember too that leaders don't just lead, they are also led – political leaders are elected by their colleagues and CEOs by boards of management. They have to manage above as well as below, and getting the balance right isn't easy. However, what it does mean is that there are terms and conditions attached to the powers they are given. Leaders need to be fully aware of these, relaxed about what they mean and confident of their capacity to fulfil them.

Leadership and the individual

At the heart of the matter is the individual leader and his or her self-awareness, integrity and empathy. It's the key that connects technical, managerial and political skills to the task at hand – or to put it another way, our technical, managerial and political skills are a necessary but not sufficient condition for leadership.

In our democratic society, talking about leadership means talking about effective and sustainable leadership. Effective leadership is that which produces good outcomes for the community and sustainable leadership is that which lasts long enough to embed those good outcomes into the fabric of institutional life. Let me put it this way – it's possible to have technically competent, politically smart leaders who achieve very little – so too is it possible to have leaders who achieve a good deal very quickly but who lose it all just as quickly.

In saying this, two important qualities come to mind: conviction and integrity.

The decisions leaders make have consequences – for the organisation and its success or failure; for the leaders themselves; and for those on the outside who are affected by what the organisation does. It may be the case, for example, that a business does very well for its shareholders but at the expense of the health and wellbeing of its workers or the community within which it operates.

Ethical leaders will cast the net as far as possible so that all factors – and not just their organisation's narrow self-interest – are taken into account. In government that means acting in the public interest, which doesn't just involve the interests of the majority (democracy), but also of minorities (human rights), the past (our heritage) and the future (sustainability). Equally, we can't define human welfare just in terms of our material interests; the natural environment has to be taken into account as well. After all, it is the foundation stone for life and liveability.

There are a number of interesting connections at play here. First, it can be observed that well-led organisations usually have a sense of purpose that goes beyond their narrow self-interest. This sense of purpose helps morale and fosters trust from the wider world. What makes such organisations well led is the attention paid to internal processes, as well as end goals. It is understood that a victory today on the basis of unethical or devious behaviour may very well mean a defeat tomorrow. In other words, in today's world of accountability, good practice and sustainability are bed partners.

Second, leaders will be affected by the decisions they make – or are asked to make. We live in a competitive world and we need to take risks in order to survive. However, if those risks involve crossing the threshold between right and wrong or, at the least, crossing that threshold as it is understood by the person concerned, there will be consequences. Integrity matters, along with pride and self-respect, and all of us have to pass what Peter Drucker has called the 'mirror test'. He writes:

> What ethics requires is to ask oneself: 'What kind of person do I want to see when I shave in the morning, or put on my lipstick in the morning?'

This is, he says, not just a case of ethical considerations as we normally think of them, but also of our own understanding of how we believe organisations should function. Do we prioritise the bottom line at all costs or do we value 'caring and sharing'? He concludes:

> To work in an organisation the value system of which is unacceptable to a person, or incompatible with it, condemns the person both to frustration and to non-performance'.[1]

Self-awareness

Each of us – leaders included – will have weaknesses as well as strengths. Each of us has our own emotional architecture as well as our own aptitudes and values. However, it's one thing to understand this reality in general terms, but quite another to know what it means for *you* and the way *you* behave.

When someone takes on the mantle of leadership, self-awareness can be the crucial difference between success and failure. A leader may stubbornly refuse to acknowledge that he or she has weaknesses and take no steps to overcome them. This oversight might be due to poor communication or negotiation skills, or perhaps an inadequate knowledge base in an area that matters to an organisation.

The very fact that someone has power doesn't mean they are omnipotent. Inadequacies that are acknowledged can be addressed either by taking steps to learn and adapt or by bringing to the team those with skills that complement those of the leader. This is easier, of course, if the areas of weakness are more in-house rather than displayed on the public stage. In fact, communication and presentation skills generally can't be ignored by anyone seeking leadership, be it political, business or community, in today's media-saturated world.

Awareness of one's own character and the strengths and weaknesses associated with it really matters. Leadership involves decisions, and at least some degree of conflict is inevitable. Leaders have friends but they also create enemies, sometimes from among those they thought to be friends. Leaders will be criticised and some of that criticism will be personal – and possibly nasty. Sometimes feelings will need to be suppressed – leaders need to guard against letting their feelings out in the heat of the moment and saying or doing things they regret later.

This is where what management theorists call 'emotional intelligence' comes into the picture. It means being in control, being fully aware of the dynamics at play and not being carried away by any of them. It means being able to understand what others are feeling and thinking, by properly listening to and observing them. It means being able to consider matters objectively and not rushing to judgement.

Some might say that such skills are nothing more than a subset of the managerial and political skills I mentioned earlier. To some extent that is true, but what is missing in that assessment is the more deeply personal element associated with self-awareness or a lack thereof. Managerial and political skills are needed to keep the ship afloat and moving forward, but that assumes the captain is not distracted or inflexible. It means being healthy and alert to the detail that has to be addressed. It means being clear-sighted in the face of changing conditions – and agile enough to change course when required. There is just as much psychology in all of this as there is intellect.

Perhaps the greatest personal challenge associated with power is the potential for hubris. Those who possess power have status in society; so too do they have the potential to do things that help some and harm others. Not all those who gain power cope with the associated flattery. They may start out humble but finish as arrogant and uncaring.

In many ways all these character issues come down to balance – pride in achievement but not arrogance, willingness to make decisions while caring about their effects, and political awareness and judgement but not as ends in themselves. All good leaders should have friends and mentors who can keep them in touch with how these balances are being drawn and whether the lines between right and wrong and effectiveness and ineffectiveness are being crossed.

However, mentoring can only go so far and it is important that leaders take an interest in these matters themselves. This has to mean room for reflection and, most importantly, self-reflection. We all need to know when the processes of leadership are beginning to overwhelm us, and this can happen as easily to those who appear strong and invulnerable as to those who don't.

Wellbeing

We now have evidence about what being employed in high-powered professions can mean for people who are anxious or who have a predisposition to depressive illness. In a survey conducted for *beyondblue* by Beaton Consulting, higher than average levels of depressive symptoms were found among professionals when compared with the wider population. What we are finding here is that the mix of unbridled ambition, a perfectionist attitude, stress and overwork can be dangerous, with a significant proportion of the survey also reporting that they 'used alcohol and other (non-prescription) drugs to manage symptoms of depression'.[2] These are the very people from whom we draw our leaders in the government, not-for-profit and profit sectors.

It's true of course that stress (and its management) is not the same as depression and that each needs to be managed differently; however, one can be a precursor to the other. It's important, then, for *all* who are involved in leadership to be concerned about their mental health and wellbeing. For most it's a case of managing time and its demands with a view to keeping on the ball, but for some it's a case of managing mind and body to avoid illness.

The fact that we live in a world that stigmatises all forms of mental illness doesn't help. It makes it harder for individuals to face up to their conditions, and all too often feelings are suppressed in ways that bring even more pain and distress. Some in society still adopt the 'pull yourself together' approach to those who are mentally ill.

If interpreted as recognition of the need to seek medical treatment it may be useful but if, as is more often the case, it is linked to an unsophisticated belief in strength of will it can, as indicated above, complicate matters even further.[3]

Leaders too need to understand that strength is conditional and, in personal terms, a capacity we can develop through self-reflection rather than a given we can call upon without complications and qualification. All of us have a mind *and* a body, and they are connected in ways that even today we do not fully understand. Care and attention to the health of both is important – not just for a leader but also for his or her employees. This is not just a personal matter but a management requirement in today's competitive and fast-moving world.

Leadership does require knowledge, capacities and skills, but the key to effectiveness is the way the *individual* understands and applies them in the wide range of circumstances that can exist. It's all about *you*, your convictions and your character, your strengths and weaknesses and your awareness of all of the above.

---

1 Drucker, P, 2001, *Management challenges for the 21st century*, p.176.

2 beyondblue, *Annual Professions Survey – April 2007*. www.beatonglobal.com/pdfs/Depression_in_the_professions_survey.pdf.

3 Gallop, G, 2013, 'Fighting the stigma of mental illness', *WA Today*, www.smh.com.au/comment/fighting-the-stigma-of-mental-illness-20130218-2encu.html.

Broaden your perspective and find your path

Andrew Hughes

Andrew Hughes is the principal of Andrew Hughes Training. With degrees in economics and law, and a masters degree in international law, Andrew has had varied exposure to the corporate legal world before turning to his current role. Known as Australia's most inspirational mindset coach for professionals, Andrew is an international speaker, corporate trainer, and executive coach. His courses in human potential and transformational leadership have been enthusiastically received. He is passionate about developing talent, increasing employee engagement and creating leaders.

Leadership is a concept generally associated with and spoken about in the context of a business, a cause, an organisation, a field or an idea, but this limits what leading is really about. Leadership transcends these contexts and concepts – a great leader is not defined by what he does, nor by where she does it, but by what she embodies, nurtures in others, and authentically lives.

Great leaders acknowledge the primacy of life over any career, cause or organisation – the latter serves, and is an expression of, the former and not vice versa. Guided by their calling, great leaders observe the drama of life with perspective, and respond with wisdom rather than cleverness. They approach the experience of life as an opportunity to express potential and live authentically, just as Steve Jobs did in his short but emphatic life.

This approach to leadership, as embodied by great global figures such as Gandhi, Mandela, Martin Luther King and Aung San Suu Kyi, is the way of being that the world needs now. It's a model of behaviour that is in stark contrast with the self-interested and destructive approach that commonly pervades public life.

I am not bound to win, but I am bound to be true. I am not bound to succeed, but I am bound to live up to what light I have.

—Abraham Lincoln

When Einstein was asked to pose the single most important question facing humanity, he is said to have replied, 'Is this a friendly universe?' The answer to that question for each of us is profound, for it determines the lens through which we experience life. It is this perspective that will determine whether we experience life as a struggle or a breeze, whether our glass is half empty or half full. The facts of life are irrelevant – it is what we make of them that determines our reality. Perspective is everything.

Public debate is an airing of perspectives. The broader and more balanced those perspectives are, the greater the quality of the debate. That means it is incumbent on anyone who wishes to enter public life (and so assume a leadership position in society) to question, and in doing so broaden, his or her perspective. That requires more than getting another academic gong – which, in many cases, only hardens a person's views. The real broadening in perspective that is required is at the scale considered by Einstein.

As everyone knows, perspective shifts with experience. Profound experiences can induce seismic shifts in perspective, examples being the birth of a first child, the 'overview effect' (experienced by astronauts who have seen Earth from space) and near-death experiences.

Luckily, you don't have to nearly die or have a Virgin Galactic ticket to broaden your perspective. You can simply ask profound questions about life, just as Einstein did. They lead to alignment with your highest values, and ultimately to the discovery of your *telos* or life purpose. This kind of openness creates a radically different, inspiring and compassionate lens through which to view life and engage in public debate.

The alternative is to continue a public debate characterised by narrow-mindedness and entrenched positions – hardly a great model for our children.

Leading is not following

Since the 1990s, we have been exposed to a public debate that has undeniably shifted to become more personal, sensational and position based, and less willing to consider different points of view. Spin and the media are used as tools of persuasion, to the detriment of genuine considered debate. It is all head and no heart. There is a lot of cleverness, but not a great deal of wisdom. Debate is about winning and being vindicated, with the ends justifying the means.

When debate is driven by polls and self-interest, it is analogous to a flock of sheep swept along by the one most scared or making the most noise. As the son of a sheep farmer, I promise you this seldom leads to wise choices. In public life it leads to clever, populist and divisive debate, often devoid of compassion and wisdom.

The truth is, cleverness and hard-hearted public debate are failing us. Recent gifts include the global financial crisis, painful corporate collapses, a warming environment, an epidemic of mental health complaints, and a myriad of wars and environmental disasters.

The system we created through our cleverness has developed a life of its own, and is now broken. The only way to change what we are currently reaping is to change what we sow. Change must come from within – in the form of a shift in perspective about life, its meaning and our potential.

Leading requires service, not self-service

As Nelson Mandela said in his inauguration speech, each of us has a light within that we are obliged to bring forth. By honouring that light we serve the world. It is in 'service' that we find a place of fulfilment and wisdom – the true place of the self-actualised individual. Fear stops most people from being vulnerable enough to share that gift, to listen to their heart and intuition and be guided to that place. But it is this inner world of peace, acceptance, and honouring their value in the service of the greater good that is the real secret to the success of the transformational leaders and business people of our time.

Public life and debate ought to set an example to the community of what it means to be true to that potential – to the light within. If you are in public life your challenge is to look beyond self-service and make the world a better place. You'll only get there if you open your heart, listen to your intuition and decide to serve the expansion of life. If *So you want to be a leader* helps just one person start that journey, it has been worthwhile.

I'm contributing to this book because it fits with my *telos*. In 2007 I left a secure and successful career in the legal industry to discover what it was that I could do to better serve the world. It turns out honouring my light involves me encouraging and inspiring others to find and pursue their potential. Given my background, my focus is especially on you – a leader in a system that needs your wisdom now.

Public debate reflects public perspective

As levels of affluence have increased in Australia, society has become focused on 'having' (as opposed to 'being') as the key to a better experience of life. Public debate reflects this, both directly and indirectly, by focusing on 'having' or 'not having'. In doing so, public debate has become entrenched in a drama cycle.

The drama cycle goes something like this. The public or the business community is unhappy about not having enough (the victim) and demands the government do something about it (become the rescuer). The government then takes action (as a rescuer) such as lowering or raising taxes or cutting or starting funding programs. In doing so, someone is always adversely affected. The government is now seen as the persecutor. The adversely affected parties then complain (playing the victim), blaming the government and allowing the opposition to promise it would do it better (becoming the rescuer). The roles in the drama cycle may change but the treadmill continues.

In this cycle there is always a persecutor, a victim and a rescuer, and who that is depends entirely on perspective. It might be a union, a business, boat people, bureaucrats, the Greens, banks – the list is endless and the roles interchangeable.

In the drama cycle personalities are fickle, no one is ever happy for long, someone is always to blame, stress is chronic, busyness is pervasive, spin is paramount and stated positions can shift dramatically.

The hypnosis of justification and blame

The consequence for public debate and leadership is that it is often framed in terms of blame, justification, and demands for and promises of rescue. The 43rd Australian Parliament illustrated this point.

Politicians and commentators alike described the atmosphere of the 43rd Australian Parliament as 'toxic'. All participants called for change and yet few were able to break their addiction to blaming, exaggerating claimed misdeeds, minimising genuine achievements and attacking character whenever possible. Parties began to believe their own rhetoric, claiming a monopoly on good character, decency and common sense. Debate became mean-spirited, ego driven, position-centric and solely about winning – individual vindication and power at the expense of the common good.

And so the 43rd Australian Parliament presented a leadership model of personal success at any cost – a model that has proven through history to be divisive, demoralising and on occasion demonic. The 112th Congress of the United States proved no better, being the least productive and most divided in history, with less than 10 per cent of the US public approving of its behaviour. Each governing house was afflicted with self-importance, self-righteousness and ultimately self-destruction.

The unwinnable game

The irony of this pattern of existence is that it creates an unwinnable game, both at the public and private level. At its core, the desire to 'have' is a desire for pleasure or a flight from pain. For the majority of Western society, 'having' is simply a means to feel better.

Inherent in this paradigm is the flawed premise that pleasure or happiness is dependant on what is external. In fact, only 10 per cent of our happiness can be determined by external factors – 90 per cent is determined by what is going on internally, as superbly demonstrated in *The happiness advantage* by Shawn Achor. That means what is external to us is almost irrelevant when it comes to being happy. Isn't it odd then that the predominant focus of individuals and public debate in Western society is on what is external? The majority have placed all of their eggs in a very small basket.

As a coach, I regularly witness the demoralising nature of this way of being. Workaholics begin to break down mentally and physically from chronic stress, but can't stop working because they only allow themselves to feel happy when they're 'getting things done'. Successful entrepreneurs go from conquest to conquest, building wealth but feeling empty. Parents exercise extreme control over their children, demanding behaviours that help them feel like good parents. Pleasers exhaust themselves trying to keep everyone happy and are hypercritical of themselves for not achieving what is an impossible task.

For each of these archetypes, internal turmoil comes from the individual's perception, rather than the situation itself. The antidote – and the means to escape from the drama cycle – is a change in perspective.

Perspective is everything

There are no facts, only interpretations.
—Friedrich Nietzsche

Psychological pleasure and pain, once you move beyond survival and the meeting of basic needs, is a matter of perspective. Lock a person convicted of a crime in solitary confinement for two years alone with his thoughts and he may lose his mind. Do the same to a Buddhist monk and he may thank you. Perspective is not only personal – it determines behaviour.

In the context of public debate, the more you are drawn into the drama cycle and succumb to the collective hypnosis of self-importance and busyness, the less perspective you will have. Before you know it, you'll believe your own press, demonise anyone who disagrees with you and become trapped in your ever-narrowing views. All of a sudden you'll be part of the problem and you won't be able to see it.

The importance of open-minded reflection becomes obvious. Quality public debate and great leadership start with perspective – an ability to remain removed from the turmoil and drama cycle that typically preoccupies most. Equally important is the ability to access happiness internally, rather than needing to win or be proven right to feel valued, approved of or worthy. Too often it seems public debate is all about the latter.

It's not that important

One of the symptoms of an approaching nervous breakdown is the belief that one's work is terribly important.
—Bertrand Russell

The first way to 'keep your head when all about you are losing theirs and blaming it on you' (as Rudyard Kipling put it) is to contrast the drama that confronts you with the totality of life. The comparison is humbling.

You are one person on a small planet populated by seven billion other humans whose concerns are no more or less important than yours. You have a life span of 50–100 years on a planet that is 4.5 billion years through a 13 billion year life cycle. You are not even a blip on the cosmic radar.

If that isn't putting things into a bigger perspective for you, remember that while our sun is more than one million times larger than Earth, on a cosmic scale it is tiny. In our galaxy, VY Canis Majoris is the largest known star, with a diameter of 2.8 billion kilometres, and a volume up to 9.3 billion times greater than our sun!

Add to this that Earth is one of 100 billion earth-like planets in our galaxy[1] and there are over 500 billion galaxies in the known universe. That's 5×10^{22} planets similar to Earth that could sustain life.

In truth, we are smaller than small. If you think about your reality in this context, you'll find that your worries, concerns about what others think about you, attempts to prove yourself worthy, feelings of righteousness, etc., are trivial. They are also the source of suffering, and a symptom of a narrow perspective.

You are a walking miracle

Once you can rise above the life drama that surrounds you, you'll find clean air. It may also dawn on you that you are part of a much larger and grander game of life than you imagined. Your body is composed of mostly oxygen, carbon and hydrogen. There has been no hydrogen created since the big bang some 13 billion years ago, and all oxygen and carbon were created 7–12 billion years ago from collapsing stars. Your body is literally stardust.

At a cellular level, your body is an electrochemical miracle comprised of 50 trillion or so cells, each one experiencing potentially millions of chemical reactions per second. Somehow, all of this works harmoniously, directed by a brain described by some* as a complex quantum computer. Your brain has 85 billion neurons constantly firing and connecting in different patterns, forming a million new connections every second of your life.[2] It's constantly changing. As Sir Roger Penrose says, 'Compared to the complexity of [your] brain, a galaxy is just an inert lump.'

So while on the one hand your troubles and concerns are trifling, arising from your internal fantasy of reality built on the illusory truth of your thoughts, on the other you are provided with a vehicle that is akin to space-age technology at its finest. Can it be that you

* Stuart Hameroff and Roger Penrose came up with this idea, saying the quantum process exists in the microtubules, where we see nonlocal behaviour. See www.youtube.com/watch?v=jjpEc98o_Oo.

were provided with this marvel in order to primp, preen, belittle, obfuscate, bully, scheme, grandstand, spin the truth, manipulate and otherwise add to the stinking pile of public debate that has dominated recent history? It's impossible to imagine that anyone could not make better use of his or her talents.

Where do you fit?

If you wish to find yourself, you must first admit that you are lost.

—Brian Rathbone

If you are not to become another cog perpetuating the maladies of the system, you might ask yourself, 'Where do I fit in the game? What is the meaning or purpose of it all?' If you do that, you're at the beginning of your journey to becoming a great leader.

Saints, sages, seers, clerics and philosophers have been ruminating on these questions for at least the last 4,500 years. The answers they found have a common thread, one illustrated daily all around you in nature. Everywhere on earth there are plants, animals, insects, fish and other organisms all striving to do one thing – thrive. A dandelion stretching out from the crack in a footpath, a seagull unerringly seeking out chips at a local beach, a resolute tree in an ancient rainforest, an eagle circling in a hazy summer sky. All are wired to be the best they can be in the environment they're in. The dandelion has no aspiration to be a tree, the seagull no aspiration to be an eagle – all are in the moment, dedicated to being the best of what they are.

What about you?

Joseph Campbell got it right when he said, 'Life has no meaning. Each of us has meaning and we bring it to life. It is a waste to be asking the question when you are the answer.' What Campbell is alluding to is the reflection of what we see in nature – what you bring to life is you. Your journey is to be you; to be all you can be. You get there by finding and living your 'calling'. History has revealed that this is the place from where you can begin to do justice to the mind-boggling magnificence of life. This is the space from which you just might begin to fulfil your potential.

If your purpose is to be all you can be, what does that mean about the purpose of work, leadership and public debate? The question reveals that each process is not a means in itself. Rather, each is the servant of life. They are processes and forums that allow you to express life, vehicles through which you can express the best of who you are. Great leaders such as Gandhi, Nelson Mandela, Dr Martin Luther King, Abraham Lincoln and Aung San Suu Kyi illustrate the point. The same can be said for Bono, Michelangelo, Steve Jobs, JK Rowling, Fred Hollows, and many more across all walks of life.

As Steve Jobs said, 'We're here to put a dent in the universe. Otherwise why else even be here?'

Accepting the primacy of life over work is a very different lens through which to consider public debate and your role in it, as well as the obligations and role of a leader. Not surprisingly, it can deliver radically different results.

As Einstein intimated, in the end, it's all about perspective.

Finding your *telos*

If you ask me what I came to do in this world, I, an artist, will answer you: I am here to live out loud.

—Émile Zola

In modern society, looking for your calling is seen by most as being unrealistic. Those who search for it are often ridiculed and called dreamers. Working in one's calling is considered an elusive luxury for a select few. This is one reason why so many people settle for second-best. If ever there was a mindset that holds the planet back from achieving the apparently impossible, this is it.

What is certain is that you have a calling, and only you know what that calling is. If you take a closer look, you'll see that your life already embodies it. Notice what excites and inspires you, what it is that you love to do. What do you like to read about? Who do you look up to and what about them inspires you? You don't create or make up your calling. Rather, you detect it.

Humanity has been talking about this calling for centuries. The ancient Vedas, which were written some 3,500 years ago, refer to it as *dharma* – each person's perfect place in the cosmic cycle. The great Greek philosophers called it *telos* – your end purpose. All of the great mystery schools, philosophies and religions of the world fundamentally agree on this point.

Your calling is your gift to the world, your greatest expression of the life force you represent. It's where you will find the elusive 'flow' – where creativity flows effortlessly through you while time stands still. It's where you'll consistently stumble upon great insight, and find the resilience to face your greatest fears.

You have a calling, and your task is to find it.

Run your own race

To be yourself in a world that is constantly trying to make you something else is the greatest accomplishment.

—Ralph Waldo Emerson

Once you find your calling, your obligation is to pursue it, *your* way. Just as the seagull won't thrive by trying to be an eagle, you won't thrive by trying to be someone you're not. As simple as this may sound, it's not, because there's every chance you've been trained to fit in since birth. The pressure to curb your behaviours and desires to obtain approval started with your parents and was enforced by the education system, modelled by your peers and perpetuated by your community.

It's hard to run your own race if you've been trained to think like a lemming. So, just like the hippies of the 60s, if you want to be all you can be you need to 'find yourself'. In the absence of the pharmacological support of Woodstock, the following four steps are essential to your journey.

Step 1 – Discover your own wisdom

If you're going to do it your way, you have to start taking your own advice as to what your way is. The truth is, no one else is you. No-one else knows what you are thinking, what really matters to you, how much courage or determination you have, what your true strengths are and how deep they run – so what's the value of their advice when compared to your own? They might be able to give you the benefit of their experience and tell you what they would do, but that's as far as anyone can go. Only you can know what's best for you.

My boss once told me I needed to be more serious at meetings. I realised I was being provided with a very clear choice. I could either accept the advice and stop being me, or I could trust my instinct, ignore the advice and do it my way. I chose the latter. From then on,

I listened more intently to my own advice. My career accelerated rapidly.

Listening to your own wisdom is not a rational or logical process. As seers, saints and prophets have been telling humanity for millennia, it's a process of quieting your mental chatter long enough to allow your inner wisdom to be heard. Far from being the result of thinking, your inner wisdom is likely to be the result of non-thinking. For example, reflect on how many times great ideas or solutions to problems have popped into your head when you haven't being thinking about those problems. Neuroscience has recently confirmed that insight is much more likely to come from and be heard by a relaxed and calm mind.

So find time to be still. Whether through meditation, yoga, long walks in the park, knitting or staring at a warm fire, you need to find a way to relax deeply and quiet your thinking. After that, trust your instincts and take action accordingly.

Steve Jobs got it right when he said, 'Have the courage to follow your heart and intuition. They somehow already know what you truly want to become. Everything else is secondary.'

Step 2 – Consider the great questions of life

One of the reasons many fall short of their potential is that they fail to ask the big questions of life until the winter of their lives. When they do finally ask those questions, most look back with regret.

Bronnie Ware[3] was living on the east coast of Australia, struggling financially while engaged in unfulfilling work. So she asked herself some of the great questions of life and decided to pursue a job with heart. A short while later she found herself – despite having no relevant qualifications or experience – working as a palliative nurse caring for patients in the last weeks of their life.

As death loomed, Bronnie's patients shared their regrets – what they wished they had done but hadn't. What she noticed was that their biggest regrets weren't long and audacious bucket lists of things to be had and experienced. Rather, they were simple themes that defined how they lived. What's more, those regrets came up time and time again.

Bronnie Ware: top five regrets of the dying

1. I wish I'd had the courage to live a life true to myself, not the life others expected of me
2. I wish I hadn't worked so hard
3. I wish I'd had the courage to express my feelings
4. I wish I'd stayed in touch with my friends
5. I wish I had let myself be happier

These regrets reveal our cultural propensity to fall into the patterns of the past without question, only waking from the dream of our self-perpetuated 'reality' when it is too late to do it differently. The way out of this pattern is to challenge your thinking before it's too late.

The great questions of life require that you reflect on your perspective and question what you believe to be true. Such questions define who and what you will allow yourself to be. Einstein's pondering on the friendliness of the universe is an example of the power of such questions.

Here are some great questions to get you started.

- Who am I? (identity)
- Why am I here? (purpose)
- Where am I from? (heritage but not ethnicity)
- What can I do? (potential and mission)
- Where am I headed? (destiny)

Consistent reflection on these questions will lead you to a clearer and expanded understanding of who you are and what's possible for you. These are necessary markers for leaders in any field and will automatically raise the quality and content of your communication, internal and external.

Step 3 – Challenge your thinking around what you can and can't do

There is no man living who isn't capable of doing more than he thinks he can do.
—Henry Ford

You are boxed in by the boundaries of who you think you are and your actions are limited by what you believe is possible for you to achieve. Those who break free of these limiting bonds often do remarkable things. The Wright Brothers refused to believe man couldn't fly. When Henry Ford's engineers told him it was impossible to build an affordable, mass-produced motor car he refused to believe them.

Your actions are a product of your thinking and so you are exactly where you think you ought to be. Talented people are regularly overlooked for promotion because they don't truly believe they are good enough and so don't put themselves forward effectively, if at all.

It's essential that you begin to dig into what you really think of yourself. The questions in Step 2 will start that process. Then you need to take absolute responsibility, break free of the victim paradigm, and accept you are where you are because of what you think you're capable of. Make a list of what you must think about yourself and your capabilities in order to be where you are. Now challenge those ideas wherever they limit you.

Step 4 – Connect and work with your calling every day

Nothing inspires or energises more than working with your calling. It is what Maslow called 'self-actualisation', and it will lead you to profound insight, deep fulfilment and remarkable achievement. Not surprisingly, your brain is programmed to help you find and follow your calling. Glial cells in the brain create a myelin sheath that allows neural impulses to travel faster and habits to form. Those glial cells are heavily stimulated when you experience your calling. In essence, your brain is actively working to get you started on your life's work. Reality TV programs like *The Voice* and *MasterChef* demonstrate the point. When people find their purpose, their ability to learn, stretch and improve is turbocharged.

Those who find and live their calling also experience a great sense of service to the world, as their efforts become more acutely focused on others rather than themselves. Service is always a predominant aspect of the self-actualised individual. Working with your calling is a place of generosity and passion, open-mindedness with discernment, compassion with determination.

Conclusion

The quality of public debate in Australia has definitely deteriorated in recent years, which is a reflection of our community, caught in the drama cycle of life and the battle to be a 'have' rather than a 'have not'. To improve the debate the first step for you, as a leader, is to do what Gandhi implored – 'be the change you wish to see'. This means you must change your perspective.

Imagine a public debate and a public service dominated by people working in their calling and finding deep meaning in their roles. Imagine if all of those players took the time to quiet their minds, listen to their inner wisdom and connect with life every day. Imagine if those players approached their roles and all their communication as an opportunity to express the best of themselves and add to life on a cosmic scale. And imagine if all of those leaders refused to be constrained by limiting beliefs of the past, choosing instead to forge their own journey of service to their community.

It seems to me this would lead to vastly different public debate. The issue is, are *you* up for the challenge?

---

1. Yock, P, 2013, 'Extending the planetary mass function to Earth mass by microlensing at moderately high magnification', *Monthly Notices of the Royal Astronomical Society*, 431: 2975–2985.
2. Philips, H, *The Human Brain*, www.newscientist.com/article/dn9969-introduction-the-human-brain.html?full=true#.UwQet3nfI-A.
3. Ware, B, 2012, *The top five regrets of the dying: a life transformed by the dearly departing*, Hay House, San Francisco.

Being the leaders we want to see in the world

Cassandra Wilkinson

Cassandra Wilkinson is a social entrepreneur, political commentator and newspaper columnist. She was formerly a senior political adviser. Her book *Don't panic: nearly everything is better than you think* (2007) discusses how doomsayers from both the left and the right seek to make us panic in pursuit of their agendas and argues that the world is a nicer, safer, cleaner place than we think.

Cassandra is the co-founder and president of Australia's only dedicated Australian music radio station, Sydney's FBi Radio 94.5FM. She is also a director of contemporary music peak body Music NSW and a director of the Human Capital Project, a personal equity finance provider for Cambodian university students.

Cassandra argues that our community is full of great leaders – but not always in the places we expect to find them. These people show us that real leadership doesn't wait for permission and it doesn't need an audience. By grasping the opportunity to take on leadership roles that are small and local we can grow into the leaders we've been waiting to follow.

Be the change you want to see in the world.
—Mahatma Gandhi

The 2013 election saw an outbreak of exasperation about the state of Australian leadership. Bernard Keane described the leaders' debates as 'sterile rituals designed to avoid errors', which could have summed up the entire campaign.

It's timely to reflect on the state of leadership in Australia. The lack of it in public life is the obvious place to start but that ground is well covered. George Megalogenis' *The Australian moment* gives a good account of how Australia's leaders ran out of steam on making the economic progress that we need to preserve our standard of living. If you find time to curl up with Sally Warhaft's *Well may we say – the speeches that made Australia*, you'll get a good sense of the diminished rhetorical charms of today's politicians. Whatever your view of today's civic leaders, the purpose of *So you want to be a leader* is to inspire and guide us to something better.

If you want change, the easy option is to wait for a leader you can throw your support behind. That's what I did as a young activist – I joined the Australian Labor Party under Paul Keating and served diligently on the Young Labor executive, which in plain English means I licked a lot of stamps and letterboxed a lot of flyers. The harder option, but the one this book encourages you towards, is – to paraphrase Gandhi – to become the leaders we want to see in the world. In fact, it's also important to become the leaders we don't see – the leaders who make their workplaces, schools, neighbourhoods and communities better places for others to be.

I've spent half my adult life working for leaders and the other half being one. In my professional life I've advised professional leaders including Michael Costa (variously NSW Treasurer and Police Minister) and NSW Premier Kristina Keneally. In my private life I've been a director of an education charity and two community sector peak bodies, and most rewardingly, co-founder and president of community broadcaster FBi Radio – Australia's only dedicated Australian music station where more than 2,000 young volunteers have come to make music and friends and general mayhem since 2003.

While I enjoyed working for politicians, and highly recommend it, of the two experiences I've found the second infinitely more rewarding. It's from my experiences of the community sector, rather than professional politics, that I draw my faith in our ability as a community to repair the malaise in our nation's public leadership.

Why Australia deserves your leadership

In my not-too-short yet not-too-long life, I have loved a small assortment of people, a lot of great music and a few dogs. But what I've loved every day – from the moment I knew how to love anything at all – is Australia.

Thanks to an accident of birth and geography I was born in the greatest country in the world. A place where I would never fight or flee a war, never know hunger or the darkness of illiteracy. Of all the luck I've had – and I've been very lucky – the greatest piece of luck in my life was being born Australian.

I don't subscribe to the view that our luck has run out, but I do see structural problems emerging that we need to fix if Australia is going to continue to be a lucky country. Much like Gina Rinehart, we've all been born on a big pile of minerals and relied on it to stay rich through global and historical shifts in wealth and power.

The luck under the ground won't run out for a while, but the luck we make is only as good as the leadership we demand. Living standards were at risk in the 1970s and it took two generations of politicians from both sides to make difficult reforms that put our luck back on track.

Underneath our present high standards of living there are challenges with education, productivity and sustainability, to name a few. If we want to stay lucky we will have to provide the leadership to address them.

Keeping our luck is not just about managing our mining wealth and the swings and roundabouts of global commodities prices. It's also about keeping our democratic and social institutions strong, and that relies on good people caring enough to get involved in leading them.

We're a weird mob, it used to be said, and it's true if you consider how little time we spend in our schools, homes or civic places reflecting on how it got so good and how to keep it this way. We don't talk about how great this place is because we're not 'up ourselves' like that. We've never claimed to have God on our side, let alone truth or justice. We don't ask the world to speak our language, fear our gods or salute our flag.

But our healthy cynicism for politics and our democratic distaste for empty patriotism has begun to take on a resigned and bitter quality. It's not surprising people are losing faith in our leaders – our leaders seem to have long since lost faith in us. Leaders no longer lay out a dense and detailed manifesto like John Hewson's *Fightback!* or Paul Keating's *One nation*. They don't have the courage to tackle big debates or seek the authority for complicated reforms. Instead the seven-second grab, the tweet, the selfie and the five-point plan have replaced the 150-page manifesto as the standard communication tool of modern leadership.

The politicians blame the 24-hour media cycle and social media as if 24-hour talkback radio and the television news hadn't been around for decades. And as if the birth of newspapers hadn't frightened the hell out of their predecessors. Politicians were so panicked that the British parliament imposed a newspaper tax in 1711 which shut down the first *Spectator*. Notwithstanding this assault on the press, the number of newspapers printed annually in England rose to 14 million between by 1780.[1] Here in Australia, by 1886 there were at least 48 daily papers, according to the Australian government's 'About Australia' website.[2]

While the politicians blame the 'modern media' for their lack of courage, the media blames them for cheapening public debate – as if they have no obligation to be putting fire to the feet of politicians giving them 'grabs' instead of intelligent responses.

And slowly but surely, everyone blames the voters. Which is all of us really. Only they call it 'marginal seats' or 'western Sydney' or 'aspirational suburbs'. But it's in those very places that real leadership is being demonstrated every day.

Real leadership does exist

To state the obvious, what's happening in our national politics isn't leadership. Our governments are generally adequately managed by generally adequate people, but as long as a quarter of young people are missing out on work or study, as long as Indigenous kids suffer violence and illiteracy, and while ever there are families wondering where they will sleep in the luckiest country in the world, you'd have to score them 'can do better'.

Higher points can be allocated to some individual politicians who work hard, take chances and think deeply. One thing I admire about Tony Abbott is that he took the effort to detail his thinking in *Battlelines*, both because it took intellectual effort and courage and because it meant people knew where he stood. The most recent Labor leader to do that was Mark Latham, whose *Civilising global capital* was a dense and thoughtful work which I think stands as testament that he peaked too early to make the contribution he could have made.

Many politicians are hard-working, but so are shift workers and carers and single mums. Leadership isn't just a matter of putting the sweat in – it's about delivering new solutions for old problems, and bringing the community together to achieve them. The National Disability Insurance Scheme is the only radical political reform of the last decade. Politicians got on board, but it wasn't a solution devised by the leaders we elected to improve social welfare – rather, it owes its genesis to the community of carers who campaigned for it.

Real leadership abounds in Australian life, and the kind being demonstrated by those outside the political circus shows us the way to something better. Average voters patrol the beaches. Average voters fight the bushfires and clean up Australia. They run the 600,000 not-for-profit organisations across our nation. They volunteer at the RSPCA; they care for the disabled; they repair wheelchairs in Men's Sheds and pick up syringes in parks on Clean Up Australia Day.

More than a third of us belong to some kind of volunteer organisation. In these community endeavours many of us are providing leadership that is anonymous, results-focused and respected by the people we do it for. At the grass roots of Australian society, leadership is inspiring and humble. It is effective and accountable, and it gets results.

Some years ago I went to a meeting to start a radio station to play Australian music. We raised money from friends and supporters and we built a community enterprise that this year celebrated 10 years of full-time broadcasting. We now have a regular listenership of 250,000 people and have been recognised as a major factor in the current resurgence of Australian music. More than 2,000 volunteers made this possible, many of them taking quiet unrecognised leadership roles to make their community better.

When we could see bushfires from my home in Bundeena, my husband Paul, and what seemed like half of our neighbours, were out in their bright yellow uniforms saving people and homes. They were never paid … they never asked for thanks. They and the rest of their rural fire service mates get up every Sunday and get ready to do it again.

So why is political leadership different? A lot has been written about the structural factors diminishing the quality of leadership in politics. The decline in class loyalty to parties, the too-short length of the federal electoral cycle and a general decline in respect for institutions are all cited with varying degrees of justification. Among the theories is the growth of politics as a career in itself, where once it was usually a second career after people had earned a reputation at some substantive endeavour like business, union or community leadership, military service or science.

In truth, there have always been political careerists, but certainly the new trend of entering parliament with no experience of life outside the citadel has contributed to distrust between the elected and the electors. Most of the members of parliament who make business regulations have never had to prepare a business activity statement. Those who make laws for the charity sector haven't had to deal with the coalface impacts of volunteer regulations. Two quick examples of this are the need for formal qualifications and licences that have reduced charities' ability to accept donated food, and the 'working with children' requirements which have resulted in children being banned from many volunteer sites where checking everyone is too difficult. This often means parents have to quit volunteering. Onerous risk-management requirements have seen school swimming programs nearly wiped out in the ACT and Queensland because too many people in power make rules for people they have never met doing things they have never done.

Importantly for me, most have never tried something difficult and failed at it. While most of the inspirational CEOs you'll see on a TED talk or *Harvard Business Review* profile will stress how important it is to understand failure as part of innovation and change for the better, contemporary politics rewards a life of caution.

Contemporary political wisdom amounts to pleasing most of the people most of the time. I've done party political training and it's largely comprised of advice given by the cautious to the cautious. In a decade of working with politicians, my observation is that the cautious often prosper but make little impact. Every parliament in the country has 20-year veterans you've never heard of but very few Don Dunstans, Nick Greiners, Jeff Kennetts or Paul Keatings.

Menzies had such confidence in his ideas that he made his case directly to the people on his radio shows. Hawke trusted in his 'great love affair with the Australian people'. The current batch often seem afraid of the voters and prefer to analyse the electorate through focus groups than talk to them over a beer at the surf carnival. I can't imagine Menzies asking an advertising executive or party official to edit his famous 1942 address on 'the forgotten people'.

Real leadership starts with trust, not, as is often said, with the voters trusting the leader, but rather with the leader trusting the voters. Trusting them as Menzies did, to care about making a great country greater and to grasp the structural and ethical foundations of his approach to delivering it for them.

Leadership starts with big ideas

It is sobering to listen to or read Curtin's war speeches and then consider the nonsense being peddled by contemporary politicians that this or that campaign is the most important election in history, that the challenges facing the nation are unprecedented, or that recent global circumstances constitute an emergency of some kind unseen in political history.

Two generations without war, a quarter century of economic growth and the continuing blessings of our natural wealth suggest that the challenges set for this current generation of politicians have been modest at best by historical comparison. It's possible that's a factor in itself.

When you look at Canberra on a map, it's easy to see why it inspires conspiracy theories about Masons and Theosophists writing spells for its glorious future into the very bone structure of the streets and buildings. Obelisks and monuments to human endeavour form the geometrical points of a city of grand boulevards which were intended to be bustling by now.

When I was born there in 1971, Canberra was still a stationery cupboard in a sheep paddock. It had a hospital, in which I arrived, and a university, but it was and remains a dormitory for bureaucrats rather than the teeming centre of commerce and culture which was originally envisioned.

Tasmanian MP King O'Malley had originally declared 'it would be a black crime against posterity if we chose any place but Bombala' to be our capital. Yet he became, as Minister for Home Affairs, the overseer of the building of Canberra. He hired Walter Burley Griffin to build a city to initially house only 25,000 people, but hoped that 'the children of our children will see an Australian federal city that will rival London in population, Paris in beauty, Athens in culture and Chicago in industry.'

At the time of Federation, many Australian leaders were creating the architecture for governance of what is today called 'big Australia' – the dream of a populous and powerful Australia; the kind of dream about which most contemporary politicians express discomfort or outright rejection.

What makes early Australian political speeches a pleasure to read is their optimism. Sir Henry Parkes, during the Federation debates, surveyed the vast natural and human riches of Australia and asked rhetorically, 'What is there that should be impossible to those people?' Generations later, it turns out he was right, as we are still among the world's richest people. The question is, can we stay that way without more leaders like him?

Compare this to current public debates centred on how needy and weak we are. Everyone seems to be doing it tough or working harder than ever or facing the greatest challenge to living standards since the depression.

It may be that the times make the leaders. In these prosperous and peaceful days, ideas matter less because they can. Perhaps the very ease with which Australia can be adequately governed has allowed careerists and show ponies to take on responsibilities which would have taxed their limited abilities too far in tougher times.

In my better moods I see the convergence of contemporary political parties as a fitting reflection of the cohesion and prosperity of our nation. We are a united people with broadly shared goals, so the lack of competition in grand theories makes sense – nobody wants to fix what ain't really broke. The mainstream parties' unanimity on most policy issues reflects both the shared values of the population and the fact that most of our services are pretty good and our civic challenges less than dire.

In my darker moods I think that, though there's an element of truth in this idea of cohesion, it is starkly at odds with the broad view that the parties are out of touch with voters. Surveys of voters suggest they crave a much better kind of politics. One explanation for this is that just as we have a two-speed economy, we have two-speed politics.

There are those for whom the basic economic problems of life have been solved – they have homes in the inner cities; jobs; good-quality public hospitals and schools. Their 'Maslow's hierarchy' needs are for a politics of identity. For these people, gay rights, asylum seekers and self-actualisation in personal and professional life matter more than tax policy.

At the other end are people in the one-hour commute zone; people with disabilities; people on the unemployment line. For these people the cities feel full, the jobs taken, the services manifestly inadequate.

Whatever you think are the most important issues – the environment, the economy, refugees or education – there is no shortage of challenges left to resolve. As society becomes more complex and lifts its expectations, there are arguably more ways than ever that you can personally make your contribution to our country.

Some tips for young players – listen a lot then speak up

What I've learned from the leaders I've worked with is to start at the grass roots. When I started work with Michael Costa (when he was Police Minister), he told me to start arranging visits to police stations. He then announced that he wasn't going to set foot inside headquarters until he'd been to every local command in the state. I remember arriving at Manly police station to a very formal reception with tea and cake presided over by a high-ranking officer who was promptly asked to leave along with all the senior staff so Michael could hear the constables and sergeants talk frankly.

What Michael learned by talking to the people at the grass roots led him to make huge changes to everything from the promotions system to search powers to replacing their polyester 'McDonalds' pants with comfortable cargos. Once people got wind of these changes, our office was inundated with information and ideas because people trusted him.

What I've learned in my own leadership roles is to ask for help. Most of us get little done by ourselves – we need friends, we need advocates and often we need money. To become a good leader you need to learn how to get all those things for the people or causes you have chosen to represent. Once you start, you'll be amazed how many people are happy to help you. After many years of campaigning, I opened the mailbox one day to find a licence to broadcast a metropolitan FM radio station. FBi had $400 in the bank and I had a new baby daughter two days home from hospital. After many calls to many people I met with a music festival promoter called Brandon Saul who shook my hand and immediately took charge of raising a million dollars to set up our radio station.

Volunteer. If you want to develop your leadership skills and show off what you can do, don't wait to get paid for it. As a volunteer you will be given more responsibility, take more risks and manage more people and resources than you would likely be trusted with as a young person in the paid workforce. Everything I learned about earning trust and respect, I learned at FBi. I helped make it and it helped make me.

Often as a young leader you will be told to be quiet. You will be told to be polite, be a team player, work with the power structures or otherwise blend in and take instruction. For some this works. For most it does not. Sharing your ideas, especially in writing, helps you get clear about what you think. It also helps raise your profile. Far more importantly, it announces your presence to people who may help you. I didn't start writing until I was 35, but once I did, I attracted hundreds of new friends and supporters who have brought me great new opportunities. Having spent many years in youth politics, I have seen too many bright young leaders spend a year as president or secretary of this or that only to disappear into obscurity because they made no waves and consequently made no opportunities for themselves. So, finally – speak up, and keep speaking up until people listen.

---

1. Black, J, *Newspapers and Politics in the 18th Century*, www.historytoday.com/jeremy-black/newspapers-and-politics-18th-century.
2. Australian government, *The birth of the newspaper in Australia*, http://australia.gov.au/about-australia/australian-story/birth-of-the-newspaper.

Letting in the light – finding your tragic hero

Nadja Alexander

Nadja Alexander is professor of conflict resolution and law at Hong Kong Shue Yan University and visiting fellow at the University of New South Wales in Australia. She is active as a conflict intervener, speaker, coach and trainer in the Asia–Pacific, Europe and Australia. She has been engaged as a government policy adviser on dispute resolution in more than 10 countries and facilitated public conversations about how we engage with conflict in more than 30 countries.

Professor Alexander is co-developer of the REAL Conflict Coaching model* upon which parts of this essay are drawn. She edits the Kluwer Mediation Blog and the book series *Global Trends in Dispute Resolution*. Her books have appeared in the English, German, French, Russian and Chinese languages, with one, *International comparative mediation*, winning the international CPR Institute award for outstanding dispute resolution book.

This essay is about you, your brain and the stories you know. In this essay Nadja Alexander explores the melodramatic nature of the tales we tell when we are stuck in difficult conversations and tense situations. Whether in public or private life, when we find ourselves in conflict we tend to use particular storytelling patterns called melodramatic narratives. Here we explore the potentially destructive nature of these conflict storytelling patterns and consider the extent to which they are wired into the default mechanisms of our DNA. Drawing upon ideas from the practice of storytelling, narrative structures and conflict coaching theory, Nadja shows how we can mindfully engage our emotional intelligences, to find our own inner hero – the tragic hero. In doing so, we can shift the way we think about conflict from the blame pattern of melodrama to the problem-solving yet realistic structure of tragedy. Yes, life wasn't meant to be easy, but it doesn't have to be a melodrama.

Nadja explains how we can use the narrative of tragedy in

* See http://conflictcoachinginternational.com/coaching. 'REAL' is an acronym for 'reflection, engagement, artistry, learning'.

the conflicts of public and private life to engage even the most challenging of adversaries.

Forget your perfect offering
There is a crack, a crack in everything
That's how the light gets in.
—Leonard Cohen

When I was young, I wanted to do something important, something meaningful that would make a contribution to society. Like many of you reading *So you want to be a leader*, I yearned to make a difference and right the wrongs of the world – or at least some of them. Back then, I was able to tell right from wrong, good from bad, legal from illegal. Some three decades later, I continue to try to make a difference in the work that I do, but I have moved in my life from that youthful place of bold certainty in search of 'perfect offerings' to one of reflective curiosity. And it is from this place that I write to you.

As you read this essay, I invite you to recall the last time you were involved in a conflict. Although it might not be comfortable, try to remember what it was like for you. How you felt (were you anxious? angry? disappointed?), how you reacted physiologically (were you flushed or perspiring? what was your heart rate?), what you thought ('you idiot, I knew you weren't up to it'), and what you said … or didn't say.

Go on … take a minute.

Most of us, when we find ourselves involved in a conflict – whether it be an argument with a family member, a difficult conversation with a colleague, a tussle on the sporting field or a well-articulated legal dispute – tend to fall into certain unconscious patterns of storytelling behaviour involving melodramatic narratives in which we are the passive victim and another person is the active villain. In these polarised conflict stories of right and wrong, of black and white, we fail to 'let the light in' (to adapt Leonard Cohen's words) to reveal the paradoxical complexity associated with our conflicts. We fear losing control of the situation and being swept up into a whirlwind of uncertainty and unknowingness.

In this essay I will explore these melodramatic narrative patterns and suggest a different way of telling conflict stories that is more constructive for negotiations in both private and public life.

The stories we tell

Stories are powerful. The practice of storytelling is fundamental to the way we interact socially and make meaning of situations and events. As social beings, we tell stories to make sense of the world and to understand one another.[1] So much of what we 'know' comes from stories. In part this is because when we feel something we remember it. Our capacity for memory is linked to our limbic system (also called our emotional brain) and its ability to connect information through stories and visual and emotional associations.

Storytelling has a long and impressive history across human cultures. The sharing of stories has traditionally formed an essential and integral part of the patterning of life and law for many indigenous cultures. For Indigenous Australians, the Dreamtime explains through mythological stories how the world was created, while stories of the Dreaming establish the structures of society and rules for social behaviour, and set out the rituals performed to ensure continuity of life and land. Dreaming stories can be about the creation of sacred places, land, people, animals and plants, law or custom.

World religions also were handed down in the form of stories. Jesus Christ was said to speak in parables – simple stories used to illustrate a moral or spiritual lesson. The stories of Jesus Christ and other great religious figures are as influential today as they were when they were first recorded. Consider the parable of the good Samaritan, in which a traveller is beaten, robbed, and left half dead along the road. First a priest and then a Levite come by, but both avoid the man. Finally, a Samaritan comes by and helps the injured man. Today, more than 2,000 years later, the colloquial phrase 'good Samaritan' is used to refer to someone who helps a stranger.

From religion we move to politics and reflect on the famous storyteller, George Washington. In 1783, his revolutionary army was on the brink of mutiny. Washington at first attempted to quell the mutiny with rational arguments; however, it soon became obvious that the would-be mutineers were not listening. He then changed tack, squinting and pulling out his glasses, indicating that he wished to read out a letter from a congressman: 'Gentlemen, you will permit me to put on my spectacles, for I have grown not only grey but almost blind in the service of my country.' At this point, a number of officers started crying. He read the letter, which contained the congressman's personal and deeply felt reflections, and then walked out without further discussion. George Washington knew he had convinced his army not to mutiny, and the rest, as they say, is history.

Today, each and every one of us continues the oral tradition of storytelling – whether in coffee shops sharing with friends, or at political rallies addressing thousands of people. In addition, we make use of technology to tell our stories by sharing on Facebook, by blogging, by contributing online news stories and by making films with our smart phones. In these various ways, storytellers can take on the transformative power of chameleons, slipping in and out of a variety of roles such as negotiator, lobbyist, activist, diplomat, trickster, conciliator, teacher, student, entrepreneur and agent of change.

Communications technology effectively suppresses space through time so that the sharing of stories between people at opposite ends of the earth and even among strangers can be instantaneous. Our stories become at once connected with others' stories and networked. In many ways this connectedness is a good thing that spreads ideas and brings people together. In other ways the intensity of story exchange through technology leads to information overload and misunderstandings, as we struggle to make sense of a never-ending shower of headlines and storylines that ultimately overwhelm us. Scientists tell us that our brains streamline information so that we can cope with it and effectively ignore what we cannot compute. In other words, we simplify the stories we hear in order to make sense of them and remember the information they contain.

Stories make us feel

While technological innovations may have changed the power and politics of storytelling, the patterns of how we tell stories have largely remained the same. More than 2,000 years ago, Aristotle argued that we make decisions based not only on logical–rational factors (logos) but also on factors that appeal to our feelings and imagination (pathos) and our sense of ethics and integrity (ethos). The great philosopher recognised that we are not purely rational beings responding to reasoned argument and evidence – a reality with which some mainstream economic theorists, who remain committed to ideal rational human actors, still grapple.

Similarly, politicians, entrepreneurs and other persuaders have always known that logical argument will only get you so far. They tell stories their listeners can relate to on an emotional level, using narratives laced with personal storylines and enhanced with symbolism and metaphor, to amplify the impact of the story and the message embedded in it. For example, Barack Obama's inaugural speech told a powerful personal story of an underdog winning an election race against all odds, and wove the tale into a greater social narrative of shared stories of triumph of freedom over slavery, justice over injustice, democracy over communism, hope over pessimism. 'Yes, we can.' These are stories of which we are all part. Half a century earlier, John F Kennedy used similar techniques in his *Ich bin ein Berliner* speech of 1963, and we have seen how George Washington connected with his soldiers by framing his message as a personal story.

In another illustration, Steve Jobs has been hailed as the greatest corporate storyteller of all time. When introducing the first-ever iPod to an audience, he didn't talk about the technology or the physical dimensions of the iPod. Rather, he simply got excited about the idea of having '1,000 songs in your pocket'. So 1,000 songs in your pocket became a story. It fired up people's imaginations. Moreover, Jobs' personal excitement was contagious and was picked up by audiences all over the world. People listening to Jobs felt what he felt – excitement, anticipation. They felt part of the story. How did this happen?

Studies in neuroscience have shown that emotions are contagious, that is, they can move between us without us being consciously aware of it. This process is made possible by mirror neurons in the brain, which fire up and 'mirror' the physical signals of another. In other words, when we watch others' facial and body expressions, our brains – through the firing of mirror neurons – mirror what they perceive and thereby practise ways of relating to these expressions. This phenomenon helps to explain how we can have empathy for people we encounter without even speaking to them.[2] It explains how we can be moved to tears by the story of a stranger, and how, in a short period, Steve Jobs can leave us nurturing the desire for 1,000 songs in our pocket. It also goes some way to explaining why it is difficult to sustain confrontational behaviour towards someone who is 'nice' to you. Empathy is one of the most subtle yet effective techniques of persuasion.

Telling stories about conflict

When we are embroiled in conflict, sharing stories of loss, injustice and betrayal may be more constructive than angrily rejecting the other's story. Genuinely engaging in listening to others' stories as well as telling our own seems to release a dose of what Southern Africans call *ubuntu* – humanness – into an otherwise hostile dynamic that can easily escalate. It's what makes it possible to move past a deadlocked situation and engage with someone we feel has wronged us.

In contemporary times the most famous illustration of this principle is Nelson Mandela's negotiations with the apartheid government in South Africa, which ultimately led to his release from Robben Island prison and facilitated his rise to power as president of South Africa in 1994. During his 27 years in prison, Mandela learnt not only the language of his oppressors, he also familiarised himself with their poetry, their literature, their music and their rugby. He got to know his jailers and in some cases their families. He learnt their stories. As a result, he was able to negotiate a new inclusive political climate for his country and avoid the bloody civil war that so many had assumed would be inevitable.

Mandela's political genius lay partly in his ability to understand the stories of the Afrikaners – and hence their culture and way of thinking. But his genius lay also in his own storytelling. Rather than reacting with angry stories of victimisation, injustice and persecution, as many black South Africans expected and even desired, Mandela offered stories of a future South Africa where no one would suffer because of the colour of their skin. Rather than stories of despair, he shared stories of hope. Rather than stories of revenge, he offered stories of reconciliation. Mandela's narratives were not always well received. Initially, many did not understand their leader's conciliatory approach and willingness to collaborate with 'the enemy'. They were confused and disillusioned; some felt betrayed. Amid tensions that brought South Africa dangerously close to civil war, Mandela stuck to his storyline. He emerged as a tragic hero who saved a nation and sowed the seeds of reconciliation. Upon his death in late 2013 he was celebrated as a giant of history. What Mandela did was extraordinary in the circumstances because it defied our human instinct to tell stories that polarise, demonise and justify revenge.

The melodrama of conflict storytelling

Let me explain. Our patterns of telling stories about conflict seem etched into our DNA. As children we instinctively respond to stories about beautiful princesses, noble knights, wicked witches, dragons and dungeons – a classic pattern of conflict storytelling featuring terrible villains, virtuous victims and well-intentioned heroes, referred to as the melodramatic genre. Just think of Cinderella. Cinderella is the innocent victim of her wicked stepmother, the arch-villain of the story. Prince Charming is our hero – well-meaning, morally upright yet at the same time naive. He does not recognise villainy when he comes across it and is susceptible to manipulation by evil characters such as Cinderella's stepmother, who refuses to allow her to attend the ball. In this sense the prince is fairly useless to Cinderella, at least at the start. This inability of the hero to immediately save the victim is essential in the melodramatic narrative as it ensures that the unfair conflict situation continues for a while and the victim gains even greater sympathy. Do you remember who it is that, at the eleventh hour, makes it possible for Cinderella to get to the ball? Yes, it's the famous fairy godmother, who with a wave of her magic wand whips up a ball gown and carriage suitable for a princess.

The melodramatic narrative form is familiar to us all. Its ubiquitous structure has filled our minds from childhood fairy tales to adult television soap operas and political rhetoric. When we tell a story about a conflict in which we are involved, we tend to slip into a structure comprising a combination of some or all of the elements of melodrama without consciously choosing to do so.[3] The melodramatic narrative offers a structure for us to organise our thoughts and feelings about the conflict. Think back to when you have confided in someone about a problem or conflict. How did you tell the story? Hold that thought for a moment.

As storytellers, we typically portray ourselves as the person who has been wronged. We play the innocent and passive victim in our own personal melodrama. We find ourselves effortlessly adopting a narrative structure of melodrama to describe the other person as the active cause of the conflict, and as someone working against us, harbouring unethical, illegal or otherwise bad and unjustifiable intentions. For example, they may be negatively judged as stubborn (rather than principled); as foolhardy (rather than courageous); as irrational (rather than passionate). The characters in our conflict story are morally polarised and they demonstrate little complexity. As a result, the storyline is thin and the sequence of events is presented as unfolding quickly and sometimes suddenly. The storyline is not always logical, as it may be accompanied by strong emotions such as confusion, disappointment, sadness, shock, a sense of injustice or disbelief. The conflict, as we tell it, plays out externally among the characters rather than internally or intra-personally, so that there is not much scope for soul-searching or self-reflection. We are convinced that, if we could turn back the clock or make our villain disappear, everything would work out perfectly. The search for a happy ending is referred to as 'dream justice' in the melodramatic genre.

Accordingly, when we tell the story of our own melodrama, the structure of the narrative form dictates that we are more likely to focus on the wrongs we've suffered than to reflect on our own contributions to the problem or on what we can do to sort things out. By focusing on the 'what' rather than the 'why' of people's behaviour, we are less likely to acknowledge the complexity and potentially paradoxical nature of their motivations and intentions. Rather, we make assumptions about intentions and motivations, deleting or glossing over what doesn't fit neatly into our world view and our preferred view of ourselves. Psychologists call this the 'fundamental attribution error'. Coming back to Cohen's lyrics, the melodramatic narrative steers us away from exploring the 'cracks' in our own perfect story.

Now consider again the conflict story that you told your friend. Be honest with yourself. When you talked about your conflict – either to yourself or to others – were any of the elements of melodrama present such as a positive, morally praiseworthy description of your own faultless contribution to the situation, in stark contrast to the blame attributed to the other? Did you mind-read and assume certainty about the others' intentions and motivations, in line with the stock characterisations that you adopted? Did you yearn for a dream justice, where everything would go back to the way it was? Did you … even just a little?

Confidence, conflict and storytelling – the plot thickens

Why is it that we intuitively rely on the narrative of melodrama to tell a conflict story? In his award-winning book, *Thinking, fast and slow*, Daniel Kahneman puts forward the idea that 'the confidence that individuals have in their beliefs depends mostly on the quality of the story they can tell about what they see, even if they see little'.[4]

So stories reflect our confidence in ourselves and how we are perceived to fit into groups, communities, organisations and other tribes. For most of us, this means being right rather than wrong, winning rather than losing and being liked rather than loathed. Melodramatic narratives offer an ideal vehicle for transporting this message to the world.

But melodrama is not just attractive for storytellers. When someone is appealing to us with a melodramatic narrative, it's easy to blame the villain, to sympathise with the victim and to wish for dream justice. There is no expectation that we will have to get involved, dig deeper, take on responsibilities, actively engage in problem solving and mediate between the victim and villain. Rather, it's the unrealistic dream justice or nothing.

Intuitively, we know this. We sense that our task is to listen, sympathise and side with the victim. You see, the narrative form not only helps storytellers organise the information in their conflict story; it also helps the rest of us to recognise the type of story it is and know how to culturally respond.

Open up the newspaper on any day of the week and count the melodramatic narratives. Here are a few that I found after a couple of minutes on the internet.

From the Australian press:

> Tony Abbott's business adviser says Australia taken 'hostage' by 'climate change madness'[5]
>
> Libs vs Nats: GrainCorp stoush shows cracks run deep in the Coalition.[6]

And from the international press:

> China slams US for sending Chinese terrorists to Slovakia[7]
>
> Obamacare failing: registration still 80% below expected[8]
>
> Licence to maim: courts were easy on McNeil.[9]

Turn on the radio and listen to politicians telling stories involving themselves and the opposition, and you will hear perfectly pitched melodramatic narratives beckoning you to side with a victim and blame the identified villain.

In the same vein, John Dewar observes:

> As a nation we pay too much attention to the sensational and the short-term. Whether it's a social media spat, a gaffe in question time, or a political interview that runs off the rails – our national discussion is increasingly derailed by a sideshow of daily crises and spin.[10]

Dewar, who is on the board of the Australian Futures Project, argues that Australia's most serious problem is the absence of a constructive process for consensus building and decision making. In other words, Australians are locked into a sensationalistic, melodramatic pattern of storytelling that distracts us from talking about how to manage the big ticket issues, such as environment, energy, economic structures, the ageing population, health-care costs and education, that will shape the quality of our lives and those of future generations. And it's not just politicians. Civil society, media, business and professional groups, civil servants and academics are all happy to blame one another for the problems they face. In the melodramatic narrative, we look to others for solutions – for example, to voters, to the legal system, to law enforcers, or to those with power, resources or authority to step in and fix things for us. In political narratives, almost everyone seems comfortable blaming political leaders for everything from climate change to stock market crises. We look to politicians to solve our problems, rather than taking time to reflect on our own contributions to them and what we might do differently to improve the situation.

In short, we lack a constructive narrative for capturing difference and working through the difficult conversations that we need to have. Former Prime Minister Malcolm Fraser famously proclaimed, 'Life wasn't meant to be easy'. Yes, it's no picnic. But it doesn't have to be a melodrama. Melodrama doesn't help us solve conflict – it exacerbates it. Melodrama demonises and depersonalises the person on the other side, deepens and reinforces differences, and limits the scope for constructive engagement with the conflict.

We need a better way to organise our ideas about managing conflict and creating better futures. Recognising the traps of melodrama in our personal and political stories is the first step towards changing how we talk and think about conflict and, as a result, how we engage with the present to shape the future. Moving away from melodrama involves asking the 'why' question; it requires a shift from a place of certainty to curiosity; it involves acknowledging the gaps in the storyline, welcoming complexity and accepting the tensions of paradox. How can we begin to make this shift?

Shifting to tragedy as a more constructive and realistic storyline

While it's easy to view conflict as something negative to be avoided, conflict management professionals are trained to look for the positive in conflict. Conflict coaches, for example, may help people look for opportunities in conflict to make choices which will transform their destructive conflict energy into realistic, constructive outcomes.

Similarly, tragedy is often thought of as something negative, something bad. You might be surprised to learn that, as a narrative form, tragedy offers more useful structures than melodrama for constructively dealing with conflict.[11] Why is this so? In stark contrast to the one-dimensional characters of melodrama, tragic characters are imperfect creatures who contain contradictions and inconsistencies and experience the tensions of competing needs, values, desires and ideals. Typical character flaws include jealousy, ambition, naivety, pride or greed.

These flaws are internal to the character rather than being externalised to a villain as in melodrama. They sit alongside positive qualities such as diligence, generosity, kindness and honesty. We are able to empathise with tragic characters because we recognise our own human weaknesses in them. Consider the characters of Frank and April Wheeler, played by Leonardo DiCaprio and Kate Winslet in the 2008 film, *Revolutionary Road*, based on Richard Yates' 1961 novel of the same name. Frank and April share aspirations to make something different out of their lives together, to stay true to their independent and non-conformist ideals, despite the suffocating social conventions of 1950s middle-class America. However, they soon find themselves living a perfect life in a nice Connecticut suburb with young children, both desperately bored. They cling to fragile optimism that they will realise their hopes and ideals one day, while compromising these same values day by day and slipping into a deep relational malaise. Most of us can relate to the ambiguities and contradictions of Frank and April at some level. As they make the mistakes that precipitate their downfall, we are able to reflect on our own flaws and foibles. This is the essence of the 'tragic tension'.

It's at this point that tragedy becomes really interesting for us as a practical paradigm for conflict management. For it's precisely these internal paradoxes that give rise to the idea that 'as we move into the future, however bleak it may appear, there is choice'. April makes a choice to move the family to Paris for a fresh start and so that Frank can find his passion. Frank agrees. Then, when April discovers she is pregnant, Frank chooses to take a job promotion in Connecticut, while April chooses to abort the baby, with fatal results. In their tale of conflict, Frank and April make choices, and these choices have serious consequences that affect the lives of many. There are no evil villains, happy-ever-after heroines or voiceless victims in *Revolutionary Road*. It is a story of deep conflict with a different narrative structure featuring tragic heroes who make their own fate.

As heroes in our own personal conflict or 'tragedy', we can take up Leonard Cohen's poetic challenge by acknowledging our own imperfection and boldly shining a spotlight of curiosity on it. We can choose to take responsibility for our own fate and make decisions by actively engaging with people and circumstances that we perceive are less than ideal. It's not about making right or wrong choices – it's just about taking a piece of the future into our own hands, and making a choice. Alternatively, we can refuse to recognise our own role in the conflict, to question our perception of things, or to change our story and, in doing so, we continue to make the same mistakes. In the tragic narrative, the inability to make these kinds of shifts, or recognising too late the need to make them, emerges as the flaw that leads to the fall from grace, and sometimes the death, of the tragic hero.

In contrast, melodramatic victims are passive and weak, unable to make choices, hoping against all odds to be miraculously saved from the fate to which they are otherwise ultimately resigned. While melodrama demands either total victory or defeat, tragedy rejects such dichotomies as being fundamentally false. In the tragic tale, victory can sit with defeat, however uncomfortably. Optimism never frees itself from realism. And in a conflict setting, cooperation goes hand in hand with competition. Paradox is triumphant.

Set against the deep social conflict of 19th century France,

Victor Hugo's classic novel, *Les Misérables*, offers a profound and timeless illustration of choice in the tragic narrative. The central character, Valjean, is an honest man yet a thief, a doer of both selfless and selfish acts, a man capable of great compassion and intense jealousy, a man who believes in God yet who also believes he can make and change his own fate. By any measurement, Valjean could have considered himself a victim in a major melodramatic narrative and behaved accordingly. Among other injustices, Valjean is sent to prison for 19 years for committing a petty theft in order to survive. And that is just the beginning. However, as the complex and dramatic plot unfolds, Valjean continues to reflect on his actions. He keeps learning from his experiences and makes choices – some better than others – about how to engage with diverse challenges as they emerge in his and others' lives. Valjean's story does not deliver dream justice. It continues a tumultuous path. However the path is one of Valjean's choosing. And this is the defining aspect of the tragic narrative as a conflict management tool.

As described earlier, Nelson Mandela employed a tragic narrative that gave his country choice, rather than the melodramatic storyline that many expected and felt was justified. After his presidency and his death, South Africa remains a nation managing complex tensions: division and unity; optimism and apathy; peace and violence; love and fear. The difficult conversations continue, in some cases using narrative-based facilitation, mediation and coaching tools to encourage the structured sharing of stories in diversity.

Practical steps to find your tragic hero

So how do we avoid engaging in the culturally ubiquitous conflict narrative of melodrama and begin the journey to discover our inner hero, who can accept the tragedy of the conflict and actively try to make the best out of it?

A good place to start is to use the following guidelines and sets of questions – drawn from the REAL Conflict Coaching System – to talk your friends and colleagues through their own melodramatic conflict narratives. Practise this a few times. It's easier if it relates to a conflict or situation that you are neither involved in, nor feel strongly about. When you are involved in conflict yourself or have a strong view about a public interest conflict, it may be challenging to coach yourself from a melodramatic to a tragic narrative. Ideally, a conflict management coach or a skilled friend would help you make this shift.

Once you become familiar with helping others work through their own tales of conflict, you will be able to take yourself through the same process, and in doing so, find your own tragic hero in every conflictual situation.

As we have seen, a melodramatic narrative thrives on sweeping generalisations, polarised positions, stereotypical characterisations and a superficial story line. The questions below offer a starting point for unpacking these narrative elements in ways that enable you to offer storytellers greater clarity and comprehension about the conflict, to assist them to see that they do have choices and to identify what those choices are. This, in turn, leads to more confidence in engaging with the conflict and others involved in it.

1. Goal setting

What does the storyteller want to achieve by telling you the story? What is their goal in relation to the conflict? For example, do they want a greater sense of clarity and comprehension about what has happened and why? Do they want to identify their choices? Do they want to identify some strategies and skills to deal with the situation? Do they want all of these things or something quite different? Helping the storyteller continue to focus on their goal through the rest of the questions will help them make the narrative shifts they need. A particularly useful question might be, 'What needs to happen in this conversation so that you can say it was worth your time?'

2. Storytelling

Invite them to tell you the story. For example, ask, 'What happened?' Let the storyteller tell the tale in their own way without censorship or judgement from you. If it's a melodramatic pattern, then let's hear all about the victim, the villain and all the other characters. Notice the main theme of their story. For example, is it a 'What's happening?' story? Or could it be a 'Why me?' story? Is it a 'There's no hope' story or simply a self-righteous rant.

3. Explore and challenge

Now explore their story. Be curious, not judgemental. Identify possible gaps or cracks and shine a light in there by asking the storyteller to tell you more. What's missing in terms of time frames, people involved, history and related events, their action (or inaction). You want to be able to see the movie of what the storyteller says happened. Until you can see the story rolling out in front of you, keep asking questions. Encourage them to develop the plot and thicken the story. Unpack their generalisations. Encourage them to be as accurate as possible. For example, instead of talking about 'him' or 'her' or the 'new boss' and depersonalising the story, encourage the storyteller to use the real names of people and places. Challenge the storyteller – 'let the light in', as Cohen would say. Are there any inconsistencies in the story? Was it really like that? Could there be another explanation? When the storyteller does not have all the details, encourage them to notice the assumptions they are making. What evidence is there to back up the tale as they have told it?

4. Why does it matter?

The next stage involves digging deeper and asking the storyteller why the story matters. These questions begin to get at the issues of emotions, identity, power and values. Questions that may be useful include: 'Why does this matter so much?', 'What is it about the situation that is most important to you?', 'How is this situation getting in the way of your goals?', 'How is this affecting you?', 'What needs do you have that are not being met in this situation?'

5. Different perspectives

These questions are about considering different perspectives. In any conflict situation, there are three main perspectives:

- the storyteller's perspective
- the other person's perspective
- an objective perspective.

This stage is difficult. People in conflict are unlikely to be ready to consider a different perspective until they have had time to fully explore and explain their own perspective. When you think they are ready, then try asking questions like: 'What story do you think the other person would tell about what happened?', 'In what ways do you think the situation matters to the other person?', 'What do you think the other person would like to happen?', 'What are the other person's needs, identity, emotions, power?', 'How can you achieve your goal, taking into account the other's needs and other factors?'

6. Alternative futures

Next, your role is to assist the storyteller to identify and develop other ideas and options – in other words, a new story with expanded choices. Try asking a 'wonder question', like: 'Suppose you woke up tomorrow and the conflict was miraculously resolved, what would you notice that would tell you something was different?', 'How would you notice?', 'Who else would notice?', or 'What would they notice?'

Supporting the storyteller to develop a future story is not about narrowing the client's future to one neatly packaged scenario; rather, it is about increasing complexity and including variations and alternative stories, before evaluating whether and how those preferred futures can be achieved. Here it is equally important to 'reality test' the future story to ensure that it is not completely unrealistic. It is a careful balancing act to be able to do this without crushing the storyteller's optimism and vision entirely.

7. Steps towards the preferred future

By this stage, the storyteller should have a clear idea about what happened, why it matters, and what their preferred future would be like. Now it is time for the storyteller to develop action steps to work towards that preferred future. Your task here is to ask questions to support the storyteller identifying and committing to action steps. Action steps should be:

- specific (e.g. not just 'talk to Joe', but include details of time, place, what topics will be discussed, etc.)
- ordered logically (e.g. are the different steps staged or dependent?)
- reality tested (e.g. are the steps achievable?, what might their consequences be?)
- placed within a particular time frame
- reviewable.

Questions to ask the storyteller might include: 'What would be your first step that would make a difference?', 'What can you do yourself?', 'What do you need from others?'

As indicated previously, points 1 to 7 are guidelines that may offer some insights into how to shift from a 'going nowhere' melodramatic conflict narrative to a tragic conflict narrative that can offer different perspectives and choice in a less than ideal situation.

So next time you feel stuck in what seems to be an intractable conflict, overwhelmed by the enormity of a problem that is not of your doing, confused by a plethora of conflicting scientific data, or daunted by insurmountable challenges that threaten your own interests, know that you have a choice. You can take the predictable path of the melodramatic victim. Alternatively you can choose to tell a different tale and in doing so, find your own tragic hero.

---

1. Bruner, J, 1990, *Acts of meaning*, Harvard University Press, Cambridge.
2. Goleman, D, 2007, *Social intelligence: the new science of social relationships*, Arrow Books, New York, pp. 29–35.
3. Hardy, S, 2008, 'Mediation and Genre', *Negotiation Journal* 24(3): 247, pp. 251–3.
4. Kahneman, D, 2011, *Thinking, fast and slow*, Penguin, London, p. 87.
5. Swan, J, 2013, 'Tony Abbott's business adviser says Australia taken 'hostage' by 'climate change madness', *Sydney Morning Herald*, 31 December, www.smh.com.au/federal-politics/political-news/tony-abbotts-business-adviser-says-australia-taken-hostage-by-climate-change-madness-20131231-303qw.html#ixzz2pLCiBAal.
6. Botterill, L, 2013, 'Libs vs Nats: GrainCorp stoush shows cracks run deep in the Coalition', *Foodmagazine*, 19 November, www.foodmag.com.au/features/libs-vs-nats-graincorp-stoush-shows-cracks-run-dee.
7. 'China slams US for sending Chinese terrorists to Slovakia', Ecns.cn, www.ecns.cn/voices/2014/01-03/95283.shtml.
8. 'Obamacare Failing: Registration Still 80% Below Expected', The emergency email & wireless network, www.emergencyemail.org/newsemergency/anmviewer.asp?a=3513&z=48.
9. Fife-Yeomans, J & Wood, A, 2014, 'Licence to maim: courts failed to punish one-punch coward Shaun McNeil on previous assaults', *Daily Telegraph*, 4 January, www.dailytelegraph.com.au/news/nsw/licence-to-maim-courts-failed-to-punish-onepunch-coward-shaun-mcneil-on-previous-assaults/story-fni0cx12-1226794625132.
10. Dewar, J, 2013, 'Forget the Sideshow: Australia needs better decision-making for a better future', *The Conversation*, 2 August, http://theconversation.com/forget-the-sideshow-australia-needs-better-decision-making-for-a-better-future-16535.
11. Hardy, S, 2008, 'Mediation and Genre', *Negotiation Journal* 24(3): 247, p. 263.

Tales of public policy formation

Daryl Dixon

Daryl Dixon is Executive Chairman, Dixon Advisory and Superannuation Services. He is an investment expert, and a well-known writer and consultant on investment and superannuation matters. He previously worked for the Australian Department of the Treasury and Department of Finance and for the International Monetary Fund (IMF).

Daryl has extensive experience in public finance, taxation and retirement income theory and policy as an academic at the ANU and the University of Calgary, Canada, and at the IMF, the federal Treasury, the Department of Finance and the Social Welfare Policy Secretariat within the social security portfolio.

Daryl Dixon's essay contains a number of anecdotes and reflections from his long and distinguished career. He expresses the hope that those aspiring to public leadership will have the courage of their convictions, study some positive examples of courageous and rational decisions in the area of public policy, and – while taking account of the practicalities and necessities that hedge such decisions – still prefer the well-researched and longer view of public policy. He counsels that you give yourself every opportunity to learn – not just how to make decisions, but how to determine what decisions to make. Inevitably, because of the global financial crisis, governments will be forced to live within their means. This will require hard but by no means traumatic decisions because of the still considerable scope to avoid overlap and duplication and achieve efficiencies. If our new leaders are prepared to step up to the plate and understand the fundamental public policy issues that need to be addressed, it will be possible to achieve progress.

Since a politician never believes what he says, he is surprised when others believe him.

—Charles de Gaulle

High office teaches decision making, not substance. [It] consumes intellectual capital; it does not create it. Most high officials leave office with the perceptions and insights with which they entered; they learn how to make decisions but not what decisions to make.

—Robert Francis Kennedy

Informed decision making comes from a long tradition of guessing and then blaming others for the inadequate results.

—Scott Adams

With such wit and wisdom at our googling fingertips it is no wonder that many a person new to a public leadership position will take the easy way out, 'go with the flow', do what is expedient. My fervent wish is that those new to such positions will have the courage of their convictions, study some positive examples of courageous and rational decisions in the area of public policy and, while taking account of the practicalities and necessities that hedge such decisions, still prefer the well-researched and longer view of public policy. What I have learned along the way is that this is indeed possible despite the observed truths of the above quotations.

My good fortune as a serious young student was being pipped for a Rhodes Scholarship by an inappropriate (as it was seen) answer to a question about leadership abilities. I responded by referring to Hitler as undoubtedly a strong leader and suggesting other attributes than leadership were equally important. Fortunately, not long afterwards, I was awarded a Shell Scholarship to Cambridge University and consequently became undergraduate secretary of the Political Economy Club established there by John Maynard Keynes.

Not only was I thus provided with a thorough education as an undergraduate in Cambridge, but I was able to meet and mix with the famous economists of the time including Joan Robinson, Nicholas Kaldor and James Meade. Joan's most memorable advice was a quote from Maynard (as all disciples called Lord Keynes) that you can have all the theories in the world but unless they work in practice you are a failure.

Little did I know at that time of the rare and privileged opportunities that would follow for me in the formulation and implementation of public policy, and subsequently in building a successful advisory business. After a short academic career, the International Monetary Fund (IMF) hired me as a fiscal policy specialist.

From a technical perspective, the IMF as an institution suffers both from an over-reliance on the member countries for the provision of key information and from an unwillingness to challenge the perceptions of its largest contributors. This is demonstrated quite clearly at the moment by their chief economist, Olivier Blanchard, being unable to provide a viable and acceptable solution to Europe's financial woes.

Back in the 1970s, the Australian Treasury was a more policy-conscious organisation than it is today. Treasury recruited me from the IMF to assist in the preparation of 15 Treasury taxation papers providing technical assistance to the Asprey Review of Taxation. Unlike the in-house Treasury input to Kevin Rudd's Henry Tax Review, this was a totally transparent process where all the Treasury arguments were revealed publicly.

The Asprey review and Treasury analysis showed Prime Minister Gough Whitlam that increasing personal marginal tax rates by allowing inflation to compress taxation brackets was detrimental both for tax collections and the economy, and this discovery led him to commission the Matthews Committee on Inflation and Taxation. This period in our public policy history was one where detailed research and analysis had a major impact on political decisions.

A key element in this rational policy development was Whitlam's decision to involve seasoned and experienced policy makers including Nugget Coombs, Trevor Swan and Fred Gruen in the policy process. Treasury secretary Fred Wheeler, not fully trusted by Whitlam because of his (correct) opposition to the Connor/Khemlani loans proposals, kept a Treasury eye on Whitlam's committee by seconding me to act as minder for Swan and the committee.

It's a previously unreported story, but that committee helped Treasurer Bill Hayden to bring in a responsible budget, the only one of that government, which among other things freed 500,000 low-income earners from paying tax and introduced the sole parent rebate for the first time into our tax system.

As budgets go, it was a rare exercise, with the overall tax changes resulting in more losers than winners. Gough, Frank (Crean) and Bill understood this when making the decision to proceed, but still concluded, the winners were deserving of assistance and the losers lost out from changes of real merit resulting from lateral thinking by Professor Swan.

Swan's proposal was an excellent example of lateral thinking, incorporating, in the tax-free area, a life insurance tax deduction that, because of the high commissions paid to agents, only provided benefits to tax shelter-seeking higher income taxpayers. The government could have removed that deduction to raise revenue, as was recommended by the Treasury's John Stone in an earlier review. But Crean and his colleagues agreed with Swan that it was far better politically and economically to incorporate the life insurance deduction in the tax-free area and thereby extend it to all taxpayers. Using the revenue savings from effectively abolishing the life insurance deduction, the Whitlam government was able to lower the cost of a large increase in the tax threshold and still bring in its only fiscally responsible budget.

My message to young leaders follows directly on from that government decision. There is no substitute or alternative to the thorough analysis involved in obtaining and presenting essential information to help decision makers review all the available options before they make the final decision. No matter how experienced and expert policy advisers may be, their agendas and objectives can be and often are different from yours. In government especially, their jobs and futures are not as crucially dependent on the outcome of their recommendations as your future will be on the decisions you make.

The Whitlam ministers all knew that they would suffer politically from a budget with more losers than winners but proceeded nevertheless against formal Treasury advice not to increase the tax-free area. The then commissioner of taxation, Ted Cain, came to the aid of the ministers by highlighting a major flaw in the formal Treasury advice, namely that it cost more to levy tax on the relevant low-income earners affected than the actual tax collected.

There's always a role for rational and detailed analysis of the possible results of policy action under consideration. Moreover, when thoroughly briefed on all options, including those that may involve difficult policy decisions, politicians who have to face the electorate on a regular basis are capable of making sensible decisions. Compared with the bureaucrats assisting them, politicians have a much wider information base and are capable of making informed judgements in reaching decisions.

Even when working in a largely negative and short-sighted Treasury and subsequently over the years, I've always been attracted to seeking out options which offer carrots instead of using sticks to achieve desired outcomes. Where possible, it is preferable to avoid the gallows when alternative actions can produce a better and more acceptable outcome. Also, spending a dollar to save even more dollars in the future can produce more lasting and better outcomes than negative attitudes to all new initiatives.

This leads me to advice provided by Trevor Swan, whom Whitlam rewarded with an appointment to the Reserve Bank Board. I had continued working on social welfare and superannuation policy in the government and kept in touch with Trevor. At one meeting, he highlighted the need to understand the strengths and weaknesses of your situation. Rational analysis of the options does not mean that you can afford to ignore political and other constraints on the decision makers.

He used an example of a colleague on the Reserve Bank Board, a former president of the Australian Council of Trade Unions (ACTU), who told him that when he became prime minister he would never lie to the Australian people. Swan, who had, along with Nugget Coombs, worked in the Chifley War Cabinet, told me that this attitude would not survive long in the real life situations that can face decision makers.

He used his experience in the War Cabinet to illustrate the point. The cabinet understood fully how serious the situation facing this country was but concluded that its tasks would not have been helped by the immediate releasing of details of a series of incidents including bombings in Northern Australia and military setbacks. Information was held back and managed as required.

Trevor Swan's advice was that even in such circumstances, there was a need to always be aware when you are lying or gilding the lily and the reasons for doing so. Hopefully as a young leader, you will not be faced with such circumstances and will be able to publicly canvass and review the available options.

Lately, with the intense pressure on decision makers to choose between competing priorities, it has been far too easy for governments and their policy advisers to avoid difficult decisions with complicated consequences and to ignore rational and researched options. One such example (which in my private sector life I am attempting to focus attention on) is the inadequacy of federal government funding arrangements to ensure that the lifetime pension benefits funded from the Consolidated Revenue Fund promised to former employees are honoured.

With a demographic background of increased longevity and an ageing population, there is an increased risk that future budgetary problems will ultimately lead to retrospective adverse changes to the pensions promised to former employees. This has certainly been the experience in parts of Europe and for a few state and municipal employers in the United States.

The funding challenges posed by these lifetime indexed pension plans will, if anything, become more serious. All of these benefits were designed and the promises made when life expectancy was much lower than it is today.

For example, even the most recent 1990 Commonwealth employee scheme, closed in 2005 to new entrants, provides an annual lifetime indexed pension determined by dividing the alternative lump sum option by 10 at age 65 as well as providing a two-thirds pension to a surviving spouse. Latest available life expectancy tables suggest that there is a 60 per cent chance of at least one of the two partners surviving for longer than 24 years.

It is hardly surprising with such unrealistic actuarial assumptions that the federal government's unfunded superannuation liabilities have blown out to around $200 billion. It will continue to do so unless action is taken now to ensure that it does not.

In justifying my case for changes now, I focused on a report in *The Economist* that the last pensioner from the US Civil War, which ended in 1865 – a soldier's widow – died in 2005. That pension extended over three centuries. It has since been pointed out to me by a reader that googling reveals that the United States is still paying two Civil War pensions (to living children of soldiers).[1]

—∞—

Failing to properly quantify a new public policy is a high-risk strategy. It is even more risky to not acknowledge this fact and not even be prepared to consider obvious ways to start reducing the size of future obligations. One such initiative would be to transfer the actuarially based charges levied on Commonwealth employers to cover the on-costs of membership of these defined benefit funds into the Future Fund as they are received by the Department of Finance.

The Future Fund was established with part of the proceeds from the sale of government assets to help fund unfunded pension liabilities, but so far the unfunded liabilities have increased faster than Future Fund earnings. This situation would change dramatically if instead of using employers' on-cost receipts as a below-the-line funding source, Finance transferred these receipts to the Future Fund.

Another area where an apparently attractive decision brought with it longer run funding problems is the three-fold increase in the personal income tax-free area to $18,200 annually. Over the next 20 years the percentage of working-age people will decrease, while the percentage and absolute number of older residents (on reduced incomes) will rise. As a result it will be much more difficult to maintain, let alone increase, personal income tax collections.

Currently, a couple with income split equally between them only start paying income tax when their family income exceeds $40,000 a year. As a consequence, as our population continues to age, the percentage of the population paying income tax will continue to fall. In the future, the income tax burden will fall primarily on the working population, who will face higher marginal tax rates on their incomes. Indeed, this process has already started through the decisions not to index tax brackets for inflation and to apply a discretionary 0.5 per cent increase in the Medicare levy from 1 July 2014.

Professor Ronald Henderson, whom I was privileged to work with at the Brotherhood of St Laurence in the late 1980s, was farsighted and foresaw this problem much earlier in the 1970s. He proposed linking the income tax and social security systems via a negative-income tax concept. Social security payments are in essence negative income tax collections. The more the two systems of collecting tax and making transfer payments can be integrated, the greater will be the possibilities for avoiding double dipping and lowering the tax burden on the working-age population.

For example, for income tax and social welfare purposes any group of adults (including a same-sex couple) could choose to merge their finances, and along with their dependents be treated as a unit. Any adult who chose to do so would be a single person tax/welfare unit. As at present, there would be a needs test taking into account relevant circumstances to determine the amount of money needed by that unit to live at a 'comfortable' level. There would be different amounts for single parents and people with disabilities, adjustments for regional locations and special costs for people supporting other relatives. Each unit would pay tax at a fixed rate on income in excess of the assessed normal required level and receive transfers (negative taxes) probably at a higher percentage of the shortfall in their income.

Henderson's message was that the benefits to be gained from avoiding overlap and duplication in the tax and social security systems would provide additional funds to help alleviate poverty. Our current system has moved in the opposite direction by having both a generous social security system and a high tax-free area. This will inevitably complicate future funding problems for our ageing population.

Nevertheless, I am confident that if you, as our new leaders, are prepared to step up to the plate and understand the fundamental public policy issues that need to be addressed, it will be possible to achieve progress. Inevitably, because of the global financial crisis, governments will be forced to live within their means. This will require hard, but by no means traumatic, decisions because of the still considerable scope to avoid overlap and duplication and achieve efficiencies.

I conclude using one big ticket item as an example of where major improvements may be possible. The government offers assistance to retirement in two separate ways, which are not integrated. The first is via generous tax concessions to superannuation savings during working life and in retirement. The second is via the provision of a generous age pension to those who qualify under a means test.

There is no formal mechanism to protect against double dipping whereby, by dissipating their assets before and after retirement, taxpayers get the benefit of both the superannuation assistance and the age pension. One possible method of removing or reducing this overlap is limiting the government assistance provided to the superannuation savings of any individual or family to the actuarial value of the age pension benefit that would otherwise be available. The actuarial value of the age pension made available at retirement would then be reduced by the value of the superannuation tax concessions utilised during working life.

There would be transitional problems in introducing changes along these lines, including a need to ensure that sufficient superannuation assets were preserved in retirement to provide an annual income at the level of the age pension. But there are also alternative, more limited, possibilities for reducing the scope for double dipping, including limiting the lump sum withdrawals.

As leaders, give yourselves every opportunity to learn not just how to make decisions but how to determine what decisions to make. By doing so you will indeed believe what you say because your informed decision making comes not from guessing the short-term outcome but from taking all rational thinking and research into account to determine the long-run outcome.

---

1. Fox, L, 2012, 'U.S. government still pays two civil war pensions', *U.S. News and World Report*, 9 February, www.usnews.com/news/blogs/washington-whispers/2012/02/09/us-government-still-pays-two-civil-war-pensions.

Painting politics in a positive light

Ray Groom

Ray Groom AO was a member of the federal and Tasmanian parliaments for a total period of almost 24 years. He served as a federal government minister in the Fraser government. He is a former Premier of Tasmania and held senior Tasmanian portfolios including serving as Treasurer and Minister for State Development.

Ray Groom is also a lawyer, and following his retirement from parliament he was appointed deputy president of the Australian Administrative Appeals Tribunal. He was the sole assessor of claims under the *Stolen Generations of Aboriginal Children Act 2006* (Tas) and the sole independent assessor of claims by individuals who had suffered abuse when in state care in Tasmania.

In his youth, Ray Groom was a nationally ranked athlete and played AFL football for the Melbourne Football Club. He won the club's best & fairest in 1968. He represented both Tasmania and Victoria in Australian rules football and was inducted into the Tasmanian football hall of fame.

Ray Groom addresses what he knows from experience to be some of the serious concerns of young people contemplating a career in politics. In most societies and eras, politicians have routinely been criticised as venal and incompetent. Ray explains the reason for, and value of, criticism of politicians. At the same time, he argues that politicians should be seen in a more positive light; that if one actually gets to know a politician, generally one finds they are likeable and approachable. It is politicians who make the really big decisions affecting our society, and Australia's high standing in the world is testament to the wisdom of past decisions.

Ray Groom appeals to talented, young Australians to consider a career in politics – ideally starting at 35 or 40 – and offers some valuable hints for political aspirants.

On we march
With a midnight song
On we march
With our lanterns on
—Birds of Tokyo

My experience of political life was most interesting and satisfying. It was, at times, demanding. There were highs and lows. It was always full of excitement and drama.

Without hesitation, I would encourage young Australians to seriously consider a career in politics.

The word 'politics', of course, has a wide meaning. In this essay I focus on our parliaments because that is where I experienced the practice of politics.

I will endeavour to paint politics in a more positive light than that portrayed in the daily media and in 'café talk'. I will explain the important role played by politicians and put the constant criticism of politicians in a historical context. I will provide my tips and thoughts for young political aspirants. Finally I will present evidence of the success of Australian politics.

Politicians make the important decisions

Being a participant in parliament and a minister in government are two of the most influential roles to be played in our community. It is, after all, the politicians who ultimately make the significant decisions affecting our society.

The politician will receive advice from a range of sources but the final decisions – on whether, for example, Australia should go to war; a hospital or school should be built; teacher or police numbers increased; the dollar floated; a highway or port upgraded; and on issues such as Mabo, climate change and the National Broadband Network – are made by the politicians we elect.

Aristotle called politics the 'master science'. I doubt that its practice is a science in the modern sense of the word. I believe, however, that being a member of parliament is an occupation of the utmost importance in any democratic society. That said, our politicians must understand that they are servants of the people, and the only source of their power is the people. Their occupation may be of the utmost importance but *they* are not. While politicians should always take their role very seriously, it would be most unwise for them to get carried away with their own station or sense of self-importance.

If politicians consider themselves to be in a class above their electors, and speak down to them, they are bound to be short-term members of parliament. To be effective, a politician must be a good listener, have genuine regard for constituents and respect their views.

Criticism of politicians in context

Criticism of politicians is healthy in a democratic society. Indeed, it is absolutely essential. If people become afraid to criticise their politicians, and particularly political leaders in government, it is a sure sign that true democracy is on the wane.

But I want to put political criticism into context. Undoubtedly there is a risk that if a political aspirant is constantly reading and hearing criticism about politics and politicians, he or she may be dissuaded from pursuing a political career – it is therefore important that we understand the true nature and value of criticism in a democracy.

Public disappointment in the perceived behaviour and incompetence of politicians presently abounds, but is not a new phenomenon; when humans first began to organise the public affairs of their communities, those making the decisions almost certainly became subjected to personal criticism. In fact, from the earliest recorded statements about politics right up until today, we see frequent criticisms of the politicians of the time.

Socrates, who disliked democracy and believed only wise philosophers were really fit to govern, said some 2400 years ago, 'The greatest rogue of all is the man who has gulled his city into the belief that he is fit to direct it.'

Napoleon Bonaparte, emperor of France, who would have worked closely with many leading French political figures, said, 'In politics stupidity is not a handicap.'

In 1944 the American poet e e cummings (as he was popularly known) wrote most tellingly:

> A politician is an arse
> upon which everyone has sat
> except a man.

One only has to read any current Australian newspaper to see examples of Australian politicians of every persuasion being ridiculed and vilified, and often in the most outrageous way. Cartoons, in particular, can be hard-hitting, and often make their point in a cruel but quite brilliant way. I think we are at a high point in the cartoon business in Australia. Present-day newspaper cartoons are very nasty and mean-spirited, but also most insightful.

In all this, it's important to remember that politicians are criticised by the people because their source of power is the people. In past ages, absolute monarchs and other despotic rulers did not allow criticism because the source of their power was not the people but was gained by the sword. It is interesting to note that even today the offence of *lèse-majesté* (an offence against the dignity of a reigning monarch) still exists in Thailand, but also in a number of European countries including Spain, Norway, Denmark and the Netherlands. But in a true democracy, a politician would not dare legislate to protect himself or herself from the verbal barbs of the masses or the media as rulers have done in the past. The politician must realise that some criticism will flow no matter how well he or she performs.

And anyway, public criticism is often directed at the whole body politic rather than at an individual politician. That has been my impression over the years. A person you meet in the street may express great disappointment at the conduct of politicians generally but then tell you that you are doing a good job and encourage you to 'keep up the good work'. Most parliamentarians would have had a similar experience.

It is important for someone entering politics to make sure they take notice of constructive and reasoned criticism. But they should not be put off by nonsensical ridicule directed at the body politic or personally at them. They should simply cop it, smile and move on.

A thick skin can be grown and is a good shield in public life.

Advice and thoughts for political aspirants

I would like to offer a few tips and thoughts for those considering a political career.

Get some life experience first

I believe you are more likely to be an effective representative of the people if you have had some broad experience of life before you seek to become a member of parliament. Those who have worked solidly in an occupation, business or profession for a reasonable period of time prior to entering parliament bring a better informed and more mature approach to the practice of politics.

A young person who, for example, goes to university and then immediately after graduation becomes a political staffer and then a short time later seeks preselection is likely to have, in my view, a very narrow perspective on what political life is about. Those with that limited experience will be more inclined to want to be involved in the games of party politics rather than work to promote the general public good. It is vital to get good life experience first.

In my view the ideal age to enter politics is probably between 35 and 40 years. By that stage, people usually have had reasonable life experience but are still young enough to learn the political ropes and have enough time ahead to make a substantial contribution in parliament and government.

Have standards

It is important to have personal standards and to maintain them. You will live in a goldfish bowl and people will notice everything you do. There will be temptations. Resist them. Sometimes there will be pressure from others to do something that deep down you are not happy with. It may be a policy issue, a statement you are asked to make or something more sinister. Again, resist. If necessary, speak out. Integrity is essential in life and particularly in public life. A person of integrity may, at times, upset some but will be respected in the long run by most colleagues and the public.

Read widely

It is essential that young people contemplating a political career read widely and think deeply about what they would like to achieve for the community and what differences they would seek to make to improve society. Political aspirants should have a clear understanding of their personal ideals and policy, and parliamentary interests and goals.

Avoid personal attacks

My view is that the most effective politician is the person who expends his or her energies concentrating on policies and programs of action rather than indulging in personal attacks on opponents.

You will be more highly regarded by your colleagues, opponents and the wider community if you refrain from personality politics and personal attacks. Sure, strongly criticise your opponents' policies and statements, but avoid criticism of a purely personal kind. If an opponent is involved in, for example, corruption or some other serious misconduct, then obviously you are entitled to be critical of that conduct. That, in my view, is not criticism of a purely personal kind.

Don't become a puppet of the press

When he was prime minister of Singapore, Lee Kuan Yew warned politicians not to 'become a puppet of the press'. This is wise advice for any young politician.

The media tends to dominate modern politics to an unfortunate extent. Ministers and members of parliament and their staff spend far too much time trying to manage the daily media. They are often satisfied if the minister or member has had a good run on TV, the radio or in the newspaper. Too little time is spent on actually governing or in attending to the genuine problems faced by constituents.

Most of the media are essentially involved in entertainment and ratings. The danger is that politicians can be lured into becoming entertainers. For example, they may get involved in stupid gimmicks to get a run on television.

My advice is to avoid silly acts and strange hats.

Be serious and genuine

Some years ago I met a senior US naval officer who was visiting Hobart. He was also a highly qualified political scientist and was keenly interested in how Australian politics was practised. Immediately prior to his Hobart visit the officer had taken time to attend Parliament House in Canberra to watch question time and to meet some leading politicians. He told me he was amazed at the joking style of our politicians in question time and said it all appeared to be tongue in cheek.

He felt that it would improve the image of the Australian Parliament if members and senators were more serious and genuine in the way they communicated their views. I found this to be a most interesting and insightful comment.

It should be acknowledged, however, that humour can be very helpful in lightening an otherwise tense moment. It can, without doubt, be beneficial in a serious business like politics. Answers and explanations may be provided with some humour as long as the politician actually means what he or she is saying.

Parliament is not a debating society

I have offered some criticism of the way politicians communicate but I also want to make the point that parliament is not a polite debating society.

Our parliaments would be failing the people if they did not permit very vigorous and passionate debate. Voices will be raised, verbal clashes will occur and it will not always be polite and civil. This is democracy at work. It is far better than what it replaced – armed, murderous conflict.

People are critical of the adversarial nature of our politics. They wonder why members of parliament argue so much. 'Why can't they simply agree?' is a common question. But having two sides contesting issues, asking questions and debating policies is critical to the democratic process. If all sides of politics reached agreements behind closed doors and there was no public criticism, there would then be a much greater risk of corruption. Total unity of the polis is not democracy. Wrongdoing is uncovered through determined probing and questioning in parliament and by the media.

The Australian parliaments have a different character to those of other countries. This is because we are a different people. Australians are strongly egalitarian. We often produce characters and larrikins – a parliament elected by the people of Australia will inevitably include some of those interesting people and reflect our unique national characteristics.

There is no doubt, however, that our politicians do need to improve their conduct. Behaviour in parliament and in public should be generally more courteous with less vitriol and name-calling. I am sure this will happen over time because that is what the people want. Hopefully these improvements will not make our politicians too virtuous or sanctimonious and we will still see plenty of vigour, emotion and passion in our parliamentary debates.

The success of Australian politics

Although not widely recognised, the truth is that our politicians have achieved great success in their policies and actions over the years.

As I have already pointed out, it is the politician who ultimately makes the significant decisions affecting our country. As a direct result of the cumulative decisions made since our colonies attained self-government in the 1850s, we now live in one of the world's great democracies.

It has to be recognised, of course, that the success of a nation is not solely the result of the work of political decision makers. The excellent democratic institutions we were gifted by our forebears, our abundant natural resources, the dedicated efforts of our public sector and especially the skill and hard work of the wider Australian community have obviously played major roles. Nevertheless, as our politicians ultimately make significant national state and territory decisions, they should be given their fair share of the credit for Australia's undoubted success.

It can be argued that Australia is now one of the most civilised nations of all time. In the context of constant criticism of our politicians, this may seem to be an extraordinary claim. There is, however, cogent evidence to support it.

There are many reports and surveys that attempt to rank the best-performing countries in the world. Some of them concentrate on very specific factors. For example, the World Bank provides comparative data on 331 separate indicators covering such disparate topics as cereal yield and the prevalence of HIV in a country. A few recent reports have looked very broadly at the relative performances of countries across a wide range of factors, including quality of life issues as well as material living conditions and economic performance.

In 2013 two authoritative broad-based reports were published by the United Nations and the Organisation for Economic Co-operation and Development (OECD). These reports rank Australia number two and number one respectively in the overall performance of the world's most advanced countries.

Human development index

The Human Development Index published in 2013 by the United Nations, which uses a complex formula to assess comparative economic and social factors, ranks Australia number two of 47 'very high human development countries'. Norway was ranked number one.

Better Life Index

In a thorough and objective evaluation of 34 of the most advanced countries in the world conducted in 2013 by the OECD (the Better Life Index) Australia is ranked number one. That survey considers a wide range of factors such as housing, income, jobs, education, health, life satisfaction, safety and work life balance and governance.

Best-performing countries in the OECD survey

1. Australia
2. Sweden
3. Canada
4. Norway
5. Switzerland
6. United States
7. Denmark
8. Netherlands
9. Iceland
10. United Kingdom

If we take these contemporary rankings alongside the fact that current community standards, in most respects, generally exceed those of past ages, it is arguable that contemporary Australia is now one of the most advanced and civilised nations in the history of humankind.

So despite the widespread criticism of Australian politicians, they must have represented us and led us rather well over the last 150 years or so to have nurtured a nation that now has, overall, such a high standard of living and quality of life.

Conclusion

In the future, those who undertake a parliamentary career in Australia clearly have a lot to live up to. But of course, as in any human endeavour, further improvement – to Australia generally and to the lot of particular groups within the Australian society – can and should be made.

As I have explained, not only is politics vitally important to our nation's future but it also provides individuals with the opportunity for a most interesting and satisfying career.

I urge young people to seriously consider a career in politics. If they do take the plunge they will then have the opportunity to make a significant contribution to the future of Australia and its people.

Escaping the trap of our own creation

Greg Rudd

Greg Rudd was an independent Senate candidate for Queensland in the 2013 federal election. He was previously an investment consultant based in Beijing and Canberra. He founded and led a political lobbying consultancy in Australia for over a decade. Greg was a former chief of staff in the Hawke and Keating Governments, general manager of the Queensland Ballet and the TN Theatre Company,* a teacher and university lecturer, a writer of fiction and non-fiction – and always a thinker. His novel *The two heart conspiracy*, the first in a planned trilogy, was published in 2014.

Greg's essay outlines how to improve our parliamentary democracy through commonsense structural reform that puts Australia's interests first rather than the interests of political parties or career politics. Greg argues that we need to create a structure owned by the parliament, rather than political parties, to protect and quarantine vital medium- to long-term economic policy currently being polluted by shallow and artificially antagonistic 24/7 political and media short-termism.

Greg argues Australia is a lucky country but it won't stay lucky unless we work at it. If you are reading this – aged between 15 and 40 – you may be one of Australia's future leaders. Know that you are not powerless. With logic, common sense, maturity, manners and willpower we can improve the way our democracy works, and build a remarkable Australia.

Australia can do better. The only thing stopping us is us.
—the author

Understand one thing: none of us is powerless – but most of us choose to be powerless. It's safer to receive and complain than to create and be judged.

If you're reading this, aged between 15 and 40, it's likely you're part of a small cohort of future Australian leaders. You are

---

* Originally the Twelfth Night Theatre Company; the theatre itself retains the name 'Twelfth Night Theatre' (ed.).

not powerless. You care and want to contribute, and for that my generation thanks you.

Most people want change but leave it to others to be the change agents. Australia has so much unrealised potential it's frustrating. By now, we should be the Switzerland of the Asia–Pacific, with a highly sophisticated economy complementing our natural advantages in mining, agriculture and tourism.

Long ago, we should have created a sovereign wealth fund that funds infrastructure and innovation. It could have been the making of Australia. Instead, today's economy is strangled by lack of infrastructure and we starve innovation through lack of capital. Party politics constantly constrain us.

Imagine if our federal parliament truly worked together to realise Australia's potential, rather than slicing and dicing us with slogans into competing tribes. Imagine if we put country first instead of party, career and personality politics. Imagine if we focused on commonalities rather than manufactured differences.

With logic, common sense, maturity, manners and willpower it's possible to improve the way our federal parliament works by 30 per cent.

Imagine a marriage vow where we swear to oppose for opposing's sake, highlight every mistake made, have dirt files on each other, character assassinate and prosecute different ways to raise kids. No marriage would last – yet that's how we run our federal parliamentary democracy.

In a public or private company, do we insist on two boards where each board's job is to tear down the other board, to constantly demonstrate to shareholders and the public why the other board is running the company into the ground? How the hell can you grow a company that way? Yet that's how we run our federal parliament.

We have the temerity to advise China on how to run a population of 1.3 billion people when we can't even maximise the value proposition for 23 million.

As Australians we laud a community coming together to fight a bushfire. We laud a community coming together to recover from devastating floods. But we choose not to come together as a parliament to do the best for our country. Instead, we trap our progress within ageing structures that we created to protect ourselves.

Young Australians have a false sense of security. You were lucky to be born and nurtured in good times so you think the good times will last. Wrong. Our parliamentary democracy is a piece of machinery. Don't romanticise it. Don't see it as sacrosanct. If not serviced and upgraded, it will rust and fall apart.

In coming years, young Australian leaders have much work in front of them. Don't be daunted. The purpose of life is to try and improve what has come before you. And for heaven's sake don't believe everything current leaders tell you. You should know by now all adults have vested interests.

Australia is a mere 200 years old in commercial terms. We're the new kids on the block, embedded awkwardly within a region that's traded successfully and cunningly for thousands of years. We play by different rules from our neighbours – we're perceived to be arrogant; we're slow moving and expensive. Just because we're a lucky country, via geography and geology, it doesn't mean we will stay lucky unless we work at it.

Australia has never truly suffered. Relatively little ethnic violence. No civil war. No invasion. No starvation. No pestilence. No revolution. Some say we won't wake up to our squandered economic opportunities until our standard of living declines. I'm counting on the fact that future Australian leaders aren't that stupid. At the end of the day, if you have zero interest in public life, it's akin to seeing cancerous spots on your body and not caring. Everything eventually needs fixing.

While the laconic 'she'll be right mate' attitude was endearing in the last century in Australia, that attitude is half-hearted at best in this very competitive 24/7 global 21st century. The days of jobs for life and job certainty are over. Modern economies are fluid and ever-changing. More than ever we live off our wits.

Yet Australian graduates often expect a job delivered to them once they have finished their education. This is yesterday's world. Today, graduates need the skill set, the mindset and the confidence to create their own job if not offered one. This is difficult because many of our teachers go from primary school to high school to university then back into primary school, high school or university. They are institutionalised, as is our parliament. Teachers and politicians often live in an academic or political world, and lack the brutal commercial life experience in how to create, defend and grow businesses. There needs to be a far greater interaction between education, industry and government. You can't have employees without employers and you can't collect tax without both. Tax revenue is the lifeblood to Australian opportunity.

Many young Australians tell me it's far more interesting to watch a YouTube clip of a guy with a fork stuck in the eye of his penis while a cat plays with a ball of string than it is to listen to a politician talk about policy. This may be true for some, but it highlights the crippling dilemma of modern-day politics. Because we haven't suffered enough, we're increasingly focused on the game of politics rather than the purpose of politics. It's like *Game of thrones*, where key players are so self-absorbed they don't know 'winter is coming'.

'Politics is a wank,' young Australians have told me over the years. 'It doesn't affect me so why should I be forced to vote?'

'It's like when you build your first house,' I often reply. 'The architect asks you what you want – you shrug and say you don't care. The builder asks you what roof you want and how big you'd like the rooms – you shrug and say you don't care. Your designer asks what carpet, tiles and wall colours you want – you shrug and say you don't care. Only when the house is finished, you say "what the hell" and start complaining.'

Australia's parliament creates the laws we live by. It builds the house around us to protect us as a nation. It's incumbent upon us all to not only show interest but to be informed and give direction to those who build our national house. So instead of complaining later, take a constructive interest now.

Australia cannot afford an ageing population, yet the younger generation is substantially disengaged. 'It don't affect me.' It does. My generation is leaving your generation with what is colloquially called a shit sandwich. We've been too gutless to make politically hard decisions so it will definitely affect you.

History shows us that humans are flawed. We want what we don't have. We like tension and conflict. Mostly we have good intentions, but greed and ego often drive us. We strive for peace but get bored by too much peace. We own things for status yet too often our things own us. We're frightened of death so we create structures, codes and systems and form relationships to give life meaning.

We are a speck of dust within the universe yet we think we have more answers than questions. We're the only species on Earth entertained by watching fellow humans murder, betray, maim, torture or seek revenge on each other in the name of art, literature and cinema. Imagine if we saw giraffes watching other giraffes slaughter each other and cheering – we'd think they were psychotic.

I was born on a dairy farm where life seemed simple. Later I realised that was because farm life was repetitive. No threats, just routine. However, when I was 14 my dad was killed in a car crash. We got turfed off the farm we didn't own. My simple farm life went out the window. Life was suddenly about change and uncertainty.

Yet we learn important things about ourselves through times of upheaval and failure more than we do through success. Success is easy to handle, and often has more to do with luck and timing than strategic brilliance. It's when our world falls apart through death, accident, bankruptcy, ill health, bad luck, greed, violence or betrayal – that's when we find our true selves in the mirror.

In short, shit happens. Life's journey, whether as a person or a country, is essentially about preparing for, protecting yourself from, and dealing with shit-happens moments, whether personal, commercial, societal, cultural or political. Protecting yourself from shit-happens moments is often about strengthening structures around you, like building a better fort. Unfortunately our political fort in Australia, our federal parliamentary democracy, is in disrepair.

The trick in life is not to panic when unexpected rips take you out of your comfort zone. Panic in a rip and you're dead. The float now, swim later method is best, but eventually you do have to swim. In that non-panic floating moment we analyse, learn and reform behaviour to lessen the likelihood of being taken out in a rip next time.

In other words, we try to be smart enough to learn from our mistakes. Yet we don't seem to be smart enough to see that our current political structures and modus operandi constrain us from achieving optimum results for Australia. Labor hates Tories, the Coalition hates Labor, Nats hate Libs, Libs hate Nats, Greens hate everyone, left hates right, drys hate wets, independents hate major parties, career politicians hate rivals. Personality politics is the new cocaine – throw more mud while everyone dances to the 24/7 media drum.

This is juvenile. It's akin to a community fighting a bushfire that threatens their town. Instead of working together they divide into competing groups and attack each other while simultaneously trying to defeat the fire. As each group is hurt, hit, sprayed or thwacked they retaliate. The focus is soon on scoring points against competing groups rather than fighting the fire. Meanwhile hungry flames move ever-so-much closer to town and sleeping children.

If life is the best teacher then why do we learn so slowly? For a country of 23 million people and one that's 200 years commercially young, Australia has a terrific chance not to repeat the mistakes of older underperforming democracies. This requires young adults and future leaders to step up to the plate of public office.

Don't be sucked into thinking our current political and public structures are the best we can deliver. Have at your core the words logic, common sense, maturity and manners. I believe that in our hearts, most people want to do good – public office gives you that opportunity. A healthy foundation stone of society is believing those who laugh together can live together.

So why do we focus so much on hate, differences and tribalism in our political systems in Australia?

Australia is a new political experiment. We're a young country. We're mainly migrants. We know what we don't like in other countries. Australia should be leading the world, not following the world. We need tolerant commonsense leaders – not narrow-minded complaining followers – to realise our future.

I started reading outside my dairy-farm comfort zone in my late teens. I was shocked to find in Aeschylus, Sophocles and Euripides that Greeks in 500 BCE dealt with the same issues of humanity as we dealt with in the 20th century. The 21st century is no different. The 25th century will be no different.

Humanity knows itself. We create systems and institutions to protect ourselves from ourselves. Democracy is one such invention. In Australia we maintain a faith in democracy. Most believe the democratic system will always work sufficiently well to keep some kind of workable balance in play, no matter how dysfunctional the operation or outcomes.

This is a misplaced faith. Greece is much older than Australia.

Greece was the cradle of democracy. It was a centre of culture, power and wealth. It built the bright new democratic car still lauded today. But Greece did not service the car. It did not fix and replace parts when obviously broken or working below capacity. It did not roll out new improved models of democracy to move with the times. Hence Greece is now an economic basket case.

Just because something works for a period of time it doesn't mean it will always work. It's no different from that horrifying moment as kids when we realise parents are fallible and occasionally full of bullshit. Suddenly our child's world seems less secure.

This reminds me of a great story told by a retiring CEO. 'You've been around awhile,' I said. 'You've got a good reputation, so at 70, tell me what you've learnt about life.' I love asking these types of questions.

'I was always a high achiever at school and university,' he replied. 'I was champing at the bit to get on the bus of life and prove my worth. Finally after my economics degree I hopped on the bus and sat in the back row. Ten years later I got my first CEO job and moved a few rows forward from the back. I was exceptionally keen to keep moving forward. As the decades rolled by I got better CEO jobs and moved closer and closer to the front of the bus. It was in my late 50s when I got close enough to look over the shoulders of the few in front of me and then I saw it.'

'Saw what?' I asked.

He smiled sadly. 'There's no-one driving the bus.'

This makes people feel uncomfortable. It's probably why so many people find solace in religion. They still want to believe that parents know best, that the system knows what it's doing, that the federal parliament largely gets it right. If only it was true. The system is only as good as the sum of its parts. This is why we all have to be vigilant and guard against greed, corruption, ego, complacency and unchallenged stupidity. In short, we have to stump up and use our collective talents to continually renew and revitalise our public institutions. If you have talent and don't use it, that is the worst sin.

Many global leaders over centuries have labelled democracy the best of the worst systems of government. That's code for 'we can do better'. Today's democracies around the world are stuttering and underperforming. Is Australia learning from this, or do we think our Aussie founding fathers were so smart they got our UK–US parliamentary hybrid system of democracy right from day one? Our founding fathers (no mothers) were a bunch of bearded frontier dudes who did their best to pull a federation together in difficult times. Hats off to them but I don't think they would have thought, 'That's it – forever – no changes – no improvements!' Surely Australia and the world in 2015 are substantially different to Australia and the world in 1901.

I haven't met one Australian in any state or territory who thinks our federal parliament or public institutions are delivering the best outcomes for our country. I haven't even met one politician in federal parliament, from any side of politics, who thinks parliament is humming sweetly on all cylinders. Yet during the 2013 federal election, not one member of a political party, not one member of the press, and not one member of a peak body ever mentioned the need for structural reform in Australia's parliamentary democracy.

Does that mean everyone thinks it's all tickety-boo?

No. It simply means it's easier to focus on Hollywood-style personality politics than on boring structural reform. We've become addicted to reality TV entertainment politics. Thus it's simpler to change the actors on the stage, while still producing the same underperforming show, rather than hire fresh scriptwriters and designers. It's simpler to rearrange the deck chairs (yet again) on the *Titanic* than to find ways to iceberg-proof the unsinkable ship that sank. And to continue the other analogy ... the bushfire gets closer to town.

Structural parliamentary reform is essential, but Australia hasn't suffered enough yet as a country to see it. Also, structural reform crosses many lines of self-interest for party elders and career politicians, thus making it difficult to achieve. But by constantly avoiding hard decisions, Australia is constantly weakened. For example, we've had 10 major tax reviews in 50 years with thousands of sensible recommendations. Yet each government enacts only one, two or three, because the others are too politically difficult – yet vital for the country. Meanwhile our Tax Act grows to thousands of pages of mind-boggling complexity and inefficiency.

History is repeating itself with the Gillard and Rudd governments prior to the 2013 election, and the Abbott government post the election, timid about proposing any review of the GST. Nothing to do with common sense or putting Australia first, but all to do with shallow politics and the fear of losing votes.

I've been constantly told by the press and old political hands that structural reform is not sexy and won't capture the modern imagination. Where's the grab, they say. You have to explain it. God forbid! John Hewson proved once and for all in politics, if you have to explain it, forget it. You can't tweet structural reform. You can't twerk it while taking selfies. What funny hat do you wear for structural reform? Where's the photo opportunity? And there's no character assassination involved! It's playing the ball not the man, so it's definitely not suited to today's instantaneous 24/7 action-reaction-comedy-attack political cycle.

Have you noticed how much 'news' these days has to be 'funny' to get a run? Public policy as entertainment is killing us.

Let me give you two recent examples of how dumb we are as a country. One side of politics introduces a carbon tax knowing full well the other side of politics has made a virtue of killing it off if they're elected. Thus Australia spends billions of dollars, consumes enormous airtime and energy, divides a country, wastes uncountable public service hours, sets up whole departments, devises and implements a complex scheme, then dismantles everything, costing billions more dollars, to end up at groundhog day. A decade of getting nowhere!

We need a structure where the federal parliament, not political parties, owns these nation-building decisions. These nation-building policies need to last beyond changes of government or, after substantive debate and majority decision, to not happen in the first place.

Political parties have successfully turned a minor refugee problem into a major issue in terms of cost, national divisiveness, international standing and distraction from core economic issues. Refugee policy must be a national policy owned by the parliament on behalf of the people. It needs to survive any change of government. It demeans us to turn people's suffering into a political football. It demeans us not be consistent in both policy and enforcement.

Our Australian parliamentary democracy is sick. How many times have we said to a sick friend, 'you'll be right', knowing deep down we don't think they will? Far too often we simply 'hope' things will get better. A symptom of this sickness is the rise of new political parties.

New political parties are not long-term solutions. They're born from dissatisfaction. Whether it be Don Chipp keeping the bastards honest, Bob Brown seeking balance, Pauline Hanson demanding plain talk, Bob Katter kicking Canberra in the nuggets, Clive Palmer wanting a revolution, the Motoring Enthusiasts wanting to bush bash in national parks with their four-wheel drives, or the Sex Party wanting more sex – the desire in all of us is the same. We simply want our parliament, and more specifically, the two major sides of politics, to deliver better outcomes for Australia.

After the 2013 election the major sides of politics belatedly talked about parliamentary reform, but only after minor parties won positions in the Senate via chaos mathematics preference flows. It was reform talk born from party self-interest rather than concern for country. There is still no party talking about structural reform of our federal parliamentary democracy even though its need stands out like the proverbial low-hanging fruit on male dogs.

Movies brainwash many voters into believing a hero will emerge to save the democratic day. Impossible. The structure within which these showbiz leaders operate doesn't allow them to deliver on their over-egged promises. Charismatic leaders put the high-jump bar of expectation too high while the democratic structure within which they work keeps delivery of outcomes low.

Believe it or not, most politicians are decent, hard-working people, but the structure they work within makes it difficult for them to deliver their best.

So let's alter the structure to protect and enhance Australia's future. Let's put structures in place to make sure 30 per cent of our policy is bedrock economic policy that puts country first, thinks long term and is owned by the parliament and not by transient political parties. This leaves a whopping 70 per cent of less important policy for parties to play silly buggers with during their ongoing game of manufactured branding differentiation to win votes.

How do we create a structure to house and quarantine the 30 per cent long-term bedrock economic policy from day to day politics? Simple. If we stimulate an economy by injecting more money then let's stimulate an underperforming democracy by injecting more democracy. 'Noooo!!' scream party leaders who want party members to vote how they're told. But common sense says yes.

Let's give the 150 members and 76 senators elected to federal parliament a greater democratic voice. Let them truly represent their constituents rather than just voting along party lines as directed by party powerbrokers.

Let's define the 30 per cent bedrock economic policy vital for Australia's long-term prosperity by bringing in experts from all over the world. Remember, politicians are rarely experts but they are mostly sensible. They know how to read briefs and come to logical conclusions. Let this debate last for two years. And let the media keep the public informed so politicians are answerable to constituents.

Then parliament legislates the 30 per cent bedrock economic policy by using the ultimate form of democracy – a majority conscience vote of all 226 members and senators. Remember the alternative to a conscience vote is a vote without conscience, which is why our parliamentary democracy is currently struggling.

In reality we're asking 226 democratically elected parliamentarians – at least for part of the time – to think like independents, and do what's best for Australia based on factual evidence rather than party or personal ideology. For the sake of Australia, we ask politicians to take off their party hat, take off their career hat, take off their self-interest hat and put on their what's-best-for-Australia hat. After all, that's why we elect politicians.

Bedrock economic policy will grow the economy with long-term economic certainty. All sides of politics will benefit, as will the country. Bedrock economic policy will stimulate growth, increase our revenue base and target core spending and savings initiatives more efficiently. We'll become the envy of the democratic world by putting common sense and country before party partisanship and self-interest.

This new commonsense 30 per cent bedrock economic policy can only be enhanced through majority conscience vote amendments every four or five years and only after a further two years of open parliamentary debate. This amendment period could be timed to avoid federal election cycles so that it did not become a political football.

Imagine where Australia would be today if 30 years ago we'd laid down a 30 per cent bedrock economic policy. The major issues dividing our country would hardly exist. Bedrock economic policy includes core tax, infrastructure, education, health, defence, immigration and welfare policy. It makes it possible to make hard decisions vital to Australia's long-term future. It takes the politics out of politics. All sides of politics wear the public odium for sensible clawback and public accolades for sensible nation building.

For 30 per cent of the time, our federal parliament won't be Libs, Nats, Labor, Greens, Katter's, Palmer's, Sex, Motorists or independents. It will be Team Australia fighting the bushfire together that threatens our town and kids. We will protect the lucky country using logic, common sense, maturity, manners and good will. We will be breaking the unproductive mould of hate, tribal and divisive parliamentary democracy ... at least for 30 per cent of the time.

Of course there are other reforms to be tackled; for instance, culling career politicians by limiting 80 per cent of politicians to serving 10-year periods divided into two five-year terms. If you can't achieve for your country in 10 years, you won't do it in 15 or 20. And we need to ban those ridiculous Dorothy Dix questions to stop the parties from using question time purely for self-promotion, and allow the general public to ask genuine questions through the speaker.

The Greeks built the first democratic vehicle, while our whiskered founding fathers designed the houses of parliament within which our democratic car first roared its engine. Now the engine is spluttering and we have an ongoing responsibility to all Australians, now and in the future, to keep servicing that democratic car and keep refurbishing the two houses within which it operates.

So, young adults of this lucky country, your job is to make sure we stay lucky. Get involved. And remember, we created and own the parliamentary structure that runs Australia, it does not own us. Learn how it works and make it work better. People only have power over you if you let them. With logic, common sense, maturity, manners and good will we can secure Australia's future.

Part 2: INFLUENCE

Mea culpa – failure as the foundation of leadership

Peter Shergold

Professor Peter Shergold is the chancellor of the University of Western Sydney. He was a senior Commonwealth public servant for two decades, becoming the nation's most senior administrator as secretary of the Department of the Prime Minister and Cabinet from 2002 to 2007. During that period he was responsible for the report of the Task Group on Emissions Trading (the 'Shergold Report'). Peter was made a Member in the Order of Australia (AM) in 1996 and received the Centennial Medal in 2003. In 2007 he received Australia's highest award, the Companion in the Order of Australia (AC), for his significant leadership of change and innovation in the public sector. He now serves on the boards of AMP Ltd, Corrs Chambers Westgarth and the Prime Minister's Indigenous Advisory Council. He is chair of the NSW Public Service Commission Advisory Board and Patron of the Left Right Think-Tank.

This chapter contains reflections on a career in public service. In it, Peter Shergold argues that while admitting systemic failure is relatively easy, acknowledging one's personal contribution to it is very much harder. Yet this is vital if we are truly to learn from our mistakes – and then, undaunted, try again.

Success is stumbling from failure to failure with no loss of enthusiasm.

—Winston Churchill

It is hard to fail, but it is worse never to have tried to succeed.

—Theodore Roosevelt

All of us live with our failures. From our earliest years we say things to our loved ones that we later realise were wrong or cruel. We get in with the 'wrong crowd'. We don't perform as well in exams or interviews as we would like. We don't listen enough to what others are telling us. We don't intervene when we should or, conversely, we become involved when we should walk away. We act too fast or procrastinate too long. Or, in these days of social media, we don't realise the long-term career implications of an embarrassing photo on Facebook.

Failures have consequences that we carry. The most profound remain with us until the end of our lives. Our feelings of regret take many forms: 'I wish I had done better'; 'I feel ashamed that I did not live up to my personal beliefs'; 'I hope I get to make amends'; or 'I'd like the right opportunity to admit I was wrong'.

The problem is that most of us qualify our regrets, even to ourselves. This is particularly so in the workplace. Mistakes may be readily acknowledged, but personal responsibility is often softened by a cushion of mitigating circumstances. When I'm providing performance feedback I'm often struck that self-awareness of individual failure gets lost somewhere in the system. 'Others didn't provide the support I needed'; 'The time frame was unrealistic'; or 'No-one would listen' – such rationalisations, which I've heard frequently, could take up the rest of this essay. Excuses are made. Blame is spread around. Personal responsibility for failure becomes diffused. (By the way, I don't think this applies only to public life; I have seen this behaviour just as much in the private sector and perhaps even more in academia.)

This represents an abnegation of leadership. It is a truism of contemporary management-speak that we must all 'learn from our mistakes'. It's a credo to which we willingly subscribe. Unfortunately, the commitment to self-improvement is often half-hearted. We are generally willing to recognise mistakes, just so long as the learning doesn't get too personal.

Now, basking in the late youth of my life (aged but not yet frail), I have reflected at length on why, on occasion, things went wrong when I was a mandarin in the Australian Public Service. Today I chair or sit on the boards of a university, private businesses, a law firm, a capital start-up, not-for-profit organisations and multifarious government advisory bodies. They are important positions but, as one of my wife's colleagues asked, somewhat enviously: 'So he actually gets paid for attending meetings?' Indeed I do, and amid discussions of organisational strategy and financial sustainability, I get time to think. In the modern world, that's too rare an experience. One savours it like a guilty pleasure.

Contemplating the past, I have discovered that I'm able to learn more from the failures that I suffered as a public sector CEO than from the successes I enjoyed. Equally important, I have found that the public servants to whom I speak at workshops and conferences prefer to hear about the failures. The stories are often much funnier. Of greater significance, listening to an erstwhile leader fessing up to moments of incompetence is a liberating experience. It helps people feel authorised to be more honest about their own mistakes and – supported by colleagues – consider how best to make use of those experiences in the future.

It takes a determined display of leadership to acknowledge personal responsibility for occasions when things haven't gone to plan. We know that entrepreneurial prowess is generally built upon repeated failures and that mistakes (rather than necessity) are the mother of invention. Unfortunately, the story of achievement is often told from the perspective of eventual success. A hero emerges.

Life's not always like that. Families split. Businesses go bust. Projects fail. The reality is that many of us battle against the odds and at the final reckoning try to balance the pluses against the minuses, and hope that we've ended up on the positive side of the ledger. Kind words at farewells help to persuade us that we have. Even greater generosity of spirit is displayed at funerals but unfortunately we don't get to hear in how many ways our estimable qualities will be sorely missed.

I know from experience how fraught it can be to admit personal failure. In 2013 I wrote a foreword to *In black and white*, a book on Indigenous policy.[1] This is an issue I've had a lot to do with, as CEO of the Aboriginal and Torres Strait Islander Commission and then, successively, as secretary of the Department of Employment, then of Education and ultimately of the Prime Minister and Cabinet.

I took the opportunity of writing the foreword to muse on what I perceived to be a generation of failure in public policy. In my view, successive governments had, with the very best of intentions, created the very worst of outcomes. I argued that Indigenous Australians are rightly provided with government payments and programs to address the appalling scale of their disadvantage, but the manner in which services are delivered treats them as beneficiaries, recipients and dependents. They become cases to be managed. As a result, Aboriginal people have become further disempowered, learning the helplessness of 'sit-down money' and 'go-round-in-circles' training. They are caught up in the safety net.

Perhaps I am right in my criticism of passive welfare. Perhaps I am wrong. That is not the issue I want to address. Rather it is that in identifying mistakes of policy, I emphasised my 'failure, personal and systemic'. These four little words (but in particular the second) were picked up by Patricia Karvelas in *The Australian* and become a report headlined 'My 20 years of failure to close gap: Shergold'. The story became my mea culpa. In a follow-up piece the redoubtable Noel Pearson only half-jokingly suggested that my 'seminal admission' should require that I be obliged to 'answer for these failures before an appropriate tribunal'. Later, more kindly, he wrote that I 'was in fact one of those rare gems who sought to deploy the power of government for good'.[2]

Public admission of mistakes, I discovered, is no act for the faint-hearted. Yet I don't resile from my admission. My view is straightforward. If you hold positions of situational authority then you cannot simply justify and explain failure in terms of the system and process of decision-making. You are – as I was – an integral component of the structure. An indication of true leadership is the willingness to hold oneself *personally* responsible for mistakes and, *on that basis*, to learn. To do so is as rewarding as it is discomfiting.

I enjoyed my time in the Australian Public Service. I left happy with what I had achieved. Yet, looking back on my career, I can now see how particular qualities of character may, on occasion, have weakened the likelihood of success. Confident, passionate if not charismatic, I sometimes failed to listen enough to the views of others. I didn't always walk in their shoes.

My natural tendency was to make decisions rapidly and to rush to solutions which would 'fix' the inevitable crises of the political environment. Sometimes this meant I could get things wrong. Equally important, it meant that I failed adequately to create collective ownership of the approach among my colleagues. A good storyteller, I was sometimes not empathic enough to the narratives of others. My reputation as an energetic 'can-do' guy had both positives and negatives. I nearly always got things done. Sometimes they were the wrong things.

At certain times, always reluctantly, I was too cautious – after all, the default position of public service tends to be risk aversion dressed up as prudent management. At other times I was too ambitious, failing to properly gauge the scale of the execution challenge or to identify clearly the unanticipated consequences of policy implementation.

As I've expostulated to critics on previous occasions, I do believe that as the head of a range of government agencies, I was frank and fearless in the advice I gave to the ministers and prime ministers I served. At least behind closed doors I did possess the courage, ego or foolhardiness to speak truth to power. In retrospect, however, particularly in the public arena, I sometimes hid or moderated my doubts about policy positions that were generally accepted as self-evident truths. While it was important not to criticise the government's position publicly, I now wonder if I could have done more to challenge prevailing assumptions privately.

In short, I now see that I personally contributed both to the achievements and failures of the development, design and delivery of public policy. Sometimes I had a large role, often not. I like to think that my qualities of character had a positive impact on beneficial outcomes: ergo, I have to accept that my flaws may have influenced the likelihood of blunders.

If I seem to have recited my failings at excessive length, then I hasten to say that I do so for a reason. I am now convinced that the most important ingredient of leadership is the willingness to admit that one's nature and actions affect decisions, whether they are taken for good or ill. It is relatively easy and non-threatening to learn from a generic category of 'mistakes'. It is much harder to learn from one's own mistakes. It is far more confronting. Yet it is the key to developing and honing one's leadership qualities so that next time around one doesn't, at a personal level, repeat history.

A few years ago I was asked by the management guru Avril Henry to write a foreword for her book,[3] identifying the most important ingredients of leadership. I emphasised resilience, by which I meant the capacity to keep on keeping on in the face of rejections and obstacles. I actually prefer the Victorian term, doggedness. 'It's dogged as does it' captures the sense of gritty determination necessary in the face of repeated knock-backs.*

---

* The phrase comes from Anthony Trollope, *The last chronicle of Barset*, first published in 1867, chapter LXI, available at eBooks.adelaide.edu.au/t/trollope/anthony/last/#.

While I continue to hold that view, I now more fully appreciate that resilience needs to be embedded in self-awareness. It's important to recognise how one has unwittingly helped to ensure failure and to learn from that experience how to modify behaviours and attitudes for the future. Leadership begins with finding the courage to say, 'I accept personal responsibility for contributing to the failures to which I was a party'. That recognition can steel the resolve to make changes, try again and do better. Acknowledging errors publicly is a form of self-improvement, not self-abnegation.

To do so is liberating. It can even create opportunities. Having headlined my admission, *The Australian* then offered me the chance to contribute an opinion piece setting out in more detail my views on failure in public policy on Aboriginal and Torres Strait Islanders. I was happy to do so.[4]

I was also asked to join the Prime Minister's Indigenous Advisory Council. I attended the first meeting in December 2013. I was welcomed for my experience. I saw it rather differently – I made it clear that I sat at the table as someone able to reflect on why failures had occurred in the past and what I had learned from my personal contribution to that unsatisfactory experience.

No-one asked me to leave. I hope it was because they appreciated that the ability to learn from earlier mistakes can contribute to leadership of change in the future. Failure, and how we respond to it, is where leadership is born.

---

1. Craven, R, Dillon, A & Parbury, N (eds), 2013, *In black and white: Australians all at the crossroads*, Connor Court Publishing, Ballan, Victoria, pp. ix–xii.

2. Karvelas, P, 2013, 'My 20 years of failure to close gap: Peter Shergold' *Weekend Australian*, 1–2 June, www.theaustralian.com.au/national-affairs/my-20-years-of-failure-to-close-gap-shergold/story-fn59niix-1226654821728#; Pearson, N 2013, 'Recent indigenous policy failures can't be pinned on Aborigines', *Weekend Australian*, 15–16 June, www.theaustralian.com.au/opinion/columnists/recent-indigenous-policy-failures-cant-be-pinned-on-aborigines/story-e6frg786-1226664090788#; Pearson, N 2013, 'Yes Minister, we're trapped by bureaucracy', *Weekend Australian*, 20–21 July, www.theaustralian.com.au/opinion/columnists/yes-minister-were-trapped-by-bureaucracy/story-e6frg786-1226682223648#.

3. Henry, A, 2005, *Leadership revelations: An Australian perspective*, CCH, Sydney, pp. vi–vii and 145.
4. Shergold, P, 2013, 'The best of intentions, the worst of outcomes for Indigenous people', *Weekend Australian* 8–9 June, www.theaustralian.com.au/national-affairs/opinion/the-best-of-intentions-the-worst-of-outcomes-for-indigenous-people/story-e6frgd0x-1226659582763.

The path to leadership – reflections from a public service career

Tom Sherman

Tom Sherman AO had an extensive career in the Australian Public Service, serving as Australian Government Solicitor (1984–89), chairman of the Electoral and Administrative Review Commission of Queensland (1989–92), chairman of the National Crime Authority (1992–96), president of the ACT Legal Aid Commission (1998–2004) and chairman of the board of the Credit Union Dispute Resolution Centre Pty Ltd (2003–09). In 1992 and 1993 he was also president of a Paris-based G7 task force of 27 leading countries developing and implementing measures to counteract global money laundering. He has conducted 20 inquiries and reviews in Australia and overseas, including two inquiries (1996 and 1999) into the deaths of Australian-based journalists in East Timor in 1975.

In this chapter Tom Sherman reflects on a career in public service – a career characterised by great changes in technology, patronage in the public service, and the role of women in the workplace. He reveals some important lessons – first for anyone embarking on such a career, then for those in middle-management positions, and finally for those at the top. Above all, service involves acting in the public interest, being conscious of what that entails for your organisation, and giving frank and fearless advice – even to prime ministers.

You get nothing for nothing, and very little for sixpence.

—A common expression in the Great Depression

I was employed in the Australian Public Service from 1961 to 1997, and then worked for another 10 years conducting inquiries and reviews for Commonwealth, state and territory governments as well as inquiries in South Africa for the United Nations and the Commonwealth Secretariat.

When I started my career, it was a very different world. The internet did not exist, and external communication was by landline telephone or by letter or telex. I did not see television until well into my teenage years. Photocopiers did not exist and you treasured your carbon copy among the few copies returned to you from the typing pool.

I never had a woman boss and I doubt if many young men could make that claim today, particularly in the public service. My early career was in competition law, a completely new field which was not taught when I studied law only a couple of years earlier.

These reminiscences have a purpose. A young person today aspiring to a career in public life will inevitably experience even greater change in the course of their working life than I did. Those who can identify and ride the waves of change are more likely to enjoy success than those who don't – or worse, those who resist legitimate change.

My focus is on the public service. I have had no experience of working in politics or non-government organisations (NGOs). There is a critical difference between the public service and those other forms of public life – politicians are focused on political advantage; NGOs are focused on the particular cause they represent. Public servants should be focused on the public interest. They are, as former governor-general Sir Paul Hasluck once said, 'the custodians of the national experience'.

Early career advice

There are a few points I would make to young people who are seeking a successful career at a senior level in the public service.

Obtain the best education you can. It is becoming increasingly rare for persons to reach high levels in public life without a university education. In most professions, such as law and medicine, it is necessary to achieve a professional qualification. You can survive without a degree but tertiary education provides knowledge, research skills, mental acuity and hopefully wisdom. Avoid specialisation too early at university. A solid liberal arts foundation will pay dividends later because it enables breadth of vision and creativity. The friends you make at university often stay with you throughout your career.

A good degree will certainly help the start of a career. Most employers rely on grades and the quality of degrees at the base levels, for the reason that they are a good indication of an applicant's capabilities. Grades will often be the determinant in the initial cull, particularly when there are large numbers of applicants. After that, performance in interview and psychological tests come into play.

Poor degrees tend to condemn young people to less prestigious jobs. You can recover, but it will take time and effort. Be very wary of what you put on Facebook and other forms of social media. Many employers check out the pages of applicants for jobs.

Once you have entered the workforce, grades and degrees will become progressively less important. It will be your performance in your chosen field that will become increasingly relevant over time. It is possible to gain some success by connections and other means – remember the adage 'it's not what you know but who you know'. But my experience is that people who do not or cannot perform are eventually exposed for what they truly are. This applies to prime ministers as well as lesser mortals.

Good bosses are important in early career. There are many skills which cannot be learnt from books. My first boss taught me two valuable things. First, to write clearly so the recipient is in no doubt about what you are saying. (The same applies to other forms of communication.) Second, to understand the importance of meeting deadlines. There is no point in producing the best work in the world if it arrives too late to be of any use. It is a question of producing the best you can in the time you have.

Many young people suffer from poor bosses early in their career. If you encounter one, get out of there as quickly as you can. They will make your life a misery and destroy your confidence. More importantly, you will learn nothing worthwhile from them.

I cannot stress enough the importance of performance at all stages of one's career. If you perform the tasks assigned to you well, it will be noticed. People who make decisions on promotion and prospects look for proven performers. Good performers will be noticed, even in a team environment. Performance in a team is just as important as individual performance.

Don't shy away from difficult challenges. It is in the difficult situations where the good performer stands out.

There is nothing wrong with ambition. Indeed, we are probably hardwired with it. But where ambition overshadows everything else, it tends to produce behaviour which becomes counter-productive.

Responsibility for others

As you progress in your career other qualities become important, but they build upon those qualities I have already described.

You will reach a stage where you will manage and become responsible for others. Initially this will involve responsibility for small teams. At this point it becomes a question not only of how well you perform as an individual, but also of your ability to lead others and inspire them to perform. There have been many definitions of leadership, but a simple one I always liked is 'the leader is the person who knows what to do'. Staff respect the leader who can give them good advice on how to deal with the issues and problems which arise daily in the workplace.

It can be a difficult balancing act to be loyal to your small team and defend them to your bosses, while at the same time recognising and implementing the requests of the boss. Honesty, clear communication and a clear-sighted approach to the issues will assist. It is also important to avoid being two-faced – that is, saying one thing to the boss and another to your peers or subordinates. It reflects a serious weakness of character and such inconsistency is often exposed at cost to the individual who indulges in it.

Communication is always important. Staff must have all the information they need to perform their work well. As a boss, sometimes you won't have all necessary information, but you must try to get it; otherwise your work and the work of your staff will suffer. Regular meetings with all staff are important so they understand what the context is and what the group priorities are. I once headed an organisation of 40 people engaged in important and demanding work. We had a meeting of all staff first thing every Monday morning. The only exception was a person to answer the telephone. This produced the result that everyone understood what needed to be done that week and most importantly, why it needed to be done. This may be more difficult to achieve in larger organisations but the same principles apply.

When you are responsible for the work of others, it is important to turn matters referred to you around quickly. There is nothing more debilitating for young people than to have to wait around for a response from those higher up. Delays of this kind can corrode morale. In my leadership roles, I tried whenever I could to turn matters around within 24 hours – it is not always possible, but it is surprising how often it can be achieved. If things take longer, let the person concerned know the reason. Many years ago I sent a submission to the then Attorney-General Lionel Bowen, one of the best ministers I ever encountered. After about a week I telephoned him and asked if he had seen it yet. (He was usually very prompt.) He said, 'Tom, I have an IN Tray, an OUT tray and I have the floor behind me. Yours is on the floor behind me.' I said, 'Is there something wrong with it?' He said, 'No, the floor is for those matters which time will solve.' He then proceeded to explain why it was on the floor. This indicates that a quick turnaround isn't always the best course, but that you need wisdom and experience to see what the best course is. Lionel Bowen had plenty of both.

At middle-management level, other skills become important. Recruiting the right staff is critical. Mr Honda (of motor car fame) once said he always picked people who were smarter than himself. Ability is an important criterion in selecting staff. It is also important to assess the applicant's performance in their other work. Treat references critically; you may be being sold a person who someone wants to be rid of. It is always important to test and assess a person's character, particularly their honesty and integrity. Referees should always be asked about the person's character; for example, whether or not they are honest and trustworthy.

Life is so much easier if you select good staff

The capacity to listen is important at all levels of a career. The best ideas often lie within an organisation. Staff should know their work and often have good ideas on how to improve things. Be receptive to new ideas and encourage debate and discussion. No-one has a monopoly on wisdom.

One common fault among managers is the failure to develop succession planning. If you have recruited well, there should always be people capable of taking over from you. It is important to develop successors. A key factor in decisions to promote is whether the person being considered can be replaced. An irreplaceable person will be difficult to promote. So it is not only a good thing, but it is in your interest to encourage and develop staff to replace you.

Don't, however, fall into the trap of playing favourites. It is a sad fact that in some areas of public sector organisations, preference is given to staff because they socialise with the boss, are friends or relatives of the boss, or share the boss's sexual affinity. In my early career there were some departments which favoured Catholics and others which favoured Masons. As a matter of law, public service organisations are required to select and promote on the merit principle. If you sense, at any stage of your career, that these unlawful considerations hold sway, get out of there. It is a sad fact that fighting these forms of discrimination is likely to be a pyrrhic process unless you have good evidence, a very good lawyer and plenty of money.

Speaking truth to power

I spent most of my early career in organisations of lawyers where speaking truth to power was not often an issue. Lawyers are, by nature, argumentative, and the most junior lawyers will tend to argue with more senior lawyers if they think their legal opinion is wrong. But this has not been my experience in other organisations where there is less of a tendency to question opinions and decisions. Robust debate is critical to good decision making. It is important to say what you believe is true, otherwise there is not much point saying anything. A word of warning, though – don't press your views beyond the point where it is clear your views will not be accepted. You have had your say and given your advice. Leave it at that.

In the course of my career I have had to advise the prime minister of the day on several occasions. Sometimes my advice was contrary to what they wanted to do. They were formidable men and needed convincing to change their course of action, but they followed my advice on each occasion. In one instance, it wasn't a question of legal advice but of what was an appropriate course of action. Some might say that this is all right for lawyers because one is reluctant to act against legal advice. But the public service is also a profession, and frank and fearless advice is a core value of that profession.

At the top

If you manage to reach the top of a public service organisation you will need to be conscious of a number of things.

First, what is the organisation trying to achieve and what are the challenges in the environment in which it is operating?

Second, is the organisation addressing the right priorities?

Finally, how do you measure its success?

Once you have correctly identified these issues, you will be in a much better position to take the organisation to where it needs to be. Don't be a caretaker; an organisation which cannot be improved doesn't exist. The organisation I headed in Queensland was a new organisation that was enthusiastic about its mandate to implement major reform in that state. It was the most enjoyable experience of my career. However, these opportunities are relatively rare. In the case of the other two organisations, I had to drive significant change to revive them. It is not for me to assess how successful I was, but in each case I left satisfied with what I did. Change isn't always popular. But if the reasons are carefully explained, and you consult widely with both staff and stakeholders prior to change, the chances of success improve greatly.

A broad experience

One of the things I admire about the United States is the seamless way in which people move from the private sector or academia to the public service and back again. Individuals may do it more than once in a career. This produces a number of benefits for each sector. First, it results in much greater understanding between these sectors. Second, there are clearly benefits in cross-fertilisation of ideas and experience. Finally, it gives the individual involved a broader perspective and a greater understanding of the strengths and weakness of each sector. Regrettably, this doesn't happen as often as it should in Australia. I would encourage young people to broaden their experience in more than one of these sectors and seek out opportunities to do so.

Life beyond a career

I look back, in my early seventies, having had a good career. I went much further than I ever expected. Many young people today will probably live to over 100. That is the good news. The bad news is you will probably work until you are 80. So don't be in a hurry.

Life is becoming increasingly stressful, particularly if you have to support and raise a family while coping with demanding work. The great public servant HC ('Nugget') Coombs was asked towards the end of his life what his greatest achievement was. His answer was, 'The fact that my children still talk to me.' What this means is that a life has to have balance. You must have some interests and passions outside work. If you don't find time for these when you are busy you will reach the end of your career and find yourself bereft. Don't be one of those people whose work defines their being. Life is much better than that.

Four lessons for real leaders

Sue Vardon

Sue Vardon AO spent 23 years as chief executive of state and Commonwealth agencies and departments and, notably, was CEO of Centrelink from its inception in 1997. Subsequently she was CEO of the South Australian Department for Families and Communities, which brings together housing, disability, domiciliary care and family services. She was the inaugural Telstra Business Woman of the Year in 1995.

Sue presently has a portfolio of interests, including senior voluntary roles in the Red Cross, chairing Connecting Up and being part of a local fire protection group. She is also active in raising funds to keep children in school in Ghana. From time to time she does work for governments at all three levels.

Sue has a passion for public service being delivered to the highest standards, and for implementing the policies of the government of the day as they were intended. She understands the connection between the elected politician and the electorate, and the importance of making transactions as helpful as they can be.

Sue Vardon's chapter discusses making the public service work environment as positive as it can be for staff, so that their creativity can be unleashed to make the public service the best it can be.

From her experiences both in leading and in supporting those who lead, Sue distils four tenets of good leadership. First, taking control of the things we can control (and learning from the things we can't) is necessary if we want to operate optimally within an organisation. Second, to steer a business safely it's important to maintain a broad overview of the business and its context while keeping in mind its ultimate purpose. Third, to help our colleagues reach their potential we must treat them with respect and give them opportunities to take risks and challenge themselves. Finally, self-awareness, compassion and courage are central to all aspects of good leadership, and will have a ripple effect throughout the organisation.

If we want to change things, we must first change ourselves.

—Paul Rusesabagina

The leader I respect has no particular personality style or rank. This leader can be noisy or quiet, forceful or reserved, leading from behind or in front, passionate or dispassionate, traditional or very modern.

A good leader is reflected in the people they lead. I know an organisation is well led when people understand the big picture, can see the way forward, have the freedom to experiment within known boundaries, are challenged to effect positive change and are supported when things go wrong.

I am not sure how much of leadership is innate and how much is learned. I do know that given the opportunity to lead, we can make choices about how we do it and we can continually learn. I have used Paul Rusesabagina's words as an introductory quote to emphasise the importance of taking responsibility for one's own leadership journey. It is a quote that has been in the forefront of my mind throughout most of my time as a chief executive. The purpose of *So you want to be a leader* – to nurture a new generation of leaders – resonates because we do not have to accept that bad leadership prevails. We each have it within us to provide a better example.

Leadership is also about perspective. We may face difficult challenges and complexities that appear insoluble, but that's what leaders take on. When things appear impossible, it is useful to stand back and reflect on the fact that we live in a great country where solutions are possible. I remember a woman visitor from Africa whose department was trying to house thousands of homeless refugees with little money, and whose people in the villages were starving. Sitting in on one of our leadership meetings, she listened politely to a corporate challenge we were trying to solve, and at the end said: 'You worry about such little things!' Compared with the human disasters she was facing on behalf of her government, our worries were as nothing.

Successful leaders leave behind a better place; they achieve something worthwhile. Those they lead will remember being encouraged to do their best as well. I call this the 'wash' the leader leaves in his or her wake – rather like a boat travelling through waters that can be rough or smooth, but which manages to get to its destination.

We are all influenced by factors beyond our control – our family, our early life experiences, the role models of our parents and teachers, accidents, economic conditions, our inbuilt personality. We build our base on these and then we add things we can control – seizing opportunities, continually learning, identifying role models, accepting challenges, thinking and reflecting, and observing the impact of others on us and our impact on them. From all these things we draw lessons, and I want to share the lessons that were most powerful for me.

Early in my career, when I was 36, a young minister of the Crown agreed with a selection panel that I should be his director-general. He wanted to put a stamp on a portfolio and thought I could fit the bill. He had choices and I was forever grateful to him that he chose me. Many years later I was given the opportunity (with the help of many others) to create the Commonwealth Services Delivery Agency, which became Centrelink. This idea arose from the alignment of new Commonwealth ministers wanting to reduce duplication of effort and improve Commonwealth services. They were aided by influential secretaries of Commonwealth departments who made sure that a new agency was created to implement the ministers' policies. This unique agency – created as a one-stop shop for Commonwealth services – reduced the number of places people had to go for employment opportunities and unemployment benefits and created a customer focus that respected the worth of those people who were in difficult circumstances, such as single parents, older citizens and young people who were looking for opportunities to study and work. It helped them all to navigate the complexities of getting assistance.

The creation of Centrelink was a bold move requiring leadership at both the political and administrative level. It worked because leaders at every level – including throughout the agency – were committed to a single purpose.

There have been many moments in Australian history when leadership of this kind makes a difference in a positive way. There are just as many lost opportunities when leadership fails.

Leadership challenges are found in many arenas: in innovation, in new product design, in research, in education, in disaster relief and so on across the range of human endeavour. For years I have attended the Telstra Business Women's Awards and sat amazed at the stories of women who saw opportunity on a small scale to make an improvement and then battled extraordinary odds to create jobs, good solutions and wealth by growing their businesses or improving public services. For years too I have been amazed at the capacity of an organisation like the Red Cross to mobilise humanitarian effort when Australia needs it – because of leadership from both volunteers and staff.

There will always be challenges to confront 'wicked' or impossible problems,* and opportunities to anticipate events and prepare for them. Some people will take up the challenges and others will follow. The important thing is to be a leader who takes us forward and acts with integrity.

Paradoxically, my preparation for leadership came not from great mentors but rather from my experience of being led poorly. In the days before the unfolding of fairness in the workplace through equal opportunity laws and a greater emphasis on diversity, the world was a tough place for working women. The serious 'boys' clubs' were based on religious affiliation, allegiances to factions, closed door discussions, withholding information and antiquated rules. I was lucky in a sense that my social work training had taught me the importance of analysis, observation and reaction. I observed and felt the results of terrible leadership myself and vowed that if I ever had a chance to lead, I would remember the lessons and do things very differently.

I can remember as a young social worker trying to get some help from a state government department. I was left with an overriding impression that I was dealing with a steel-cased marshmallow. It was almost impossible to get through to someone who could help – the steel barrier – and then, when I did, I felt as though I was wading in marshmallow because no-one could make the decision I wanted.

I have seen awful things happening in bureaucracies: people claiming credit for other people's work; people lying; people creating crises then moving in to be the hero to save the day; people blaming others† and people treating other people in ways I can only

* There is a literature on so-called 'wicked problems' in social planning: they are difficult or impossible to solve. It is, furthermore, hard to even define the problem and hard to know whether a solution has been reached (ed.).

† On one infamous occasion, when public servants had been cleared of responsibility for a citizen's misbehaviour, a minister said, 'I would like to have been able to blame someone but I can't'.

describe as domestic violence in the workplace. I have observed the 'oak tree' syndrome – a strong, impressive person, well able to impress upward with glib tongue and comforting words, but whose subordinates could not grow in the shade they cast. This style of leadership is often associated with people who talk big and switch jobs frequently, but leave little in the wash. A real leader presents and represents behaviours which are the opposite of this syndrome. Unfortunately, I still hear about too many examples of this kind of behaviour; and we all see it in public life when our political leaders lower, rather than raise, the standard of public discourse.

As the years went on I learned four important lessons, and if I were to summarise them for future generations they would look like this.

1: Take control of the things you can control

Many aspects of the work environment are out of our control. Good and bad things will happen to us and around us. On the other hand, all of these experiences will help us learn when and how to take control.

In my first years in a state government department in New South Wales I learned a very big lesson. I had arranged to get Treasury support (and political support) for a matching grant for the newly emerging women's refuges. I was told to get the request in my department's budget (I was a middle manager) and it would get the nod. I duly prepared the submission, forwarded it through the right channels and waited optimistically for the good news.

When the budget came down in parliament there was no mention of any money. Aghast, I rang the Treasury contact who said it had not been forwarded to them. I tracked my submission down and found the finance officer responsible. He said he worked for a church group as a volunteer and didn't believe in women's refuges and therefore had not included my submission!

I was finally able to get the proposal through with help from my contacts, but this very big lesson taught me that I had to understand how every element of the department worked and follow through on everything. Our organisations are large interlinked systems, and the clever leader will know that they must understand the interplay and manage the whole. I also learned that not everyone is interested in you succeeding, even if they appear to be. A good proposal does not automatically prosper on its own merit. You have to be proactive, constantly checking on its progress. Focus on all the determinants of its success and follow through to the end.

Understanding how systems work is closely associated with learning about the technical aspects of management, including project management, program management, risk, audit, the laws around your space, human resource rules and so on. There is a textbook for everything and they are easily accessible. I look to find one good idea in each one.

There was a time when I read two or three management texts a week. From each of these I would draw at least one important lesson. I would recommend that future leaders read widely – not to copy slavishly but to collect inspiration and stimulate useful ideas in your work space. One of the most exciting ideas I gleaned from reading was the concept of 'waste'. I also learned that two-thirds of all process does not add value and that we create unnecessary work for ourselves and others. From this starting point I explored process redesign, reference suites of material, customer focus and accuracy and quality. I decided that we all have the power to remove the overlays, often historical, that inhibit fluid transactions and processes by thinking carefully about service delivery from the point of view of those we serve.

Some people (and this often applies to women, although not exclusively) have a tape running in their head that limits their courage and confidence. The tape says 'I am not good enough' or 'I have to try harder' or 'It isn't fair'. While it's true that life isn't fair, we tend to place as many limits on ourselves as others do upon us. For a long time I thought I could only be a social worker because that was what I was educated to do. It took some time to realise that this was a starting point for me, and that I could actually do anything I wanted to do.

One of the qualities of a good leader is the ability to tell a story that will cause people to understand the purpose of their work and where the organisation is headed, and to give them a value proposition which they can accept as their own. Simple concepts, repeated, are much more effective in driving change than lengthy mission and vision statements. Many private sector agencies have learned this lesson.

Unfortunately, leaders in public sector agencies don't do enough to prevent the use of unclear and confusing language in their documents and other written communication. Politicians really dislike obtuse language in submissions sent to them or in correspondence to citizens. Clear speaking and writing can be learned with effort, and good writers hired. If a document has no meaning to the reader then it has no value and is a waste of government money. It also fails to deliver the purpose of a policy decision or implementation strategy.

I sat recently as a citizen listening to young people explaining an environmental strategy, using technical language that went right over the heads of the audience and wasted the time of those present. The government certainly didn't get the feedback it needed. Unfortunately, the young people presenting were pleased because there had been no comment. They thought that everyone therefore agreed with their propositions. A few moments spent thinking about the audience first would have made all the difference. In the early days of Centrelink, all new forms were tested first in focus groups of customers to see if they made sense, and were subsequently altered if necessary to use language that had meaning for their intended audience.

At a personal level, aim for the truth in what you say or write, even if the message is difficult.

2: Understand your business and stay focused

The good leader understands what the business is about and also understands that people in different parts of the business see it from different aspects. There are always competing demands and the world moves fast. This is particularly so in the public sector. In the private sector, profit is the driver – businesses can choose their customers and there are fewer agencies to account to. By contrast, the public sector has a complex array of stakeholders – electors, government and opposition, competing thoughts about priorities, the widest possible range of customers (the whole population with all their cultural, social and economic differences). The most important skill in this space is that of listening and building an understanding of the different expectations of all parties. All views are important but there comes a time when you have to settle on the way you want to approach the business, and commit to the choices you take at each step.

In my leadership roles, at the end of every week I would ask myself these questions: 'Has my work been in balance? Have I concentrated on the expectations of those who give the organisation validity? Have I paid attention to the expectations and capacities of the customers? Do I understand the strengths and potential of the members of the organisation who are working with me to achieve our purpose?'

We need to allow ourselves moments for quiet reflection to check that we are still on the right path. Are the many distractions and competing demands making us lose our focus on the choices we have made for the journey ahead? Focus and follow-through are the touchstones of effective leadership. In the end, we have to deliver.

John Kotter, of the Harvard Business School, once wrote that a characteristic of a good leader is the capacity to have an outsider's perspective and an insider's credibility. At the edge of all our work are horizons – new technology, new challenges, new research, new competitors. Leaders can read all the signs and think about how all the pieces fit together. They can keep an objective view about how the organisation is coping in the wider world and whether it is moving fast enough to adapt to the forthcoming changes. Some people call this the view from the helicopter. Looking out, looking back and looking around are critical leadership skills. The capacity to anticipate comes from this type of thinking.

However, there is no point in having this capacity if your people don't understand your vision and its context. Your credibility comes from people believing in you because you can clearly articulate the way forward, drawing together all the elements in the mix, including the over-the-horizon challenges. They must have confidence that you understand all these things and that you can position the organisation – and them – for the future. They want to be assured that you have made the right choices and that you understand how each person can contribute. Your people want to hear from you directly if possible. Nothing beats face-to-face communication from a leader who talks about the vision in language that resonates. In these ways the real leader aligns the whole organisation behind a purpose. It is even better if the key concepts of the vision have been drawn from ideas from the people who will be delivering the results.

3: Respect the people you work with

I have learned that the culture of an organisation stems from the top and the most important personal characteristic for a leader is congruity. There must be an absolute alignment between how I behave and how I expect others to behave. Along with this lesson is the one that says that if you look after your people, they will look after the citizens we are serving.

I once overheard some staff members saying to each other that I expected them to provide an education program for their customers but I did not care about educating them. This was one of those 'aha!' moments, which led me to a lifetime commitment to education in the workplace. On another occasion, a staff survey marked us down on staff development at a time when there was more staff development going on than in any other department. Listening to people when I followed up led me to understand that short courses without accreditation are not seen as real education. In fact, the introduction of accredited articulated courses that went up to tertiary level had a much greater impact on organisational improvement than any other single factor.

Another one of those moments came when I read about 'driving out fear' – perhaps one of the most powerful post-war slogans for industry. Organisations that are poorly led have frightened people in them – people who are frightened for their jobs, frightened to innovate, frightened to improve – all of which leads to loss of confidence in their capacity to solve problems. At worst they can be frightened of the people they are set up to serve. People in organisations then misread the messages from above. Conspiracy theories develop. Gossip becomes the alternative form of communication and the great divide of 'them' and 'us' appears like a huge crack in the organisation. Innovation disappears as people keep their heads down for fear of being noticed and somehow punished. When there is no transparency of process or recognition of good work, people's disaffection grows.

In the public service, where every taxpayer dollar is precious, an environment based on fear reduces the value of each dollar significantly, perhaps by 50 per cent. In the early days of Centrelink, when we depended on innovation to deliver the speed and service improvements the government was looking for, people had to be free to experiment with service improvement, so we did everything we could to remove fear by respecting initiative, acknowledging improvements, and giving managers permission to try new things.

We all know that corporate plans rarely make money. They can set general direction and boundaries but it is innovation and local problem solving within the workplace that open the door to improvement. People need a sense of excitement and adventure in their workplace: this can entail taking risks, which can sometimes lead to failure – but more often leads to success.

Let me give an example. The Centrelink board once travelled by small plane to Maningrida, an Indigenous community about as remote as one can get in Australia, right at the top in Arnhem Land. We were going to the opening of an office there – the first-ever Commonwealth building in the community. We heard on the plane that some very clever IT people in Canberra had worked out a way to access the mainframe by satellite. The community members were being trained as part-time employees and for many this was their first employment. There had been great cooperation with the elders to get the project off the ground. Amazed, I asked the young community worker sitting beside me how this had all happened and who had given permission for the new office. She turned to me and said, 'I asked myself, what would you have wanted to happen? Using your authority, I negotiated everything'. She had achieved the near impossible because she knew she could and persuaded her manager with her arguments.

Bob Joss, of the Stanford Graduate School of Business, once said: 'Strong leadership is not about authority. It's about making it possible for your most talented staff to reach extraordinary heights.'

That is my conclusion too. Many people underestimate their potential and good leaders find ways to stretch them with challenging projects. A good leader finds ways to help everyone work to their personal best. Indeed, many Commonwealth secretaries were given opportunities as middle managers to lead cross-departmental teams to find solutions for 'wicked problems'. They not only had to think and collaborate but it gave them a chance to be noticed.

4. Manage yourself

Aristotle said a good leader demonstrates courage, wit and self-knowledge. It was right for his time as it is right for ours. Emotional intelligence matters.

We all carry baggage, some bits heavier than others. It's worth finding out about the inhibitors to best performance. When we understand the things we cannot control, we have a much greater capacity to manage the things we can. We know that the mood of a leader determines the mood of the organisation or team.

I can remember a boss who was always cranky and unhappy. He hid in his office while files grew in piles on his desk. In fact, he had to have an annexe attached to his office for the overflow. His secretary, a long-suffering saint, was always sending out 'mood messages', and we had to anticipate when we might be able to get something approved. As a consequence, of course, little happened in a timely manner and people spoke in whispers around his office. In another 'aha!' moment, I realised that a constant happy personality was much more effective for keeping things happening and a sense of energy flowing through the universe. And to be constant, we have to understand those triggers that send us over to the dark side and bring out our worst behaviour.

I have learned to live with 24-hour turnover on my desk and am inspired by the goal to touch each piece of paper only once. Of course I can never be perfect, but timeliness around the CEO can lead to timeliness throughout the organisation. This flows into managing meetings on time, purposefully and with follow-up. So much time is wasted by poor personal performance in this area. I am a great writer of lists – things to do today and things to do in the next few months. Things written on a list get done. It is so easy to procrastinate.

I believe compassion needs to infuse our approach to everyday work and to relationships with people around us. You can tell the difference between a member of a group who thinks, 'What is in this for me?' and one who is thinking, 'How can I give my best thoughts to finding a way through this challenge?' A compassionate approach takes out the need for self-promotion with its consequent short-term effects and looks to longer-term solutions. I have found that, as a general rule, people in the public service are motivated by a sense of the public good. This is especially true for direct service workers who every day look for ways to make life easier for the people they serve. This compassion can be easily taken for granted unless they understand that the hierarchy also endorses it as a value, and act congruently by being compassionate themselves.

Courage is a good friend to compassion. Nothing much would change in this world if someone didn't first take a stand and show courage by fronting bad behaviour or insisting on trying a new way. Courage is having the ability to take a position on social injustice and make a difference. It always pleases me to hear people who have worked with me say, when they are facing difficulty, 'What would Sue do?' A leader has a set of behaviours that can be relied upon to hold steady through all circumstances, especially when things are challenging.

Of all the behaviours I have observed that cause confusion and debilitation, panic is at the top. There are people who resort to panic and noise when things get tough. The immediate impact on everyone else is an escalation of worry and concern. The best leaders show deep calm at times like these, and through that calm, spread the message that there will be a solution in the quietness if everyone's energies are directed to purposeful intervention.

Sometimes awful things happen to good leaders. The ones who prosper approach adversity with grace and dignity. They are remembered for how they handled adversity, not for what befell them.

My final message comes as a result of people saying to me, 'You must have had a blessed life. You were appointed to a senior position early and you just kept going.' I recently heard a young woman say, 'I don't want to hear about high-achieving women anymore. We can never be like them.' Both these thoughts are uncomfortable. First, no-one sails to the top on a gust of wind, and second, every high achiever I have met started life with drive and determination, and worked hard in all the jobs they did. Of course there aren't enough spots at the top for everyone, but remember that a leader can operate at any level of an organisation. Every story of success is inspirational and can lead to those moments of clarity that can be incorporated into our own journeys.

About 30 years ago I conducted a small study of women who were chief executives. While each had a very different personality, they had many things in common. They all had a drive to make the world as they saw it a better place; they had interests outside their work; they were leaders in more than one sphere; they read; they moved on from adversity; they took people with them; they focused on issues, not on the game to be played; they could put their point of view clearly; they had a personal sense of integrity that others recognised. None is still a chief executive but they are all still in positions of influence.

Leadership is not for everyone. Being a good follower and concentrating on improving the space you are in is just as important for many. Being able to recognise and experience good leadership is a powerful motivator. Power comes from choosing the leader you follow and not allowing yourself to be demoralised by a bad leader. Bad leaders have the power to erode confidence and motivation by their toxic behaviour, so my message is to get away from them before they totally remove your self-confidence.

There are always serendipitous moments that provide the circumstances for a leader to be chosen, but you may not always recognise them, or be able to control them. I have always believed that women can prepare themselves for leadership opportunities and be ready to step up when the moment presents itself. However, it is up to leaders to provide opportunities for all their people, not just the ones who look like them or who have had the same life experiences. There is enough evidence now to show that diversity in organisations adds value to the nature of service and to the bottom line. Unfortunately, there are still diversity filters in organisations, and the closer you get to the top the more likely people making appointments will pick from a limited pool of people like themselves.

You may choose to be a leader or a follower. Each requires special knowledge and stamina. For those who have the potential to be leaders, there are choices about the type of leader you want to be. Thinking about the experience of being led is a good start. Was the experience one that left you with a sense of worthlessness and reduced confidence and an inability to take the calculated risks that you need to take to achieve results? For the lucky ones, were you empowered to do the best you could and did you have a sense of pride in your work? The good examples are there to watch and follow but so is the constant learning and self-knowledge that a positive leader can exhibit.

It takes strong inner strength and courage, mixed with compassion, to navigate the future. And it is in your hands.

When to step away and when to step up

Tania Sourdin*

Professor Sourdin is the foundation chair and director, Australian Centre for Justice Innovation at Monash University where she leads a number of research teams. She is a part-time member of the Administrative Appeals Tribunal (AAT). She is an active mediator, conciliator and adjudicator and has also conducted research into dispute resolution and conflict perceptions in a range of courts, tribunals and schemes. She wrote the National Mediator Accreditation Standards. She is widely published in several areas of conflict resolution, artificial intelligence, technology and organisational change. She has practised and worked in many jurisdictions within Australia, in the Asia–Pacific region, North America and the Middle East.

Conflict is a feature of public, private, professional and social life. In this chapter Tania Sourdin argues that how we handle conflict and negotiate through it defines us as individuals and as a community. To negotiate well, we need to consider the strategies and processes that we use, and think and operate in counterintuitive ways. Moving from more primitive styles of negotiation to more sophisticated styles and considering the perspective of others are markers of wise leadership. How we deal with high task complexity and high behavioural complexity conflict will determine how well we succeed as leaders.

People will forget what you said, they will forget what you did, but they will never forget how you made them feel.

—Maya Angelou

Introduction

One of the hardest decisions in negotiation and in life is when and how to pursue an issue and when to let it go. As in the song 'The gambler' (performed most notably by Kenny Rogers):

---

* Parts of this chapter are drawn from Sourdin, T, 2013, *Alternative dispute resolution*, 4th edn, Thomson Reuters, Sydney.

You've got to know when to hold 'em
Know when to fold 'em
Know when to walk away
And know when to run.

Mostly, what drives decision making or a response in a negotiation is not well thought out, strategic, logical or rational. More often than not, the choices made in negotiation are the result of learned responses – that is, we consider the situation and then, without conscious choice, use a style or approach we have used before. Or our reaction is driven by our emotional or neurobiological response to the situation (including the degree to which we consider that we have been respected or dealt with 'fairly'). As a result, we may also not act strategically (or usefully) and may persist with an issue, or let it drop, where there may be a better strategic approach.

Many responses in negotiation are driven by basic reactions to conflict that have developed from a young age, when we first reacted to fear or anxiety with a primitive 'fight or flight' or even a 'freeze' response – a state where the body prepares to cope with a threat. Undoubtedly, our responses to negotiation and our communication styles are also derived from the approaches that we learn from our family groups. Some families have passionate nightly dinner-table discussions, others may scream and yell, while some will adopt a 'silent treatment' approach to conflict.

A conscious awareness of how to negotiate, over what, when, how and why requires self-awareness, an understanding of negotiation and process skills, and is the hallmark of quality leadership. Good negotiators and leaders need to be able to read a situation, consider a strategic response, communicate well, and know when supported negotiations and facilitated options would be useful.

In many situations, preparing – even if only briefly – for a negotiation and being able to use strategic negotiation responses can support better outcomes and the realisation of mutual gains. Where competitive negotiation is the best or only option, assessing and tracking the negotiation process can mean that, despite disagreement, options and outcomes can be realistically discussed. However, in some situations, using a facilitator to assist in discussions can prevent negotiations from becoming either sidetracked, or consciously or unconsciously sabotaged.

What drives responses in a negotiation?

Negotiations can become difficult partly because most of us, when in a negotiation situation, automatically assume an approach that's familiar to us without realising that other strategies may be of greater assistance to either resolve the issues or prevent a conflict from recurring. Many people's responses to negotiation can be aggressive. For example, it has been suggested that those who are repeatedly stressed as young children can end up with overdeveloped stress responses, which means they may be more likely to overreact to situations or be more aggressive in stressful situations that occur when conflict is present. This finding has been linked to higher levels of the stress hormone cortisol and even changes to the brain and the way in which the *corpus callosum* assists in passing messages from one part of the brain to another.

Our responses and reactions in negotiation are also thought to be a reflection of our personality, preferences, experiences, culture, values, education and training. In addition, the way we respond is determined by our health (mental and physical) and whether we are rested or tired. Other differences may be gender- and age-related. We may, for example, be more likely to be competitive (and less likely to submit or avoid) in our late teens and early twenties. Our approach is also determined in part by how we perceive comments and the actions or inactions of others. Our perceptual filters (affected by age, health, education, culture, etc.) may encourage us to respond in a certain way.

It may be that the context of a situation leads us to interpret an event in a manner that is entirely different from the way in which others might interpret the same event. Our response to an issue can also determine or heighten the response or reaction of other individuals. For example, if the approach that is adopted is unconditionally constructive despite great aggravation and irritation, it is likely that the process used to deal with the negotiation will involve more cooperation. On the other hand, if the response includes a raised voice, a heightened sense of stress, and an approach where personal insults are traded, it is more likely that the process used to deal with the issue will be competitive, and less likely that it will result in an outcome.

Culture also plays a role in how we negotiate. In some societies, there has been a far greater emphasis on collaborative problem-solving approaches and the facilitated resolution of disputes (rather than someone else deciding the dispute for you). There may be a greater tendency in some cultures to submit to something in a negotiation or avoid some issues altogether. While this tendency appears to stem in part from a greater emphasis on social harmony and the role of the society (rather than the individual's rights), the approach also stems from some fundamental differences in communication and negotiation patterns, and from cultural contexts that have become more apparent as our world has become more globalised.

In some parts of Asia, for example, it would be unusual for a young person to ever challenge the view taken by a respected older person, even if the view was wrong or the younger person considered that there was a better way of approaching an issue.

Negotiation patterns

Negotiation and conflict theories abounded throughout the Cold War as nations and individuals struggled to deal with repeated impasse issues, and to negotiate complex situations and difficult behaviours. A greater emphasis on negotiation strategies and theories emerged in the early 1970s to assist with planning and strategy development, and to manage the more complex international and cross-cultural relationships that were becoming an increasing feature of modern business activities. A close examination of the factors that surround a negotiation was seen as essential to determining appropriate negotiation strategies.

This led to the evolution of interest-based negotiation or bargaining by a number of negotiation theorists. For example, Harvard University academics Fisher and Ury wrote the book *Getting to yes* in 1981.[1] In that work, a method and process of negotiation were developed. Movement from hard or soft positional bargaining could be achieved by using a method that Fisher and Ury called 'principled negotiation' or 'negotiation on the merits'. The Fisher and Ury model of negotiation was said to be a collaborative or cooperative model that promoted a 'win win' outcome.

In *Getting to yes*, the four fundamental elements to achieve a successful negotiation were distilled as follows:

Elements of successful negotiation

1. *people* – separate the people from the problem
2. *interests* – focus on interests, not positions
3. *options* – generate a variety of possibilities before deciding what to do
4. *criteria* – insist that the result be based on some objective standard.[2]

These basic approaches were used to promote a different and more collaborative approach to negotiations.

More recently, theorists have also suggested that there are a variety of approaches to any given negotiation:

Approaches to negotiation

- *avoidance* – where the issue, dispute or conflict is avoided. In a family or workplace dispute, for example, this could be characterised by a lack of contact or withdrawal
- *submission* – where a party 'gives in' and decides not to pursue an issue
- *compromise* – where 'give and take' outcomes are suggested
- *competitive* or *positional* – where one party seeks to 'win' and adopts a 'position' without exploring the other parties' needs or interests
- *interest-based* or *collaborative* – where the parties' needs and interests are explored and the options that are developed address those needs and interests.

The first four approaches are understood by all of us at a very young age. The fifth (interest-based) approach usually requires more work and is a more sophisticated response. In any negotiation, the choices that are made about which approach to use can be explored using simple preparation tools (see below). For example, it may simply not be worth your time to negotiate about some issues, or your prospects of success may be so insignificant that it is simply better to 'let it go'. In other circumstances, it might be appropriate to use a more competitive negotiation approach, for example, where there will be no continuing relationship and if you can protect your reputation.

Many people can effectively negotiate a matter without needing to have someone else assist them. However, some people may not achieve useful outcomes in the negotiations or they may find that issues are not resolved. Sometimes, giving up or avoidance approaches can have disastrous long-term consequences, lead to strained emotions or exacerbate a dispute. Other people may need to resort to courts, and a lack of negotiation skills could also hamper people in social, work and other situations. In these circumstances, it can be useful to work through the issue with the help of a trained negotiator.

Given that we all negotiate issues on a daily basis, there was surprisingly little attention given to negotiation processes until the latter half of the 20th century, when there was an increased focus on the way negotiation takes place within the business setting. Some of this negotiation material focused on the strategies, tactics and styles used in negotiation. Other material focused on developing a process of negotiation and an understanding that negotiations could deliver better outcomes for all involved if they were interest-based. The story most commonly used to explain the difference between the two major styles in negotiation – competitive and interest-based – is the orange story.

The orange story

The orange story is often used to illustrate the basic problem-solving and interest-based approach in negotiation. In the orange story, Fisher and Ury in *Getting to yes*[3] tell of two sisters who each wanted an entire orange. Only one orange was available and it was cut in half to satisfy them. One sister squeezed her half for the juice and threw away the peel. The other sister grated the peel from her half to use in a cake and threw the rest away (including the juice). Neither was satisfied or had their needs met with the 'solution'. Both girls had wanted the whole orange, but one needed (or had an interest in) only the juice whilst the other needed only the peel. Both of their interests could have been satisfied more fully if they had been explored, with one sister taking the juice and the other taking the peel – each maximising their gain, and not to the detriment of the other.

The orange story suggests that interest-based negotiation can result in more effective outcomes for all concerned, and shows how in negotiation the most important question to assess is why someone wants something (that is, what the underlying needs or interests are).

Addressing this question will usually mean that in a negotiation you explore the most important needs or interests, rather than focusing solely on positions (what it is they say they want). This process of identifying parties' underlying needs (interests) often results in the discovery of several needs which, even if they are not common to both parties, may not necessarily be in conflict with the needs (interests) of the other party. For example, in a family dispute over parenting, the reasons (interests) a mother may have in wanting the children to reside with her may not be incompatible with the reasons (interests) that the father may have. It is important to recognise that not all disputes can be resolved using interest-based negotiation. However, supporting an interest-based negotiation approach can assist the parties to negotiate more effectively.

Interest-based approaches are also more likely to support continuing relationships. This is partly because a conversation about underlying interests can be more respectful and can also enable future arrangements to be discussed. A critical question is: when should this type of negotiation style be used, and under what circumstances might it be better to avoid, submit, compromise or even compete? To answer this question, many skilled negotiators will prepare for a negotiation (even if only briefly) and this will help them to know how best to respond.

Choosing a negotiation approach

In thinking about how to negotiate, it is useful to think about how and where the negotiation will take place and to ensure that, where appropriate, there is a structure, guidelines and time frame for the negotiation. The time spent preparing may vary according to the complexity of the problem. In preparing, the negotiator can consider and take notes about a range of factors.

Determining interests

This requires each negotiator to explore their own interests (not positions) and to consider the interests of the other parties they are negotiating with. In addition, the negotiating party should consider the interests of others who may not be present at the negotiation. For example, in a salary negotiation an employee may consider their own interests (for example, economic needs, housing, profile, promotion, work tasks, flexibility, etc.), their employer's interests (for example, having motivated staff, ensuring profitability, staff retention) and the interests of others who may be outside the negotiation (such as senior management, other employees, families). In considering other interests, media and key stakeholder interests can shape negotiation outcomes (or may potentially derail negotiations). Considering or at least mapping these interests is critical in ensuring that negotiation can stay on track.

Determining alternatives

If the negotiation does not produce an agreed outcome, what is the alternative? This requires the negotiator to consider not only their alternatives but also to consider the alternatives of the other party. The question to ask yourself is, what will happen if there is no agreement? When negotiating, it is worthwhile to explore these aspects and to determine how your alternatives can be improved, particularly your 'best alternative to negotiated agreement' (BATNA), and your 'worst alternative to a negotiated agreement' (WATNA). In addition, the alternatives of the other party (their BATNA and WATNA) need to be fully considered. Options to strengthen your alternatives and to weaken those of the other party should also be considered.

What options exist?

That is, what ideas could be used in the negotiation? In a salary negotiation, for example, there may be options other than money that might be appealing, such as time in lieu, added flexibility, work opportunities and other such benefits that may improve the status of an employee.

What information and process are required?

Are there questions that can be asked and, if so, what are they? Are there any standards that can be used to assist in measuring the agreement or any options? What can you do to help persuade the other side or those outside the negotiation? Are there other processes that could be used to help reach an agreement? How will the negotiation take place, at what time and with what expectations? Is there a better time or place? Should the negotiation be conducted face to face?

How are you going to communicate?

What messages will you send? How can they be framed? A message can be framed in many ways. For example, sometimes it can be useful to frame a message in terms of mutual interests. In other circumstances the message might be framed in terms of more detailed information. The central approach requires that the impact on those you are negotiating with is considered and that the message is framed in a way which is responsive to the other participants in the negotiation. There may be particular communication strategies that can be explored. For example, creating a useful agenda, and summarising main points and areas of agreement and disagreement, can be useful in more complex negotiations.

What relationship issues exist?

How can the relationship be improved, and what type of relationship will be important into the future? If there are relationship issues (for example, a lack of trust), what might the cause be and how can this be addressed? The relationship can impact on long- and short-term outcomes, and many negotiations can be adversely affected by perceptions about reliability or perceptions of behaviour. Unless such issues are attended to, the negotiation may not produce an outcome.

What are the products of the negotiation?

What needs to be agreed? How will it be followed up? Who will take action in future and how will they do it? Implementation is sometimes forgotten in a negotiation. An agreement may say something is to happen 'as soon as possible', but if the parties are in dispute, this lack of certainty can lead to further communication breakdown. If it is unrealistic to expect sign-off after one meeting, considering multiple sessions can be useful. Variations in the outcomes of negotiation can be related to a vast range of options that include timing, apologies, understandings, provision of additional information and new agreements, as well as options of high value to one negotiation participant and of low value to another.

Preparation ensures that you understand the approach that will work best in relation to the problem. In general, where there is a continuing relationship, it will not be supported by competitive approaches to negotiation. Compromisory approaches can be problematic as they may mean that better options and solutions (that meet the interests of those involved) remain unexplored. Avoid and submit responses may be more appropriate where your alternatives are limited or non-existent. Preparing can help with this assessment and also assist in your actual negotiation as it will help you to put forward ideas and discuss matters in a way that might satisfy the other person's interests. In general, when you approach a negotiation in an interest-based manner, the other person is more likely to follow this approach.

Styles and behaviours

Some negotiators use aggressive behaviours in negotiation in an attempt to extract better outcomes, and these behaviours may make it difficult to maintain an interest-based approach. The behaviours will lead to particular negotiation patterns unless they can be dealt with. However, often the behaviours used are unconscious. Sometimes considering the behaviours can assist a negotiator to frame their responses, or can be used to help analyse the approach of others in a negotiation. An individual negotiator may also adopt one stance or style in relation to an issue or at a particular time in a negotiation before shifting approaches. For example, a negotiator may adopt a competitive stance towards one issue and a more collaborative stance towards another. Similarly, the stance a negotiator adopts may be unconscious or alter if they are tired, hungry or uncomfortable.

Where teams of negotiators are engaged, negotiation styles may be influenced by the team dynamics as well as by different negotiator characteristics. In one negotiation I was involved in, a person from one team of negotiators started the conversation with a fairly insulting remark. This made it difficult for the other team to maintain their composure and made it more likely that the negotiation would be conducted in a competitive manner. Fortunately, the structure and ground rules in the negotiation (as well as good preparation) made it less likely for the remark to have a lasting impact and derail the negotiation. The style you adopt may also be influenced by lateral, vertical or other pressures. The audience, constituents and the relationships may play a central role in influencing the styles you choose to adopt.

One approach used by some negotiators can be defined as a tactical adversarial approach and involves competitive negotiation strategies and tactics. In this 'give and take' approach, 'what one party gains the other must lose'.[4] For instance, one party states a position: 'I want that orange.' The other says. 'I want the orange.' Rather than exploring why either party wants the orange, one or both parties seeks an outcome where the whole orange is obtained by one party. This type of approach more often than not will lead to no outcome (the matter may need to progress to court or end in a stalemate) or to an outcome where one side is left wanting to exact revenge into the future.

Sometimes 'dirty' tactics will be used. These can vary from personal insults, omitting or distorting information, putting ridiculous offers on the table, claiming lack of authority (or saying 'I'll need to ask someone else' when an offer has been put within a bargaining range) or making you feel uncomfortable in some way. These tactics can readily distract you from the subject matter of the negotiation and might prompt you to respond in a competitive way or avoid the negotiation altogether. There are some approaches that can be useful. First, understand that the behaviour by the other person may not be intentional. At times, aggressive and competitive negotiators can be unaware of the impact they have on others (although some may enjoy causing others discomfort as a result of sociopathic or psychopathic tendencies).

Second, it is sometimes useful to clearly raise or 'surface' the tactic. For example, you might say, 'I am finding the way that we are talking with each other to not be very productive. I would like to make sure that we can have a productive conversation. Can we agree not to use personal insults?'

Where the tactic involves an extreme demand or offer, it can be useful to seek more information – to say, for instance, 'Can you help me understand this better so that I can explain this to our organisation? They will need some detail to understand your thinking.'

Sometimes the styles or behaviours may be compromisory, that is, using an approach most classically demonstrated as a 'bidding approach'. Using the orange example above, the orange could be cut in half. This can occur when one party seeks to 'win' and adopts a 'position' without exploring the other party's needs or interests. This is also referred to as distributive bargaining – essentially, a fixed amount of benefit is divided among those negotiating. A characteristic of compromisory negotiation can also be the presence of confronting and personal attacks and a series of offers (also known as the 'high–low game'). Where extreme 'bidding' becomes a feature of these types of negotiations, it can be hard to remain respectful, and it is important that these types of tactics and strategies do not become distracting. In many negotiations, after four bidding rounds are concluded it can be hard to achieve an outcome so it is important that you consider these styles and plan appropriately. Again, to support a resolution and a more constructive conversation, it can be important to gather information and attempt to ensure that positions are not discussed until after information about the problem and the problem's impact have been discussed.

It is important to understand that sometimes people will put an extreme position to 'anchor' you to a different bargaining range, and that with good preparation, it is less likely that these approaches will lead you into a 'tit for tat' response that distracts you from what you need to achieve.

Sometimes, respectful compromisory bargaining can result in a good outcome and can even be useful where the relationship with the other party is less important, for example in a one-off transaction or where ethical issues are not relevant.[5] If you find yourself in this type of negotiation, maintaining a more interest-based approach and asking to hear more about how the situation has affected the other person can sometimes assist to create a more interest-focused environment (and therefore be more likely to result in an agreed outcome).

In terms of interest-based negotiation, behaviours are of critical importance. It is said that the likelihood of reaching agreement is greatly increased if an 'unconditionally constructive' approach is adopted by the negotiator.[6] This has certainly been my experience, regardless of the style of negotiation used by the other side or even in circumstances where disruptive behaviours and tactics are present. By far the most successful negotiators are those who maintain constructive approaches and remain positive, respectful and assertive. This means that the issues remain the focus, rather than the people involved in the dispute.

Planning for complex negotiations

Planning for a more complex negotiation includes considering the environment, the timing (including time of day and scheduled sessions), the people attending and whether guidelines or preparatory documents will be helpful.

In terms of the actual negotiation, clear communication is a critical aspect. To create a respectful environment, it is useful to be able to create a neutral and mutual agenda, to listen, to ask useful open questions that enable you to check assumptions and understandings, and to 'summarise back' to ensure you have accurately understood the issue and message. Where competitive negotiation tactics are used, good preparation can help you determine when and whether to negotiate at all, and can also ensure that you are not derailed by dishonest or positional tactics.

In some negotiations, participants may decide to use a 'collaborative' process model where lawyers and all experts are trained in interest-based negotiation, are focused on the negotiation process for two-hour periods, and follow guidelines for gathering and exchanging information (participation agreements normally require the withdrawal of lawyers and others if the negotiation does not succeed).

Using a third party

Sometimes a third party is used to assist in the negotiation and may support a focus on less linear constructions of negotiation. Often the third party will be a facilitator or mediator who will design a process for the negotiation in consultation with those involved. Ordinarily, the third party under these circumstances will not have an advisory role in terms of outcomes but may advise about the process. A third party can help move beyond a competitive construction of negotiation and be more focused on problem-solving processes that 'subordinate strategies and tactics to the process of identifying possible solutions and therefore allow a broader range of outcomes to negotiation problems.'[7]

Using mediation models

Mediation models are used because advisory, hierarchical, adjudicative and rights-based processes of dispute resolution may not be sufficient to deal with negotiations that involve a careful consideration of future options and interests. Mediation processes are usually designed to support interest-based negotiation and often assume that some preparation will take place and that agreements about confidentiality, authority and exchange of material will operate in the lead-up to a meeting. In accordance with interest-based negotiation models, there is a focus on exploring the problem, underlying interests and issues before considering options.

Facilitation or mediation can be adapted to multi-stakeholder conflict and negotiations in a range of settings. Although these models are used frequently in social, business, industry, and complex negotiation areas (including with environmental and intractable conflict) they have been less well used in the political area (in particular in relation to internal conflict). In the government area, many government departments are now focused on how early dispute resolution can take place, and dispute-management plans have been developed by some lead government agencies (such as the Australian Tax Office (ATO), the Commonwealth Attorney-General's Department and the Australian Competition and Consumer Commission (ACCC) that are all directed at using effective dispute resolution at the earliest possible time. Over the past decade, literature and research about these types of dispute-resolution processes has proliferated. While many of these processes now are required to be used before litigation has commenced, often they are also required once litigation is on foot.

Future developments

The developments in the negotiation and dispute-resolution area are being informed by neuroscience, neurobiological and behavioural research as well as by significant developments in technology (that can support decision making as well as remote access and other issues). These developments suggest that negotiation styles and processes can be varied to produce better outcomes in different circumstances. There is much research that suggests that joint outcomes are more likely to be achieved where interest-based negotiation processes are used. In addition, this approach is said to enhance both relationships and satisfaction.[8]

In government, wise negotiation processes may make all the difference in whether and how policies can be created, implemented and embedded. The personal qualities and styles adopted by leaders when negotiating or adopting facilitative approaches can influence perceptions about the content of policy initiatives and about the individuals and political groups involved. While skills in analysis, reasoning and decision making are required in leadership, communication, negotiation and process skills, knowledge and understanding can ensure that potential leaders are not hampered by barriers and that they are driven by strategic considerations rather than instinct.

---

1. Fisher, R & Ury, W, 1981, *Getting to yes: negotiating agreement without giving in*, Houghton Mifflin, Boston.
2. Fisher, R, Ury, W & Patton, B, 1991, *Getting to yes: negotiating agreement without giving in*, 2nd edn, Random House, Sydney, pp. 56–57, 73.
3. Fisher, R & Ury, W, 1981, *Getting to yes: negotiating agreement without giving in*, Houghton Mifflin, Boston, p. 100.
4. Menkel-Meadow, C, 1984, 'Toward another view of legal negotiation: the structure of problem solving', *UCLA Law Review*, 31: 754, p. 755.
5. Lewicki, R, Saunders, D & Minton, J, 1999, *Negotiation*, 3rd edn, Irwin McGraw Hill, Singapore.
6. Fisher, R & Brown, S, 1999, *Getting together: building a relationship that gets to yes*, Business Books Ltd, Great Britain, p. 38. See also: Schneider, A, 2002, 'Shattering negotiation myths: empirical evidence on the effectiveness of negotiation style', *Harvard Negotiation Law Review*, 7:1, pp. 143–233.
7. Menkel-Meadow, C, 1984, 'Toward another view of legal negotiation: the structure of problem solving', *UCLA Law Review*, 31: 754, p. 755.
8. Atkin, T & Rinehart, L, 2006, 'Research report: the effect of negotiation practices on the relationship between suppliers and customers', *Negotiation Journal*, 22:1, p. 47.

Civic dialogue – leading respectful conversations

*Margaret Halsmith**

Margaret Halsmith is principal of Halsmith Dispute Resolution. She has almost 20 years' experience mediating disputes in a range of contexts, including interpersonal and relationship, family and extended family, community and government, and business and commercial. Her areas of particular interest include the language of peacekeeping and peacemaking, standards of dispute resolution, dispute resolution for entrenched conflict, apology in dispute resolution, and participants' overall wellbeing during and after dispute resolution. She chairs the entity (as yet unnamed) formed on 1 January 2015 from the merger of the former LEADR: Association of Dispute Resolvers and IAMA: Institute of Arbitrators and Mediators Australia. Other current roles include member of the former National Alternative Dispute Resolution Advisory Council (NADRAC); vice-chair of the International Mediation Institute's Independent Standards Commission and, as part of that role, chair of the Standards Design and Implementation Committee; and deputy convenor of the Western Australian Dispute Resolution Association (WADRA).

Civic dialogue is constructive conversation between leaders and stakeholders that takes place *prior to* leaders' decision making. It is the kind, gentle and potentially robust exchange of ideas about public issues among people, including leaders, who attribute value to their own and to others' perspectives. Participants in civic dialogue aim to broaden and deepen their learning, and to influence and be open to the influence of others. Their relationship dynamics generate dynamism and stasis, consonance and dissonance, and creativity and conflict, which integrate to create a realm of procedural and substantive possibilities. Civic dialogue contributes to participants' confidence and resilience by meeting their needs for acknowledgement and connection. Leaders who participate in civic dialogue know a group well and can represent it with confidence.

---

* The writer acknowledges the assistance of Tom Howe QC in the preparation of this essay.

In this chapter Margaret Halsmith discusses how selecting the language of civic dialogue, as one factor among many, aligns intent with integrity and leaves influence to (almost) look after itself. She shows how to choose language that speaks to each person and to people collectively.

---

suspend certainty
create possibilities
person to person
—the author

I understand the incredible power of language and how it shapes ideas.
—Tim Minchin

The self and others in conversation

Each person on this small planet – whether follower or leader – wants to know themselves and wants to be known by others. In conversation, we tell of the meanings that we make of the world, and become known to others through their listening. Equally, in our telling we learn about ourselves. We listen to the discourse of others to recognise aspects of ourselves. In hearing others we also learn about them. Our telling, our listening and our learning create opportunities to build connections of mutual acknowledgement. Our private recollections of telling and listening record the evolution of our identity. In speaking, we tell something of ourselves; in listening, we hear something of ourselves. To others, what we tell and hear may range from incidental to profound, whereas to ourselves the private significance of what we tell and hear may range quite differently from incidental to profound. What we tell and hear may be crucial to our sense of self and to connecting with other selves. Conversation is, in part, an intimate exchange of vulnerabilities. Safety in conversation comes from respect, which is another way of saying reverence for the vulnerable, intimate selves of fellow communicators.

Often in politics, as it is currently practised, respect is the exception. It was not always so. As this excerpt[1] from the memoir of the only daughter of Sir Robert Menzies records, in 1941 John Curtin and Robert Menzies exchanged intimate, personable and kind correspondence at a time of likely vulnerability for each.

Correspondence between Menzies and Curtin, 1941

My dear John,

I have ceased to be Prime Minister and we shall therefore no longer be opposite numbers at the table.

I want to thank you for two years and four months in which my task, always difficult, has frequently been rendered easier and at all times more tolerable by your magnanimous and understanding attitude.

Your political opposition has been honourable and your personal friendship a pearl of great price.

Yours sincerely …

Dear Bob,

Thank you for your letter. I appreciate it more than I can say. On my part I thank you wholeheartedly for the consideration and courtesy which never once failed in your dealings with me. I wish you good health and fair going. Your personal friendship is something I value, as I hope and know you do, as a very precious thing.

Yours faithfully …

Leaders

This essay regards leaders as role models. When among followers, good leaders listen with respect for the variety of opinions and meanings, and speak with respect for a variety of possibilities. Respectful listening affirms both the leader's and followers' sense of self and strengthens their sense of affiliation. The tone having been set, the exchange of ideas is likely to continue, enriching both the dialogue and the experience. The connection between leadership, dialogue, its lexicon, the listener and the speaker is the 'human connection', a connection of relationships. This essay proposes that leaders can influence the outcomes of their cause through their approach to dialogue and by their choice of lexicon.

Leaders are leaders because they make decisions that achieve outcomes for causes in ways that resonate with others. Followers look to leaders for outcomes that improve their wellbeing or the wellbeing of others, through means they value. We support leaders whose decisions bring distributive justice, procedural justice and interpersonal justice. Leadership that is just recognises the intrinsic value of listening and telling, as well as the significance of how ideas and meanings are heard and told. Just leadership flows into a style that is fair and into decisions that are wise.

A cause is usually identifiable by its relevance to a definable group. In the 21st century, all causes, all leaders and all followers have a meta-cause: governance for the sustainability of Earth and its creatures. Perhaps the imperative of sustainability will be the catalyst for the revival of widespread energetic and respectful dialogue on public issues. Perhaps such dialogue will result in improved governance for sustainability on the basis that the richer, the more robust and the more respectful the dialogue, the more it will meet people's need for affirmation and affiliation. The more those needs are met, the more resilient and peaceable people will become. More peace will mean better distribution of resources and more resources to care for the planet. The more care is taken of the planet, the more sustainable the global ecosystem will be. And the more sustainable the ecosystem, the more energy and inclination there will be for rich, robust, respectful dialogue. Civic dialogue has the potential to become both a contributor to and an indicator of the wellbeing of people, humanity and the planet. Once established – and that is the challenge to leaders and followers – it perpetuates in a positive feedback loop.

Each day as a mediator I 'wage (procedural) peace'* so that participants can reach distributive, procedural and personal outcomes that they each assess are in their individual and collective interests. My practice is informed by three ideas that relate to the human needs for affirmation and affiliation. The first idea is that each exchange, each message, affects the people involved: the sender, the receiver and, importantly, any bystanders. The second is that all exchanges have the potential to engage people and to contribute to their wellbeing and to the wellbeing of others. And the third is that the first two ideas are inextricably connected. These ideas are probably part of human consciousness. As ideas, if they are radical, it is only in their simplicity. In practice, as civic dialogue, they can be radical in their transformative ability – such is the power of language.

---

* I adapted this expression from the title of Anne Deveson's memoir *Waging peace: reflections on peace and war from an unconventional woman* (2013).

Politics

This book, *So you want to be a leader*, is timely because many Australians are disengaged from established electoral decision-making processes.[2] It is my impression that many are engaged in protective apathy and disengaged from the current political discourse because to engage is to accept that after an initial period of limerence, current political discourse neither affirms nor affiliates. This is because to engage politically is to publicly endorse one view and to oppose all others. It is to claim moral superiority; to frame 'facts' so that they clash with those claimed by others; to defer to power cabals, deifying some people and demonising others. It is to be profligate in the use of terms such as 'back down', 'attack', 'scare tactics' and 'in tatters'. In this environment, the focus of political parties and politicians is 'politics', a euphemism for 'power struggle'. Australians, especially those under the age of 29, are asking for public engagement, for focus on policy and for global perspectives. Instead of being front and centre, each of these priorities is marginalised, lost to public one-upmanship and naysaying. 'Decide politically then defend passionately' and 'if in doubt, oppose' are two among the political truisms of much of the public Australian political discourse. Disengagement from this sort of depleting interaction is self-protective. Protective apathy is understandable and deeply regrettable. Australian citizens of the world, namely, people for whom 'public issues' and 'global issues' are synonymous, are atypical in the Australian political scene.

The choreographed and public arm wrestle of Australian 'politics' normalises incivility. Terms of engagement are rigid, excluding, competitive and fragmenting. Outcomes are brittle. Abrasive language reflects its mindscape, tending toward bombast and hyperbole. Denigration is formulaic: blame, minimise, justify and deny; all are prominent features of public political discourse in Australia. When the opposition see it as their task to oppose first and think later, the public are treated to a gross oversimplification of the complexity of the issues to be considered and the decisions to be made. Dissent is distinct from opposition. Dissenting opinions add to complexity which adds to the creative possibilities.

Meanwhile, behind the public political scenes, politicians, and in civic spheres, other Australians, continue to generate wonderfully adaptive, creative and inclusive ideas and to cooperate to bring them to fruition. Among the arts, the sciences and the humanities, for example, there is an enormous diversity of goals, resources and opportunities. Within and among each, significant difficulties arise and are mostly addressed through collegial relationships with the common goal to make creative sense of complexity. This is civic dialogue.

How can potentially constructive 21st-century political ideas be similarly and publicly nurtured and challenged? What can Australians do to participate in the generous and constructive robust national conversation aspired to by this book. This book encourages the considered exchange of ideas through universally affirming terms of engagement. It endorses the place of caring, enriching, wide-ranging and challenging conversation which focuses on the important issues and comes from a platform of respect. It looks to new leaders to initiate and maintain this approach.

Communication

Conversation is comprised of numerous linguistic elements, one of which is messages and another of which is the lexicon of the messages. Leaders who express their messages and invite comments in ways which meet the needs of followers are leaders who will be heard – leaders whose ideas will be considered and responded to. That perhaps goes without saying. More subtly – and just as importantly – leaders who take the next step and align their lexicon to be consonant with their messages are even more likely to engage followers. Too often, however, leaders' respectful messages include words which undermine their message. Such messages are at risk of conveying ambivalence and of eroding the potential for civic dialogue.

Consider two speakers' responses when a discussion is getting heated. One says, 'I would like us to continue this discussion, knowing that we each see the situation differently.' The other says, 'I will let this discussion continue, knowing that we each see the situation differently.'. The words 'I will let …', in particular, the word 'let', convey a relationship which has a conditional, authoritarian element. 'I would like us …' conveys an affirming, reciprocal relationship of civic dialogue.

When followers evaluate leadership, their first measure is often 'interpersonal justice': how have relationships been managed? Next is often 'procedural justice': how fair have the processes of communication been? The processes of decision making? And next, to what extent has the outcome met their (distributive) expectations? This is 'distributive justice'. When leaders look after interpersonal justice, procedural justice largely looks after itself and distributive justice follows on. One aspect of interpersonal justice is communication. The first speaker above is alert to how communication can affect interpersonal justice.

Communication, as it is used here, is a collective noun for all that is involved in listening, speaking, hearing, being heard and making meaning. If communication were a ball game and each message were a ball, the ball that is thrown would rarely, if ever, be the ball that is caught. The ball that is thrown is one created from the perceptions and needs of the thrower. The ball that is caught is held within and shaped by the perceptions and needs of the catcher. When one is the leader and another a follower, a particular dimension of perception is added: the dimension of influence.

Leaders perceive opportunities for fulfilling goals and outcomes, have needs for affirmation and achievement, and have authority. Followers perceive opportunities for relationships through participation, have needs for affiliation and identity, and follow authority as a conduit to fulfilling goals and achieving outcomes. Bob Geldof, one of the leaders of the 1985 Live Aid, and the audience at that concert provide an example of perception possibilities. He announced: 'Please. Please. Please. Give us as much money as we know you have. Thanks.'

Geldof's is a goal-fulfilling and outcome-oriented message: Give us a lot of money. We know that you know that you have ample.

The audience hears 'please', 'us', and 'thanks'.

Geldof used his authority to throw a largely goal-oriented, outcome-focused message-ball: Give us as much money as you can. Concert-goers accepted Geldof's authority and are likely to have filtered his message and heard it as one of relationship building. That is, many of the audience are likely to have caught and held that ball largely by reference to the words 'please', 'us', and 'thanks': the relationship-focused aspects of the message. The message-ball that was thrown was quite different from the message-ball that was caught and the needs of each were met.

As well as sending messages that transform in *meaning* as they are received, leaders send messages that can be transformed in *significance* as they are received. Bob Geldof may have intended to make a request: 'Please. Please. Please. Give us as much money as we know you have. Thanks.' One concert-goer may have heard those words more strongly than as a request: they may have heard them as an entreaty. Another may have heard a demand; another, an obligation. The weight of a message-ball is due in part to the authority that the catcher attributes to the thrower, in part to the needs of the catcher and in part to many other factors. The corollary is that when followers throw message-balls, there is a chance that leaders will catch them more lightly than was intended.

Experienced leaders catch followers' message-balls heavily and intersperse the goal-oriented message-balls that they throw with relationship-oriented message-balls: 'I've just realised that today is the best day of my life. Now I'm going home to sleep.' (Bob Geldof, still at Live Aid.)

Civic dialogue

Civic dialogue is conversation that is guided by interpersonal justice shaped into procedural justice and motivated by public justice. It is entered into with the aim of clarifying and influencing participants' opinions.

Civic dialogue could qualify to be the next addition to the 'slow movement'.* It is dialogue at a thorough pace and through an inclusive process. It is characterised by open-mindedness and the aspiration to become well informed. During their immersion in exploring, explaining, challenging, hypothesising and distilling big ideas, each participant tells something of themselves and hears something of themselves and of others. Each influences and is influenced by others. Doubt is respected. Participants are likely to both create and contribute to resolving some doubt. Civic dialogue is communication that is experienced as reciprocal and patient, and which imbues the participants with a residue of confidence.

* The Slow Movement was founded by Italian Carlo Petrini in the late 1980s in response to 'fast food'. The Slow Movement establishes, maintains and develops connections with the fundamental constructs of life, creating conditions for shared and individual meanings to evolve through opportunities for affirmations and affiliations.

What is communication when it is not civic dialogue? It could be a parallel monologue; it could be a debate; it could be an argument; it could be a soliloquy. It could be a lecture; a tirade; an ultimatum; a stipulation; a demand. It could be declaratory speech; it could be graffiti.

Observers and participants each experience civic dialogue from different perspectives. A distant observer sees and hears conversation which flows through open questions, around silences and reflection, over time and sometimes into joint endeavours, with a tone of mutual empathy, acknowledgement and respect. From a distance, an observer hears the percussive rhythm of message-balls as they are thrown and caught.

An observer who is nearby sees and hears message-balls being thrown and mostly being caught, but some bouncing and some falling short. They see people listening with concern and curiosity and they see and hear people speaking, mostly moderately, with periodic passionate deliveries. They hear a range of voices speaking the language of peers, and hear participants gradually distilling disparate topics into cohesive issues of concern. They notice participants getting along with warmth, consideration and humour. Although not the intent of civic dialogue, a nearby observer may hear agreed recommendations for decision makers being reached by consensus.

A participant engaging in civic dialogue implicitly joins a three-part 'perception pact': first, that they and each other participant will throw and catch message-balls with care and confidence, keeping an eye on the ball, rather than 'playing' the person; second, that ideas are communal; and third, that the experience is an iterative one of learning and relearning about public issues and privately about self and others. As a result, the participant expects that the message-balls they throw will be caught and held differently by the receiver. They perceive the differences as rich with possibilities for deepening the dialogue. The participant respects their own and others' ambivalence, uncertainty, paradox and contradictions, regarding each as opening new trajectories for dialogue. Changes of mind are regarded as evidence of sophisticated thinking and a resilient sense of self.

The outcome of the 'perception pact' is that the participant is inclined to listen generously, to think constructively and to speak moderately.

Most often the participant feels acknowledged, validated, affirmed, confident, connected and comfortable. From time to time, due to the nature of communication in identifying vulnerabilities, inevitably they may feel affronted, dismayed, doubtful, frustrated or hurt. The participant takes responsibility for their role, their choice of expression and their feelings in civic dialogue. They know themselves and the process well enough to know that dismay and its close relatives are harbingers of lateral thinking. At the time and in hindsight they feel satisfied with the interpersonal and procedural flow, having had the opportunity to suggest modifications during discussions.

Words

Expressing ideas and meanings involves a multitude of interacting linguistic variables. Choice of words is one. The extent to which a particular word affects civic dialogue depends on many factors including the substance of the message, the use of figures of speech, the disposition of the listener, the context, the tonality and the body language of the speaker. Even amid the infinite variety of circumstances, there are some words that have a tendency to foster civic dialogue and others that are at risk of stifling it.

As eyes are windows to the soul, so words are to the mind. A speaker's choice of words conveys nuanced insights into their perception of their relationship with the listener. Words which convey a dimension of mutuality, as if from a peer, can evoke feelings of safety and invite cooperative responses. Words which convey an authoritarian dimension, as if from status or position, can evoke distress and activate competitive reactions. Listeners are attuned to words that affect their sense of self (whether affirming or depleting) and those that affect their affiliation (whether belonging or alienating).

How people disagree is an indicator of a relationship. The choice of the words of disagreement is key to this. When disagreeing with a peer, words such as 'decline' rather than 'refuse', 'question' rather than 'reject', and 'request' rather than 'demand' are likely to keep the civic dialogue ball in play. 'Refuse', 'reject' and 'demand' are likely to shift the focus of the conversation away from the subject matter and towards the relationship paradigm of power and authority; the civic dialogue ball is at risk of being thrown out of bounds on the full.

I shall consider 10 words that originate from criticism, resistance and contempt as often as from commitment, passion and determination. They are words which, because they can convey the speakers' self-conferred apparent authority over the listener, are at risk of being heard as being inappropriately authoritarian. Use of these words can denote a transaction premised on I-know-you-better-than-you-know-yourself, invoking a fight or flight reaction in the listener.

Considerable personal integrity and experience are called upon to respond to authoritarian pronouncements with issue-focused civic dialogue rather than reacting with relationship-focused sparring. Words with potentially authoritarian overtones are 'no', 'but', 'should', 'obviously', 'concede', 'eligible', 'allow', 'submit', 'position' and 'back down' and, importantly, their many synonyms and derivatives. For each word, a gentler, more inviting expression can be employed to promote civic dialogue, keeping the dialogue on the issue and affirming all participants. Another significant benefit of using an inclusive, peer-oriented, positively-phrased approach is that just as the listener is more able to hear civic dialogue than authoritarian directives, so the speaker is more able to hear themselves. It is from listening to oneself and others that insights, including leadership insights, germinate.

Let's look at 10 reaction-provoking words and plausible response-inviting alternatives, one by one.

No

Authoritarian: 'No, I can't see the relevance of that idea.' The word 'no' is often significantly more influential than 'yes'. 'No' often has the power of status quo: dismissing consideration of change. It often denies the receiver the opportunity to be heard.

Synonyms: 'forget it', 'no way', 'never', 'veto', 'whatever'.

Civic dialogue: 'Can you tune me into some more of what you are thinking?'

Recommendation: First show that you have heard the speaker then find out more; consider the situation then provide your considered response.

But

Authoritarian: 'Your idea has promise, but can you see how so many people would be worse off if it went ahead?' The word 'but' is often an oblique way of saying no.
Synonyms: 'however', 'although', 'nevertheless', 'yet'.

Civic dialogue: 'Your idea sounds to me like it could have promise and I'm cautiously interested to hear more.'

Recommendation: Substitute 'and' for 'but'. It can sound a little odd and the results are often pleasantly surprising.

Should

Authoritarian: 'You should have found a better source of information. I'd be interested to see what you used.' The word 'should' is often a reprimand, implying a relationship of superiority and inferiority and suggesting blame. It can imply that the speaker knows the listener better than the listener knows themselves.
Synonyms: 'must', 'ought'.

Civic dialogue: 'Would you like me to send you a couple of links that I find useful? I'd be interested to see yours too.'

Recommendation: Ask a question or make a comment that is future focused and involves each of you as peers, whether or not you are peers.

Obviously

Authoritarian: 'Obviously this disaster could have been averted.' The word 'obviously' is usually redundant or incorrect as well as often implying a relationship on the superiority–inferiority scale.
Synonym: 'clearly', 'of course'.

Civic dialogue: 'This situation might have been averted. I wonder what the decision makers were considering … and not considering.'

Recommendation: Leave it out.

Concede

Authoritarian: 'You would concede then that if it were not for the election, Australia would be in dire straits now.' The word 'concede' is often heard as an expectation of acquiescence. This conveys a relationship on the superiority–inferiority continuum.
Synonym: 'admit'.

Civic dialogue: 'Where could Australia be, do you think, if not for the election?' 'I wonder whether we would be thriving, struggling or in some sort of new paradigm.'

Recommendation: Express your point of view and ask the other person for theirs, expecting it to be different from yours and regarding the difference as a potential source of civic dialogue.

Entitled

Authoritarian: 'You were late, so you are not entitled to hold the floor now.' Here, the word 'entitled' implies a relationship of privilege.
Synonyms: 'have a right', 'permitted'.

Civic dialogue: 'The discussion on item two ended before you arrived. Item three is now under discussion ...' 'What are your thoughts about where your points would fit later on the agenda?'

Recommendation: Explain process; identify the procedural problem to be solved jointly.

Allow

Authoritarian: 'I won't allow you to speak to me that way.' 'I will allow you to put your case.' The word 'allow' often conveys power, authority and privilege.
Synonyms: 'let', 'authorise', 'tolerate', 'permit'.

Civic dialogue: 'I am concerned about this conversation. I feel offended and hurt. I'd like to make a time that works for each of us to talk about the issues we were discussing when I'm feeling more composed.'

Recommendation: Express your own concerns and describe your suggestions for a way forward; invite others to do the same. Use 'allow' only when it is an accurate use of authority.

Submit

Authoritarian: 'I'm waiting for you to submit your reasons for what you said.' Using the word 'submit' is a way to exercise power over a person.
Synonyms: 'defer' (in some uses of 'submit').

Civic dialogue: 'I'm interested to hear the thoughts that led to you saying what you did.'

Recommendation: Assume merit until you discover otherwise; put the onus of proof on yourself, not on others.

Position

Authoritarian: 'It is my position that all children must be reading effectively by the end of year three.' Using the word 'position' puts the speaker on a precipice: there is only one way to go: someone will be right and someone will be wrong. Declaring a position is akin to stating that you have stopped listening.
Synonym: 'judgement'.

Civic dialogue: 'I think it's important to find teaching techniques to maximise each child's chance of learning to read to the best of their ability by year three.'

Recommendation: Have a long discussion followed by a short decision rather than a short decision followed by a long defence.

Back down

Authoritarian: 'I agree with the opposition putting the pressure on them to make them back down.' The term 'back down' is indicative of capitulation, which is a transaction of power.
Synonyms: 'capitulate', 'give up', 'surrender'.

Civic dialogue: 'I think that both the government and the opposition need to find out what matters to all the stakeholders. Something needs to change.'

Recommendation: Provide others with the opportunity to consider changing their minds. You may be able to do this by giving them more information, or by giving further explanation. Find out the best way by listening for longer than you speak.

Conclusion

Leaders and followers are in partnership. Each complements the other. It follows that communication – between leaders and followers, and among followers – that meets the interests of all is in the interest of the cause. Civic dialogue is such communication.

Leaders are leaders because followers regard their processes as just, their decisions as wise and the outcomes of their decisions as satisfactory. A significant contribution to leaders' wisdom is the feedback, opinions and concerns of followers. Collectively, through rich and robust civic dialogue, followers add breadth and depth to leaders' repositories of information. Through civic dialogue the wisdom of followers becomes the wisdom of the leader.

In practice, civic dialogue is discussion of public issues in a way that demonstrates self-respect and peer-to-peer respect for followers and non-followers alike. One way for leaders to initiate and maintain civic dialogue is to model conversation in which people weave together three strands: listening generously, thinking constructively and speaking moderately in a ratio of approximately 3:2:1.

The ecology of civic dialogue is such that it sustains participants, is itself self-sustaining and has a role to play in the sustainability of the planet. Along with leadership, widespread civic dialogue is crucial to good governance for the 21st century.

---

1. Henderson, H, 2013, *A smile for my parents*, Allen and Unwin, Sydney.
2. The Lowy Institute 2012, *Public opinion and foreign policy*, 5 June, www.lowyinstitute.org/publications/lowy-institute-poll-2012-public-opinion-and-foreign-policy.

Toxic leadership – psychopaths and psychopathic behaviour in organisations

Charmine Härtel

Charmine EJ Härtel is professor of human resource management and organisational development at the University of Queensland Business School. She is a registered member of the College of Organisational Psychologists (Australia), fellow and past president of the Australian and New Zealand Academy of Management (ANZAM), fellow of the Australian Institute of Management (AIM), and fellow of the Australian Human Resources Institute (AHRI). She has substantial experience in senior management roles and almost 30 years of experience working in the public and private sectors, including consultancies in Australia, Europe, Asia and the United States. Charmine is recognised internationally as a leader in developing and translating new knowledge into management practices to create and maintain jobs and workplaces that foster the opportunity for all workers to contribute to their potential. She has won numerous national and international awards for her research, including five awards for innovation in organisational practice.

Toxic behaviours do enormous damage, both public and private, within organisations. The damage is worse where the offender has charmed their way to a position of leadership. Often the most vulnerable are the ones who get hurt.

Charmine Härtel's chapter offers important insights about psychopathic behaviours, and strategies to combat them – such as the creation of a positive work environment. These insights will help protect you in navigating your path to leadership, and enlighten you as a steward of the wellbeing of those affected by your leadership.

Do not believe in anything simply because you have heard it. Do not believe in anything simply because it is spoken and rumoured by many. Do not believe in anything simply because it is found written in your religious books. Do not believe in anything merely on the authority of your teachers and elders. Do not believe in traditions because they have been handed down for many generations. But after observation and analysis, when you find that anything agrees with reason and is

conducive to the good and benefit of one and all, then accept it and live up to it.
—attributed to Hindu Prince Gautama Siddharta, the founder of Buddhism, 563–483 BCE

Bullying behaviour isn't just found in the schoolyard. There is growing awareness that mean and scheming behaviours are all too common in our workplaces. No area of work is immune – toxic behaviours are reported across private, public and not-for-profit sectors including volunteer organisations and charities.

For those contemplating a career in public life, the problem of toxic work environments has two-fold importance. The first consideration is how to manage one's career, from first role to formal positions of leadership. The second is the policy implications for a healthy society. Sadly, the workers most vulnerable to experiencing and enduring toxic work environments are first job holders, unskilled labourers, stigmatised group members and casual workers. Lacking the power and status of other members of the workforce translates for most into a heightened sense of fear, but also into perceived and often real limitations to stopping the mistreatment. The dilemma is worsened when the offender is your boss.

The aim of this chapter is to help you gain insight on the nature of psychopathic leaders and leadership behaviour, and contrast it with the features required for positive work environments. In doing so, you will learn the antidote to psychopathic behaviour at work, gaining an important tool for choosing where you work, developing as a positive leader, and understanding the elements required to grow a healthy organisation and workforce.

The corporate psychopath

To put the issue into some context, it is useful to consider the enormous cost of 'corporate' psychopaths and toxic leadership. According to Dr Paul Babiak and Dr Robert Hare, authors of *Snakes in suits*,[1] corporate psychopaths 'can do immense amounts of damage to those who cross them, or frustrate their goals. They can cost companies millions'.[2] Most recently, Babiak and Hare were part of a team comparing the effects of corporate psychopaths in a private financial services organisation and a public organisation. In both organisations, subordinates of leaders who scored high on corporate psychopathic behaviour reported the same damaging effects on job satisfaction, and employees of the public organisation also reported psychological distress.

My own research reveals that toxic leaders serve as negative role models, with evidence showing that their followers are more likely to engage in self-serving and deviant behaviours. The public cost of toxic leadership is made clear in a 2014 newspaper article[3] which highlights growing anger and loss of confidence and trust in the ethics of politicians, public officials and bankers.

At this point, you are probably wondering what a corporate psychopath is, especially as most public portrayals and indeed research focus on the criminal psychopath rather than the type of psychopath that can survive and even thrive in an organisation. Defining a corporate psychopath means not only understanding their dark characteristics, but also the strategies by which they survive in the business world.

Babiak and Hare's extensive work on the topic identifies six dark characteristics of corporate psychopaths.

Babiak and Hare: characteristics of corporate psychopaths

1. they are insincere, arrogant, untrustworthy, manipulative, and insensitive to the thoughts and feelings of others
2. they are inclined to blame others
3. they have a low tolerance for any sort of frustration, and are therefore impatient
4. they are erratic, unreliable, and unfocused
5. they are selfish and parasitic; they take advantage of the goodwill of people they work with as well as the company itself
6. they are inclined to treat people, including their families, like objects.[4]

Psychopaths and their protectors

Although psychopathy has only recently been examined by management research, Babiak and Hare's work indicates that most psychopaths gravitate to high-powered or high-authority vocations like law, politics, entertainment, the church, the military, trade unions, the media, academe, charities and the arts. Highly functioning corporate psychopaths, they say, have 'a veil of normality' and are liked by many others and by organisations, due to being perceived as charming, persuasive and charismatic.* They avoid detection by finding protectors or people who can help their career. These protectors operate at all levels of the organisation. For example, protectors more senior than the corporate psychopath defend the person against any criticism, whereas those more junior protect the corporate psychopath by excusing their behaviour and covering for them by doing work they are unable to do. The tactic of finding protectors makes it challenging even for senior people to disarm a psychopath they uncover in their midst.

Babiak and Hare's case studies uncover examples of ethical leaders trying to address the destructive effects of a psychopath, including one where the attempt was thwarted by the psychopath who successfully convinced his protector to dismiss the leader who posed a threat.

Understanding the psychopath's use of protectors is useful in thinking about the potential risks in some common organisational practices. For example, when a new leader is appointed to a department or organisation, it is not uncommon to see turnover among staff to make room for installing workers from the new leader's former place of employment. This can be a positive practice if the change is effected to address toxicity, corruption or incompetency. It could, however, be effected for the purposes of bringing in protectors to cover for a corporate psychopath.

Another common organisational practice is mentoring. Career counsellors advocate for the benefits of mentoring, and indeed there are many such benefits, including the development of networks, career planning and problem solving. There is a potential dark side, however. What if the mentor is a psychopath looking to develop a protector from below? Or the mentee is a psychopath looking to develop a protector from above? These are real issues of which one should be mindful when seeking a mentor as well as setting up and evaluating mentor programs.

Psychopathic behaviours

Babiak and Hare developed a taxonomy of corporate psychopaths,

* One group in particular is likely to be taken in by a corporate psychopath. You might like to guess which group. I will disclose the answer in a moment.

which distinguishes between three types of psychopathic behaviour or strategy:*

The con

A person identified as a con 'deals one-on-one with individuals, primarily tries to exert influence over them, and then swindles them out of something. It's a very simple process, and they may not make it into the high levels of the corporate structure, but they can do some serious damage.'

The bully

A bully is 'a person that influences others by intimidation. It could be overt, verbal threats, maybe even physical violence, but it can also be very covert intimidation.'

The puppetmaster

'That's an individual who is very savvy, is quite a student of human behaviour, is quite capable of manipulating individuals into hurting other people. So it's a two-step process. The puppetmaster manipulates individuals and these people whom they are manipulating do the dirty work for them.' Interestingly, evidence suggests that clinical psychologists are among the most vulnerable to being exploited by this category of psychopaths due to the psychologists' close adherence to clinical expectations of normal human behaviour.

At this point, it is important to note that not everyone engaging in the behaviour described above is a psychopath. To meet Babiak and Hare's diagnostic criteria, they must have the six dark characteristics I described at the beginning of this chapter. If a person does not meet Babiak and Hare's criteria but engages in the psychopathic behaviour above, the damage is equally harmful. Such persons are referred to as toxic or destructive co-workers or leaders. Drawing on the broader literature on psychopathy including that of Dr Hare, the list of psychopathic behaviours in the workplace can be expanded to include aggression, lying, exploitation, conniving, rationalising corrupt or disrespectful behaviour, insincere flattery, discrediting others' reputations to bolster one's own, dishonesty, creating power networks for personal gain, smooth-talking with the appearance of

* Quotations in this section are from Babiak, P & Hare, RD, 2007, *Snakes in suits: when psychopaths go to work*, HarperCollins, New York.

caring, a sense of entitlement, duplicitousness, changing emotional displays to create desired impressions or gain and maintain control or power over others, creating false relationships to obtain some advantage, distorting or hiding information in order to influence others' choices, taking credit for others' work, not walking one's own talk, having hidden agendas, sending messages that create fear or guilt, having a win-at-all-costs attitude, retribution, taking more than giving, being unapologetic for bad behaviour, and blaming others for one's shortcomings rather than taking responsibility. Although this is not an exhaustive list, it captures the essence of the activities that constitute psychopathic behaviour.

The case of 'Bob'

Consider the example of Bob, who had a meteoric rise in the public sector. Bob was considered very intelligent and a rare and valuable talent that his organisation needed in order to succeed. His manager thought very highly of him and identified him as his eventual successor, subsequently grooming him for the role. He had had responsibility for a few subordinates but these employees never lasted long, seeking transfers to other roles or leaving the organisation. He explained each case to his boss and HR as being due to his high standards and to these employees lacking the drive and talent required. He correctly judged that this would impress his boss, who was keen on improving the standards of the department and having a reputation as the best. The boss also only knew Bob as a friendly, sincere and committed person. When my consulting team was involved in leadership profiling to identify individuals to fast-track, Bob was put forward as a candidate.

During the assessment, Bob's reactions to the evaluation exercises were to aggressively challenge when confronted and to glare. These displays of hostile and intimidating behaviours during assessment were recorded as part of the feedback report and submitted to HR. Upon learning he was not selected for fast-tracked leadership development, he requested a meeting with the HR director, saying he wanted to discuss his feedback report. During the meeting, Bob appealed to the director's background and desire to help by describing a difficult childhood and some social awkwardness including what he claimed were people's misinterpretations of his difficulty expressing emotions and use of eye contact as intimidating and uncaring.

When he left the meeting, the director felt pity for him and was convinced he wanted and would respond positively to help. After she conveyed this to my team, a meeting was scheduled for us to review his assessments and identify a developmental plan to assist him. At the meeting I was confronted – not by a willing participant, but rather by a cold individual with a hard, intimidating stare. Bob denied he had said he was concerned about his ability to deal with emotions and refuted every piece of feedback presented. He made it clear he was not interested in pursuing a conversation or development in this area.

The strong incongruence between the person the HR director experienced in her office and the one that presented to me was a clear sign of psychopathic behaviour. The way he controlled his boss, his HR director and others suggested he was playing the role of a puppetmaster. He was never identified by the organisation as a problem, but in retrospect, a review of the evidence suggested that the department and his co-workers had been damaged by his behaviour. Despite HR having access to all of these records and being aware of his history, Bob managed to keep them on side and have them serve as protectors. A key lever that psychopaths play on is people's strong preference for praise over criticism.

The trouble with most of us is that we would rather be ruined by praise than saved by criticism.

—Norman Vincent Peale

Ethics and the positive work environment

If you pursue a career in public life, the knowledge of what constitutes psychopathic workplace behaviour carries not only personal meaning for managing your own career, but also responsibility, as befits your role as a steward of national wellbeing. There is an important public interest in holding organisations and their workers accountable for creating workplaces devoid of psychopathic behaviour and ensuring vulnerable workers can avoid coming under the destructive hold of toxic leaders.

At this point, you would be right to ask why organisations would hire and even promote psychopaths and why non-psychopaths would engage in psychopathic behaviour. It turns out that it has to do with the type of work environment the organisation has created or let develop.

Negative work environments are characterised by unethical practices, toxic emotions, bullying, discrimination and destructive leaders. In contrast, positive work environments are characterised by psychological wellbeing, work–life balance, a sense of meaning at work, and ethical behaviour.

When we look at organisational incentive systems and how leaders are selected and trained, we often see a fixation on performance and growth at the expense of staff; sycophancy; treating workers as a means to an end; and neglecting the emotional, ethical, and spiritual dimensions that make up human beings. These sorts of incentives promote toxic leadership, reward psychopathic behaviours, overlook the importance of character – instead focusing on the *appearance* of authenticity and morality – and in so doing foster negative work environments. Interestingly, recent research by my team conducted with a government department revealed that training in moral reasoning and authentic leadership, while generally very beneficial, does not solve the problem with psychopathic behaviour, as psychopaths can leverage these skills for their own schemes rather than for benefiting others and the organisation.[5]

People displaying these psychopathic behaviours simply should not be put in positions of power or authority as the risk for destructive consequences for others and for society is too high. In contrast, positive work environments have reward systems that foster other-interest (in contrast to self-interest), collegiality, honest and open dialogue, and ethics in leaders and co-workers alike. They also have procedural transparency such that practices related to promotions, performance appraisals and increments are standardised and transparent. Additionally, positive work environments use leadership selection methods that include rigorous assessment of ethics, authenticity and character. This truth is captured by the following quotes:

Character is higher than intellect.

—Ralph Waldo Emerson

You can easily judge the character of a man by how he treats those who can do nothing for him.

—variously attributed to Johann Wolfgang von Goethe, James D. Miles or Malcolm Forbes

Because power corrupts, society's demands for moral authority and character increase as the importance of the position increases.

—John Adams

Neutralising or avoiding the psychopath

Understanding the context in which corporate psychopaths and psychopathic behaviour thrive provides an important lesson in how to avoid coming into contact with toxic individuals in your career. The fruits of positive leadership are positive work environments, so investigating a potential employer to determine whether they offer such an environment is an important tool for finding a healthy place to work.

My research[6] and my consulting on positive and toxic work environments provide useful indicators of the characteristics and drivers of such cultures. For example, positive work environments exist when employees see their workplace as respectful, inclusive and psychologically safe, policies and decision-making as just, and leaders and co-workers as trustworthy, fair and open to diversity. Positive work environments provide the set of emotional experiences necessary for employees to flourish. That means positive emotional experiences outweighing negative emotional experiences, and an absence of emotional game playing and manipulations. It also means a special kind of leadership: one that focuses on the needs, concerns and growth of followers and that sees the role of leader as stewardship, making a positive difference and upholding the principles of social justice. Tellingly, this type of leadership is not described or labelled as 'charismatic' in the academic literature, but rather as 'servant leadership'. This is in contrast to the pure focus on performance and success pursued by many organisations.

Try not to become a man of success, but rather try to become a man of value.

—Albert Einstein

The real antidote to letting psychopaths reign is keeping the focus of one's career, organisational incentive systems, and indeed governmental and national culture, on service to the wellbeing of others and society.

---

1. Babiak, P & Hare, R D, 2007, *Snakes in suits: when psychopaths go to work*, HarperCollins, New York.
2. Radio National, *Background Briefing 18 July 2004–Psychopaths in Suits*, http://netk.net.au/Psychology/Psychopath1.asp.
3. Vogl, F, 2014, 'Stop corruption—anger to rise in 2014', *The World Post*, 2 February, www.huffingtonpost.com/frank-vogl/stop-corruption-anger-to-rise_b_4498875.html.
4. Radio National, *Background Briefing 18 July 2004–Psychopaths in Suits*, http://netk.net.au/Psychology/Psychopath1.asp.
5. Härtel, C E J, Butarbutar, I, Sendjaya, S, Pekerti, A, Hirst, G & Ashkanasy, N M, 2013, 'Developing ethical leaders: a servant leadership approach', in Sekerka, L (ed.), *Ethics training in action* (IAP Ethics in practice series), Information Age Publishing, Charlotte.
6. Härtel, C E J, 2008, 'How to build a healthy emotional culture and avoid a toxic culture', in Cooper, C L & Ashkanasy, N M (eds), *Research companion to emotion in organizations*, Edwin Elgar Publishing, Cheltenham.

Asking for trouble – standing in the headlights of confrontation

Tim Mendham

Tim Mendham is an experienced journalist, editor and copywriter, with more than 30 years in business-to-business publications. He has written extensively on IT, technology, research and development, business finance and marketing issues. During his career he has edited a number of publications, including *Lab News*, a technical journal for the research and development community; *CFO*, the then premier professional magazine for senior finance executives; *Fast Thinking*, a quarterly publication devoted to innovation issues; and most recently *CIO*, Australia's leading magazine for senior IT management. In 2000, he was joint winner of the Australian Business Publishers' Bell Award for best analytical writing of the year. In 2006, *Fast Thinking* was named best business-to-business publication in the same awards. He is also a life member of Australian Skeptics, a body established to investigate pseudoscience and claims of the paranormal. Since 2009, he has been executive officer of the association.

For better or worse, for those wishing to put themselves into the public arena, confrontation is a fact of life. Dealing with confrontation is a skill that needs to be learned, but sometimes it's necessary to put yourself consciously and purposely in controversial situations where there will inevitably be confrontation based on emotional responses rather than rational debate, and this is particularly fraught. This requires great sensitivity in balancing one's personal ethics and convictions while dealing rationally with another's strongly held beliefs, at the same time being able to influence and convince third parties. Representatives of Australian Skeptics regularly find themselves in such situations, dealing with issues of misperception of 'truth' and fact, based on an audience's misunderstanding of probability versus possibility, coincidence, the reliability of first-person observation and anecdotal evidence, and the need to distinguish between faith and investigation.

I believe in evidence. I believe in observation, measurement, and reasoning, confirmed by independent observers. I'll believe anything, no matter how wild and ridiculous, if there is evidence for it. The wilder and more ridiculous something is, however, the firmer and more solid the evidence will have to be.

—Isaac Asimov

We have all heard the warning for dinner table conversation etiquette – no mention of sex, politics or religion. All of these topics have a strong emotional attachment, and often one without a lot of rationality behind it, so raising them over dinner could lead to a bad case of indigestion, at best. At worst, red wine stains are hard to remove from the wall.

Any sort of confrontation between those of opposing philosophies is not pleasant, and for many people it's something to be avoided if possible. But avoiding all unpleasantness all of the time is extremely difficult for anyone; for leaders and prospective leaders, it's downright impossible. Anyone who wants to deal in contentious issues is bound to find themselves in heated discourse with those who strongly disagree with the point of view being expressed. But it is a rare person who throws themselves knowingly into confrontational situations, not necessarily with relish, but with determination and confidence.

This happens with representatives of Australian Skeptics, who regularly find themselves up against antagonistic views and view holders, sometimes by choice and sometimes thanks to third parties such as the media, who love nothing better than a live barney on TV or the radio.

About the skeptics

Firstly, a bit of background on the skeptics. Australian Skeptics is the second oldest skeptical group in the world, having been founded in 1980 following a series of tests of water diviners set up by Australian entrepreneur Dick Smith and American conjurer and skeptical investigator James 'The Amazing' Randi.*

Randi received great public attention in Australia during a subsequent visit when he confronted TV talk show host Don Lane

* As an aside, no diviner was able to successfully pass the tests, which both sides had agreed prior to the events were fair and above board. Within hours of the event concluding, many diviners found excuses as to why they had been unsuccessful on that occasion.

about Lane's belief in self-proclaimed psychics Doris Stokes and Uri Geller. When Randi replicated their 'skills', Lane was outraged, knocked a glass to the floor and stormed off his own program. Ever since, this event has been a highlight of any retrospective history of Australian TV.[1] It's a good example of real-world high-profile confrontation in action.

The skeptics investigate a range of topics, focusing on 'pseudoscience and the paranormal'. These are defined as areas outside the broadly accepted areas of scientific knowledge and processes, and they range from more amusing areas such as UFOs, astrology and unknown creatures such as yetis and Loch Ness monsters, to more serious topics of psychic powers and clairvoyance, where people can be milked of money for little benefit. Then there are those areas where the results can be very serious, even life-threatening. These latter include the fundamentalist religion and creationist movements, which can have a serious impact on education; many areas of alternative medicine, where 'patients' may forego established and effective treatments in favour of unproven and disproven methodologies; and conspiracy theories, which have been known, in extreme cases, to have led to terrorism and mass killings.

The key criterion for skeptical investigation is that 'extraordinary claims require extraordinary proof'. This means that blind faith is not enough to prove anything's existence and, as skeptics would say, an open mind should not equate to an empty head.

While the emphasis on pseudoscience and the paranormal gives skeptics a specific set of topics, the basic tenet of skepticism is critical thinking, which is something that can be applied widely, and in fact is practised every day by most people (perhaps to their surprise).

Critical thinking is the application of research, review, appraisal and either acceptance or rejection of particular theories, arguments or claims – in other words, thinking with your brain rather than your gut.

There are many areas where people apply critical thinking. When we make a choice between going to work by bus, train or car, we take into account the costs involved, the time it will take and the scheduled time of arrival, the reliability of the service, the comfort of the journey, the distance from the final stop to our destination, and the costs associated with parking versus foot-slogging. These are all criteria for decision making, and often ones we can analyse quickly and painlessly because doing so is a fairly common process.

Therefore, the concept of critical thinking can (and should) be broadly applied across most activities, lifestyles and professions. In leadership it is a vital skill, important in separating out substantiated claims and demands from those with little or no foundation.

As a leader, you will be challenged on many areas and topics; your skill in separating the wheat from the chaff and your ability to act upon that understanding will determine your future success and, particularly, the way others see you and trust your judgement.

In skeptical circles, the main process underpinning the assessment of extraordinary claims is scientific method, which means repeated investigation and review of claims, undertaken by those with knowledge and experience in a particular area. In most areas of science, this means dealing with physical phenomena, often involving laboratory or field work, where the results are presented in a format where others can assess, discuss, debate and sometimes debunk them. This can be a hard school for presenting ideas, but it is the best way of weeding out the unfounded and substantiating those claims that have a greater likelihood of being true.

The same process can be applied to some areas of the paranormal and pseudoscience, and in ways that are readily understood and indeed practised by the general public. For instance, someone comes to you and says they can fly; your response is no doubt: 'Show me.' Simple and straightforward – that is critical thinking, and it is also the skeptical approach. Note that it is up to the claimants to prove their claims, not those who question them. If the person can't fly under controlled conditions, then we can safely say it is unlikely that they can do what they say they can.

As formal as these processes are, the approach and the topics covered put the skeptics in the direct line of fire of those who have beliefs in which they have invested much emotional collateral. Such people are often unwilling to hear opposing arguments, no matter how much the counter arguments may be based on critical thinking and hard evidence.

Skeptics, thus, often find themselves dealing with people in a confrontational (and often entirely non-rational) atmosphere. No matter how much evidence skeptics can bring to suggest that specific claims may be unfounded, believers will often stick stubbornly to their beliefs, and describe anyone who suggests that those beliefs might be unfounded and based on 'dodgy' evidence as spoilsports (at best), 'doubting Thomases' or ignorant enemies (or worse).

Note that the view taken by skeptics is not that these things are not and cannot be true; the view is that they are unproven.

So how do skeptics then deal with contentious situations that have social, personal and even political aspects? How do you couch your argument so that personal ethics, evidence and critical thinking are not compromised, while also allowing for sympathy, empathy and diplomacy? Skeptical discourse often has implications that run well beyond the skeptical arena.

These interactions have a strong dependence on the aptitude of people to assess their own claims. This may require methods that might be difficult for the general public to understand or apply. They may not have the education or experience, or they may simply be unwilling to hear the opposing view – they might stick their fingers in their ears, or they might go on the offensive and actively confront those who present what skeptics would consider a more measured view.

But leaders will not shy from such situations. In public life, and particularly in such areas as health policy, leaders will come up against many conflicting claims about a specific event or treatment's efficacy and, in fact, its very existence. In such situations, leaders will need to both understand the basis for claims, and develop methods for dealing with them.

You should be aware that by being in leadership positions, you will not necessarily be immune to the odd strange belief. You, too, can be taken in by a hustler or a well-meaning but deluded person.

Former Queensland premier Joh Bjelke-Petersen was an enthusiastic supporter of cancer cure claims made by Mylan Brich, who claimed medical qualifications he did not have. Bjelke-Petersen also supported a hydrogen-powered car put forward by Stephen Horvath. Neither of these developments were ever substantiated.

Similar stories abound. Noted racing driver Peter Brock supported an 'energy polariser' designed to improve car performance, but the invention had no scientific basis and any performance enhancement was more wishful thinking than real.

In 1988, a 'channeller' named Carlos raised great interest and endorsement in the media and among noted celebrities, saying he had surprising accuracy in his psychic powers. He attracted large audiences at public functions, including at the Sydney Opera House, and many media appearances. But he was a fake – set up by Randi – and his qualifications and history could have been easily debunked by any reporter with an ounce of effort and skepticism. They didn't investigate, and when the truth was revealed, journalists and the like were more outraged at being offered a fake celebrity than embarrassed at their own credulousness.

Arthur Conan Doyle, author of the Sherlock Holmes books, expressed strong beliefs in communication with the dead and some specific claims of fairies literally at the bottom of a garden. We would suggest that Doyle was less skeptical than his creation.

Currently, a number of universities in Australia run courses in alternative medicine, despite serious doubts about those subjects' veracity. The skeptics would support research into these areas, but training practitioners in areas that are still highly suspect is a path which could severely damage the institutions' reputations. There are obvious pressures on universities to maximise income, but succumbing to 'market demand' rather than academic probity is not the way to ensure long-term success.*

Confronting probability and counter-intuitive thinking

Notions of probability and associated statistical analysis are one area where skeptics often come up against a brick wall, one built of perplexed looks and, ironically, responses of 'that can't be right!'

Coincidences are a classic example of people finding significance in apparently non-significant events. Many people refuse to believe that there is nothing more to coincidence than two things happening at the same time – coincidence. They insist there must be a relationship, a cause and effect, that simply cannot be put down to dumb luck, thoroughly misinterpreting what coincidence actually means. The issue here rests on the difference between possibility and probability.

For instance, there is the *possibility* that the world is flat (and, for the pedants, I mean flat, not oblate). However, based on empirical and historical evidence, we can say that the *probability* of the world being flat is zero. The world is not flat, it is pretty much a sphere,

* For more information on this, see Friends of Science in Medicine, www.scienceinmedicine.org.au.

and you'd be hard pressed to find anyone outside of a very tiny fringe few who would suggest otherwise.

(By the way, throughout most of recorded history, most people believed – knew? – the world was round, despite what you might have been taught in school. In the same way, it was not Copernicus who first visualised the earth as orbiting the sun; that idea goes back at least to Aristarchus in the third century BC. Columbus was sailing around the world, not to the edge, and the fear of ships falling off the edge was not taken seriously.)

There's no great problem here distinguishing between possibility and probability – probability being simple evidence with broadly accepted results.

But let's get into murkier areas of probability, a field rich in results that even intelligent people find counterintuitive.

The birthday paradox

How many people do you need in a room before there's an even chance that two people will share the same birthday? Note we're asking for the same day and month, not the same year.

Intuitively, many people would say that you needed 367 people to ensure that two people matched (allowing for leap years). But in fact, you only need 23 people to give you 50 per cent probability, and you would only need 57 people to give you 99 per cent probability. This statistical 'anomaly' is called 'the birthday paradox', and is widely known in statistical (and gambling) circles. But it is obviously counterintuitive for most of us who don't have a detailed understanding of statistical analysis.

But try explaining that to your audience at a political rally. The response of most would be disbelief, perplexed looks and the occasional thrown pie or expletive. The leader's response would be that 'you don't have to take my word for it; I can show you the evidence'. But those without a strong mathematical background would not understand the evidence.

Between the flat earth and the birthday paradox lies a long landscape of odd and quirky beliefs that stretch the boundaries of probability and possibility. Critical thinking is based on the concept that anything is possible, but that in some cases the probability of something being true is so infinitesimally small that we can confidently say, for all intents and purposes, that it does not exist.

'But it's still possible, isn't it?' desperate believers in pseudoscience and the paranormal might suggest, and that small opening is enough for them to storm like soldiers through a breach in the wall.

Standing in opposition, defending the breach, is neither easy nor comfortable. Despite knowing that you have the best evidence to support you, facing up to misguided mass opinion requires great courage in one's convictions. Leaders will do that. Followers will move to one side and allow the hordes through, despite the obvious and often devastating consequences that that might have for an honest appraisal and a rational approach to dealing with problems that face us in the future.

Climate change is a good example. Despite the best evidence and broad consensus supporting man-made global warming, many people would just let the negative approach ride: 'I don't understand all the science, there are some people objecting to it, so I won't take a stand.' The consequences of such inaction and timidity may be the most serious mankind has ever faced.

But overwhelming odds in confrontational circumstances do not mean you give up. Skeptics would say it is worth the effort, despite regular battles not won and no positive result in sight. Eventually the 'mob' will come around, though it might leave many bashed and bleeding bodies in its wake.

Without scientific evidence, pseudoscience and the paranormal are not supportable. When they are supported by reliable, repeatable and reputable evidence, they are no longer pseudoscientific or paranormal. They are welcomed into the body of scientific theory. They might be tossed out again if they are subsequently proved incorrect, but as good evidence piles up on top of good evidence, the move from possibility to probability becomes less controversial, and defence against violent assaults on logic is no longer needed.

Challenging observations and witnesses

Police and lawyers will tell you that eyewitnesses to events are unreliable. Yes, they are used in court cases, trials and discussions, but their accounts can be assessed and brought into question.

Accounts made of the same event by different people often differ markedly. How many people were involved? How were they dressed? What did they look like? Who else was present? Did you actually see what you claim to have seen, or are you bringing others' accounts ('hearsay') into your own? These problems only increase the longer the time between the event and the recounting of it.

The invisible gorilla

In a famous and regularly used test of people's ability to closely observe a situation, participants in a study have been shown a video of a group of people in a circle passing a ball back and forth. The viewer is asked to count how many times the ball is passed. At the end of the viewing, the witness is asked what the gorilla did.

Unless they have been forewarned, the common response is 'Huh? What gorilla?' But a second viewing will clearly show a man dressed in a gorilla suit wandering through the scene, behind the players. But the observers don't normally notice it because they are concentrating on something else.* While a gorilla wandering round in clear view is not a normal event, it should still have been noticed.

Picture, then, observations which are highly out of the ordinary – unpredictable – where the observers are often taken by total surprise, and where the event in question may be extremely brief and occur under difficult circumstances, and may certainly involve the observer dealing with a phenomenon which they do not have the experience or training to properly assess.

These might include a UFO. Unlike astronomers, people do not normally stare at the sky; they see it, but it is not a subject of constant observation. Seeing something in the sky, particularly at night, may reveal bodies that people might not be familiar with but which are quite fully understood by experienced observers in that particular field.

Reports of such incidents, particularly in the paranormal world, often refer to the 'authority' of the witness. Police officers are often cited as being trustworthy witnesses because of their (assumed) respectability and probity and supposed ability to weigh claims through training in observation and assessment of evidence. The fact that they don't normally deal with UFOs as part of their day-to-day activities seems to be beside the point.

One of the more curious uses of authorities is quoting celebrities – film stars, politicians – as if they are better placed to com-

* You can see the 'invisible' gorilla at www.theinvisiblegorilla.com/gorilla_experiment.html.

ment on alternative medicine and the paranormal. Supporters of homeopathy often mention that the royal family, particularly Prince Charles, use homeopathic treatments. But why the royals should be seen as medical authorities because of an accident of birth is anyone's guess.

Dealing with such claims is difficult, particularly as they involve personal anecdotes. The witnesses might claim 'I saw it with my own eyes', and ask why one would doubt them. There are obvious problems dealing with anecdotal evidence – you weren't there and there is usually no hard evidence you can use to assess, prove or disprove a claim. But no matter how many observations are made, poor evidence piled on poor evidence does not make something true. It just remains poor evidence.

To suggest that claimants might be mistaken is to cast negative aspersions on their abilities and even their character, and this is never seen as a sympathetic situation.

Skeptics and confrontation

Top of the list of confrontational situations is one which goes to the core of a claimant's very being, that they're 'not thinking straight' – that they are mistaken, they are not qualified and, ultimately, they are wrong.

Issues of blind faith, by definition, do not require proof, and no manner or amount of evidence will generally dissuade people from their beliefs.

How do you deal with someone who flat-out refuses to discuss an issue with you? When negative results about a claim are presented, skeptics are often accused of having no values, of being amoral iconoclasts bent on destroying precious and long-held beliefs, putting nothing in their place. This is about as far from the truth as you could get.

Skepticism is not nay-saying cynicism, it is merely applying the mantra of 'prove it' – nothing more, nothing less. Whether someone is claiming to be able to fly, lift objects with mind power, predict your future from cards, or cure cancer with some sort of miracle treatment, it is perfectly reasonable – even advisable – to ask the claimant to prove it.

But that doesn't mean there won't be a dispute. Despite all the best evidence you can muster, there are situations where confrontation is still encountered. You will need to decide whether to cut your losses and leave, knowing how that will give your opponents ammunition, or to stand your ground and support your position. How you do the latter is the key consideration in all of the circumstances described in this chapter.

Evolutionist and atheist Richard Dawkins says it's not necessary to convince an individual that your argument is sounder than theirs; rather it is the audience to that confrontation that you need to convince.

One important issue is to avoid *ad hominem* arguments, i.e. that the person is wrong, not the claim; that person is stupid, therefore the claim is wrong; that person looks weird, so their position must be wrong as well. Believers use their beliefs to define themselves, so arguing against them personally is not going to convince them, or the audience, that you are right.

In an address to a gathering of skeptics in 2010, astronomer and skeptic Phil Plait asked the audience, many of whom had already agreed they once believed in a paranormal claim, 'How many of you no longer believe in those things and became a skeptic because someone got in your face, screaming and calling you an idiot, brain-damaged and a retard?'

Very few raised their hands and, as Plait suggested, most of those who did so would have been joking. He went on to ask, 'How do you convince someone they're not thinking clearly when they're not thinking clearly?' It takes practice, and you need to ask yourself what you are trying to accomplish.

'Everyone knows a hammer is for pounding nails, but not everyone knows how to wield that hammer,' he said. 'You don't swing wildly and you don't use all of your strength – you might pound in your nail but you're also likely to destroy the wall. Sometimes a focused movement is more effective; smaller swings that are aimed well take more swings to accomplish your goal, but in the end you have a nail in the wood with minimal damage to that wood.'

Anger is a natural reaction, especially when dealing with unfounded and illogical claims that have been made repeatedly and just as often debunked. But it is not productive. Our demeanour is vital, Plait said, famously adding, 'don't be a dick! All that being a dick does is to score cheap points. It does not win the hearts and minds of people everywhere, and winning those hearts and minds is our goal.' Plait says he believes that it is more important to teach people *how* to think, not *what* to think, and that means teaching critical thinking.

Critical thinking is the basic tenet of the skeptical approach, and it is or should be intrinsic to presenting a good argument in confrontational situations. (In fact, it is the best approach in all situations.)

While many groups, such as cults and fundamentalist religions, actively discourage apparently aberrant and individual thinking, most of us realise that, if we're making an important decision, it's important to use a little brainpower, a little discernment, some critical thinking. And the application of critical thinking has always been a vital part of the human makeup – and it should remain so as long as we have brains to use and good sense to guide us. The problem is that, like common sense, critical thinking is nowhere near as widely practised as it should be.

In summary, what do leaders face in such circumstances?

Certainly you have a specific audience that is emotionally tied to a particular topic, much more than they are logically tied to it. This is not surprising, considering the dearth of good evidence for many 'alternative' pseudoscience and paranormal claims. They will also have a hazy understanding of the difference between possibility and probability, and associated statistics that go with this. They will have an overestimation of the value and reliability of observation and witnesses. And they will not take kindly to any attempt at dissuasion.

But you must do it, and you must do it well.

Consider the issues you face when challenging your audience's own beliefs, bias and prejudices – the unreliability of their own 'experiences'; the lack of means to assess claims or an unwillingness to do so; an emotional attachment to a particular belief; and a fear of loss if their beliefs turn out to be untrue.

You are dealing with human beings here, a sensitive situation, so your manner, demeanour, presentation and good evidence are critical to establishing your credentials and maybe – just maybe – winning them over.

Good luck!

---

1. Youtube, *Don Lane loses his temper with magician*, www.youtube.com/watch?v=PIvolhx8yJA.

Many small things make an economy

Peter Strong

Peter is currently CEO of the Council of Small Business Organisations of Australia (COSBOA) and has represented the organisation since June 2010 in public forums. This includes an address to the National Press Club on 8 August 2012 and appearances in main stream media as a commentator and advocate for the small business community.

Previously Peter spent 30 years consulting on change management at business, community and national levels, and at an international level with the United Nations, the World Bank and NGOs. His areas of expertise range from small business development, industry restructuring, microeconomic reform, local economic development and development and assessment of government services. Peter was also the proprietor of Smiths Alternative Bookshop in Canberra for over seven years until he sold the business in early 2014 to concentrate on his COSBOA role.

Peter Strong's contribution is a plea for politicians and decision makers to consider the 'small' people in the community who are often forgotten. He argues for more understanding for the challenges faced by small business people who make up the majority of employers. He also argues that the people who actually live in a community are best placed to deal with changes to their economy, and that our political leaders should provide the tools, resources and information to empower them to develop and implement policies for managing change.*

Great things are done by a series of small things brought together.

—Vincent Van Gogh

The title of this essay conveys an important truth. A great deal of politics is conducted by and for the 'big end' of town – those who can afford to descend regularly on Canberra, business class. The result is a plethora of rules and systems that favour big business,

* Parts of this chapter are adapted from Peter Strong's address to the National Press Club on 8 August 2012, www.cosboa.org.au/Post/PeterStrongsAddresstotheNationalPressClubon8August2012.

bureaucrats and powerful vested interests. I am not going to argue here for specific policy solutions – this is not the proper forum and, in any event, the issues are too many and various. My essay is a general plea to policy makers to spare a thought for the smaller end of town: firstly the small business men and women who are in many ways the backbone of the economy; and secondly the local communities that together make up our economy and our culture but that are too often overlooked as individually unimportant.

—∞—

There is no culture on earth, and no ethnic group, that does not have traders and business people. If there had been, that culture would have disappeared and that ethnic group would have been quickly sorted out by natural selection. The Phoenicians, the Romans, the British, the Chinese, the Americans and others have all triumphed in their time as much through their traders and their business people as through their military might. As the Soviet version of communism found out, if you suppress those who wish to do their own thing in the world of business then economic failure will follow. The latest Chinese vision states loud and clear that 'you can't have communism until everyone is affluent' and so they foster and promote the business people, big and small, in their country.

As executive director of the Council of Small Business Organisations of Australia, my concern is with the condition of the small business community in Australia today. We make up 96 per cent of all businesses. There are some 2.5 million small business owners, and nearly one million of us employ some five million other people. That is at least 7.5 million people who rely on small businesses for their living. There are at least 700,000 people running their business from home. There are another 900,000 independent contractors making their living in other people's workplaces. We are the majority; we are the innovators, the risk-takers, the people who provide the culture of many communities – and yet we are too often forgotten. And because people in a small workplace are so close to one another, if we are victims of neglect and a lack of care then so are our employees, our co-workers, and the people who we work with day in and day out.

Let me relate two stories to illustrate the point. Both experiences suggested that, for some in positions of power and influence, we in small business do not exist in any real sense as people. And coincidentally both incidents happened on the same day.

In the morning of that day I met with a representative from the federal Department of Health to discuss the involvement of small business in their healthy workers program *Promoting Good Health at Work* – an excellent program in which they were having trouble getting small business involved. I gave some advice on ways to do that and then we discussed the merits of the program. The program would pick up everyone in the workplaces of Australia. I pointed out that this program missed 2.5 million people – the self-employed. There was no mention of the self-employed except as an employer who would be responsible for other people's health. This major oversight was corrected when the joint statement from the government and from industry and employee representatives was released. But a health oversight of the needs of 2.5 million people needs to be investigated. The senior bureaucrat I was dealing with was appalled and asked, 'Why did we miss these people?' An excellent question. A question even more compelling when you realise that the advisory group for this program included people from the Australian Council of Trade Unions, Australian Industry Group, the Australian Chamber of Commerce and Industry and the Business Council of Australia.

That afternoon I received a phone call from the Human Rights Commission. An official informed me that the commission had a program aimed at helping workers with mental health problems, but that they were having difficulty getting small businesses involved. Again I provided advice and information on how to do that. Then I asked: 'If an employer has a mental health problem, is this an issue for the Human Rights Commission?' There was silence at the end of the phone and eventually the official replied that she would have to check. Why? Could there be any other answer to that question besides 'yes'?

So those two stories highlight the fact that we had somehow lost our right to consideration as members of the human race. We were employers with responsibilities; we were not people with health needs like anyone else.

I am happy to report that subsequently we have had much better engagement on these issues. In part, this reflects the receptiveness of

Allan Fels, the chair of Australia's Mental Health Commission, with whom I have had some fruitful discussions.

But please remember these two stories. They help reinforce the fact that we in small business are regarded by some as secondary to other, more important groups. This fact underpins our arguments for policy changes. This is not the place to argue for specific solutions, but I will make some important general observations which I hope will be food for thought.

Many of the regulatory systems in Australia are designed for 4 per cent of businesses – the big end of town with experts and time and resources and money. The tax system, the corporate system, the financial system, most compliance demands, competition policy, contract law, work health and safety, and the workplace relations system are all about the big end. Complexity often suits them, for it offers opportunities to 'game' the system; for tax avoidance, competitive advantage and rent-seeking. Sadly, complexity often suits the bureaucrats too, for it cements their advantage over anyone who comes under their authority.

Let's look at some examples of how things are designed for big business and not for the majority – small business people.

There are some 700,000 corporations in Australia that are small. The great majority of corporations have one or maybe two shareholders. I have a corporation of which I am the only shareholder, a not uncommon situation. But the process and communications imposed by government are based on the needs and behaviour of large business. For example, by corporate law I have to have a meeting with myself every year. I have to send myself a letter 21 days prior to that meeting and I have to inform myself that I will attend that meeting. I have to propose resolutions, vote on them, and tell myself later what was decided! What if I can't attend? Can I send a proxy? If I nominate myself for chair who will second that nomination? And so it goes on. This is obviously silly, and rather reminiscent of the delightful scene from the Gilbert and Sullivan comic opera, *Iolanthe*, in which the Lord Chancellor, after long argument with himself, persuades himself that he should permit himself to marry his ward, Phyllis.

No-one has been fined, that I know of, for not meeting with themselves! But it does highlight the fact that designers of policy and process do not 'get' the fact that we are people and we are the majority. And it points out the crying need, when designing regulations and compliance regimes, to distinguish between smaller businesses and large businesses of a size to employ a paymaster, a human resources department and a chief financial officer, with accountants and lawyers on tap.

As further illustration of that, let me take an example from the federal workplace relations system. The Fair Work Ombudsman had conducted a retail campaign, which determined that some 26 per cent of retailers contacted in the campaign were not compliant with the workplace regulations. What did this mean? That the system had failed? That natural selection picks 'incompetents' to get into retail? Or perhaps that the retail sector was under stress? So, to help inform my comments on the policies, I asked them to provide a breakdown of the size of businesses that were not compliant. To my surprise, they had not kept data on the size of the businesses. How do you plan an education campaign when you don't know the size of the businesses? Again I am pleased to say the approach has changed and they now collect data on business size, but the fact that they didn't collect that data in the first place shows a lack of understanding of the difference between big and small. It turned out later that when you looked at the performance of department stores alone, the level of non-compliance was only 2.5 per cent. This amply illustrates the difference between a business with a paymaster and other expert support, and one without these resources. The system was, and still is, designed for paymasters and experts.

Under the current systems, it is enormously difficult to employ your very first employee and get everything legally correct – especially if you are in need of help now, not in a month's time. You will have to get your head around pay rates, tax rates, award conditions, public holidays, unfair dismissal laws and superannuation, just for starters. I have first-hand experience of this. For over seven years I was the proprietor of Smith's Alternative Bookshop in Canberra. We were not just a bookshop, but more besides: a wine bar and coffee shop and a popular venue for book launches, with live music. This meant that there were multiple rules applying to the business, and it was not always clear how we were to be treated for our various legal purposes.

Of course there are official 'helplines' that the small business person might call. But somewhere in the course of the experience you are likely to get a recorded message to the effect that any information provided is not a substitute for legal advice, relies on the accuracy and completeness of information that you provide, and could be affected by changing circumstances or changes to relevant policies, laws or judicial interpretation. What if you want to employ someone for one day? Should you really have to spend between $800 and $5,000 getting legal advice over pay of perhaps $300? The system has failed. No wonder then that some take a risk and fly beneath the radar and do a 'cashie' (which incidentally I do not endorse).

The small workplace in Australia is full of people working together to make a living. When we go into business in Australia we have to do several things. We have to collect GST and fill out our business activity statement and send the GST collected to the government. When we employ someone we have to collect 'pay as you go' tax and send that to the government. We must have workers' compensation and a safe workplace. We are required to collect superannuation and send it to multi-billion dollar superannuation funds, and we have become the conduit for paid parental leave. For all of this we are paid precisely nothing. That is our contribution to a civil society. In return we ask that governments and their agencies accept that it is their job to make it simpler to do these things.

On my own journey of understanding policy development and implementation, I discovered that the people who actually live in a community are best placed to deal with changes to their economy, and that with the right tools and information they can deliver most important policies and deal with the ongoing change that is a constant of the modern world.

Up until the 1960s the rate of change of technology, industry and of jobs was relatively predictable. People held career jobs, big business was the main focus of employment, small business people dominated retail and hospitality, and communities were normally friendly places with friendly faces. With the advent of microchips, the increased access to work and careers for women and globalisation, there have been major changes in the way we work, the level and frequency of change, and in planning and policy development processes.

So we may ask: how good are the policy development, planning and implementation processes for dealing with change? My message for the readers of this book – some of whom may become the next generation of leaders – is that you must understand, embrace and value the word 'local'. Local economic development; local empowerment; local politics; local community.

I was first engaged with policy for local economic development and labour market reform when I moved to Canberra from Goulburn, New South Wales, in the late 1980s. I joined a group of public servants who were a small but significant part of a large department. We worked with regions, enterprises and the people who were most affected by John Button's industry restructuring of the late 1980s and early 1990s, prompted by the dropping of tariffs for the passenger motor vehicle and for the textile, clothing and footwear industries. These changes caused job losses and major changes to communities from Geelong in Victoria to Elizabeth in South Australia, as well as many areas of Melbourne and Sydney and throughout regional Australia.

In response, the government decided to set up a network of local economic development projects as well as providing assistance to the workers and enterprises most affected. The assistance was in the main positive – major outcomes for workers were retraining and re-skilling, and enterprises were able to restructure and develop new products or processes.

The main focus of activity was around local economic development. We provided access for key community stakeholders to information, to experts and to funds. These stakeholders then decided what retraining was needed for displaced workers, how downsizing would take place (who would go first, how much notice could be given), what new business opportunities should be investigated and which job creation schemes best suited their situation. We did not blindly approve what was suggested by local people but we did value their opinions and work towards outcomes that communities wanted. Where we had success there was always a local driver, a person or people with vision and passion who grabbed this opportunity with open arms and worked hard for what they saw as the future for their children. We made sure we supported these people with secretariats and project funds.

But the empowerment of local communities was always a process that would be resisted. Not long after starting in this job I received a phone call from a senior person in the now defunct Federal Office of Local Government. Geelong was a major centre of industry reform at the time (nothing changes), and this senior public servant's opinion was that the people in Geelong did not have the capacity to respond to the crisis and that we could fix Geelong from Canberra. I told him firmly that our process of local empowerment was the best way to deal with change. He wasn't convinced and never would be.

In my time with this work, there was (and still is) an ongoing and powerful tendency to centralise decision making and project management in Canberra.

After the change of federal government in the mid 1990s, and after I left the public service, Amanda Vanstone became responsible for labour market reform. She understood the need to empower locals, but her public servants resisted her approach. Ms Vanstone had some 60 Area Consultative Committees scattered around Australia, run by local business people who volunteered their time to develop and influence local economic planning to better their own communities. Administrative support for these committees was funded by the federal government. I worked with many of the committees and found frustration from all of them with the way Canberra dominated their activities. Most, if not all, believed that they were being held back by those in Canberra. I then met the public servant in Canberra who was responsible for funding and management of the committee process. She told me she was frustrated because the committees 'would not do as they are told'. One person in Canberra truly believed that she knew better than the hundreds of business people involved in their own community's development and welfare. This is paternalistic centralism which must be overcome if we are going to better predict and manage change.

It may be true that the centralised decision maker will have a better understanding of macroeconomic reform and levers, but they are still remote from the effects and cannot apply microeconomic solutions from afar. The danger of centralised decision making is that those making the decision and designing responses are distant from the problem and, more importantly, they and their families are very unlikely to be impacted if the response is wrong or creates unfairness. The motivation for success is more one of performance and pay than of ownership of outcomes.

A key to local success is that local business people must be accepted as crucial stakeholders and drivers of local economic planning, as they are the ones who will have access to the funds to risk. There may be government funds spent on feasibility studies or research into new industries or business ideas, but in the end if a business proposition is to start and grow it will need money from investors.

In the early 1990s there were few local councils that could embrace local economic development. That has changed and more and more local councils have appointed local economic development officers. These people need good skills and knowledge but can help a council become one the hubs of local empowerment.

Of course the public servants giving out the taxpayers funds are ultimately responsible to their minister and the parliament for the proper and effective expenditure of those funds. But accountability should not be a replacement for good planning, for local involvement and for developing opportunity for all parts of the country.

As I acknowledged earlier, macro policies are vitally important. National leadership needs to give leaders in local communities the confidence to become involved. The decision on interest rates, large infrastructure projects, changes to tariffs, competition policy and many other areas are the domain of national leaders and agencies, but once they have made those decisions they should do all they can to empower local people to better understand policy, plan their communities, develop an economy, identify opportunity and deal with necessary but difficult change.

It is the constant instinct of centralised decision makers to try to make the world into something they prefer and something they think will work; something that suits their ideology. Extreme examples of failure of centralised economies based on ideology include the Soviet Union, and China under Mao Zedong and his supporters. Interestingly, China is expanding and changing as the state gives more economic power to the regions and cities (while maintaining a ruthless hold over communications!).

Understanding and managing local politics is another key to

success. There is no community that doesn't have politics of some sort or another. Most communities, the vibrant ones, will have many committees and groups striving to do good for the community for one reason or another, for business, welfare, sport, politics, special interest groups and others. Sometimes I hear people complain that there are too many committees and that people should cooperate more. The only places I have been where there are few community committees are communities that are lethargic and directionless or in communist countries and dictatorships where only sanctioned committees and groups can exist, and non-sanctioned groups will be liquidated or removed with force. I prefer our system, but only if the locals, the people in their own community, have the chance to participate and make decisions that will affect their lives.

The more involved the locals are, the less stress and uncertainty will exist and the more likely new and innovative ways to manage change or create jobs or develop a community will emerge.

Reclaiming politics, democracy and the third sector

Craig Wallace

Craig Wallace is the president of People with Disability Australia – a peak national cross-disability rights organisation – as well as deputy community co-chair of the ACT Disability Expert Panel and a member of the ACT Inclusion Council.

Craig is a well-known community leader in Canberra and served two terms as chair of the ACT Government's Disability Advisory Council as well as serving as president of the peak body People with Disabilities ACT. Craig was a member of the ABC Advisory Council for four years. He has written opinion pieces for *The Australian*, *The Australian Financial Review*, *The Guardian*, the ABC's *Ramp Up* and in Fairfax online, as well as blogging at craigwallaceontherecord.com.

Craig was awarded a Centenary Medal in the Australian Honours List in 2003 for service to the community, especially on access issues, and was featured in the Australia Day Awards four times for work with the Australian Public Service. Craig was the winner of the 2014 ACT Inclusion Awards Chief Minister's Award for Excellence in Inclusion. He has had a career spanning government, not-for-profit and the business sector. Craig has a disability called central core disease and uses a wheelchair for mobility.

Many commentators have observed that young people are disillusioned with traditional politics. Craig Wallace says this is not surprising in the current climate where managing opinion seems to have become a dominant project ahead of nation building and constructive change. While the media cycle is focused on colour, movement and set pieces such as question time, emerging leaders might reassess the many places where politics occur and develop an understanding of the power and influence within third sector organisations as a real engine for democracy, noting their powerful role in driving reform in areas like the National Disability Insurance Scheme. These organisations in turn need energy and a clash of ideas to drive cultural change and achieve their potential.

We disregard the things which lie under our eyes; indifferent to what is close at hand, we inquire after things that are far away.
—Pliny

The multitude which does not reduce itself to unity is confusion; the unity which does not depend on the multitude is tyranny.
—Pascal

It is not surprising that many young people feel alienated from the conventional political process. One of the aspects of this phenomenon, which has also been noted by President Obama, is that we're experiencing a coarsening of our political dialogue with the loudest, shrillest voices gaining the most attention.[1]

In Australia the manifestations seem to be a very toxic and angry political climate driven through online platforms and social media, and the rise of opinion as a commodity and a source of authority. The new toxic body politic crosses the divide. Neither the Left nor the Right are covered in glory by the kinds of inflammatory statements and imagery that adorned either the Carbon Tax Rallies of 2011 and 2012 or the 'March in March' in 2014.

While the unique circumstances of a hung parliament where everything was on the line all the time turned the volume full pitch over the term of the most recent Labor government, the drivers of underlying anger run deep, especially in Western Sydney: a mix of housing stress, Sydney commuter hell, discomfiture about rapid cultural change, the white noise of information overload and the pressing demands of a 24/7 do-more-with-less work culture. Some of us just aren't getting enough sleep.

There is also a gap between expectations of government and what it can actually do, as outlined in Laura Tingle's expanded essay: 'Great expectations: government, entitlement and an angry nation'.[2] This is a compelling and worthwhile read.

But there is also a legitimate critique to be made of the outcomes and the political narrative we now have. Looked at through a century's sweep of history, Australian parliamentary democracy in the opening years of the 21st century looks very stuck.

Between 1900 and 1915, the new Commonwealth of Australia created a defence force; founded a navy; conducted the first census; set up the Commonwealth Bank; established wage arbitration and set a minimum basic wage; set up the High Court; sorted out excise and customs arrangements; created the Northern Territory and the Federal Capital Territory* and chose the site and design for Canberra; and established arrangements to regulate commerce between the states. Many of the arrangements put in place during that period remain in place today. Most of it happened with hung parliaments, fractured coalitions and prime ministerial swaps and changes that make the parliament elected in 2010 look like a bedrock of certainty.

Since the 2000 Olympics, by contrast, our national discourse has foundered on unsuccessful attempts to solve a small number of reactive issues: finding a way to manage refugee intakes arriving by boat and responding in a settled way to climate change. Both issues have bounced back and forth between competing partisan approaches that don't always seem geared to the national interest.

These issues have also sucked the oxygen out of the room when it comes to dealing with other challenges that Australians might be worried about, like getting a transport system capable of linking a 4,000 km-wide island continent with distant capitals and urban centres; fixing the health system – especially in regional Australia – as well as preparing for population ageing; getting to a real place of settlement and material progress with Australia's traditional owners; plotting a future beyond the resources boom and the rise of China's consumer class; and getting to grips with the economic and strategic challenges that come with being a middle power in the Asia Pacific.

Meanwhile, the proceedings of our parliament stand in increasingly tawdry, embarrassing contrast to the reflective and probing conversations that can be seen during prime minister's questions in the United Kingdom House of Commons. Debates in the UK do not always swing on party lines and there is a surviving moderate liberal position within the parliament, as the recent debate on same-sex marriage illustrated.

It is hard to name standout examples of poise in the Australian system under any kind of political pressure. Name-calling and undergraduate student political tactics seem to be a default setting of Australian politics. Rarely has this been better expressed than by

* In 1938 the territory was formally renamed the Australian Capital Territory.

the ABC's Jonathan Green in his excellent, humorous pastiche of a maiden speech on the ABC's *The Drum*.[3]

The reality is that watching proceedings in the UK House of Commons side by side with the Australian House of Representatives on just about any given day is a sobering experience. Saying that it's just a fraction of the parliamentary day is no excuse; that's the fraction that people watch, and so it deserves a higher standard.

An exception to all of that – an issue which found clear air, civil conversations and a consensus (even to the point of politicians from both sides congratulating each other) – has been the drive to found a National Disability Insurance Scheme (NDIS).

Action here was driven largely by an unlikely line-up of heavyweight politicians, hardworking officials, service providers, advocacy organisations and online activity joined with real world networks and ordinary people working in a mix of new and traditional ways.

My organisation, People with Disability Australia (PWDA), is a not a new organisation. We began in 1981, which was International Year of Disabled Persons. Many of our members have been involved for a long time. We're active on social media and online, and combine old and new campaigning methods, but in other ways we are traditional. We have a board elected by members and survive from a melange of project work, volunteer goodwill and dedicated people. We scrape through on the familiar bits of string and glue which somehow keep organisations together. They shouldn't work at all, yet somehow they do.

It would be an unwise organisation which claimed the laurels within a collective campaign involving thousands of Australians and coordinated by the 'Every Australian Counts' campaign. Yet I do believe that our intervention at a critical point, which started with an article I wrote in April 2013,[4] was a seminal moment in the conversation about funding the NDIS through the tax take.

Over the following days the opposition came aboard too, and suddenly an idea that we had agonised over taking into the public domain was a reality, with a 0.5 per cent addition to the Medicare levy a settled matter on both sides in the space of a few weeks.

During the second reading speech for the Medicare Levy Amendment (DisabilityCare Australia) Bill 2013 in the House of Representatives, Prime Minister Julia Gillard noted our words summarised the argument well in favour of a levy.[5]

Many made the argument, but looking back, I'm not sure that anyone but a longstanding consumer organisation like PWDA could have taken that issue and run with it.

Who knows, and in the end, who cares? All that matters is that the thing was done. And yet there was leverage here at a critical point – one that neither a public servant nor a parliamentarian could have wielded on their own. It surprised me then. It surprises me still. This should give pause to those who believe that the days of organised lobby groups are past and that the whole future lies in online petitions, snap protests and viral videos.

Lobbying, research and media management retain their power and freshness when done in the right way and put in agile hands. Despite the occasional sneering comment about interest groups, they remain a legitimate tool of democracy: a way for governments to receive focused advice, a pressure valve and a focal point for people with a cause and a passion to pool their energies, time, corporate knowledge and intellects.

If you are a young person seeking ways to create the world you want to live in, I would invite you to reconsider engaging in community through these civil society organisations and remaking them in forms of your own choosing. By 'civil society organisations' I mean a sweep of organisations which exist outside government and business, ranging from associations, service clubs, youth development and sporting organisations, advocacy groups, church communities and charities to Parents and Citizens associations. There are also emerging arrangements like 'social enterprises' that blur the boundaries between community organisations and enterprises.

In other words, the choice doesn't have to be between standing for parliament or being a 'slacktivist' who shares things on Buzzfeed and signs the occasional online petition. Those tools have a place, but much real political democracy still occurs *within* organisations. I recommend being on boards, getting a handle on the way they work and gaining a perspective across human, material and policy management. This offers insights that people rarely get from just being in a public service position, doing industrial advocacy, practising law or parachuting straight into parliament.

Community organisations can also see politics at its most essential. For those with a literal bent, politics (from Greek: *politikos*, meaning 'of, for, or relating to citizens') is the practice and theory of influencing other people on a civic or individual level.

In these times we seem fixated on the idea that politics, and those who practise it, are a class apart. Influenced by a vocal angry commentariat, we seem to have adopted the maxim of Ralph Waldo Emerson, who described politics as 'a deleterious profession like some poisonous handicraft'.[6] We see it as a dark art practised by someone else – usually those people in far-off Canberra.

In reality, politics, in its broadest sense, is happening all around us and in every family, retail district, body corporate, office, school and community. Politics is everywhere and part of the normal healthy spectrum of behaviour. Only the least of it is about being elected to a narrow range of public offices through parliamentary politics. And even in parliament there is a big disconnect between the reality of things and the branding we see on the nightly news.

The long-haul project of most people in this kind of politics isn't about cutting ribbons or plotting in dark corners – it's about getting things done, answering a call to service and reworking the world in a better shape along the way. Often it's about convincing people to take a broader view. Many of the long days are counted in constituency work and individual advocacy and inquiry. There is much that is ordinary, decent and mundane happening within the endless marble corridors of the parliament in my home city of Canberra.

During my time in the Australian Public Service I had cause to meet with a few parliamentarians, parliamentary secretaries and ministers – not that many, but enough to see some patterns over the lives of three governments. A common refrain from new ministers, especially in the social policy areas where I worked, was genuine surprise at how *little* they could actually do in their policy areas and how constrained they were by process.

Many of these areas involved what some people call 'wicked problems' – issues with no clear causation, disputed ownership, no neat solutions and where sometimes the people with the power to fix the problems were also the ones causing them.

The nexus between income support and work is a classic example – the more you means test to ration some programs and meet public expectations that programs will be delivered against need, the more perverse incentives you can create *against* participation.

In some, I watched as bright eyes grew visibly dimmer as they confronted the scale of these issues amid a wall of briefs and daily bushfires, while others who were determined to reform came to see how reliant they were on civil society organisations and lobbyists to ginger up debate, create spaces for conversations and create a climate for breakout change.

Increasingly, volunteering and third sector organisations are the doers by proxy for government and actually deliver programs – a strong trend started by the Howard government and continued since then across the spectrum. We are told by reports on volunteering trends that long-term engagement with one organisation in civil society has fallen out of favour with many generation Xers in favour of short projects which meet private passions.[7] The National Volunteering Strategy consultation conducted by the Department of Prime Minister and Cabinet and released in 2011 identified that young people may feel alienated from traditional models of volunteering.[8]

And while all this is understandable, I would invite emerging leaders to reconsider the possibilities of building a path through organisations as a way of getting skills and making the change they believe in. Joining up, getting elected, sitting on a board, arguing your case, making compromises to accommodate other views and seeing your ideas through from beginning to implementation in a community body is a form of politics and provides skills that we all need – in business, in community and in relationships.

Feeling jaded from too much screen time? Well, civil society organisations offer a respite from the angry white noise of electronic media. They invite us to work with living, breathing people again, to test the behaviour we see in the online world with the behaviour we expect in our real world. They invite us to get real things done and gain a sense of completion.

The boards and committees of many long-term struts of civil society – from community councils, peak bodies, business chambers, political parties, sporting clubs and interest groups – are full of people who are ageing and exhausted and who wonder where the young people are.

One challenge for the future of democracy is for new generations to step up and reinvent and reinvigorate 'traditional' organisations in the shapes that they choose. Young people I know tell me that boards, committees and civil society organisations are stale and boring. But this invites the question: if they're stale, whose fault is that? Don't like the sound of getting involved in your local RSL, Apex club or Country Women's Association? Instead of walking away or ignoring them, why not join and seize the opportunity to remake them?

Are there organisations that don't step up ethically or fully include women, Indigenous people, young people or people with disability? Do they bully people, promote on patronage or maintain an old Australian booze culture? Take them over, make them professional, get them engaging well on social media, focus them on the issues that you want, get rid of the toxic culture and create one that you can thrive within while keeping that which is proven and sound.

Make them have elections and engage in a healthy clash of ideas. Take this change and form a flatter structure to share power and information and put the members back in the driving seats. And in doing so, remember that modelling good behaviour is the most powerful thing that we as individuals do to shape our world, even when we don't intend to.

As the Chief of Army, Lieutenant General David Morrison AO, said in responding to allegations of unacceptable behaviour by a group of service personnel, 'The standard we walk past is the standard we accept'.[9]

The same goes for democracy; walking past a broken system makes you part of the problem. *Carpe diem.*

---

1. Allen, M, 2010, 'Obama sees "coarsening" of national debate', *Politico*, September 13, www.politico.com/news/stories/0909/27082.html.
2. Tingle, L, 2012, 'Great expectations: government, entitlement and an angry nation', Quarterly Essay 46, www.quarterlyessay.com/issue/great-expectations.
3. Green, J, 2013, 'A maiden speech for our times', *The Drum*, 5 December, www.abc.net.au/news/2013-12-05/green-a-maiden-speech-for-our-times/5135890.
4. Wallace, C, 2013, 'Time to think about a levy to fund the NDIS', *Australian Financial Review*, 24 April, www.afr.com/p/opinion/time_to_think_about_levy_to_fund_BBrokmFSc2dSA7QZNNrZZJ.
5. 'PM introducing legislation to fund DisabilityCare Australia', YouTube,

www.youtube.com/watch?v=d8Z0MXRlOTw.

6. Wood, J, 1946, *The Nuttall dictionary of quotations*, F Warne, London, p. 352.
7. Wesley Mission, *The faces of volunteering*, www.wesleymission.org.au/publications/volunteers/youth.asp.
8. Australian Government: Department of the Prime Minister and Cabinet, *National Volunteering Strategy Consultation Report*, www.dpmc.gov.au/publications/national_volunteering.
9. 'Chief of Army message regarding unacceptable behaviour', YouTube, www.youtube.com/watch?v=QaqpoeVgr8U&feature=youtu.be.

Obstacles on the way to reform

Bruce Chapman

Bruce Chapman AM is professor of economics, Crawford School of Public Policy, ANU. He holds a Bachelor of Economics (first class honours) from the ANU (1973), and a PhD from Yale (1982). He was president of the Economics Society of Australia (2007–13) and president of the Australian Society of Labour Economists (2003–06). He is a member of the executive committee of the International Economics Association (2011– present). He was an invited participant at the 2020 Summit in March 2008.

Bruce was named the 'person with most influence in higher education in Australia' by *The Australian* in February 2012. He identifies as a 'naïve academic'. Yet he played an instrumental role in the establishment of the Higher Education Contribution Scheme (HECS) in 1989, and was senior full-time economic adviser to Prime Minister Paul Keating from 1994–96.

Beneath the visible drama of politics there is invariably a series of subsidiary battles going on – sometimes personal – involving politicians, their advisers, bureaucrats and people whose interests are affected. In this chapter Bruce Chapman gives an academic's account of lessons learned from his involvement in two major reform processes in the education sector. He concludes that:

- the novice policy adviser can be completely unprepared for the forces that may be unleashed by a seemingly straightforward, rational proposal
- you need to understand the institutions and interests you are dealing with
- a policy adviser should expect invective but not take it personally.

The innocence that feels no risk and is taught no caution, is more vulnerable than guilt, and oftener assailed.

—Nathaniel Parker Willis

Introduction

The Australian economy underwent profound transformation in the 1980s, including painful tariff reductions, the restructuring of the trade union movement and the resurrection of universal health care. The leaders of these changes (among them Bob Hawke, Paul Keating, Bill Kelty and Ross Garnaut) faced powerful and public opposition to reform.

Everyone knows that public policy reform is hard because it almost always involves winners and losers, and the potential losers are sometimes willing to go to great lengths to preserve the *status quo*. What is less well documented and understood is that in some reform processes there is often a series of major battles going on behind the scenes, and occasionally this can become very public and difficult for those promoting change. This essay reports one academic's experience with two policy changes which affected higher education financing in Australia in the late 1980s and early 1990s.

I was the academic involved in both reforms. The first was the design of the higher Education Contribution Scheme (HECS), which was turned into policy in 1989, and the second was the Austudy Loans Supplement, which had a real policy life from 1993 to 2004. Both experiences were very unsettling for me, both professionally and personally, because they were both so unexpected. Quiet academics have chosen research as their profession in part because it is supposed to be apolitical and not hostile. That's what makes us so unprepared for the real world of public policy, which is by its nature a tough, competitive and contested space.

My role in HECS was to prepare an options paper for the federal Employment, Education and Training Minister, John Dawkins, to facilitate the reintroduction of tuition fees (which he was strongly committed to, and believed that the Labor cabinet would support). My report, delivered at the end of 1987, started with the presumption that tuition fees would be introduced no matter what, and recognised that some form of loan scheme supported by the government would be required because of the unwillingness of banks to provide poor prospective students with loans.*

I canvassed different options and effectively recommended an

* This market failure is well understood in the economics profession and can be traced to the work of Milton Friedman.

'income contingent loan' (ICL). This is an arrangement in which all students upon enrolment could defer their tuition payment until, and only if, their future incomes reached a certain level (at the time this was suggested to be the average income of all Australians working for pay). It was recommended that the collection agency should be the Australian Tax Office, since it had the legal jurisdiction to know citizens' incomes and was collecting income taxes efficiently on the same sort of basis that was suggested for the proposed policy.

I thought at the time that there would not be strong opposition to the suggested reform, from either the tax authorities or the student body as a whole. Both predictions turned out to be quite wrong, almost laughably so, and that in part is what this essay is concerned with. The basic message is that a young well-educated economics researcher, sitting quite comfortably in a university (the ANU), can be startlingly poorly prepared for the harsh world of public policy.

The second example is that of the Austudy Loans Supplement, designed by me in 1992 and adopted by the Labor government in 1993. The idea was to allow those students on income support (then known as Austudy) to be able to access additional finances by taking (voluntarily) a trade-in option in which they would be able to swap each dollar of their grant into two dollars of an income contingent loan, to be repaid as part of, and in addition to, their HECS debt. Because the proposed system was entirely voluntary I believed, again incredibly naively, that there would be little student opposition. Sadly, this presumption turned out to be around six light years from the reality of a very public and almost entirely vengeful response.

There are several themes in what follows. Perhaps the most significant relates to the losing of innocence, or at least a diminishing of naivety, in the part played by, and the nature of, politics in an area of public policy. A fundamental point is that the 'politics of the matter' takes disparate and divergent forms, most of which I was ignorant of at the time and thus very surprised by. That political forces are hugely important and need to be understood in the process of development and maturation of leadership is a basic public policy issue.

I am not sure exactly what 'leadership' is, and even less sure whether my policy experiences and reform influence can be characterised in such a way. But I do know that there are strong institutional factors at work that can guarantee that the process of change is extremely hard, and people involved in policy disputes can make life very difficult for the proponents of reform. But it has to be remembered that in many ways those opposing change are just doing their job, and it helps to self-reinforce continually that apparent hostilities and resistance are not to be taken personally.

HECS

Background

Australian universities required students to pay fees until 1974. Even then, the vast majority of students had fee obligations exempt through the receipt of scholarships awarded on the basis of academic merit. These took two forms, Commonwealth and teachers' college scholarships, and covered around 75–80 per cent of students. Fees were abolished in 1974 for all students, meaning that from the early 1970s to the late 1980s Australian universities were financed without any direct contribution from students.

Thus the Australian higher education system in the late 1980s was one in which there was no student tuition charge – that is, universities were funded almost entirely by taxpayers. It is of interest that this was also the situation for two other countries that have introduced income contingent loans since HECS (New Zealand and the United Kingdom).

But in the Australian context at that time, there were serious forces at work for change. First, during the 1980s there was a significant increase in the proportion of pupils completing the final year of high school, but there was no commensurate expansion in higher education places. This resulted in the political problem of large and growing queues of qualified prospective students. The government clearly needed to do something about this.

Second, while this problem could have been solved with increased budget outlays, the Labor government was not prepared to spend the additional taxpayer resources necessary to finance extra university places. Similarly, this has been the case with many OECD countries since the 1980s.

Finally, and perhaps most importantly, two cabinet ministers, the Honourable John Dawkins and Senator Peter Walsh, were strongly in favour of student fees on grounds of income redistribution. Their view, supported clearly by the evidence, was that a higher education system which did not charge students was regressive: universities were paid for by all taxpayers yet students both came from relatively privileged backgrounds and as graduates received high personal economic benefits. It is important to record that Peter Walsh and John Dawkins were then respectively in charge of the critical ministries of finance and higher education.

These forces set the scene for the introduction of student charges in Australia. The Wran Committee was formed to investigate how this might best be done. The committee used my options paper as the basis for discussion, and I attended every meeting, as did David Phillips, a senior adviser to the minister and a strong believer in income contingent loans as the solution to the Australian higher education financing problem. The committee recommended HECS in its report presented to the minister in April 1988.[1]

The economics behind HECS has (mostly since) been understood to have a sound basis. It is essentially a government risk management instrument because debtors not able to afford to repay at a particular point in the future have no obligations to do so. However, there were several problems right at the beginning of the suggestion for HECS reform, although they took quite different forms. The major institution involved in a behind-the-scenes aspect of policy development and resistance was the Australian Tax Office (ATO).

Bureaucratic politics and HECS

One of the most important practical issues with the suggestion of an income contingent charging system using the income tax mechanism was that such a policy had not then been made operational anywhere in the world. Thus the agreement and cooperation with the ATO was fundamental. The ATO's initial response is now recorded.*

While the Wran Committee was deliberating on the possibility of recommending an income contingent loan, it became clear that the ATO needed to be consulted with respect to implementation issues. I can't remember if I was asked, or if I volunteered, but it was very likely the latter because I thought this would be pretty

* Some of this material draws upon a similar account from an interview with Bruce Chapman, published in Edwards, M, 2001. *Social Policy, Public Policy: From Problem to Practice*, Allen. & Unwin, Sydney.

straightforward – and perhaps even pleasant – which now seems a bit ridiculous and was testament to my youth and naivety.

So one sunny morning in autumn 1988 I turned up at the ATO with no understanding of how difficult the task would turn out to be. I was met by two moderately senior and very well-attired officials (in the conservative Treasury mode of dark suits and starched white shirts) with deceptively friendly smiles, offering cups of instant coffee and a (small) range of (mediocre) biscuits.

I argued that a charge for higher education was justified. I explained the merits of collecting such a charge depending on graduates' future incomes. The ATO was the natural (the only) collection institution available, I think I said, and had the unique advantages of knowing what graduates' incomes were and being able to easily make the relevant deductions from salaries. I argued something like, 'This is a great opportunity for path-breaking policy reform.' I thought that there would be no doubt they would be keen to be involved in the development of the policy.

The more senior of the two said, 'The tax office collects taxes, not debts. This is a basic principle.' I thought that there was also an unspoken and patronising tone, which in my projection took the form of him thinking, 'So don't bother us any more, sonny.' Raising the issue of a 'principle' seemed to be the end of the conversation, because a principle – by definition – is something that can never be compromised. I left the ATO disheartened, with my confused tail between my legs. But I knew I had to come back, maybe many times.

Preparing for the next meeting I decided to ignore the difficult issue of what a principle actually means, and instead planned on asking them to outline the practical implementation issues. At this second meeting they came up with many problems, such as:

> 'People avoid paying taxes. What does this scheme do about that?'

and:

> 'People die. How can we collect their debt if this happens? We don't have death duties.'

and:

> 'What about women graduates? Many of them won't repay because they will leave the labour force to marry brain surgeons and look after children.'

I hadn't thought much about these issues at the time. At the meeting I was not able to respond convincingly, and felt downcast and frustrated.

After this, it occurred to me one focused night that the whole process and arguments were a bit mad. The critical point was to address the policy issues in an empirical way; I decided to focus on this at the third meeting. In this discussion I suggested that none of the practical difficulties raised by the ATO were obviously important in a practical sense, and noted for example that the vast majority of female graduates would pay off most of their HECS debts well before rearing children, and that most would return to the labour force afterwards anyway. They probably knew I was right and, as a consequence, reverted back to the principle, 'The tax office does not collect debt'. Then a critical thing happened.

In a coffee break from the discussion ('battle' is probably the right word), the senior man asked me, by way of friendly conversation, who was on the Wran Committee recommending HECS. I said, Bob Gregory (who they seemed to approve of), Mike Gallagher (no opinion was expressed), and Meredith Edwards. The mention of the last changed everything.

The senior official's demeanour changed radically, and much to the negative, at the mention of Meredith's name. He turned to his offsider and said, 'We're stuffed.' They seemed then to wave a white flag.

Later I came to appreciate why Meredith Edwards being on the Wran Committee was critical to the ATO's assent. It was because, unknown to me, Meredith had been fundamentally involved the previous year in the institution of the non-custodial parenting support scheme, in which deductions are made from a person's wages, through the tax office. The ATO was already involved in doing things that were not just about taxes, and could be described as 'debt collection'. In other words, the 'principle' of the ATO not being a debt collector had already been significantly compromised well before I turned up arguing for HECS.

Essentially this was the end of my involvement with the ATO with respect to HECS. ATO officials came to the Wran Committee for discussion about administrative arrangements, but there was not strong opposition. I suspect that behind the scenes it was more than them losing the argument with me (and, indirectly, Meredith) than that the then treasurer Paul Keating, with the strong and effective guidance of the Australian tax commissioner Trevor Boucher, had made sure that the ATO complied. Later the ATO came to be a strong supporter of HECS.

It is of interest that a few years later the ATO embraced the concept of income contingent debt collection through its support of the mechanism needed to make the Austudy Loans Supplement operational, the second main policy issue examined below. On reflection it was not hard to understand why the ATO was initially opposed to HECS, before eventually embracing it. A government department is right to resist new administrative arrangements, particularly if it is obvious that they will involve greater staff input, as HECS did. After all, they may not get the required additional staff, and this would mean harder work for those there. And, much more importantly, if a public servant's role is partly about avoiding screw-ups it makes sense not to get involved too unquestioningly in some newfangled policy idea dreamed up by a university boffin who could be dangerously naive (as I was), and this they certainly weren't prepared to do. Overall, I think the ATO acted very professionally with respect to the prospective introduction of HECS, and the institution showed itself to be a model of cautious and progressive administration.

Since then I have had the opportunity to travel to many countries the governments of which have shown significant interest in the adoption of a HECS-type income contingent loan, adapted for their own political and institutional circumstances. In most of these countries I have asked if I could meet with senior tax office personnel (most usually in institutions known as the Internal Revenue Service (IRS), to gauge their reaction to the possibility of such policy reform. Almost without exception, and in Spanish, French, Thai, Chinese, English or other languages, there has been close to universal opposition from these public servants, always along the same lines that I had heard in 1988 from the ATO.

What has made it different for me post-HECS in dealing with IRS officials overseas is that when they say that it would be impossible to make it work, we all now know that this is not true, because it operates very smoothly in Australia (and now, *inter alia*, New Zealand and the United Kingdom as well). Professor Kenneth

Boulding, the late Harvard economist, once said: '… if it exists, then it is possible'. I often think that this is a profound, apposite and witty lesson with respect to the introduction of income contingent loans, given Australia's experience with HECS.

A point about leadership from this experience is that while I have been able to assist in transforming the higher education financing landscape in other countries, and with the World Bank, the important skills were developed and learned on the job, and were not part of my DNA. I had no idea what I was doing with the ATO in 1988, or how I should have been doing it. But we can all learn from direct experience, and maybe that is the only way to learn properly. Put bluntly, the message is: understand the institutions you are dealing with and what is in their interests.

The Austudy Loans Supplement

Background

In 1992 I was asked to write an options paper for the Labor government that would allow greater flexibility and fairness with respect to the delivery of income support for higher education students, a system then known as Austudy. As noted above, I suggested that students should be allowed to access higher levels of assistance by being given the option of trading-in part of their student grant in place of a doubled level of support taken in the form of an extension to their HECS debt and repaid in the same way.

Because the scheme was to be entirely voluntary, I didn't see that students would find any problem with it – after all, if they didn't like the option they could ignore it and not be any worse off. This turned out to be quite wrong and there were major, highly aggressive and very public protests in the short period between the release of my report and the adoption of the scheme announced in the 1992–93 budget by the new treasurer, John Dawkins, who understood the issues very well. The reasons for the hostilities, which seemed to become quite personally targeted, were as follows.

Student politics and the Austudy Loans Supplement

After HECS became policy it was well known that I had been an (the) 'architect' of the system, and in some indirect way I was considered to be an enemy of a major group affected, Australian university students (represented by the National Union of Students (NUS). After all, even though HECS can be seen to be a generous and gentle way for students to pay fees – certainly compared to both the up-front variety and the bank loans used extensively overseas – this was not the big point for Australian students. The point instead was that HECS was a new impost, as previously university education had been delivered free to students (or at least to those who could get a place). A conveniently ignored fact was that the additional money allowed John Dawkins to expand the size of the university system very considerably.

Moreover, NUS could see the prospects of what is known as the 'thin edge of the wedge': the notion that once a policy reform is put in place it is quite easy for governments to change it and potentially make it less generous for groups affected. Interestingly, this characterisation clearly became true with respect to HECS, which changed over time in ways that have always decreased the subsidy to university students.* As well, NUS knew that there would only be a short opportunity to stop the government from adopting the trade-in option and thus the need for strong and public action was from their point of view critical to killing it off; from my perspective, I became quite concerned about the possibility that I myself might be killed off.

This fear was not totally paranoid as there were large and physical protests at many meetings at which I spoke publicly about the trade-in option. In Melbourne, for example, about 6,000 students blocked streets, and police saw a need to lock my colleague Damian Smith and me in a basement toilet for our protection. I had a similar experience in Adelaide, being locked in a small room with students breaking windows and smashing at doors while I met with the then president of the Students' Association of the University of Adelaide (SAUA), Natasha Stott Despoja, who graciously apologised on behalf of the students acting with such apparent fury.

A number of posters were prepared as part of the NUS below. The first, printed straight after my report was made public, was

* For example, the average charges increased by about 40 per cent and the first threshold of repayment of HECS debt was decreased by about 30 per cent in 1997, and charges were effectively allowed to increase by a further 25 per cent in 2003.

headlined 'RIDICULOUS IDEAS No.1 – STUDENT LOANS' and featured a man pedalling a contraption which appeared to be a perpetual motion machine.

When I first saw this poster I thought, 'well, at least they don't mention me'. However, not long afterward it was followed by a leaflet, distributed in bulk to students, which featured a photograph of me and the text:

WANTED

FOR CRIMES AGAINST EDUCATION

Bruce Chapman

Gave us the HECS

... and now the LOANS scheme

Tuesday, October 13th, 1992

ECL Lecture Th 3, 12.30 p.m.

'It could be nastier,' I rationalised.

But soon it *was* nastier. A demonstration was organised by the Western Australia NUS to coincide with a seminar I was giving (on poverty!) at Murdoch University in Perth. The poster was a rallying cry designed to paint a fairly horrible picture of me.

Not long before my report was made public, NUS organised a national day of rage against the main proposal, the optional trade-in arrangement designed to allow students greater short-term flexibility with no long-term costs to the budget. The evening news covered the demonstrations in significant detail, and one clip included the burning of effigies of myself* and the minister responsible for the portfolio, the Honourable Peter Baldwin. My five-year old son watched the reports and said, 'Are these people angry at you Daddy?' I took the question to be rhetorical.

* I would like to note, without resentment, that the effigy of me I considered to be gratuitously very ugly.

SAC AND THE PROPHETS PREDICT
"THE EVIL ONE HIMSELF IS COMING!"

...

That's right girls and boys,

DR BRUCE CHAPMAN who brought us HECS, THE LOANS SCHEME and other really neat ways to deprive **YOU** of an education is coming to a campus near you.

Meet in the forum area (near main refec at Uni of Qld) for a forum at 11am, on Friday, 5th June. Then it's onto the Economics Dpt.

We've tangoed with Kemp, We've waltzed with Howard, now let's Dance with the Devil.

Over this period I had been attacked quite broadly by NUS so, again with considerable naivety, I wrote a short note to the University of Melbourne student newspaper, *Farrago*. Perhaps completely predictably, I received the following response from the editor:

Melbourne University
Student Union

...

Monday March 16 1992

Dear Dr Chapman

Thank you for forwarding your "Article for Student Newspapers" for consideration by *Farrago*.

We have read your paper, and regret to inform you that it fails to reach the standards we usually require of our contributors.

Further, we view your comments as a cynical attempt to dampen the co-ordinated efforts of students across the country as we prepare to crush your loans scheme proposal.

Your science is a sham. Your co-conspirators are exposed. Your motivations are perverse. Your propositions are clumsy. Your philosophy is anti-social. Your days are numbered.

Yours sincerely.

...

I heard other reports of widespread personal condemnation including that my name had been scrawled in university toilets with various uncomplimentary epithets. These actions did not deter me from pursuing what I thought the research of the matter supported: that the loans supplement would make many students better off, and that there would not be long-run costs to the budget.

But the big lesson lies in the realisation that there is a yawning (even snarling) gap between what economic analysis views as an efficient and fair way to go and the politics of the matter. And politics in part is about the real power of special interest groups and their ability to demonstrate their power. That's why public policy reform is so hard; those who believe that they will be affected adversely by change have little to lose and much to gain from resistance, but those who might be assisted may not be aware of the benefits, or may consider themselves insufficiently advantaged by the change to want to be involved.

Conclusion

Policy reform is difficult and academics by their nature generally do not have the experience or the inclination to be effectively engaged in the process. But so-called 'leadership' in the economics public policy space requires a commitment to some basic principles, and from my experience these include the following:

- It is critical to be sure that the economics of what is being proposed has been worked out properly, and that the empirical evidence used is as sound and thorough as it can be.
- It is naive in the extreme (as I have been) to believe that change can ever be seamless or easy.
- The politics of the matter is completely critical and if people want to be part of the process of economic reform, it helps to realise that even highly aggressive opposition to ideas has to be expected and is not a personal issue.

---

1. Australian Government 1988, *Report of the committee on higher education funding (the Wran report)*, AGPS, Canberra.

Part 3: COMMITMENT

Young people, change making and democracy

Lucas Walsh and Jan Owen

Associate Professor Lucas Walsh is Associate Dean (Berwick) in the Faculty of Education at Monash University. He was previously director of research and evaluation at The Foundation for Young Australians. He has published two co-authored books: *In their own hands: can young people change Australia?* (2011) and *Building bridges: creating a culture of diversity* (2008), and his research covers a diverse range of areas related to young people.

Jan Owen AM is CEO of the Foundation for Young Australians and a pioneer of the youth sector in Australia. She is a highly regarded social entrepreneur, innovator and child and youth advocate. From 2002–10, Jan was executive director of Social Ventures Australia, which increases the impact of the Australian social sector. Prior to this Jan founded the CREATE Foundation and was its CEO for nine years. She is the only non-US citizen to receive a fellowship for leadership and innovation to the Peter Drucker Foundation (United States) and has been awarded membership of the Order of Australia for services to children and young people. In October 2012, Jan was named the *Australian Financial Review* and Westpac Group Woman of Influence 2012 and the social enterprise category winner. The Women of Influence awards recognise the important contribution female leaders make to Australia's future.

Young people are often described as disengaged and immature, and as having a false sense of entitlement. Polls have suggested that many of them are questioning the value of democracy. But the reality is much more complex and hopeful. The rise of social entrepreneurs suggests a vibrant current flowing beneath much of the malaise pervading contemporary government and public life in Australia. Through innovative forms of action and technology, young people are actively seeking to address some of the key problems facing Australia and the world. We should rethink common stereotypical views of young people, and in particular their role in public life and in shaping Australia.

It's down to you, if you know about it, you want it, [then] change it.
—Young social pioneer

Introduction

On a mild spring evening on the first day of September 2013, a group of young social entrepreneurs gathered in an open second-floor space above a narrow Melbourne laneway café, the Henley Club. Sprawled amid the old timber, floor-to-ceiling art and junkyard installations housed within this converted printing press, a group of women and men aged between 18 and 29 were starting a year-long Foundation for Young Australians leadership program. The program supports 18 inspiring change makers through mentoring, peer learning, skills development, leadership inquiry and international connections so that they can improve their social impact. The Young Social Pioneers program seeks to build young people's capacity to bring about change by helping them collaborate and develop networks of key organisations, people and resources. To date, 58 young people have participated in the program, its alumni coming from around Australia. Through start-up-style projects, these pioneers work in areas as diverse as education, the environment, health, human rights, the arts and technology.

The workshop took place one week prior to the 2013 Australian federal election. The timing was coincidental but portentous. In their different ways, the pioneers represent a new wave of young people with an approach to making change outside of conventional political channels of influence. Their 'politics' – though highly engaged – were far from the noise of the electoral campaign and the jousting of political parties. In a way, the meeting and discussion sat oddly with the prominence afforded to young people by the media and some of the political parties during the 2013 campaign, because their work often eschews political processes such as elections, instead seeking to use different ways and tools.

Their approaches and ethos send a message to new leaders about the changing landscape of young people's engagement in making change. This chapter explores that landscape, from young people's increasing disengagement from conventional politics to the changing ways in which many approach social and political influence. Within a broader movement towards issue-based politics, young people are making use of technology and new vehicles for change making, such as social enterprises to find new platforms for and approaches to leadership.

The shift away from electoral politics

From the outset of the 2013 federal election campaign, Prime Minister Kevin Rudd appealed to young people for their vote. He had done so previously in the 2007 campaign and with good reason. The potential influence of young people on election outcomes is significant. Because young voters represent about 30 per cent of the electorate, a shift in the vote of this age group could have a significant impact on an election outcome. As Eric Sidoti has suggested:

> The collapse of the youth vote for Labor between the 2007 and 2010 elections, for example, saw a drop of well over 15 points among 18 to 34 year olds, and their intentions to switch to the Greens (by roughly the same number) goes some way to explaining the hung parliament ... Yet as an electoral cohort comparatively little is known [about them].[1]

What is known is that in recent elections, young people, especially women aged 18–24, have continued to favour 'progressive' parties over their conservative counterparts. According to a study by Ron Brooker,[2] men aged 25–34 are more conservative. But neither gender exhibits stable voting behaviours. Younger voters are more fluid, and vote more according to issues, 'political moments' and values, rather than along specific party lines.

What is also known is that voter registration continues to be low among 18- to 24-year-olds. Thirty per cent of the 1.4 million eligible Australians missing from the national electoral roll are young people, and only around 35 per cent of potential voters from the ages of 18 to 24 were registered to vote in the 2013 federal election. As of March that year, 493,113 young people were unenrolled.[3]

Young people's attitudes to Australian democracy itself may be shifting. The 2013 annual Lowy Institute Poll[4] found that only 48 per cent of 18- to 29-year-old Australians said they preferred democracy over any other kind of government. They appear to be turning away from democracy, or at least the distinctively Australian version of it. Have the divisive and intensely personal politics visible across the media during the last several years from politicians of all political stripes shaped this view? Perhaps their responses relate to the type of questions asked in the poll.

Nevertheless, a related question is whether or not young people see democracy through traditional institutional lenses such as voting and certain forms of civic participation. The Social Pioneers may not engage directly with these questions, but instead are passionately interested in improving social justice, itself a vital ingredient of democracy. This is what is going on beneath the currents of conventional politics, and it is a powerful reflection of a changing social and political landscape.

But this message is often drowned out by a persistent, pervasive and too often unfounded negative view of young people. Often we hear or read commentators bemoaning an apparent sense of entitlement felt by Gen Yers or millennials, their lack of interest in civic participation and general disengagement. There continues to be concern that many Australians experience apathy, lack of confidence in political affairs, personal alienation, powerlessness and exclusion from civic life.

An alternative and emerging view argues that young people are not democratically disengaged but are utilising new modes of participation. As membership levels in the major political parties experience a record decline, youth-oriented and grassroots movements such as the Australian Youth Climate Coalition are experiencing growing membership. What does it mean for key social and political structures that so many of these young people are routinely bypassing them? Conventional political pathways are not working for many young people. Which, in part, was why some of these Young Social Pioneers were gathered in the room on that mild spring evening in Melbourne.

Conventional notions of political participation are being replaced with different ways of creating change through vehicles such as social entrepreneurship and individualised responses harnessed collectively through the viral capabilities of social media.

The emergence of the politics of choice

In a time when broad political platforms have been replaced by big-ticket issues (e.g. poverty and the environment) and increasingly presidential-style and poll-driven politics within a relentless 24-hour media cycle, there has been a shift away from parties and government as the main avenue for representation, and towards informal, issue-based politics in which young people think that they might have more influence. In this movement away from institutionally-based to more issue-based participation, particularly via information and communication technology (ICT), a 'politics of choice' has emerged as the key basis for political interest, expression and participation.

Young people are civically engaged in politics more informally than has previously been the case. They are more values-driven and less attached to traditional political organisations than in the past.

A 2013 poll by the Australia Institute[5] showed that trust and integrity are important to young people. In our meeting at Henley a debate ensued about the pragmatism of politicians. One Pioneer called their integrity into question, noting a propensity to 'flip-flop' on key issues when it suits them. Another retorted that the changing and complex practical circumstances in which government must make decisions necessitates the ability to change when required – bringing to mind the famous quote by economist John Maynard Keynes: 'When the facts change, I change my mind. What do you do, sir?'

The first Pioneer voiced another concern about the lack of diversity among Australian political representatives. Despite huge strides in representation by women, Indigenous people and those in same-sex relationships, the face of politics, he argued, continues to be dominated by middle-aged white men. By extension, it was suggested that a lack of diversity would shape the capacity of many political representatives to understand, empathise and respond to key issues in their diverse constituencies.

Young people show a consistent interest in global issues such as human rights, racism, equality, the economy and, above all, the environment. Many of these issues – particularly the last two – are also highly rated by much of the older population. It's just that the views of young people are too often dismissed because they are young.

Two key drivers are altering the capacity for young people to be heard and to make change: technology and the rise of the social entrepreneur.

Young people and technology

In the Henley gathering that Sunday, notes, concept maps, laptops and handheld communication devices were strewn throughout the room – the evidence of young social entrepreneurs at work. A portable digital projector beamed onto a makeshift screen. Perversely, it rested upon a stack of encyclopaedias that came with the space. The encyclopaedias evoked a time when the room was a printing press, but its function was now digital. As with the vast majority of young people in Australia, these Pioneers were fully connected.

The internet, social media and portable devices like smart phones have opened up opportunities for new types of and spaces for participation. Through these technologies, young people feel that they can disengage and re-engage freely, as the unstructured nature of the internet allows them to have freedom over their own participation. The internet enables them to achieve a number of goals simultaneously by taking action on issues that are important to them, generating networks of new people, and identifying, exploring and responding to new causes.[6]

Web 2.0 technological platforms, tools and social media have collaborative and user-generated benefits that can help create spaces for young people's participation and engagement, in the places where they live and in forms that are relevant to them.

These tools enable a shift in the loci of power. We see this at its most extreme and disruptive in the controversial release of sensitive military information by Wikileaks. Less contentiously, the use of these technologies by social movements such as GetUp! illustrates this shift in increasingly mainstream ways. The technologies offer individuals and groups enormous constructive possibilities for democratising participation, enabling collaboration and rapid sharing of information. They are key tools of the social entrepreneur.

The rise of the social enterprise

During the last decade, the relationship between government, business and civil society has started to shift. This has enabled new opportunities, resources and spaces for young people to engage in change making on matters of importance to them. Our Young Social Pioneers operate in these spaces. Their vehicles for change making – social enterprises – seek to work in between the spaces typically occupied by government, philanthropy or corporate social responsibility. In this changing environment, young change makers pick and sample from corporate, government and third-sector resources and approaches to create more agile organisational and financial vehicles for creating social impact. As Cheryl Kernot from the Centre for Social Impact suggests, social entrepreneurs reject the assumption that governments and corporations can best determine the most effective allocation of resources.[7]

Young change makers have expressed frustration in the slowness of government processes and in governments' limited capacity to make timely, grassroots change. Social enterprises have grown as a result of a need for change making to take place in more dynamic, responsive and efficient ways. They draw upon a range of resources, networks and approaches, often to expedite the delivery of a program, campaign or initiative. Their hybrid nature reflects a pragmatic and strategic attitude prevalent among young social entrepreneurs.

Defined as a viable business with a social agenda, a social enterprise seeks to bring about social change in two key ways that differentiate it from charities and not-for-profits. First, by creating revenue from the sale of products or services and reinvesting all profits back into the enterprise; and second, by putting the tools of individual empowerment – whether financial, skills or human capital – in the hands of the 'end user' or 'program beneficiary'. A good example of this is the social enterprise café group in Melbourne, STREAT, which trains and employs young homeless people in hospitality while maintaining a fully sustainable social enterprise.

Social enterprises have been characterised as 'profit with purpose'; as prioritising social capital over hard assets. They seek to deliver social outcomes but are typically organised more like businesses – they use traditional business tools to generate dividends that are reinvested in the core social purpose of the enterprise. Social enterprises can take many forms. They can function as cooperatives, companies limited by guarantee, unincorporated associations, sole trader or business partnerships, among others. But typically, youth-led social enterprises seek to be nimble and to avoid the bureaucratic restraints of government and large non-government organisations.

Another kind of social enterprise is the growth of youth movements, like the Australian Youth Climate Coalition (AYCC), which tap into the vast networks and resources enabled by sophisticated campaigning tools that not only raise votes for petitions but also crowdfunding. The AYCC is an example of a youth-led, youth-oriented enterprise that uses ICT – in combination with conventional campaigning mechanisms and education – to engage young people in learning about and taking action in response to climate change. A key purpose is to create a social movement around responding to climate change with the aim, in turn, of bringing about lasting political change. The AYCC uses social media as a means to recruit volunteers and accept donations. In 2009, it organised 'Youth Decide', which mobilised over 37,000 young people aged 12–29 to vote online or at one of more than 300 local voting events held around the country for the future world they want to inherit.

Our change makers at Henley share similar approaches, many of which seek to address the big-ticket items discussed above. One 25-year-old Pioneer, for example, heads a not-for-profit that supports the funding, fuelling and connecting of entrepreneurial people, resources and networks. Another project researches and funds renewable energy solutions through an international network to provide electricity to some of the world's most deprived communities. Others seek to address mental health, homelessness and the social inclusion of people with disabilities, as well as body image and self-worth – issues routinely acknowledged as being important to young people in annual national surveys conducted by Mission Australia.

These entrepreneurs use a range of strategies and tools, from theatre and fashion to food, sport and print media. They target global, local and regional contexts. They reflect the diversity of change making that often goes unnoticed beneath the radar of how we understand power and influence.

This shift in the landscape of change making prompts us to rethink how we understand, describe and promote youth change making, as well as young people in general. A number of key messages emerge from this.

Rethink the 'political'

In July 2008, 10 focus groups conducted with young people by the University of Western Sydney provided insight into the broader landscape of young people's relationship to politics and participation in Australia. Participants showed a broad knowledge about how the Australian political system works. However, the existing political system was not seen to encourage or value young people's participation or provide sufficient opportunities to participate in decision making. Political structures, particularly at state and federal level, were characterised as complex and a barrier to meaningful participation.

Of particular significance is that many young people who are seeking to bring about change do not necessarily categorise their activity as being 'political'. They demonstrate an interest in political issues, but prefer to label their interests as 'making a difference' socially rather than politically. Young social entrepreneurs work to address an area of need in society rather than seeking government intervention. Politics emanates from the personal to a wider social expression. Social media enables these individual expressions to have a collective voice.

This should send a strong message to leaders seeking to mobilise young people – a message that is often overlooked.

Reimagine participation

Young people's perception of the power of participation through conventional means is complex and uneven. The Sydney focus groups in 2008 produced two contrary strands of thought. Some participants thought that Australia's democratic system was 'functional and effective'. Other participants considered that Australia's representative democracy – characterised by most as adversarial and by others as non-participatory – was flawed and needed to change to re-engage citizens, particularly beyond the community level.[8] Findings such as those published by the Lowy Institute in 2013, mentioned earlier, suggest a shift away from the first view and towards the second view of democracy during the intervening five years.

We can't help but wonder whether this questioning of democracy in Australia relates in part to a perception of dysfunction of party politics in Canberra and in the recent erosion of the status of the prime minister and government played out in the media over the last few years.

The message to leaders here is clear. The landscape of participation is uneven and changing. Active participation can and should take place across formal institutional settings, such as schools, and informal contexts, such as through voluntary engagement in community organisations, involvement in online social movements, social enterprise, or even through the exercise of market power through ethical consumption. Young people need to be able to connect the experience of participation to other parts of their lives: in work and study, at home and across digital networks. This requires us to support young people's participation in a range of ways and contexts.

Conclusion

Though gathered while an intense Federal election campaign entered its final week, many of the Young Social Pioneers had other things than the politics of the election on their minds. They were more interested in the immediate practical challenges to improving the viability and impact of their enterprises. But if certain previous social entrepreneurs are any indication, some of these entrepreneurs will move on to formal political life. Simon Sheikh, the national director of the Australian political organisation GetUp! from 2008 to 2012, unsuccessfully contested the seat of Australian Senate candidate for the Australian Capital Territory in the 2013 federal election. The former national director of the Australian Youth Climate Coalition, Anna Rose, worked on the communications strategy to elect Adam Bandt to the lower house. Both are members of the Greens party.

Given that the participants from the 2008 Sydney focus groups and our change makers at Henley expressed views ranging across the political spectrum, it is quite likely that some will also choose to enter the conventional theatre of politics via party membership or perhaps even independently.

In the meantime, the challenges faced by young social entrepreneurs in Australia reflect the experience of their peers throughout the world. Many young entrepreneurs operate in isolation without supportive networks, the wisdom of mentors, and opportunities for peer-to-peer learning. They want to harness and improve the skills and knowledge on how to lead, and at a very basic level, get the resources and financing to survive and thrive.

The first step in addressing these challenges is to recognise and value young entrepreneurs' work. This involves a fundamental shift in how we view their capacity to influence. One young female

Pioneer observed that 'I never really thought of myself as someone of influence … being a young person, and [at the] end of last year I got an award being one of the top 100 young women of influence in Australia and I was really … surprised.' Though other winners were CEOs, she had recognised that people could influence in other ways. The corollary of this was that she herself was recognised.

At a deeper level, there also needs to be a better understanding of how 'the political' is understood. The conventional lens through which we often view participation does not enable many of us to see many of the ways that young people could make change, and are seeking to do so. Social entrepreneurs like the Pioneers are keen to engage, but not in conventional pathways. They use ICT to extend their reach and impact. We therefore need to better understand the ways in which young people are participating in making change that are not recognised through the current lens.

A final key message to new leaders is therefore to hear the voices of young people through the noise of media hyperbole and stereotyping that obscures understanding and in doing so is sometimes divisive. It is time now to listen. Looking at the passion, drive and innovation of the Young Social Pioneers, perhaps this message is unnecessary, as they are the future leaders. And the future looks bright.

---

1. Sidoti, E, 2011, 'Young voters a force to be reckoned with', *The Australian*, 23 July. www.theaustralian.com.au/national-affairs/opinion/young-voters-a-force-to-be-reckoned-with/story-e6frgd0x-1226099321957.
2. Brooker, R, 2013, *Youth federal election voting intentions update: a statistical and graphical analysis of Newspoll quarterly data election poll 2010 to March 2013*, Whitlam Institute, 26 August, http://whitlam.org/__data/assets/pdf_file/0005/507803/Newspoll_Analysis_Update_Election_Poll_Update_Aug_2013.pdf.
3. Australian Electoral Commission 2013, *AEC working with Facebook to encourage young voters to matter this election*, http://www.aec.gov.au/media/media-releases/2013/06-24.htm.
4. Oliver, A, 2013, *Australia and the world: public opinion and foreign policy*, Lowy Institute, http://www.lowyinstitute.org/publications/lowy-institute-poll-2013.
5. The Australia Institute, 2013, *Youth value 'trust' but undecided on federal*

election, 14 June, https://www.tai.org.au/file.php?file=/media_releases/MR%20youth%20survey%20June%202013.pdf.

6. Collin, P, 2008, 'The internet, youth participation policies, and the development of young people's political identities in Australia', *Journal of Youth Studies*, 11(5): 527–42.
7. Kernot, C, in Walsh, L & Black, R, 2011, *In their own hands: can young people change Australia?*, ACER Press, Camberwell.
8. Horsley, M & Costley, D, 2008, *Young people imagining a new democracy: young people's voices; focus groups report*, Whitlam Institute, p. 4.

Are you cut out for public life?

Ian Harper

Ian Harper is a partner at Deloitte Access Economics and Professor Emeritus at the University of Melbourne. In a career spanning academe as well as the public and private sectors, he has worked closely with governments, banks, corporates and leading professional services firms. He was a member of the Wallis Inquiry into Australia's financial system in the mid 1990s and inaugural chairman of the Australian Fair Pay Commission from 2005 to 2009. He was a member of the Independent Review of State Finances in Victoria in 2011–12. From 1992 to 2008, Ian taught economics at the Melbourne Business School. In March 2014, he was appointed to chair the Commonwealth government's Competition Review Panel, a 'root and branch' review of Australia's competition policy, laws and regulators.

Ian Harper is a member of the advisory board of the Bank of America Merrill Lynch in Australia, a director of the Australian College of Theology, a fellow of the Academy of Social Sciences in Australia and a fellow of the Australian Institute of Company Directors. He is the author of *Economics for life: an economist reflects on the meaning of life, money and what really matters* (2011).

What does it mean to be in 'public life', and are you qualified to take this path? Ian Harper argues there should be minimal formal requirements, but you should ask yourself what motivates you to enter public life. If it is money, then public life is not for you. On the other hand, there is nothing wrong with being motivated by power in itself. But remember that the state exists to serve the people, and its authority ultimately rests on their consent. Be prepared for your family's privacy to be compromised, and to not always be thanked for your efforts. Rather, be content that public life is a high and noble calling, that you bring your best to the task, and that you seek to serve the public interest with all your heart and mind and strength.

And he sat down and called the twelve. And he said to them 'If anyone would be first, he must be last of all and servant of all.'

—Mark 9:35

Wanting to be in public life is a noble objective. At its best, a career in public life can be deeply satisfying and genuinely improve the corporate life of the community. In essence, public life involves the willing and often self-sacrificial service to others. This is what makes it noble and also personally satisfying. But, to be effective, you should be under no illusions about what public life will demand of you and those close to you.

Australians are typically sceptical of those who offer themselves for public service. There is a suspicion of authority which runs deep in the Australian psyche. Who are you to be lording it over us? Are you genuinely interested in promoting our welfare or just seeking to glorify yourself or, worse, to enrich yourself at our expense? Are you looking for an easy ride in life at the expense of the hard-pressed taxpayer?

Indeed, there is cynicism here as well as healthy scepticism. But those who offer themselves for public office should be aware from the outset that not everyone will welcome this as an act of unmitigated selflessness. And, of course, they're right: it won't be entirely selfless. People in public life have aspirations and ambitions like anyone else. When I was asked to chair the Australian Fair Pay Commission, I saw an opportunity not only to serve the lowest paid members of the community but also a chance to exercise my professional skill and to build my public profile. None of us acts from purely selfless motives – at least, no-one I have ever met, even in religious life.

There is nothing wrong with wanting to be prime minister or secretary to the Treasury or lord mayor of Melbourne. However, your career in public service will be ineffective at best, or destructive at worst, if your motivation is primarily self-centred rather than other-centred. A good place to start when contemplating a career in public service is to examine your own motivations. What are you trying to achieve? Be honest. Is this primarily about *doing* something important or *being* someone important?

If it's the latter, spare yourself and the rest of us a load of heartache and stay away from public life. Run your own business or someone else's. Become a famous entrepreneur or a sporting star – or an actor or a barrister or a surgeon. You will serve other people in those careers as well – indeed, you must, or you will fail financially. But at least you won't be hiding the fact that the primary reason you do what you do is to aggrandise your own fame and fortune. There's nothing wrong with this either, except that you may discover rather too late in life that 'all that glisters is not gold'.

Examine yourself

As you examine yourself, and seek counsel from others, a telling question to ask yourself is what you treasure, and to check whether others agree that they see this in you. Jesus of Nazareth said to his disciples, 'Where your treasure is, there your heart will be also.'[1] If your 'treasure' is money and material possessions, then public life is probably not for you. You will come to resent the fact that most public positions are remunerated less generously than their private counterparts. Worse yet, you might be tempted to corrupt your position of public authority for private gain and land yourself in serious strife.

Secretaries of government departments are often responsible for bigger budgets and more employees than the chief executives of many private businesses, and yet are paid far less. Even the chief executives and senior managers of government business enterprises, while better paid than the public servants and ministers of state to whom they answer, are paid well below equivalent scales in the private sector. Moreover, this is generally truer of positions with greater power or authority. For example, the prime minister is the most highly paid member of parliament yet is paid less than the chief justice of the High Court or the secretary to the Treasury or the governor of the Reserve Bank.

There is wisdom in this practice. The machinery of state exerts legitimate coercive power over its citizens. Such power can be turned to great pecuniary advantage, as the state does when it raises taxes to pursue legitimate public objectives. But this same coercive power can be diverted to the pursuit of private gain – a corrupt practice known as 'jobbery'. Keeping material rewards for public service below those available in equivalent roles in private life helps to deter jobbery by discouraging those whose primary motivation is pecuniary from seeking public office in the first place. Of course, neither should the rewards for public service be set so low that public officials are tempted to 'supplement' their official income by accepting bribes and favours (another corrupt practice known as 'graft'), as routinely occurs in some other countries.

If it's money you're after, stay away from public life. You'll either be resentful of the lower pay, or worse, be tempted to rort your allowances or, in some less savoury or even illegal way, profit from the power at your disposal. Abusing public office for private pecuniary gain is something our state institutions are well buttressed against and the penalties for breaching these defences are severe. There is no shame in setting out to make lots of money in life but don't ever think of seeking out public office as a way to do it – not if you want to stay out of prison!

Power not money

But perhaps it isn't money that interests you. A modest, if comfortable, material living standard is all you aspire to, and the luxurious trappings of a highly paid position in the private sector leave you cold. In that case, perhaps it's power that draws you to public office. You want to make a difference to the way people live their lives, and directing the coercive power of the state to that end appeals to you.

At first blush, this seems entirely innocuous. After all, designing and implementing public policy to enhance the public interest is surely what the best careers in public life are all about. Indeed, that's true; but power corrupts. The machinery of state can be used to aggrandise oneself and one's station just as surely as it can to enrich one's personal fortune. The defences against the latter are generally much stronger, as noted above. There are no laws against bureaucratic empire building or political grandstanding. Indeed, it would be almost impossible to formulate such laws, because so much depends on internal motivation and external interpretation.

To be fair, the system has an in-built dynamic in the form of the democratic process that helps to limit the exercise of power against the interests of citizens. Egomaniacal or narcissistic political leaders tend not to survive the political ambitions of their rivals, and bureaucrats whose power or influence threatens to eclipse that of ministers can be moved aside or even dismissed. Yet, for all this, the public interest is ill served by politicians or public officials who allow their personal ambitions for power and influence over the affairs of state to corrupt their pursuit of the public good.

If it's power rather than money that drives you, a career in public life can at least deliver what you seek. There is no doubt that high office confers power and influence over other people's lives; indeed, over the quality and direction of our corporate life as a nation. It may be you who sends your fellow citizens to war.

Former Prime Minister Paul Keating used to say, 'If you change the government, you change the country.' As citizens we allow governments to exercise such power and influence over our lives in the hope that they can improve our communal life in ways that we simply cannot when acting in our private capacity. This is the legitimate role of government: to achieve collectively what we as individual citizens wish to achieve but cannot do acting alone.

But the key is to remember whose interests are paramount when the great wheels of state are set in motion. The state exists to serve the interests of the people, whose broad consent is required even if those assigned to wield state power fear that some people don't know their own best interests. The 'nanny' state is unedifying and presumptuous. People might be ill informed but, within limits, they should be allowed to determine their own destiny.

The exceptional case of the conscientious objector to blood transfusions is just that – exceptional. Generally speaking, the democratic state is right to presume that people are a better judge of their own best interests than governments are. Of course, when interests collide, as in the case of compulsory immunisation to prevent the spread of communicable disease or conscription to military service in wartime emergency, the democratic state will override individual preference for the greater good.

For better or worse, we are lashed, like Ulysses, to the mast of the democratic ship of state. We must accept that the people will judge rightly most of the time, albeit sometimes with a lag, what best promotes the quality of their corporate life. By all means persuade, cajole and argue but give over all ambitions to public life if you cannot accept that, in the end, the will of the people prevails over all forms of self-appointed wisdom or authority. The state must remain the servant of the people and not the other way around, lest we descend into tyranny.

Serve the people

If you enter public life, understand that you are there to serve the people. Also understand that the people won't necessarily thank you for your service, or indeed show any signs of pleasure at being ministered to, even if you do so with a genuinely servant-hearted attitude. Do not expect thanks but be satisfied that you've done your duty, that is, served the people to the best of your ability.

And when your time comes to leave the stage, don't be surprised to find yourself quickly transformed from 'rooster' to 'feather duster'. You won't be the first, and better men and women than you have found themselves suddenly cast aside by an all-too-fickle, yet sovereign, public. Following his coronation, an aide to King George III remarked enthusiastically how the crowds adored his majesty, to which the king dryly replied that, given a mere year, they would be baying for his blood!

Of course, recognition may come in the form of official honours and the like, and retiring on a public service or parliamentary pension won't see you starve. But do not embark with this expectation or you will sow seeds that may germinate into bitterness and disappointment. The joy of public service is knowing that you brought your best to the task and sought to serve the public interest with all your heart and mind and strength. If you cannot conceive of this being enough to satisfy you at the end of the day, then look elsewhere. Public life is not for you.

What do you bring to public life?

If, having examined your motivations and calibrated your expectations, you still feel that public life is for you, you may well ask what skills the task requires. The answer to this question depends on the capacity in which you feel called to serve. Obviously, particular dimensions of public life require you to bring specialised training to the task.

If you want to work in public health, you'll need to be trained as a doctor, nurse or allied health professional or as a public administrator. If you want to work in the Treasury or the Reserve Bank, you'll need appropriate training in economics, finance and accounting. If you want to join the defence forces, you'll need specialist training as a soldier, sailor or airman. If you want to be a judge, you'll need to serve your time before the bench as a solicitor or barrister.

Specialised arms of the public service demand the same specialised skills as equivalent roles in the private sector where they exist. Some roles are exclusive to the public sector, like military intelligence personnel, public prosecutors and police officers. But even where the same roles exist in the private sector, the added dimension of public life is the attitude of heart discussed above. We call them 'public servants' for good reason: they're there to serve the public – not themselves – and not even their political masters, except as representatives of the wider public.

The emphasis on qualifications should not be carried too far. It's rather too easy for a younger generation raised on the need for advanced education to think that educational qualifications are essential for faithful and informed public service. Some even go so far as to say that a form of 'education suffrage' ought to apply in qualifying people to vote in elections or stand for parliament. Heaven forbid!

Our parliaments work best when they are broadly representative of the people; yes, the best and the worst of them, although clearly excluding criminals, the insane and non-citizens. For the parliament to win the consent of the people, the people must see their individual perspectives on display in the chamber, even if theirs are minority views and in some cases despised and ridiculed.

Filtering representation or participation in democratic processes to exclude the ill-educated or the bigoted or the malicious is fundamentally to corrupt and weaken democracy. Without the confidence of those whose views are excluded, the parliamentary process would sooner or later be discredited in the mind of the people, and cease to be acknowledged by them as a source of sovereign power.

The only formal requirement to enter public life in its parliamentary dimension ought to be that you are an adult citizen of sound mind who is not serving time in prison. Then come the questions of motivation and expectation discussed above. Apart from that, no-one should feel excluded from the opportunity to serve his or her fellow citizens in that most fundamental of public roles, as a representative in one or other of the chambers of parliament.

But again, even in roles that exist in the private sector, like that of a surgeon, advocate or teacher, there is an added extra when serving in public life that is missing from private life. If you work as a surgeon in the public sector, you must operate on whoever turns up at the hospital in whatever degraded condition you find them. If you are a magistrate, you must judge your fellow citizens impartially however much you despise them personally or the crimes they are alleged to have committed. If you teach in a public school, you must exercise your skill to teach whoever attends your classes, not just those you would choose if they were your private students.

If you are called to public life, you are there to serve the people without fear or favour. You do not have the luxury of choosing whom you serve, unlike your private sector counterparts. How do you feel about rushing to the rescue of a convicted sex offender whose safe house is engulfed in flames and whom you must resuscitate on the pavement before the ambulance arrives? Or allocating funds for the rehabilitation of a drug offender who has been in and out of detox units at least a dozen times in her short life? Or, as a senior public servant, crafting legislation to abolish the carbon tax which you entered public life for the sole purpose of establishing in the first place? Are you really cut out for public life?

And another thing ...

Depending on the particular role you have in public life, you may well find that your privacy is compromised beyond what you might have expected. Everyone expects politicians to be in the public eye; after all, they seek out publicity and place themselves squarely in its path. But everyone in public life is, to a greater or lesser degree, public property.

When the current governor of the Reserve Bank, Glenn Stevens, was appointed, there was some controversy about his suitability for the position. Soon newspaper reporters and television cameramen were staked outside his suburban home. Photographs of his house, his car and his family coming and going were published abroad. He didn't ask for this or seek it; quite the contrary. Nor did his family have anything to gain by this exposure; again, completely to the contrary. And yet this happened to a public official who had committed no crime or given cause for any public scandal beyond the fact that he had been selected to occupy one of the most powerful unelected roles in public office.

If you are fiercely protective of your privacy and that of your family, think again about public life. Not every public office is subject to the same scrutiny as governor of the Reserve Bank. Judges, for example, are very rarely in the public eye and have the defence of the contempt laws to protect them from overenthusiastic reportage. But at any time the public glare can light upon even junior officials.

In the final analysis, if you are in public life, you are a servant of the public, and the public can be a demanding taskmaster.

One final word

Paul Keating described public life as a 'high-wire act' – exhilarating but also involving high stakes. He also said that nothing in private life could compare with the deeply fulfilling challenge of serving the public interest. Not every former politician or public servant might agree, since many have gone on to successful and satisfying careers in private practice. I, for one, have moved from academic life, through public office and on to private practice. Many of the skills are transferable but it remains true that public office is uniquely subject to scrutiny and unwelcome invasion of privacy. If you think, with Oscar Wilde, that the only bad publicity is no publicity, then think again!

There is no doubt that public service is a high and noble calling, albeit demanding and oftentimes thankless. If you go into public life in the right frame of mind, seeking to serve rather than to be served, and not expecting recognition but accepting it graciously if offered, you will maximise your chances of making a positive and lasting difference to your own life and that of your fellow citizens. Many are called but few are chosen. If you are called and chosen, then serve well and serve truly.

---

1. Matt. 6:21.

Entering public life by accident

Melanie Irons

Melanie Irons initiated and administered the *Tassie Fires – We Can Help* Facebook page in response to the bushfires in Tasmania in January 2013. The site quickly gained support from more than 20,000 followers – many of them willing to lend a helping hand or offer shelter to those rendered homeless by fires in Tasmania – and demonstrated how communities can mobilise and work together. She is the proprietor of Booty, an award-winning personal training business, and will complete a Psychology PhD in 2015.

Melanie Irons argues, from her own experience, that the best way to enter public life is 'by accident': when you are doing something you are so passionate about so well that people want to know about you.

I will prepare, and some day my chance will come.
—Abraham Lincoln

The Tasmanian bushfires of January 2013 were Tasmania's worst in more than 40 years. Thousands of people were displaced, hundreds of homes were destroyed and thousands of hectares of bush and farmland were burnt. This is a story of a social media initiative which began in the immediate aftermath of the fires, and which continues today. The initiative facilitated a community-led response to the disaster, including the coordination of many volunteer hours, and in so doing saved property and livelihoods – and perhaps even lives. It filled the gaps left in the official response, and stands as a powerful lesson in the effectiveness of social media in times of crisis.

The emergency

Since 2006, I have been running my own personal training and fitness business, Booty. I have also been working towards completing a PhD in psychology at the University of Tasmania. These activities mean that I am out of the house for a few hours a day, but I do plenty of work from home.

On the afternoon of 4 January 2013 when the fires struck I was at home working, while also baby-sitting for a friend. I'd given myself a week off Booty to get some solid days in on my thesis. So I was listening to updates on local radio and monitoring the Tasmanian Fire Service website while pottering away at my research. I live in Mount Nelson, an area that has been hit by bushfires before. Though we weren't under any threat from these particular blazes, I was still very interested, and getting more and more worried about the people behind the fire front. Stories were already circulating about homes being destroyed, people being evacuated and others being trapped. Many of the details were murky, but it was clear a crisis was unfolding.

I had no experience in working in a fire situation, or in anything to do with emergency management in general. I was anxious to help but was limited by my lack of experience and by my immediate situation – stuck at home baby-sitting. So I posted a few questions on Facebook and details started to emerge: there was a refuge centre that needed volunteers; people were worried about their pets; others were offering donations. This was only the beginning. At the time I had no idea of the sheer quantity of information that would be requested, broadcast, shared and crowdsourced, or where my decision to voluntarily manage this information would lead. If I had I would probably have been overwhelmed by the thought of taking on a task for which I had *no* relevant experience or expertise. I merely had a strong sense that all this information – all this good will – needed to be organised. It was only a general thought, but it was enough to get me started on making the *Tassie Fires – We Can Help* Facebook page.[1]

I am not a social media expert and I still can't pinpoint why I actually acted on my desire to help. I had a thought, and I carried it out. I know I was emotionally connected to what was happening. It was clear at that stage that the worst of the fires was burning in the south-east, near the town of Dunalley. Friends of mine either lived in the area or had family there. This wasn't something happening in some far-off place on a map: in my mind I could see the eucalypts, the small country houses and the beaches. And from my house, 60 kilometres away, I could see the smoke and a huge orange glowing fireball against the black skies.

The fires in the south-east were on two peninsulas which are connected to the rest of Tasmania via the Arthur Highway. They started at Forcett, which is about 30 kilometres east of the city of Hobart, then moved into the Forestier Peninsula, which is connected to the mainland by only a canal bridge at Dunalley. Fire moved down the Peninsula and then leapt across Eagle Hawk Neck, another very thin strip of land that connects the Forestier Peninsula to the Tasman Peninsula and Port Arthur. The Forestier Peninsula was hit very hard. The Tasman Peninsula was not hit as hard but when the Arthur Highway was severed it was completely cut off. Thousands of people were stranded behind the fire-front. Homes lost power and telecommunication services were completely down. Thousands of tourists holidaying in the area were stranded. Some people had no access to conventional news sources for days in the initial stages of the disaster. There was a tremendous hunger for information – from those trapped behind the fire front, and from those trying to reach them.

Major bushfires were burning in two other areas: there was a huge fire in the Derwent Valley, which is about a 40-minute drive north-west of Hobart, and another one at Bicheno, a major tourism hotspot in Tasmania on the east coast.

The *Tassie Fires* page

I set up the *Tassie Fires* Facebook page with the vague notion that it could be something of a clearing-house. People could post with requests or problems, and solutions would be found (I hoped). I think I had expected it to be a small-scale operation, working at the local level, dealing with the sorts of smaller things that agencies and government departments weren't going to be that interested in while they dealt with the 'bigger' stuff. Perhaps we would make muffins for the firefighters! But to be honest I can't really tell you *what* I was thinking, because it seemed to just happen. I definitely felt like I was being moved forward by providence without much of my own conscious control.

I called my local ABC radio station, which at that time was providing rolling coverage of the emergency. I explained on air what I'd done and encouraged people to get involved.

Within a few hours the page had attracted 16,000 likes. Soon this number peaked at 20,815, and the page was being advertised and talked about across all different types of online and traditional media. People flocked to *Tassie Fires* to get information, to ask questions, to give support and to see what was needed. There were updates from police and emergency services, information from various charities about what they were doing and how people could contribute, while thousands of volunteers shared information about what they were up to and how others could help them. People were using the site to solve all sorts of problems – many of which I had never anticipated – like organising collection points, exchanging information with people on the 'inside', searching for missing family members, getting help with injured livestock, sourcing livestock food, and so on. Meanwhile, I was on the phone liaising with various government departments, agencies, charities, businesses and other groups to get the most reliable information available, then sharing as much information from every level as I could get my hands on through the *Tassie Fires* page.

I was on the laptop and phone for up to 20 hours a day, posting new content every three to four minutes. That became my job. I slept about five hours in the first three days, and I'm a bit embarrassed to admit I only had one shower in the first week! I sat on the same uncomfortable chair for a week before I had time to set up a proper workstation. If I left my chair for more than a few minutes I would be inundated with more posts, comments, private messages, emails, phone calls and text messages. My phone bill that month was an enormous $3,000 – which I am happy to say Telstra graciously waived.

None of this mattered; I just dealt with things moment by moment to help real people who were in real need. My job was easy compared to the challenges facing people fighting fires on the two Peninsulas, in the Derwent Valley and in Bicheno. I saw myself as helping to guide traffic, then letting everyone get on with things in an autonomous way in the real world. I would have been useless had it not been for the thousands of people coming forward to help. I was simply a switchboard helping to connect people; and they all went out there and did the hard yards. I had asked about six different people to keep an eye on the page from where they were and help answer questions they knew the answer to, so in this way, I had eyes everywhere. And without my family, best friend and partner feeding me and taking care of absolutely everything else in my life that I completely neglected for months on end, there's no way I could have kept going.

I created the page at about 10.15 pm on the day the fires struck. Here's a snapshot of *some* of things that happened on the page in the first 24 hours, adapted from the archives of the page's timeline:

Many organisations offered to care for animals; many others offered food; St Vincent de Paul's provided donation information; babysitters and child carers offered their services; private offers of agistment were made; horse floats and transport were made available; chainsawing, accommodation, transport, tents, brand new baby clothes, a water tanker and water pumps were offered; trucks and semi-trailers were made available; MP Rebecca White offered her paddock and floats; information was provided on the missing persons hotline and refuge centres; offers of help came in from everywhere (Burnie, Victoria, Mackay ...); someone bought out all the bottled water in Hobart and was told where to take it; people who experienced Black Saturday in Victoria offered advice; 20kg bags of ice were arranged; there were requests to move people off the Peninsula; there were requests about missing relatives and friends; the first organised fundraiser I heard of was announced at 11:30 pm; there were offers from WA; people made food to drop at fire stations; toilets and showers were made available at the Sorell Cricket Grounds; a balloon entertainer was organised at 1.00 am on the second day to head down to the RSL later that day; info about The Link was provided for young adults; information was shared on lost and found pets; a plumber offered his help; by 8:30 am on the second day I had spoken to the Hobart Hurricanes rep (and a coin collection was organised for the following week); Telstra made pay phones free; the Tasmania Disability Lobby gave advice for any disabled individuals affected; a Maxi Taxi owner offered his car; supplies were delivered to an expecting mum; Echidna Kids got new toys out to those affected; fire stations communicated about what they did and did not need; diabetics offered hard-to-get items to other diabetics; Nubeena Pharmacy offered assistance even though their phones were down; a builder offered his skills; Diabetes Tasmania communicated with us; the Commonwealth Bank announced that certain branches would be open on the Saturday; Chemmart Sorell donated goods; Bendigo Bank and RACT let us know they had set up their money collections; North West Community Legal Centre gave advice; mental health helplines were shared; information was shared about phone lines being up or down; doctors at the Private Hospital filled scripts free of charge ...

Let me give just one example to illustrate the role and impact of the *Tassie Fires* page. It concerns the plight of a particular oyster hatchery in Dunalley. The hatchery contained around 60 million baby oysters. About 40–45 per cent of the oysters grown in Australia come from this business. It also employs 35 people locally, and about 200 family businesses from the southern part of Australia rely on oyster spat from this hatchery. The hatchery only narrowly escaped the flames but in the days following the fire, another crisis emerged. Power had been lost, and there was nothing to keep the oysters cool or to feed them. Baby oysters are very sensitive to temperature – even slight changes cause stress and can kill them after about a 12- to 24-hour time frame. A distraught local farmer contacted me, having heard about the Facebook page. He had already seen people using the website and figured it was his last chance to get some help.

On January 6 (about 36 hours after the fire first began) I posted a message on his behalf:

> Hi everyone – posted this earlier. They have had replies which is great, they have enough electricians and engineers.
> THEY STILL NEED SOME BIG GENERATORS. Can you help? Can you call someone?
> So no electricians/engineers needed, but GENERATORS
> *URGENT* ARE YOU AN ELECTRICIAN, AN ELECTRICAL ENGINEER or OWN A BIG, BIG GENERATOR? Can you contact someone who is or does?
> Dunnalley needs you NOW
> Ben at Cameron's Oysters just spoke to me: They really need two 30 to 50 kva 3 phase generators (diesel better) – they need it because they employ 35 people in the area who are not around but ALSO they supply half the Australian industry with baby oysters – if they don't get a few generators up and running in the next 8 hours there will be no oysters next year! CALL BEN NOW IF YOU CAN HELP [xxxx xxx xxx]

Everyone got to work. Within a few hours, we had sourced three generators and got them through with police escort, while more than enough electrical engineers and electricians arrived by boat or via police escort on land. In the very early hours of Monday morning, the hatchery was back in action.

The following morning, I was able to post the following message:

READ THIS FOR SOME ABSOLUTELY AMAZING NEWS

Just speaking to Ben, the owner of Cameron's Oyster Farm. Yesterday I got on to them because they desperately needed some big generators, electricians, and electrical engineers. The word went out here and I rang the ABC too.

Here's what he had to say today:

We have managed to save an estimated 80% of our livestock at one of our sites – we are thrilled about this. 35 jobs in the local community have been SAVED. We have over 200 customers in other areas in Tassie and South Australia who rely heavily on us to supply livestock – so we have literally saved dozens of families and family businesses in regional Tas and South Australia.

This is all because the word went out and we got generators and sparkies who came out and stayed out there for hours yesterday.

So an enormous thank you to the Hobart community from Ben, the boss of Cameron's Oysters (third generation oyster farmer)

At present – they don't need anything ☺

Through everyone networking, we managed to source everything the hatchery needed. This one example showed how the page helped connect volunteers and provide immediate assistance. The owners of the hatchery are certain help would not have arrived in time if they had tried to go through the official channels.

After the fires

In the week following the outbreak of the fires, more than 26,000 different people were actively engaged with the page each day – that is, they clicked on a link, shared something or commented on a post. After 35 weeks, more than 2.6 million people were exposed to the page. The *Tassie Fires* page went through distinct phases. It was at its busiest for the first two weeks, providing support, information and deliveries when very little else was available while the roads were closed. Activity then declined bit by bit for the following weeks and months, as the recovery moved forward.

Although the news media move on quickly from one disaster to the next newsworthy story, for those who have experienced the fires, the physical recovery can be at least a 10-year process – let alone the psychological recovery, which can last a lifetime. The page is still in operation, and its following has barely dropped off. However, as at January 2015, I am posting only when really necessary. I am happy for the page to lie dormant while it is not needed, rather than posting just for the sake of it.

People know where the page is and they will presumably come back to it in the next fire season. Indeed, in May last year we had a flare up of a fire in Tea Tree, and a large local business contacted me to ask if I could help them source a generator as they had lost refrigeration power. Within 20 minutes of me posting on the page they found the help they needed.

Initially, I felt that once the emergency was over, my role would be complete and my life would go back to normal. However, as the weeks and months passed, I increasingly found myself being asked to address audiences about my experiences. Groups from charities to academics to emergency managers to governments to police forces sought my advice on their social media strategies, and how to work with the community. I realised that my role was not complete.

Several people said to me, 'Don't wait for a fire to build a fire station'. I didn't want to think there would be a next time, but I could see that 'building a fire station', even if it was never used, was better than not having one at all. And I realised that it was up to me. So I began to think about how I could improve what I had done for next time.

I knew that the Facebook page really benefited from having an attached website that had been set up in a flurry by a generous, industrious and intuitive woman in Melbourne, Linda Farrell. I knew that if we could set up a more permanent, very robust website that could work in tandem with the Facebook page, our response next time could be even better. Around March 2013 I started work on the website. This entailed a good three months of writing content, working with designers and collaborating with local businesses. In June 2013, with sponsorship from 13 local businesses, I launched the website.[2] It is to be a companion to the Facebook page, should we need to mobilise as a community again in the face of bushfires.*

* The Facebook page is an excellent vehicle for posting current problems and getting them resolved quickly. But it's not ideal for information of more permanent importance. The new website enables me to store important information in a much more structured and accessible way.

It was September 2013 before the phone calls and emails petered out (a blessing in disguise because I was exhausted!). Having had a relatively quiet bushfire season over 2013–14 and 2014-15 (so far), I feel ready to do it over again should I be needed. And this time, I will have a formal team, ready to help me.

In response to recommendations from the independent Bushfire Inquiry, our state government has since launched an excellent website called Alert TAS, which comes with a Facebook page and a Twitter feed. And the Tasmania Police have become very active in the social media landscape. Both these things have meant that we as a state are better prepared for the next bushfire emergency.

The last two years have been incredibly challenging, and yet extremely rewarding. Seeing what my fellow Tasmanians went through in 2013 and being able to help in just one small way was a moving experience. It has been an honour to have so many different groups statewide, nationwide and worldwide interested in my story and keen to learn from my new-found knowledge and expertise. And it's deeply satisfying to see people willing to move forward in a space that many official groups are exceptionally wary of and nervous about. There is considerable fear around all the unknowns inherent in social media-based responses, and the risks associated with the citizen journalist having a voice and being able to mobilise others. Spontaneity and trust are two of the many key elements of an effective community-led response – two things that are not normal ingredients in traditional emergency management command-and-control style responses. But this is changing and we are seeing more groups embrace social media, albeit slowly and with plenty of rules, policies and caveats!

About entering public life

So I entered public life, well and truly! Not as a politician or a public servant in the traditional sense, but as a public servant in another sense of the term. No selection committee appointed me to the role, and none of it was planned. But when I suddenly saw an opportunity present itself to me, I felt like I had been preparing for it my whole life, and I knew that I needed to grab it and run.

The page was such a success because it was so organic. There is an important insight to be gained here. In all my talks about *Tassie Fires*, one thing has come up again and again: I created the page because an opportunity presented itself, and because I saw only infinite possibilities, and no boundaries. If I had had experience in emergency management I think I might have only seen the boundaries, the rules, the regulations. But in my mind, we as a community could achieve absolutely anything; we could find a way to make everything work, including finding ways around those boundaries when they did present themselves. I thought – provided we use common sense and think critically about our decisions and actions – how hard can this be?

With the benefit of reflection about the *Tassie Fires* experience, some other important lessons have emerged for me.

Observations on social media

Who knew social media could have been so effective? Social media is so new that there is not much research out there yet about how it can be utilised and used for good during emergencies.

Of course it is hard to pinpoint exactly who makes what happen, but as long as the word is spread and the solution is found, then social media and the crowd are doing their job. My approach all along was to let people know we were there, but not to get in their faces and harass them.

The social media space is often regarded suspiciously by authorities and emergency services as something that can't be trusted and should be kept at arm's length. There's a view that it's too prone to rumour-mongering or the spread of false information. These fears have some merit but are usually blown completely out of proportion, and they shouldn't obscure the fact that social media can also be tremendously beneficial during times of crisis – for example, myth busting, providing psychological support, spreading information faster than any other means possible, crowdsourcing to gather intelligence or solving problems using human resources that you simply would not have access to any other way. In fluid, ever-changing environments where information needs to be shared quickly, social media is a valuable communication tool. In fact, it's essential.

Having seen the incredible ability of social media, I wanted to know more. So I've changed my doctoral thesis. Using the *Tassie Fires* Facebook page as a case study, I am looking into how social media is used and how it functions in times of crisis. I am hoping that the results of my research can add to the currently small body of knowledge around social media in times of crisis and create some insight into the real benefits of social media, using evidence rather than simple anecdotes.

Self-determination theory

From my studies in psychology, a theory that has always held great interest for me is 'self-determination theory'. This was originally developed in the 1970s by Edward L Deci and Richard M Ryan at the University of Rochester,[3] and has since been adapted and developed a great deal by other scholars.[4]

The core of the theory is that humans have three innate needs, and that if we can satisfy them we are working towards our best growth and our best functioning.

Self determination theory: three innate human needs

1. Competence – feeling that we can effectively control outcomes, have success, master our environments or tasks; feeling that we are good at what we are doing
2. Relatedness – feeling connected to others, cared for by others; being able to interact as part of a community; feeling that we belong
3. Autonomy – feeling that we have independence and freedom; feeling that we are in charge and can make our own decisions; wanting to be the causal agent in charge of our own lives.

Just as I have done for years with my business Booty, I consciously based *Tassie Fires – We Can Help* on those three principles.

Competence

I worked hard to give people plenty of volunteering options so that they could do something within their capabilities. For example, not everyone had spare money to donate to the Red Cross, or was mobile enough to volunteer, or could commit to specific hours helping for an organisation. But we could utilise their time or their information-gathering skills, or perhaps they could do one simple delivery for us or could link someone else up with someone in their own pre-existing networks. Everyone who came to the page could help in a way that suited their abilities and availability, which left them feeling like they could indeed contribute and make a difference.

Relatedness

The *Tassie Fires* page became a related community almost immediately and I made it very clear that everyone was welcome, that no one would be ignored or turned away, and that everyone could contribute. The page emphasised positivity, encouragement and support, and I continually thanked and acknowledged people and told the amazing news stories that were coming through to help inspire people and develop that pride and community spirit. No one was blocked or banned; everyone was heard. Running the page reinforced for me that even though you may not be part of a particular geographical, relational community, you can certainly create an online community where everyone feels that they belong, that they can relate and that they can make a difference.

Autonomy

Autonomy was a very easy principle to foster, as when I first started the page I had about four pieces of information and that was it! So I was relying so heavily on everyone else – what he or she could do, what information they could share, what people they knew, what connections they had. I needed everyone to be doing their thing in the real or online world in an autonomous way and then to bring that knowledge, those connections or those skills back to me so that we could pool them. Because I wasn't issuing strict instructions or making demands, and instead was making suggestions and providing guidelines, people had a huge amount of autonomy to help in ways that they wanted to. Whatever the polar opposite of micromanaging is, that's what I was doing.

Final thoughts

If *you* are fulfilling the criteria of self-determination theory in your own life – if what you are doing makes you feel competent, related and autonomous – then I would argue you are doing exactly the job that you are meant to be doing, and sooner or later you will be known for it in the public domain. Getting to this place entails having chosen the right job, the right workplace or the right hobby, *and* having surrounded yourself with the right people. If you are doing things that don't bring you excitement, that you aren't actually all that good at, that don't make you feel connected to others, that you feel you have no agency over, and (perhaps most important of all) that don't fit with your authentic values … you need to think about change.

I would never encourage someone to enter public life simply because they want to be well known or famous (or notorious!). I would argue that the best way to enter public life is by accident: because you love what you are doing so much, you are so good at it, you get so much value out of it, and it makes you feel such a high degree of competence, relatedness and autonomy that people want you for your skills. If you have that as your foundation, you will be entering public life for authentic reasons, and you won't need much guidance or mentoring from people around you. You'll be able to trust yourself that you are doing everything right because you have built your career on what really matters to you, and where your strengths lie.

Oh, and a good education, an amazing family and a whole lot of luck certainly help!

---

1. Facebook, *Tassie Fires – We Can Help*, www.facebook.com/tassiefireswe-canhelp.
2. *Tassie Fires – We Can Help*, www.tassiefireswecanhelp.com.
3. Deci, E & Ryan, R (eds), 2002, *Handbook of self-determination research*, University of Rochester Press, Rochester, NY.
4. *Self-determination theory*, www.selfdeterminationtheory.org.

Finding your voice as a leader: speaking and writing to be followed

Christopher Balmford

Christopher Balmford holds a BA and an LLB (hons) from Monash University. He is an internationally recognised expert in plain language. He is the immediate past president of Clarity, a worldwide group of lawyers and others who advocate for plain language – see www.clarity-international.net.

Christopher is the founder and managing director of Words and Beyond, a plain-language training, rewriting and cultural-change consultancy launched in 1999 – see wordsandbeyond.com. Clients include major law firms, public companies, government agencies, the United Nations, and the European Central Bank. He is also the founder and former managing director of online legal document provider Cleardocs, launched in 2002 – see cleardocs.com. In June 2012, Thomson Reuters acquired Cleardocs.

People everywhere need to improve the clarity of their communications by taking responsibility for how their message is received – whether it's received by a listener or a reader.

When we are reading or listening, most of us prefer communications with a logical structure that reflects our needs. When reading, we like frequent and meaningful headings, clear design and graphics. As readers or listeners, we better understand short sentences that use everyday words – with unfamiliar concepts explained, perhaps with an example.

Yet when we are at work the messages we write, or say, so often fail to meet the standards that we expect as a reader or listener. Indeed, the tone and style of many of our own messages would make us blush and cringe if we read them, or listened to them at home. At work, we need to prepare and send communications in a tone and style that we, as readers or listeners, would readily understand – even if we are uninformed about the topic. If we do, we'll do our jobs better. Our readers and listeners – whether they are customers, clients, colleagues, investors, suppliers, regulators, or anyone – will appreciate our clarity. The style and tone of our communications help us get our message across – they might even enhance our, and our organisation's, brand.

The world isn't made of atoms; it's made of stories.
—Muriel Rukeyser

Good writers make their readers feel smart.
—Bryan Garner

Take responsibility for how your message is received.
—Julian Canny

A place to start

If I asked you for a word – a simpler word – to replace 'numerous', you'd probably say 'many'. If I asked you for a simpler word than 'facilitate', you'd probably say 'assist' or better still 'help'. And for a simpler word than 'terminate', you'd say 'end'.

So are you someone who says:

> There are numerous ways we can facilitate the termination of [something]

or someone who says:

> There are many ways we can help you end [something]?

And which person – which leader – would you rather be? You can choose to be a wordy leader who seems to aim for pretension – perhaps unconsciously – or a direct leader, who cares more for comprehension.

To be sure, there's more to clear communication than the words we use. It's also crucial that:

- we structure our ideas – we put them in a certain order – in a way that works for our readers or listeners, or our followers
- we use visuals – the design of a document and tables, charts, images or other graphics – to help communicate our written or spoken messages.

If you're reading this book, it's likely that you're regarded as a good communicator. Fair enough, too.

Think of some great leaders. They are often the great communicators: Lincoln. Churchill. Gandhi. Most of us know at least a few lines from something they wrote or said. More recently, think of Aung San Suu Kyi, whose clear, simple statements hold our attention and galvanise wide-ranging international support.

But many leaders – even some at the highest level of politics – are renowned for waffling, or for using unfamiliar words and long impenetrable sentences, or for speaking in a tone that doesn't work for their audiences and purposes – a style and tone that sabotages their message.

To be sure, sometimes leaders are deliberately vague. They are vague for a whole range of understandable – though perhaps not always legitimate – reasons. (Usually those reasons boil down to ducking the issue, etc.) But too often leaders are wordy even when they're striving to be understood.

This is true when leaders speak and when they write. Indeed, at work many of us write documents the style of which would make us blush and cringe if we had to read the document out loud to a friend or family member.

Here's an example. Many years ago, I was employed in the Melbourne office of a national law firm. But I worked on secondment for a client in Sydney. One Friday afternoon, a partner I knew slightly in my firm's Sydney office rang and asked me to help him out. He had developed a set of documents for a client and needed to deliver them on Monday. The documents had to be as plain as could be. He'd gone way over budget – which meant I couldn't bill my time, sigh – but he still felt the documents weren't clear enough. Effectively, he asked me to give him my Sunday for free and to edit the documents to improve their clarity. I was happy to help. A few hours later that Friday afternoon the documents arrived by courier. (This was in the days before email.) There was a covering letter – typed, and printed on the firm's letterhead – addressed to me:

> Dear Sir,
>
> We refer to our earlier conversation and enclose the documents for your review. We look forward to your comments in due course.
>
> Yours faithfully
>
> [Handwritten name of the firm – *the partner hadn't even signed his name!*]

The letter irritated me. A lot. (Mind you, I edited the documents anyway.)

I would have been much happier with a handwritten note on a 'With compliments' slip. Something like:

Dear Christopher,

Thanks for this. I owe you lunch.

Cheers

[His handwritten first name]

As I see it, the letter from the lawyer was a classic example of someone automatically using an inflated overblown voice. In a Zen sense, the writer was not 'in the moment' when he wrote the letter. He did not even remotely consider his purpose (asking a favour), his audience (a colleague) or the impact of the tone of his request (irritation and delay).

Messages and stories

As humans we've evolved to tell and hear stories. For millennia, that's how we shared information, navigated, and understood the universe and our place in it – around fires on the Serengeti; on the plains of the Mongolian deserts; in the shadow of sacred rocks in the Kimberley.

People follow leaders who tell stories. Stories thread our communities and our villages together. They are the heartbeat of political movements. They generate the creative energies that initiate squillion dollar mergers of big corporations. They are the colour and texture of visions and dreams and ideals – in boardrooms, in parliaments, in articles, in proposals, in policy statements, and still around campfires and in the shadows of rocks.

People follow leaders who tell stories that are clear and strong, and whose stories the listener can both understand and find themselves in. You possibly have a message you want to share with a wide audience. To successfully convey your message and inspire others to capture your vision, you'll need to tell intelligible, engaging stories. Stories that ring true when you tell them. Stories that are consistent with who you are as a person, and with what you and your organisation stand for.

To do that, you'll almost certainly (unless you're a dancer, or painter, perhaps) either be:

- speaking – in a conversation, a meeting, or presentation, or
- writing – a 'document' of one sort or another, whether printed

on paper, lit up as pixels on a screen, or written in the clear blue sky.

Sometimes your audience, whether listening or reading, will be cheering your message. Sometimes they'll be resisting it. Or they may be doing something else – for example, checking email on their smartphone, or thinking about what to get for lunch. The clarity of your message should be the same for your audience whether that audience is cheering or booing. And the clarity of your message should keep them focused.

Regardless of your audience's response to the content of your message, you need to take responsibility for whether they understand it. For how clear it is. For whether it is meaningful to them and resonates with them, or leaves them hearing only noise.

Whether you're speaking or writing, you might have some visual, graphic support – perhaps even some dancers. That visual support is a good thing.

But let's think about words. About the sentences we build with them. And about the documents, or stories, we build with our sentences. Let's think about our voice. In particular, let's think about whether the clarity of your written and spoken voice enhances, or sabotages, your reputation.

To lead, you'll almost certainly need the 'voice' of a leader – in the same way as authors have a 'voice'. (I'm not concerned here with what you sound like when you talk – with your timbre, resonance and projection. For those, consult a voice coach. Rather, I'm concerned with the clarity of your message, with how you own your voice as being the voice of a leader – someone who believes in their subject, feels for their subject, and who wants to share that belief convincingly.)

Our voice: spoken versus written

Speaking

When most of us speak, we couch what we are saying and how we say it to suit our audience. Sometimes we do that subconsciously – for example, when we're talking to a pet. Sometimes we do that consciously – for example, when we're leading a discussion in an important meeting at work, or speaking at a conference, or maybe, one day, when we're responding to a question in parliament.

At the same time as couching our spoken message to suit our audience, we couch it to suit our purpose. Often subconsciously – for example, the voice an employee uses to talk to their manager …

- in a conversation at a social function about how great it is that their organisation just completed a major project successfully, on time and on budget, and in a way that confounded its competitors and enabled the team to grow, to learn and become stronger …

is very different from the voice that same employee uses when speaking to that same manager …

- at the employee's annual performance review when they ask for a 25 per cent bonus, a 30 per cent pay rise and whether they can work out of the Paris office for a couple of months a year, business class travel will be fine thanks.

That's how our audience and purpose help shape our voice when we speak.

Writing

When most of us write at work, we do so without thinking about the who and the why – that is, without thinking about our audience and our purpose. We put our fingers to the keyboard, and away we go. Usually, our 'work voice' kicks in and takes over. Our work voice tends to be fairly heavy, formal, traditional and impersonal. As was the voice of the lawyer I mentioned above who asked me to review his documents over a weekend.

When writing at work, most of us automatically use the same sort of voice regardless of whether we are writing to:

- a constituent to explain a policy position
- a colleague, asking them to provide us with some information
- a large organisation about a dispute between it and our organisation, or
- an individual with some good news.

Many people are proud of their work voice. It gives them confidence, makes them feel like they really are a biologist or a banker or whatever it is they are. I remember the moment in my final year as a law student when a friend of mine – a medical student – asked me a question about a legal issue he had read about in the paper. Lo and behold, I knew the answer. Even better, when I explained it to him, even I thought I sounded like a lawyer. What relief I felt: the feeling that, 'hey, maybe I'll be able to do this after all'.

Most of us are familiar with our work voice. It affects us when we speak and when we write. We especially notice our work voice when it materialises in an inappropriate context. For example, imagine you're at a social event chatting with people, as you do. Then someone asks you a serious question about something related to your area of expertise. All of a sudden you're being consulted professionally. You start to answer. You might stand a little straighter, put your shoulders back. Your work voice kicks in without being summoned. The first thing you notice is that when you start to speak, your cheeks feel a little funny and your words aren't coming out quite right – you feel a little slurry or odd. The second thing you notice is that the person you're speaking to suddenly has a baffled expression on their face because they have no idea what you're saying. That's your work voice.

Somewhere along the way to becoming qualified in our field and working for a few years, most of us develop a work voice. When we speak, we can sense from our audience's response whether our work voice is allowing us to communicate successfully. If it isn't, we can try again, say things another way, explain something that we had assumed the audience understood. The trouble is, there is less opportunity to do that when we write, usually much less.

And the double trouble is that most of us use our work voice for nearly everything we write – no matter how inappropriate it is to the audience and to the purpose of our writing.

Perhaps the reason many of us so habitually use our work voice is that we want to sound professional. Fair enough, too. Yet, if we think about the hallmarks of 'professional' writing, we often steer towards 'formal' and 'traditional'. But 'formal' plus 'traditional' doesn't equal 'professional'. It equals pompous and out-of-date. In fact, we can write something that's warm, human, clear and friendly, and still be completely professional. Indeed, those very qualities often equate with understandable, accessible, persuasive voices – with the voices of leaders who move people.

What matters is that we speak and write in a way that is consistent with our brand.

A sense of our brand, or our organisation's brand

An organisation's reputation is expressed through a clearly defined brand. That's true whether the organisation is a public listed company, an NGO, a charity or a political party. The brand represents the essence of the organisation: everything it stands for, and everything that differentiates it from its competitors in the eyes of the public, customers, clients, stakeholders or voters. To quote the global management consultants McKinsey & Company:

> A name becomes a brand, when consumers associate it with a set of tangible, or intangible, benefits that they obtain from that product or service. To build brand equity, a company needs to do two things: first, distinguish its product from others in the market; second, align what it says about its brand in advertising and marketing with what it actually delivers.[1]

Perhaps the best way to understand the concept of brand is to imagine someone offering you a sports car and asking you to choose from three leading models, each from a different manufacturer. The vehicles are labelled Model A, Model B, and Model C. The trouble is you have to choose your car on the basis of the anonymous manufacturers' vehicle specifications and performance criteria (no photographs of the cars either).

I expect you'd have trouble choosing – until I told you that Model A was a Corvette, Model B was an Alfa Romeo, and Model C was a Volkswagen. With that information alone, most of us would choose one of the cars immediately – who cares about the torque ratios, the widget factor, or the number of what-have-yous in the thingy. (Personally, I'd take the Volkswagen.)

We're able to decide which car to buy as soon as we know the names of the manufacturers because of branding – the intangible thing that influences our buying decision so much more than product specifications and performance criteria.

As individuals, we have a reputation, which is – in a sense – our brand. Think Nelson Mandela. Albert Einstein. Angela Merkel. Michelle Obama. The Dalai Lama. Roger Federer. Madonna and her ever-evolving brand.

The key point about building and maintaining a brand is achieving 'alignment' (as stated in the above quotation) between what is promised and what is delivered. That's equally true for the brand of an organisation and the reputation of a leader. If what is promised doesn't align with what is delivered, then any campaigning, advertising and marketing is undone when the audience's – the followers' – expectations are not met.

An important aspect of an organisation's brand is its documents – these form the voice of its brand. And so do yours as an individual. You need to think about the voice of your personal brand in your writing and in your speaking. You need to make sure that the claims you make about yourself are aligned with what you actually deliver – content, style and tone – when you open your mouth to talk, and when you put words on paper, on a screen or in the sky. We need to make sure our documents are clear before we send them out into the world to deliver our message.

Let's think about organisations and then apply the thinking to ourselves.

Voice of the brand

The people who create written communications for an organisation are creating the voice of the organisation's brand. The voice of the brand is vital to the success of some organisations – particularly those that provide intangibles. Their communications may be the only thing of any substance that a member, voter, client, customer or supporter has to go on when, for example, they are:

- deciding whether to support a cause, a political party, or that party's candidate or leader
- deciding whether to buy a product or use a service
- working out how to use a product, or
- trying to understand and apply some professional advice they've received.

Each time someone reads an organisation's document, they connect with the organisation's brand. Too often, that moment of truth is sour: the document is formal, impersonal and awkward. It fails to live up to the values that are the foundation of the organisation's brand.

Organisations spend fortunes on logos, visual identities and advertising. They do so with the aim of creating or refining their brand in an attempt to woo and retain members, customers, clients, voters or the like. Yet the very same organisations pay little attention to the voice of the brand, even though it is the voice of the brand that the audience has to deal with – often when the audience is busy at work, or weary at the end of the day, or would rather be doing something else.

An organisation needs to treat the voice of its brand as seriously as it treats its visual identity, its customer service, and the flowers in its reception space. A simple way for the organisation to do so is to measure its documents against its brand values, its brand promise, its mission and its vision.

Consider this simple letter from a major global organisation. (You might try to guess which one – though I'll tell you later.) The letter was sent to a former colleague of mine in response to a letter she wrote to the organisation seeking information to help with her tertiary studies. (I need to mention that the information my friend asked for was not at all secret or valuable.)

Here's the letter:

> Dear Ms X
>
> Thank you for requesting information about [name of the company]. We appreciate your interest in our company and our products.
>
> Due to the sheer volume of student requests for information we receive, we are not able to provide detailed answers to specific questions about our company. However, there is a comprehensive packet of marketing information available to students.
>
> Please note, that as we are a [particular type of company], we are not required to produce a [certain publication] and this information is considered proprietary in nature.
>
> Our student information packet is now available for review on our corporate website, www.[web address] in the section titled 'All about [name of company]'. All information contained in our student packet is available on this website.
>
> In case you do not have internet access, we have enclosed a copy of our current student packet.
>
> As most of the information published about [name of the company] is available in magazine articles, we strongly recommend that you look through the *Reader's guide to periodic literature*, which is an annual index of magazine articles. This should be available to you at a public or university library.

Thanks again for contacting us. Please call us at [number] if we may be of further assistance.

Sincerely,

Let's consider a few questions about the letter and the organisation. I need to emphasise here that I'm not concerned about the content of the letter. I completely accept that the organisation does not have to answer every set of questions it gets from students. My concerns are only with the letter's style and tone.

So to a few questions about the letter:

- *How does the letter make you feel about the organisation?* I find the letter insincere – for example, it seems to give with one hand and take with the other. Then in the last paragraph, the writer invites the reader to ring for more information, but that's the last thing the writer wants the reader to do. And to suggest a tertiary student look for information in the library is pretty patronising. Also, the letter is defensive, impersonal and repetitive.
- *Is the organisation cool?* Not at all.
- *Do you want to work there?* No. *Buy its products?* Not really. *Invest in the organisation?* Hmmm, investment is different.

When we're reading the letter, its words, structure and visuals are the voice of the organisation's brand – and that voice gives us a sense of the organisation.

One more question about the letter. *What sort of organisation might the letter be from?* Hard to tell really: maybe it's a bank, a pharmaceutical company, or a government body ...

Actually, the letter was from Levi's, the clothing manufacturer.

How did the letter measure up against your perception of that organisation's brand?

I use the letter as an example in a plain-language training course I run. Most participants on the course say there is a massive disconnect between how they feel about that organisation – that is, its brand – and how the letter reveals that organisation to be. That disconnect is so strong that when I reveal the organisation's logo, the participants nearly always respond with an audible gasp, or laughter.

The importance of your brand's voice

For some organisations the voice of the brand doesn't matter a great deal – for example, for a clothing manufacturer. We don't care too much about the way a clothing manufacturer writes to us – if it ever does, other than in advertising and labelling.

But for some organisations, the voice of the brand is of vital importance – for example, for a radio station. If we don't like the voice of the brand of a radio station, we're never going to listen to that station. The radio station has got nothing to give us other than its voice.

If we had a spectrum showing the relative importance of the voice of the brand to an organisation, we could put a clothing manufacturer at one end of the spectrum and a radio station at the other end.

At the same end of the spectrum as the radio station – where the voice of the brand is vital – are organisations like political parties, law firms, financial services organisations, many government bodies, providers of medicines, any organisation that gives its staff or its customers a set of instructions or a product manual, and any organisation that is campaigning, whether for the status quo or for change.

And for leaders, the voice of their brand is at least as important as it is for the radio station.

Consider a lawyer in a law firm and the relationships that that individual and their firm have with their client. The moment of truth comes – for the lawyer and the firm – when the client reads something, say a letter of advice, that the lawyer has written. In that moment, it doesn't matter how brilliant the writer is as a lawyer, or how pleasant they are to deal with (or how lovely the flowers are in reception). What matters is how easy it is for the client to use the letter of advice to help them make a decision about their campaign, their business or their life. And in that moment, it doesn't matter whether the client is sitting:

- in caucus contemplating a constitutional challenge
- at their kitchen table thinking about a claim against their insurance company, or
- in a huge corner office – at the top of a tall building with the

logo of their organisation in neon on the top – thinking about taking over a competitor.

That moment of truth matters to the client because the document matters to them as a reader. If that wasn't so, they wouldn't be reading the document – and they wouldn't be paying the law firm to write it.

The moment when the client reads the document is either a brand-damaging or a brand-enhancing moment. The client reading the law firm's letter quickly senses whether the way in which the firm communicates lives up to the claims the firm makes about itself in its advertising and marketing material. The reader can 'smell' whether the firm's advertising and marketing puffery reflects the way the firm provides its services.

To make that point using the McKinsey & Company language (quoted above), the reader is made abundantly aware of whether the document – a key aspect of the law firm's behaviour and of the service it delivers – is aligned with the firm's claims about itself. If the document fails to live up to the brand, then the firm's brand is damaged. However, if the document and the brand are aligned, then the moment when the document is read is a brand-enhancing moment: the client is likely to feel happier about using the firm, paying the invoice, coming back next time and referring other clients to the firm.

And these moments matter to leaders who need to use their brand-enhancing voice – both spoken and written – to engage with people and to win them to a cause. A leader's voice needs to ensure their message is easily understood, strongly felt, and passionately adopted. The moment of truth for a leader comes when a follower – or potential follower – is deciding whether to put their name to the cause, make the donation, spread the message or vote the leader's way.

Whatever your role is today (leader or not), take a look at the documents around you – especially the documents your organisation produces and, even more especially, the documents you write or approve. Check the clarity of the voice you and your colleagues use when you write or speak. Then measure your organisation's written and spoken voice against its brand values – that is, measure them against everything your organisation stands for, and everything that differentiates it from its competitors.

If brand and voice are aligned, then well and good. But in numerous organisations, brand and voice aren't aligned. There's a disconnect, and that disconnect is disconcertingly obvious to clients, customers or followers. If that's the case in your organisation (or for you), then set about reworking the voice to align it with the brand.

Going on that journey and achieving that aim will help you develop and refine your voice – a voice that likely will work for you as a leader. And when you're leading, strive to tell clear stories. Stories that will inspire people to follow you – especially people sitting on the fence, or the other side of the fence.

---

1. McKinsey & Company Journal 1997, in Friedman, A, 1999, *The Lexus and the olive tree*, HarperCollins, Sydney, p. 189.

Reflections on public advocacy

Richard Cogswell

His Honour Judge Richard Cogswell SC graduated in law from the University of Tasmania in 1974. He was awarded a Rhodes Scholarship and spent the following two years at Oxford University, obtaining an MA in philosophy and politics. He was admitted to the NSW bar in 1981 and spent 10 years in Wentworth Chambers, practising mostly in civil work with some criminal work. In 1991 he took an appointment as a Crown prosecutor and practised for the next 10 years from the Crown Prosecutors' Chambers in Sydney, prosecuting jury trials in the District and Supreme Courts and appearing regularly in the NSW Court of Criminal Appeal. He took silk in 1997 and was appointed Queen's counsel in Tasmania in 1998. In 2000 he was appointed the NSW Crown Advocate, and in that role he advised and appeared for various state government agencies, including before the High Court. He was a member of the NSW Bar Council for eight years and is a member of the senior faculty of the Australian Advocacy Institute.

Richard was appointed a judge of the District Court of New South Wales on 6 February 2007. He is actively involved in St James' Church in Sydney as well as the Christian meditation community, serving as national president for a year.

Courtrooms are public places. The discourse among lawyers, judges, witnesses and juries occurs in open court, and can provoke confrontation and high emotion. The quality of discourse can easily deteriorate. This essay offers some reflections on how courtroom discourse can be managed to ensure that the adjudicative process takes place in the most effective way. There are parallels here with politics, and lessons to be learned by those who would enter other areas of public life.

Persevere.

—the author

Introduction

If you are reading this, it is probably because you are interested in some form of public life. I am going to focus on one form: practising in court as an advocate. This article will tell you something of what I have learned from working in that arena for the last 30 years or so. I think there are also lessons here that apply more broadly to those in public life.

What I mean by 'public life' is that a significant component of your working performance is on public view. Being marked by an examiner, assessed by a supervisor or criticised by an employer is one thing. Being marked, assessed or criticised by unknown and unnumbered members of the public is quite another.

Performing in public requires a good deal of resilience, energy and ego. Our successes are lauded but our flaws are exposed. Criticism is not always fair.

We may like the idea of public life but dislike the public lives we see being lived. Perhaps we dislike aspects we see on display such as ego, drivenness, personal attacks, or the absence of a sense of a bigger picture.

I am writing this because I have spent many years working in the public arena. It is exciting and stimulating and great fodder for the ego. But as the years have passed I have had to work out my own way of performing in public – a perspective beyond the inflation and deflation of my ego. My arena has been the courtroom rather than politics as narrowly understood, but the skill sets are similar. Indeed, many politicians are former barristers or solicitors, and some choose to return to their practices after politics. If you are choosing between law and politics, or contemplating a switch from one to the other, then I hope my essay provides food for thought.

Politics versus the law

My form of public life is not in the cut and thrust of politics. It is in the cut and thrust of rational argument. You might think that the arena of a courtroom contains much more civilised dialogue than the arena of politics. It is, after all, a dialogue driven by reason and a search for the truth, not by populism and the securing of votes. This is broadly true, but there are still many opportunities for a better form of forensic discourse.

In my twenties, I made a choice. I could pursue politics as I had done as an undergraduate or I could pursue the practice of law. Politics had a certain attraction but I came to realise that I was not suited to it – I was not quick enough, nor was I fluent in the development or articulation of policy. So I opted for the law. After a few years as a solicitor, I went to the bar in Sydney. It has been a very fulfilling career. I have acted for individuals and institutions, and both have placed a lot of trust in my advocacy.

I have found that my work has a lot in common with politics in terms of its ethical responsibilities: courts are the places where the ordinary misfortunes, misjudgements and misdemeanours of humanity are dealt with; the public interest is a very common context, and sometimes courts have had to deal with public policy issues. I have acted for a woman who stabbed her violent husband to death and then claimed the widow pension. I have acted for the NSW Attorney-General in an application to keep a serious sex offender in prison beyond his sentence under novel legislation.

Looking beyond my own advocacy, the courts have a significant role to play in implementing public policy decisions. When parliament in New South Wales enacted 'standard non-parole periods' for sentences, a question arose as to whether those standard non-parole periods should bind a judge or just guide the judge in sentencing an offender to a prison sentence. The courts had to resolve that. And quite regularly the courts have to consider what is the purpose of punishing a person. Is it:

- to remove the offender from society in order to protect the community?
- to reform and rehabilitate the offender?
- to deter other potential offenders?
- to give expression to standards of behaviour that society demands be respected?
- to ensure adequate punishment for the offence?
- to make the offender accountable for his or her actions?
- to recognise harm done to the victim and to the community?

Do these purposes overlap or even conflict? These are the sorts of questions the courts grapple with daily.

Discourse in public places

Courtrooms are public places. They are also places of public discourse. Information is provided in response to questions and there are conversations, discussion and arguments about that information, as well as about matters of principle and policy.

Let me commence by contrasting courtrooms to parliament and to public transactions we personally engage in.

In appearing as an advocate in a courtroom you are participating in public life. Like parliament – another place of public discourse – the proceedings of courts are open to the public. Like parliament, courts are places of controversy: arguments for opposing views are exchanged and final decisions taken. However there is an extra dimension of real drama in court decisions. Parliamentary outcomes are usually predictable: it is the government which, by definition, commands the majority of votes and therefore the outcome. But the public announcement of a court decision is less predictable – far less so if it is a jury verdict. The tension can sometimes be palpable. There will be a winner and a loser, or more than one of each. Unlike parliament, the resolution of the discourse can be direct and personal, even immediate. People can lose children, money, freedom – sometimes immediately, or within days or months. Unlike parliament (with some exceptions) you will cross-examine people in public – that is, verbally confront them. Judicial officers in court exercise coercive power. The person on the receiving end of that power *must* answer the question, produce the documents, come to court, pay the fine or go to jail. They have no choice.

The principal areas of engagement for you as an advocate in the courtroom will be between you and your opponent, you and the judge or jury and you and the witness. Because there can be so much at stake, emotions can run high. Clashes and verbal jousting are part of the scene and are fuelled by emotion. Confrontations occur between counsel and witnesses, counsel and counsel, and counsel and judges. Features of these confrontations can include rudeness, power struggles, personality clashes and manipulation. You have a client who wants you to fight and confound the opposition and stand up to the judge. You have your own performance anxiety. You are exercising power over a person in a vulnerable position (the witness).

How can this discourse be managed so that the desirable goals of information gathering and resolution of controversies are achieved with a reduction of the undesirable features that can accompany the process?

I will propose a number of ways by which this discourse can be managed to achieve that desirable goal.

The rules of evidence

Your basic tool to manage discourse should hardly surprise you: the rules of evidence. Nowadays, a number of Australian jurisdictions have a uniform Evidence Act which has a specific provision about cross-examination. Techniques of the cross-examiner of yesteryear now come under the rubric 'improper questions' and are 'disallowable' if 'unduly annoying, harassing, intimidating, offensive, oppressive, humiliating or repetitive' or if put 'in a manner or tone that is belittling, insulting or otherwise inappropriate'. The provision is clearly based on an appreciation of the vulnerability of the person in the witness box. Cross-examination is not an opportunity to splash your client's venom or your own distaste over the particular witness. As a judge, I maintain some vigilance (as I am bound to by the Act) when questions drift towards sarcasm. There are corresponding provisions about 'improper questions' in the non-uniform Evidence Act jurisdictions.

Perspectives on your role

Another tool is keeping a firm and clear perspective on your role. As the bar rules say, you are not simply a mouthpiece for your client. You are *representing* your client and are part of a profession which has obligations of ethics and etiquette as well as a duty to the court – these obligations do not generally bind your client. Keep firmly in mind that it is not your fight: it is your client's fight. Fight the issue, not the person. Self-restraint is needed. It is important to do your job. It is *information* you want from the witness and there is no place for rudeness or abuse of your position.

Your opponent in court is doing the corresponding job of representing their client. Neither of you were there and you do not know what actually happened. (If you were there then you probably should not be conducting the case.) You are doing your best to represent your client's interests. Indeed, you are being paid to do just that (by or on behalf of your client). You are taking somebody else's money in exchange for the exercise of your forensic judgement. For that judgement you need detachment to assess how the case is to be conducted in the best interests of your client. Your assessment may not necessarily coincide with your client's assessment. When you need surgery, you pay a surgeon to do what you ask and discuss with them how the procedure will go, but in the end you rely on the surgeon's cool and calm skill and judgement. You are being paid for the equivalent skill and judgement.

Another way to keep perspective is to keep the big picture in mind. You are participating in the justice system. Only qualified persons are allowed to represent others, and you are qualified. Australia is one of the countries that have inherited a system of resolving disputes (civil or criminal) that is generally fair and untainted by corruption. This is an important and valuable quality of our justice system. The system relies on the participation of qualified people of integrity bound by ethical obligations. You are contributing to an important process – keep that in mind.

Self-awareness

Self-awareness is important to you when you are in court. By self-awareness, I mean awareness of how you are feeling and what you are reacting to. The main faculty you will be using in court is your mind: there will be a lot of thinking, planning and deciding. But your feelings will be bubbling away under the surface: mostly tension and anxiety ranging from mild to near panic.

Let me say two things about self-awareness. The first is that it's important to simply remain aware of your feelings so you can manage them and your reactions. If your opponent is provoking you or the judge is frightening you, at least be aware of this fact and acknowledge it to yourself. This will help you to manage it better.

The second point is about displaying your feelings. Be selective about what you show. You might be in a blind panic inside, but you do not have to put it on show. The classic example is when you get an unexpected answer to a question. Just proceed to the next question, contain your panic and give yourself time to think. Do not show your opponent how much they are annoying you. Try to give the impression that you are cool, calm and collected, even if you are not.

Managing your feelings is also important in maintaining your equilibrium and judgement. Always remember: you are being paid for your professional skill and judgement. Sometimes you have to give your client clear and confronting advice that they will not like. The advice often has to be given in circumstances where you are confined by time and space. You have to separate your own feelings and engage your intellect so you can provide that advice.

Maintaining your equilibrium

In court, there are various ways that your equilibrium can be disturbed. They include your level of preparation, your opponent and the judicial officer.

If you are not prepared, you will be distracted and overanxious. You will worry about the question to ask or the one from the bench that you do not know the answer to or the next step to take in the case. I found that the better prepared I was, the easier it was to manage the unexpected. If the foundations are in place, you can manage the cross-currents.

You can be destabilised by your opponent. They may be senior and more experienced, and you may feel intimidated. They may be brusque or rude or overbearing. Remember, they too have a case to run and their client to deal with. There will probably be weaknesses in their case which concern them. Remember also that the judicial officer will be conscious of your respective efforts for your clients and any imbalance in your skills and experience. Some opponents will try to throw you or provoke you or needle you. Keep your eye on the game, not the jibes from the other players. Steel yourself and conduct your case with the skill and judgement you are being paid for. You are both equal in being the professional advocates for your clients in that court on that day. Some advocates will be more skilful than you are, others less skilful: conduct your case with the skill you have. Remember that you are both members of the same profession. You are colleagues, who happen to be opposed representing your respective clients in this case.

The judicial officer will obviously affect your equilibrium. As an advocate, my anxiety would be greatly increased or relieved when I found out who was on the bench. Keep your basic perspective: you are there to exercise your professional skill and judgement to conduct your client's case. If you are well prepared, you will get off to a good start with most judicial officers. Remember you are there to help them to make a decision; to resolve the dispute. You are also there to persuade them to resolve it in your client's favour. These are generalisations, but frankness and honesty will be appreciated by most judicial officers. Take a moment to consider the judicial officer's perspective. Are they presiding over a busy daily list? In that case, brevity and efficiency may help your presentation. Are they familiar with the law and issues ('another drink driving plea')? Then go straight to what you want and why. Are they unfamiliar with this area of law – more so than you? Then take a little time to explain. Are they conscious of someone else's convenience? Here I have in mind mainly a jury. I am always aware that a jury might be waiting patiently (or impatiently – I do not know) while the advocates are developing their legal arguments at leisure.

Do not forget that there is a time to stand up to judges. Your best approach to a rude or intemperate judge is being calm and firm. You are a member of the legal profession charged with the obligation to represent your client as best you can. This can sometimes require the courage to keep the judge's attention on the relevant issues, evidence and arguments when they are hastening to a premature judgement (often because of their own anxiety to move their case load along). Also, you do not have to tolerate insulting or rude behaviour. That might need to be pointed out to the judge. Always remember you can consult a senior or more experienced colleague about handling such situations.

Role models

Observing others can teach you a lot about managing discourse. Give yourself time to go to court when you are not personally involved, and watch. See how experienced advocates manage their performance in court. Some will appeal to you, some will not. Do not be afraid to follow up and try making an appointment to see that advocate later on. Chances are they will be more than happy to give half an hour of their time to a young aspiring advocate.

Conclusion

Some of these perspectives might be relevant to other public fields of endeavour. The evidentiary rules for questioning witnesses would temper any discourse – including parliamentary debate and the exchange between politicians and journalists or broadcasters and the public. If all of us engaged in more respectful, persistent inquiry and recognised different viewpoints, then rudeness and confrontation would stand out as an unwelcome exception. Developing a longer perspective on our role promotes integrity: choices made are in the context of a bigger picture. Self-awareness and equilibrium enhances public discourse. When we become aware of deeper currents, we come to know how our own demons can sometimes drive us rather than rationality and constructive emotions. Equilibrium in public debate reduces abuse and pettiness. Finally, it almost goes without saying that we all should find our role models.

In summary, maintain respect for your profession and your role in the justice system. Keep your conduct professional much more than personal. Exercise your rights and privileges responsibly. Be well prepared, self-aware and maintain your equilibrium.

Change the world with technology

Marlene Kanga

Dr Marlene Kanga AM, Hon.FIEAust, Hon.FIChemE, CPEng FIPENZ FAICD, was national president of Engineers Australia in 2013. She trained as a chemical engineer with a specialisation in process safety and risk engineering. She is an experienced business leader and is director of iOmniscient Pty Ltd, which has developed patented software technology for automated video analytic systems, currently used in smart-city projects around the world. She is a member of the board of Sydney Water, the largest water utility in Australia, acting chair of the Board of Innovation Australia and chair of the Department of Industry R&D Incentives Committee, the largest government support program for industry innovation.

Marlene is a transformational leader and has been responsible for many changes for the engineering profession, especially to make it more inclusive and less male-dominated. Many of her changes are world firsts and are being adopted across Australia and internationally. She is a board member of the International Network for Women Engineers and Scientists and the Executive Council of the World Federation of Engineering Organisations. She was listed by *Engineers Australia Magazine* as being among the top 100 most influential engineers in Australia in 2013 and 2014, and by *The Australian Financial Review* and Westpac as being among the top 100 Women of Influence in 2013.

Engineers have an important role as leaders in developing radical innovations to create new wealth for Australia and to solve many of the problems that the world has to deal with: climate change, water shortages, depletion of natural resources, natural disasters and urbanisation. Engineering provides an opportunity for transformational change using science, mathematics and technology. In an increasingly technological world, Australia needs more engineers to claim our future, and more respect for the role they can play in bringing about lasting changes for a better world.

Enjoy failure and learn from it. You can never learn from success.
—James Dyson

Anyone who has never made a mistake has never tried anything new.
—Albert Einstein

You've got to find what you love. And that is as true for your work as it is for your lovers. Your work is going to fill a large part of your life, and the only way to be truly satisfied is to do what you believe is great work. And the only way to do great work is to love what you do. If you haven't found it yet, keep looking. Don't settle. As with all matters of the heart, you'll know when you find it. And, like any great relationship, it just gets better and better as the years roll on. So keep looking until you find it. Don't settle.
—Steve Jobs

Coming to Australia

As a child, I was always fascinated by Australia. There was something romantic and utopian about a faraway country with a large amount of space and very few people. For someone born in India, crowds were an inescapable fact of life. From this perspective, Australia was indeed a lucky country. I made my first Australian friends at university at Imperial College in London and was struck by their extraordinary generosity. What was even more remarkable was that my friends considered these acts of kindness a normal part of life. It convinced me that Australia was the place to build a life – a new country with no limitations and unlimited possibilities.

I am a proud Australian. But I am exasperated by the fact that many young people are slow to value the blessings bestowed on them by their country of birth and maximise this advantage for the benefit of our country and the world.

I had a rude awakening when I first arrived in Australia as a young engineer. Engineering was not valued as highly in Australia as in other countries, including the United States, and, especially as a woman, I had great difficulty finding a job which used my skills. It took me a while but I did not give up. I had found what I loved; I had a passion for engineering and a belief in myself. I was also sustained by an important piece of advice I received from one of my first supervisors in the United Kingdom. 'Learn everything about everything,' he said; 'make yourself indispensable.' This was a simple message but very good advice. It meant that I learnt to be self-reliant; I sought out and embraced the challenges that followed. This provided exceptional opportunities to learn and, most importantly, to lead.

I was a change maker from the start. I knew engineering gave me the skills to create solutions and I dealt with the circumstances and issues I faced with gusto. I felt empowered; engineering gave me 'the Force'.*

My advice to young people is to take responsibility. It is important for young people to feel privileged to receive opportunities to make a contribution and not feel entitled. If you want to advance in your job or your career, you must find ways to be invaluable to your employer. You should make the best use of every opportunity to learn and to grow.

In my career, I have always been grateful for those rare gifts of good advice, especially from people more experienced than me, which have provided me with an insight into what lies beyond the horizon of my own competence and experience. It broadened my perspective.

Needed: science and mathematics

For young people who aspire to be change makers, the pathway via technology is one that offers both challenges and opportunities. In a rapidly changing and increasingly technological world, Australia needs more scientists and engineers than ever before. I am constantly surprised and dismayed by the statistics that show a declining proportion of young people studying the enabling subjects of science and mathematics at school. The proportion of year 12 students enrolled in advanced mathematics has fallen from 14.1 per cent in 1995 to 9.6 per cent in 2011, continuing a long-term decline. The proportion enrolled in intermediate mathematics fell from 27.2 per cent in 1995 to 19.8 per cent in 2011.[1] Similarly, there has been a long-term decline in the percentage of students studying science from around 90 per cent in 1991 to approximately 50 per cent in 2010.[2]

It's not as though our students are not bright enough. Australia ranks among the top countries in proficiency in science and mathematics and there is no difference between boys and girls, according

* From *Star wars*; for example, Obi-Wan Kenobi to Luke Skywalker: 'May the Force be with you', etc.

to the latest Organisation for Economic Co-operation and Development (OECD) Programme for International Student Assessment (PISA) scores.[3] However, many bright young people are completing their high school certificate without studying mathematics in their final years and are embarking on careers that do not involve science and technology.

The impact of Australia's shrinking maths and science intake on our economy in the next 20 years will be significant. Australians are leaders in taking up new technology and are among the highest users of mobile phones in the world. Thirty-seven per cent of Australians have at least one smart phone, second only to Singapore.[4] Eighty-two per cent have an internet connection.[5] However, in order to lead the world and to change it for the better, we need to be participants in creating new technology, not just consumers. The world is being shaped by engineers and scientists, and Australia cannot afford to be left behind.

Technology and revolution

Engineering invention and innovation have been driving economic and social development for millennia. Around 2,600 BCE, the early civil engineers built planned cities like Mohenjo-daro, in the Indus valley, with gridded streets, grand buildings and public baths. In Roman times, civil engineers built roads, bridges and viaducts that transported Roman armies and supplies across vast distances, enabling the discovery and conquest of hitherto unknown lands. The scientific discoveries of the Renaissance were the precursors to inventions that eventually led to the Industrial Revolution.

The Industrial Revolution in the 19th century in the United Kingdom and Europe was driven by inventions, like the steam engine, that reshaped the world, giving massive productivity improvements to those who had the means and the determination to implement them. Steam engines led to rail networks and industrialisation, jet engines led to global travel, and the first computers eventually enabled global connections and access to vast amounts of information. All this has been made possible with science, technology and engineering. The creativity of these professionals changed the world, affecting the quality of life of everyone in most parts of the globe.

Engineers, scientists and technologists continue to be at the forefront of shaping our world in the 21st century, and the solutions they create will be as revolutionary as in the previous millennium. Most of the problems we face today – including the problems of urbanisation, climate change, food security, water shortages, energy and the depletion of natural resources – will be solved by engineers. For countries exposed to natural disasters and rising sea levels, engineers will be able to share knowledge to devise the type of sustainable solutions that are needed to address these issues. These are just a few examples of the enormous benefits that engineering provides to humanity.

Engineers are also facilitators for social justice and political revolutions. The invention of movable type in the 15th century led in time to profound social change, making books and therefore knowledge more freely available to all social classes. The Arab Spring in 2012 would not have been possible without the extraordinary accessibility of mobile telecommunications and inventions like Facebook and Twitter. Many developing countries around the world are benefiting from the advantages of technology, including clean water, which has eradicated many diseases such as cholera and typhoid. Indeed, the work of engineers has saved more lives than the work of doctors has.[6]

Closing the gap

However, technology has not reached everywhere. Although electricity, clean water networks and modern sewerage systems have been installed in most parts of developed countries, they are still missing in many remote Aboriginal communities around Australia and in many developing countries in the Asia and Pacific region, our nearest neighbours. It is estimated that approximately 20 per cent of the world's population – 1.6 billion people – do not have electricity in their homes.[7] The numbers for clean water and modern sanitation are similar or worse. Approximately 1.1 billion people do not have access to clean water and 2.6 billion lack access to basic sanitation. Nevertheless, the pace of change is increasing even in these remote areas of the world. If you want to change the world, become an engineer.[8]

Australians who grew up in a developing country know first-hand of the rapid pace of change that is occurring in Asia, not only in its large cities (some of which are larger than the entire population of Australia), but also in its villages and rural communities. My ancestral home, some 400 years old, in Goa, received electricity only in the 1960s and our first tap supplied from the public system was installed only in 2011.

Engineers are the people that have made the world a global village, where almost instantaneous communications are possible to nearly every part of the world. I have seen our telephone number in our home in Goa grow from just two digits in the 1990s to eight digits. While the installation of telephone landlines has been slow, mobile telephone subscriptions across the developing world have risen rapidly. There are now nearly a billion mobile telephones in India.[9] Importantly, the price is highly affordable, less than 1 per cent of the cost in Australia! The ability to communicate has profound implications for the economy and our quality of life. This has enabled new business opportunities even in remote villages.

At the same time, young people in these villages are becoming avid consumers of all things technological. They all have mobile phones and watch Zee TV.* Large numbers of them recognise that science and technology will give them the edge – they want to become engineers. While the United States and Europe have been world leaders in science and research, Asia is now emerging as a world centre of innovation and technological development. China has overtaken South Korea as a science and research producer and has recently overtaken Japan on a number of measures, such as research and development expenditure and national output of scientific publications. In 2010, Japan in turn overtook the United States to become the highest producer of triadic patent families. South Korea was fifth in producing triadic patents.†

Other emerging economies in Asia are also becoming knowledge creators. India's large and youthful population and its growing expenditure on research and development have lifted its publication of scientific papers from 2.1 per cent of the world total in 2000

* Zee TV is a Mumbai-based cable and satellite television channel established in 1992 and now watched in 169 countries with more than 670 million viewers globally, the largest media channel serving the South Asian diaspora.

† Triadic patent families are a set of patents taken at the European Patent Office, the Japanese Patent Office and the US Patent and Trademark Office.

to 3.7 per cent in 2010, a share that exceeds that of Australia at 3.4 per cent.[10] With rising wages, India is moving from being the call-centre hub of the world to developing innovative technologies for the internet, telecommunications and manufacturing.

Asian students are outperforming their European counterparts in mathematics and science, the enabling subjects for engineering, according to the latest OECD PISA scores. So the pipeline is full, the numbers will continue to grow and the demand for engineering education in Asia has never been greater.[11] The race is on, as more countries in Asia and Africa realise that engineering and technology are an essential path to prosperity. Young Australians also need to realise that we must become a smarter country and embrace science and engineering to remain a leading economy.

Our neighbours in the Asian region are already producing the largest numbers of scientists and engineers in the world. The United States, the United Kingdom and Japan produced around 70,000 engineers per year in the 1980s and were leaders in engineering. This situation has now flipped dramatically. While the numbers graduating with engineering degrees has remained constant in these countries, Asian countries are also producing the largest numbers of scientists and engineers in the world. China now produces more than 700,000 engineering graduates per year compared with just 6,000 in Australia. This translates to around 530 engineers per million people in China, up from less than 200 in the year 2000. This compares with around 284 in Australia, a figure that has remained flat over the past decade. In Korea, the figure is 1,600 per million people, up 25 per cent from 1,200 in the year 2000. In Germany, the figure has been flat at 800 per million people.[12] India, also, has more than trebled the number of engineering graduates in the past decade and now graduates around one million people per year in engineering and information technology.[13] I am pleased to say that the proportion of women in many countries in Asia who are studying and practising engineering is also increasing and outstripping the proportions in Australia and the developed world, approaching 50 per cent in some countries.[14]

Mining our intellectual capacity

Innovation is the path to prosperity and engineers are a vital part of the process that takes great ideas and scientific breakthroughs from the laboratory to the market. Innovation is vital to Australia. As a small nation that wants to remain highly educated and highly paid, Australia cannot afford to be lazy about innovation. To maintain a comparative advantage, the Australian economy must develop industries that require brainpower and enormous creativity, and have high barriers to entry. These industries have the greatest competitive advantage and create the greatest value. Even within existing industries, innovation can increase productivity – for example in manufacturing, once our largest employer. By adapting existing technologies and processes, manufacturing companies can become more efficient and create solutions for the rapidly changing needs of customers.

Australia has tremendous comparative advantages for innovation. Although we need to increase the proportion of students studying the enabling subjects of mathematics and science, we do have an educated workforce. Furthermore, we have a multicultural workforce and this diversity of intellect encourages innovation. This is a huge pool of available talent.

Australia has always been an innovating nation. We have the boomerang; the 'black box' flight recorder; the cochlear implant; the cervical cancer vaccine; even wi-fi was invented by CSIRO engineer John O'Sullivan. These innovations have the ability to transform our economy by creating new jobs and generating profits for decades. For example, an Australian icon, the Hills Hoist (clothesline), was invented more than 60 years ago. The company that was then established is publicly listed on the Australian Stock Exchange and employs more than 3,000 people.[15] It is now a diversified group in metal building products and electronics and communications with global sales exceeding $1.2 billion – a great example of the multiplier effect of innovation.

Similarly large innovating companies like Cochlear and Resmed – which were spin-offs from innovations made in the University of Sydney – are publicly listed companies with billions of dollars in revenues and thousands of employees, generating wealth for Australians with operations around the world. Their engineers are world leaders in their fields. More importantly, they are bringing humanitarian benefits to thousands with special problems with hearing and sleeping. The benefits are boundless.

We need many more companies like these. We all know that companies in the United States like Microsoft, Cisco, Google, Facebook, Yahoo and Apple have generated wealth for millions of Americans. We need this kind of wealth generation in Australia – the kind of boom that will not run out, and the opportunity to lead the world with our innovations and inventions.

Innovate when you are young

Australians must understand that engineers are indispensable to innovation – they use their imagination and their ingenuity to implement innovations that transform our world. The difference between invention and innovation is in the realisation. Engineers connect the dots and bring scientific and technological breakthroughs to the world. Engineers are the realisers, making great things possible. It is both a creative and a rational endeavour to change the world. Engineers are the bridge between research dreams and industry success.

For example, consider the simple principle of boiling water. Chemists developed the distillation process that is used to separate chemicals based on the differences in their boiling points. But chemical engineers have realised the distillation process on a large scale, and in doing so have developed the oil and gas industry. Our modern world depends on these fuels. The humble distillation process is the foundation of hundreds of industrial chemical processes and new ones evolve every day. Pills, processed foods and petroleum products are all produced by some form of distillation process.

The powerful smart phone in your pocket – a computer in the palm of your hand – is the result of innovation in information and communication technologies. The initial research into semiconductors was pure physics – and Australia does some world-leading research into the use of optical fibres for communication – but the practical applications for everyday life were developed by engineers. Over the past 40 years we have witnessed a revolution which started with personal computers, then the internet, then mobile telecommunications and now social media. These achievements have been the result of electronics, telecommunications and software engineers.

Most importantly, the best innovators are young engineers. Young people are unfazed by rules and by doubts about what might not be possible. Consequently, young people are often the source of disruptive innovations, that is, innovations that have no previous heritage. Think Bill Gates, Steve Jobs and Mark Zuckerberg,* who created whole new industries in computing, communications and entertainment while in their twenties. At a recent visit to the West Coast of the United States, I was enthralled by the buzz about new technological breakthroughs and the convergence of computer science, computer hardware engineering, nanotechnology, biotechnology and other emerging disciplines to produce new breakthroughs and new products. These discussions were not held in laboratories and offices but in trendy bars and coffee shops. The main protagonists were young people in jeans – some of them millionaires in their twenties.

Contrary to expectations, failure was almost a badge of honour – it demonstrates that one has pushed the boundary of science and technology to risk what has never been done before. As Einstein said, 'I have not failed, I have just found 10,000 ways that don't work.'

In Singapore, the National University of Singapore has established a design-led innovation program that has a similar ambition: to encourage its graduate engineers to become 'techpreneurs' and start their own businesses. These young people are dreaming up new products for the next decade and will soon be establishing their own businesses in emerging technology fields.

Innovative ideas lead to huge gains in employment, productivity and quality of life. Experiences such as those of Silicon Valley show that innovation gives rise to more innovation. There have been successive waves of new technologies emerging from this small region, impacting on and changing lives around the world. Given the right environment, opportunities and investment, Australia can also have an above-ground boom that need not be depleted. If it is to be realised, engineers must be there to make it happen.

Big risks, big rewards

However, facilitating innovation and transformation of our economy requires other factors. We need an ecosystem of entrepreneurship and venture capital that works together to bring new products to market. I am frequently asked by young Australians about the difficulties they have in landing their first job. My response is, 'Why

* They created Microsoft, Apple and Facebook, respectively.

not create one?' In the United States, more than 50 per cent of engineering graduates from the Massachusetts Institute of Technology (MIT) start their own companies. They are in an environment where they have the confidence to try, where failure is not seen as catastrophic and where capital is available to back ideas. A study in 1997 found that MIT gradates had founded 4,000 companies, created 1.1 million jobs and generated $232 billion in sales – equivalent to 15 per cent of Australia's gross domestic product. By 2006, 25,600 companies had been founded, employing 3.3 million people and with revenues of more than $2 trillion.[16] This is by living alumni. This new breed of leader will be transforming their world though technology and entrepreneurship.

Australia needs this kind of leadership and entrepreneurship in engineering and technology. Rather than wait to buy the next big thing, we should be creating it. Young Australians, men and women, should be creating their own innovations, establishing their own technological companies and creating a new future for the nation. When you are young, you can afford to take risks, you can explore your big ideas, you can afford to fail a few times, you have the potential to win big. These wins would also be wins for Australia.

Innovation and entrepreneurship need courage and vision. Most innovators have to try hundreds of times before they succeed. One of the most active and visible proponents of innovation in engineering is Sir James Dyson, and it's worth spending a moment studying his creation.

> In designing the suction capability of the DC Series vacuum cleaner, Dyson developed a total of 5,127 patents over five years, before arriving at the Root Cyclone technology that spins dirt out of the air rather than relying on bags and filters to trap debris. The AB01 hand dryer is another technology innovation, featuring a digital motor that produces a high-speed sheet of cool air that dries hands in twelve seconds, while using less energy than conventional warm-air systems.[17]

Dyson's motors will be used to develop other new products and the real leap might well be an electric car motor, demonstrating how one breakthrough can lead to others.

Dyson asserts that to compete, countries must take risks. 'Without taking risks, you don't generate long-term wealth,' he says. He argues that more innovations – and in particular, more radical innovations – are required. Radical innovations often require rules to be broken, but Dyson finds fewer revolutionaries around him as time goes by. Faced with a shortage, Dyson even came to Australia in 2012 to hire a few of our own engineers.

At the core of most exciting innovations is a new technology that is radical, that has had no previous heritage (and perhaps no obvious application) and that often requires creative destruction of existing paradigms. Steve Jobs is a great example of a leader who was an innovator in technology – an engineer who changed the world. He had the courage to destroy an existing technology paradigm, the Walkman, to create the iPod, and cannibalised the PC to create the iPad, creating a new market and a new industry. This example demonstrates that radical innovation goes beyond competitive positioning, and has the potential to fundamentally change the way the world operates. Radical innovation is responsible for the genesis of high-technology industries such as information and communications technology (ICT), telecommunications, biotechnology and sustainable energy.

Another source of innovations involves the use of resources in a frugal manner. Frugal innovation initially developed to address the needs of low-income consumers in India. But the resulting products have global applications because they make minimal use of resources and energy – two global imperatives for sustainability – to keep costs down.[18] The Tata Nano car, for example, has 34 patents, uses a minimum of resources and materials, and has been designed and built in India. The Aakash Tablet computer costs just A$50 and has much of the functionality of conventional tablet computers, but has lower energy and resource utilisation. Australian engineers have the opportunity to develop innovations appropriate to our environment and needs, for example addressing water management and the needs of remote communities, and harnessing solar power.

Of course, engineers cannot do it by themselves. In the innovation game, it is impossible to pick winners. Australia needs a culture that supports innovation; an environment that recognises the need for risk-taking and rewards success. It needs appropriate government policies to facilitate commercially relevant innovation and business that is willing to support new ideas with venture capital. Australia currently ranks 19th on the Global Innovation Index.[19] The annual reports on Australia's innovation system show mixed results despite significant public investment in mainly scientific research and development.[20] We need stronger links between research institutions and industry to ensure rapid commercialisation of new ideas, and a greater recognition of the role of engineers in the commercial realisation of scientific inventions.

Readers may wonder, 'What's your track record in innovation?' Some of you may know that my company, iOmniscient, has taken Australian research and transformed it into a world-class software product comprising patented intelligent video analysis technology. The technology we have developed is truly remarkable and is delivering solutions that even we did not imagine. The company is recognised as the leader in its field, with several triadic patents (which are granted only to significant innovations). We have encountered both failure and success, but we love what we do. Importantly, we are energised by the fact that we are implementing solutions internationally, making change for a safer, better world.[21]

Creating the next big thing

Another question is what lies ahead, and where the next big thing in technology is. This is not an easy question to answer, but it is clear that Australia should exploit the areas where it has a specific technological leadership and understanding – areas that are frequently influenced by the Australian environment. The CSIRO has identified resource exploration, the reduction in biodiversity, the growth of Asia and the demand for technology and resources from the region as key areas for innovation and growth.[22] The ageing population provides opportunities for biomedical engineering and health-related technologies. Advances in human genome mapping and reduction in computing costs will result in medical breakthroughs, which are coming about with the use of advanced technologies. The blurring of boundaries between different science and technology disciplines will result in emerging technologies such as biochemical engineering, robotics, big data* and technologies unknown. The march of the internet and all forms of rapid communication will also provide new opportunities, as well as reducing the tyranny of

* This is an emerging area of technology where large amounts of data are analysed for new insights and trends.

distance. Australia will no longer be a long way from the rest of the world and will be able to communicate instantly with partners and customers across the globe. Rising consumer expectations and appetite for new technology will also be drivers of innovation.

The scope for innovation in engineering and technology is unlimited. What is in short supply are capable young people who are willing to take on the challenge of a career in engineering, science or technology and to lead the world in developing solutions that will create a better, more sustainable future for us all.

---

1. Engineers Australia 2013, *The engineering profession—a statistical overview*, August, https://www.engineersaustralia.org.au/sites/default/files/shado/Representation/Stats/2013_statistical_overview_australia.pdf.
2. Australian Academy of Science 2012, *The status and quality of year 11 and 12 science in Australian schools*, http://science.org.au/publications/research-reports-and-policy.html.
3. OECD 2013, *OECD PISA 2012 scores*, December, www.oecd.org/pisa.
4. A faster future, *Australia 2nd globally for smartphone usage: Google*, www.afasterfuture.com/australia-2nd-globally-for-smartphone-usage-google.html.
5. Google, *Internet usage in Australia*, https://www.google.com.au/#q=internet+usage+in+australia.
6. Civil engineering portal, *Civil engineering history*, www.engineeringcivil.com/history.
7. Global issues, *Poverty facts and stats*, www.globalissues.org/article/26/poverty-facts-and-stats.
8. *Engineering for change*, www.engineeringforchange.org; Engineers without borders, www.ewb.org.au.
9. See: http://www.trai.gov.in/WriteReadData/PIRReport/Documents/The%20Indian%20Telecom%20Services%20Performance%20Indicators%20-%20July-September,%202013.pdf.
10. The royal society, *Knowledge, networks and nations—global scientific collaboration in the 21st century*, http://royalsociety.org/uploadedFiles/Royal_Society_Content/policy/publications/2011/4294976134.pdf.
11. OECD, *Comparing countries' and economies' performance*, www.oecd.org/pisa/46643496.pdf.
12. Engineers Australia, unpublished research.
13. Chaturvedi A & Sachitanand R, 2013, 'A million engineers in India struggling to get placed in an extremely challenging market', *Economic*

Times, June 18, http://articles.economictimes.indiatimes.com/2013-06-18/news/40049243_1_engineers-iit-bombay-batch-size.

14. Various research presented at the International Network Women Engineers and Scientists Asia Pacific Nation Network meetings, 2011–13.
15. Hills Holdings Ltd 2013, *Annual report.*
16. Roberts, E & Eesley, C, 2009, *Entrepreneurial impact: the role of MIT*, Kauffman, https://entrepreneurship.mit.edu/uploads/Entrepreneurial_Impact_The_Role_of_MIT.pdf.
17. Varrasi, J, 2011, 'The man behind the vacuum cleaner', ASME, December, https://www.asme.org/career-education/articles/entrepreneurship/the-man-behind-the-vacuum-cleaner.
18. See: http://www.nesta.org.uk/sites/default/files/our_frugal_future.pdf.
19. Dutta, S (ed.), 2012, *The global innovation index 2012*, www.globalinnovationindex.org/userfiles/file/GII-2012-Report.pdf.
20. See http://apo.org.au/research/australian-innovation-system-report-2013.
21. *iOmniscient*, www.iomniscient.com.
22. CSIRO 2012, *Our future world: global megatrends that will change the way we live*, 2 October, www.csiro.au/Portals/Partner/Futures/Our-Future-World.aspx.

A volunteer's perspective on leadership

Ashlee Uren

Ashlee Uren spent five years volunteering and working in education and advocacy roles with various not-for-profit organisations while studying at the University of Western Australia. In 2012, Ashlee was the recipient of the Ciara Glennon Memorial Law Scholarship. In September 2013, Ashlee graduated with a combined degree in arts (French, political science and international relations) and law. Ashlee has worked with the Global Poverty Project, as a volunteer for the End of Polio concert and later as national logistics coordinator. She has collaborated with a variety of individuals and inspiring leaders – from high-school students and polio survivors to musicians – to increase public engagement with global issues at the heart of extreme poverty. Ashlee volunteered with the World Health Organization in Geneva during the rollout of the Middle East outbreak response following the confirmation of a polio outbreak in Syria in October 2013.

Ashlee writes about the qualities embodied by volunteers and how these can inform better leadership. The best volunteers are generous in time and energy, self-aware, innovative and responsible. They are also courageous: the best volunteers are unafraid to be authentic, unafraid to demonstrate their passion and unafraid to reveal weaknesses or failings. They listen and learn from others and connect with colleagues and with the task at hand without self-interest or competition. Lessons in courage learned through the volunteer experience can be applied later in public life.

It is amazing what you can accomplish if you do not care who gets the credit.
—Harry S. Truman

A culture of disenchantment

If you were to judge 'public life' based on the majority of sentiments expressed online about Australian leaders, you would not form a favourable impression. For example, the status updates and comments that appear in my Facebook newsfeed about our political leaders and political system range from disappointed to disparaging to downright abusive. Contempt is the status quo. To dare express praise for a politician or government is to risk being met with incredulity, or worse, vitriol. Even comments that only indirectly criticise our leaders paint a sorry picture of our political system and our faith in its ability to represent each one of us.

One of my Facebook friends, Jessica, often posts status updates that begin with: 'When I become prime minister …' and follow with a description of how she would resolve a problem she has observed in the community. She suggests some very inventive solutions to local and national issues, but ingenuity is not the reason that her status updates attract a lot of 'likes' from the Facebook community. Rather, Jessica's status updates are a veiled criticism of leaders in public life – and her peers 'like' her status updates because they concur with the sentiment behind the veil. Jessica and many others our age have lost confidence that our leaders will hear or respect their views, and so the concept that their ideas could ever influence public policy is laughable to them. They therefore judge that the only way for them to shape public policy is to become prime minister! Yet, the suggestion of becoming prime minister – or entering public life in any capacity – is abstract and unappealing. For Jessica and her peers, her status updates are an inside joke about a shared feeling of being sidelined from democracy.

Jessica's attitude reveals a culture of disenchantment – a culture that is particularly strong among young people. Young people are more likely to criticise those in public life, particularly politicians, than enter public life. Perhaps we avoid political engagement and public leadership because we fear being criticised in the language that is so often used to criticise our current leaders. Equally, we are more comfortable joking about politics than we are actively engaging with civil issues.

In writing this essay for *So you want to be a leader* I asked a number of friends between the ages of 18 and 24 whether they would meet with their member of parliament (MP) to raise an issue that concerned them. Overwhelmingly, the answer was 'no'. When I asked why, the common response I received was that approaching their MP would be useless – their MP would not listen, would not take them seriously, or would not act on their concerns. I asked my friends if they thought the result would be different if they were older, and overwhelmingly the answer was 'yes'. Statistics from the Australian Electoral Commission revealed that one in four people aged between 18 and 24 failed to enrol to vote in the 2013 federal election. Indeed, in that election the lowest level of enrolment to vote was among young people.

I can relate to this sentiment, as I used to share it. Though I was excited to vote for the first time in the 2007 federal election, I was not too dismayed when I received a letter the following month saying my vote had not been counted because I had not enrolled correctly. I did not feel invested in the election result as I had not spent much time choosing my preferences; public policy and governance seemed to be something older people did and younger people observed from the sidelines.

Reflecting on when or why I formed this opinion, I recall sitting with my family and watching the leaders' debate on television in the lead-up to the 1996 federal election. At the time, I was about six years old. I decided (without logic or explanation, as children tend to do) that I liked then Prime Minister Paul Keating better than the Leader of the Opposition John Howard. When I announced as much, my beloved gran turned to me in horror and exclaimed that if I made any more statements to that effect I would be sitting on the lawn outside! Sure enough, I didn't voice my opinions around my family for some time thereafter, in case my opinion was the 'wrong one'.

Even as a young adult, when I began to form opinions that were supported by more than mere childhood logic, I had doubts about whether my opinions were credible or whether, as a young person, I had any right to express them. I doubted that a leader would listen to my views, let alone be persuaded to act on them. My doubts as to a young person's ability to shape public policy persisted until 2011, when I was called up from the bench on the sideline of democracy to enter a field of public life.

The End of Polio campaign

In early 2011, a close friend asked me to join a group of young people to campaign for polio eradication. At that time, I could never have predicted the success of The End of Polio campaign, which had a lofty aim: to gain political and financial support for global polio eradication efforts when world leaders arrived in Perth for the Commonwealth Heads of Government Meeting (CHOGM) in October 2011. In conversations with Australians from all walks of life, our team saw clear public support for the eradication of polio – a debilitating disease that mostly affects children under the age of five living in the most vulnerable communities on earth. In the 10 months leading up to CHOGM, the End of Polio team spent countless voluntary hours organising and executing a community event, The End of Polio concert, to communicate to our political leaders the public support we had witnessed.

On the opening day of CHOGM, 4,500 people – mostly young people – attended The End of Polio concert in demonstration of their support for polio eradication. The sold-out concert was broadcast to over five million people. Our plea that the Australian government help financially support global polio eradication efforts reached our political leaders and they listened. Moreover, they responded. The day following the concert, then Prime Minister Julia Gillard invited The End of Polio team to a press conference where she committed $50 million towards global polio eradication efforts. Following the prime minister's lead, the prime ministers of the United Kingdom and Canada, the presidents of Nigeria and Pakistan and Bill Gates (on behalf of the Bill & Melinda Gates Foundation) committed a total of $118 million towards polio eradication.

Lessons from the volunteer experience

My volunteer experience demonstrated to me the ability of young people to successfully engage in the democratic process and shape public policy, challenging my preconceived belief that leaders would not have regard for the views of young people. Young people represent a significant portion of the electorate and our views are powerful – when we have the confidence to voice them. Yet many a young person's confidence to engage in public life is inadvertently shaken – like mine was at age six – by the disapproval of family members and other older role models. Compounded by negative perceptions of leaders, a lack of confidence can quickly transform into disenchantment with our political system more broadly. What can be done to transform a sense of disenchantment into a sense of empowerment and proactive engagement?

First, it is the responsibility of the young voter to engage proactively – for example, by approaching their MP, or by using the internet to learn more about our political process and leaders rather than to berate them. It takes courage to engage in public life, particularly for the first time. It's much easier to adopt an attitude of detachment to avoid becoming invested, relinquishing control over others' reactions and opening oneself to criticism. Volunteering and engaging in public life at a political level are similar in that you get out of the experience what you first put in. The learning curve might be a steep one but do not delay the decision to start; you might be pleasantly surprised by others' reactions and the outcome. The investment of engaging in public life ultimately pays off with inclusion and representation in the political decision-making process.

Second, those in public life can develop and display personal qualities that have the effect of encouraging direct, meaningful engagement with young people and a more competent national conversation.

And from my experience, volunteering is invaluable preparation for effective engagement in public life, both as a voter and as a courageous leader. My understanding of the knowledge and skills needed for quality leadership in public life has been shaped by this experience.

During my time as a volunteer – and subsequently working with volunteers as state coordinator for the Global Poverty Project – I frequently heard praise for volunteers: 'There should be more people like that.' Presumably, leaders enter public life because they, like volunteers, have a desire to serve their community. Yet when I contrast this familiar discourse about volunteers with the sentiments I read about Australian leaders on Facebook, I have to wonder: what qualities do we see in volunteers that we do not always see in leaders? Perhaps we would see a gentler national conversation if leaders sought to model the qualities and mentalities of the best volunteers.

Leadership is underpinned by courage

Having had the privilege to work with a number of volunteers during my time with the Global Poverty Project, I have found that the best volunteers share four common qualities. Much like engaging in public life as a young voter, the qualities necessary to be a successful volunteer or a successful leader in public life are underpinned by one virtue: courage.

- courage to demonstrate passion
- courage to listen and learn
- courage to reveal shortcomings, and
- courage to give praise.

I believe that these four qualities in combination, as embodied by the best volunteers, are essential qualities for new leaders entering public life who aim to counter the disenchantment felt by many Australians. A courageous leader – that is, a leader who confronts their fears – invites courage from those they lead, including young voters who may be building up the courage to engage in public life.

Courage to demonstrate passion

There is much literature regarding the relationship between passion and leadership. For me, the word 'passion' describes a sense of strong emotional energy. My colleague and friend, Akram Azimi (from whom I've learned much about leadership), describes passion as 'intrinsic motivation', but the effect is the same – feeling inspired, creative, hopeful and resilient in the face of setbacks. I have worked alongside talented volunteers who are wholeheartedly passionate about ending extreme poverty and thus are imbued with these qualities. They are also extremely committed to continuing volunteering despite any obstacles in their way, because they make their passion their priority. Passion equips them with the emotional energy to surmount any challenges.

However, during a recent advocacy day at a local farmers' market it occurred to me that simply being passionate is not enough to truly succeed in public life. Watching three of the Global Poverty Project's best volunteers interact with market-goers, I realised that the best volunteers are not only passionate; they also communicate their passion to others. To do so is an act of courage, as to communicate one's passion is to lay it out in the public sphere to be tested, debated, examined and challenged. Sarah, Sophie and Fiona wove through the crowd, bravely striking up controversial conversation with strangers about their passion to see an increase in Australia's commitment to foreign aid. I have worked alongside these three quiet achievers for long enough to know that it would have been confronting for them to bare their passion to the market, thus leaving themselves open to criticism and even hostility. Yet they faced their fears and did exactly that. To their surprise, Sarah, Sophie and

Fiona were not subject to criticism or hostility, even though some of the market-goers disagreed with the proposition of increasing foreign aid. The public connected with the genuineness and generosity of the girls' passion. The gentle quality of the discourse reflected the public's respect for their courage to communicate their passion.

The courage to demonstrate your passion potentially has the added benefit of winning the support of people who are ready to be persuaded. I was inspired to join The End of Polio campaign when the team manager, Michael Sheldrick, communicated his passion for a world where vulnerable people live without threat from preventable diseases such as polio. Through communicating his passion, Michael also communicated his energy, hope, commitment and resilience to see the plan through – and inspired the support, trust and respect of the team and the wider public.

Courage to listen and learn

Courage is what it takes to stand up and speak; courage is also what it takes to sit down and listen.

—Winston Churchill

In my role as state coordinator, I once recruited two new volunteers for the same task of speaking to young adults about extreme poverty. They had very similar qualifications and were both brilliant public speakers. Each volunteer had good intentions and similar levels of commitment. Yet after a few weeks, I was receiving much better feedback about one volunteer. I couldn't place the point of difference, until I reread their position applications, which asked the volunteers to explain why they had chosen to become involved with the Global Poverty Project. The first volunteer had responded: 'I have a lot to offer and I would feel guilty if I didn't try to help out in some way.' The second volunteer had responded: 'I know a little bit about extreme poverty and my place in the world, but I want to learn more.' The second volunteer was the better volunteer because he approached every conversation and task as an opportunity to listen and learn. Doing so took courage in order to let go of the need to be heard and validated, and his readiness to listen and learn demonstrated a preparedness to be influenced by people with different perspectives. Consequently he formed genuine connections with the people he spoke to, which organically attracted support for his work. I firmly believe that each one of us has a lot to offer, but when the first volunteer approached his work with this attitude he was perceived as aloof and consequently attracted criticism, not support. Do not fear being undervalued for starting out with seemingly small, meaningless and thankless tasks – for example, volunteering! Trust the process as a rehearsal for a larger role in public life.

This readiness to listen and learn is not only vital for attracting supporters, but also for maintaining support and engagement through challenges. The best volunteers and leaders recognise that learning is a life-long process, and value self-development. As a leader in public life, demonstrating the courage to listen and learn will inspire optimism, confidence and a culture of active learning and engagement.

Courage to reveal shortcomings

If we accept that learning is a life-long process, we accept that there will be times when we come up short in knowledge, make mistakes or let someone down. The best volunteers admit their shortcomings, which is no easy feat in the age of the internet. With limitless information at our disposal, we are expected to know something about everything – and fast! On social media, we carefully curate a persona, highlighting only the good and omitting everything else. The facade of perfection in our online life trespasses into our personal relationships in the 'real world'. In the workplace, we erroneously fear that revealing shortcomings will jeopardise our reputation. Therefore, we avoid admitting when we don't have knowledge or we have made a mistake. Equally, we are uncomfortable acknowledging when we have let someone down and delay or evade it altogether, if possible. In each scenario, we are constrained by a fear-based culture where shortcomings are so often concealed and we critique our leaders with vitriol when they make mistakes.

Having the courage to reveal your shortcomings can actually benefit you in public life. First, revealing shortcomings in knowledge gives you the opportunity to connect with better expertise and resources, which enables you to complete work effectively to a higher standard. Second, when we let go of what we think we should know (or who we think we should 'be'), we are 'ourselves'. Being authentic and vulnerable in this way – in contrast to being false, scripted and robotic – inspires respect and trust. A May 2013 study by the

Australia Institute concluded that young people in Australia rate 'trust' as the most important factor influencing their vote. Finally, when we reveal our vulnerability we highlight our humanity and invite others to connect with us. Perhaps if our leaders were more forthcoming about their failings, young people would be encouraged to engage with them.

The best volunteers also work up the courage to promptly accept and acknowledge criticism and – rather than resent it – use it to constantly improve their performance. When leaders are honest and forthright about a bad decision, and acknowledge when they have let someone down, they demonstrate that they are willing to be held to account for their decisions. We continue to feel some level of input and control. We feel that our leaders respect us and we often return that respect when we have discussions with (and about) our leaders.

Courage to give praise

The importance of giving praise in the workplace is widely recognised. Showing others that you appreciate their contributions can be a strong motivating factor for them to work hard. This is particularly true of volunteers, who have no financial incentive to contribute. However, like revealing shortcomings, giving praise to others strikes fear in the hearts of many leaders. We are afraid that generous praise for others would shift the spotlight away from our good work and lead others to consider us redundant. Young people are understandably concerned with job security and do not want to risk undue competition for their position. Even more-experienced leaders are often more focused on self-advancement – from garnering support for a particular idea to securing a promotion to gaining a strategic advantage over a political opponent – than on giving credit to praiseworthy ideas.

If praise is scarcely given to colleagues, supporting the ideas of political opponents is out of the question. In 2009, Malcolm Turnbull was ousted as Leader of the Opposition when he agreed with then Prime Minister Kevin Rudd's proposals for action on climate change. This example suggests that courage to give praise is not rewarded. Unfortunately, this attitude has the dangerous effect of inhibiting the opportunity to find the best solutions through civil dialogue. In contrast, the volunteer example suggests that courage to give praise can and should be rewarded.

The best volunteers eschew ego and self-interest, and are open to discussion and collaboration in order to enhance, not undermine, good ideas, find the best solutions and achieve the best result. The best volunteers do not subscribe to adversarial paradigms. They liberally give praise to colleagues and even to organisations that are doing good work but are in direct competition for resources. Praising competitors requires you to have courage that others will also give credit where credit is due. Praise is contagious and by being generous with our praise for good ideas, irrespective of their origins, we create a culture of innovation and collaboration rather than a culture of competition.

The quality of our civic dialogue would benefit greatly if leaders were to follow the example set by volunteers and focus on praising ideas on their merit rather than dismissing them because of their origin.

True success in public life is not in the end achieved through self-promotion. This is perhaps the most important lesson I have learned from Akram Azimi, who has spent many years as a volunteer and models a very special form of leadership. By his example, Akram has taught me that the best leadership opportunities are those that afford the possibility of bettering society, not personal interest. Akram praises and invests in work and relationships and, in doing so, embodies wisdom I have heard him express from time to time: 'Leaders don't create more followers, they create more leaders.'

Conclusion

The criticism of our leaders in the online space and on social media gives an insight into young people's disenchantment with Australia's political system and process. The generally negative way we perceive our leaders is in sharp contrast to the positive perception we have of our volunteers, who we often describe as genuine, admirable human beings who contribute to making Australia – and more broadly the world – a better place.

So my message to new leaders is this: to contribute to the formation of a gentler national dialogue, take a leaf out of the book of the volunteer experience. The best volunteers communicate passion; are ready to listen and learn; reveal shortcomings where appropriate; and give praise. Each of these qualities is underpinned by courage.

Similarly, it will take courage from new leaders to actually employ an alternative understanding of leadership based on the volunteer experience. Developing the qualities necessary for courageous leadership begins with one courageous first step away from the spectator bench of social media and into a field of public life. Just one step can get the ball rolling towards inspiring courage in other leaders and encouraging young voters to actively engage in public life. After all, the etymology of the word encourage is 'to put in courage'. And in my experience, to take a courageous step into a field of public life is to step onto a path that leads to many unexpected opportunities to learn, grow and positively affect our own lives and the lives of those in generations to come.

Know where you are going and why

Fiona Jose

Fiona Jose is the chief executive officer of the Cape York Institute for Policy and Leadership, and the general manager of its parent group, Cape York Partnership, and several associated enterprises. She is also a director of Bama Services, Djarragun College and chair of Cape York's Jawun Advisory Group, each of which play an important role in the Cape York reform agenda. In these roles she has strengthened her reputation as a strong advocate for national Indigenous affairs policy and leadership development.

Fiona is of Aboriginal and Torres Strait Islander heritage and her childhood was spent mainly in Queensland. After leaving school at an early age, she spent two decades managing business entities and leading development programs in industries ranging from education to aviation before she came to the institute's Cape York Leaders Program in 2008. In 2011 she joined the institute as director of leadership. In December 2012 she was appointed as CEO.

In 2012 Fiona was named Queensland Not for Profit Manager of the Year by the Australian Institute of Management and was a state finalist in the Telstra Business Women's Awards. She sits on the boards of several community organisations.

In this essay Fiona Jose describes the important work of the Cape York Institute for Policy and Leadership, established by Noel Pearson. She relates her own process of growing into the leadership role at the institute. She explains that at the heart of the Cape York Agenda is a simple assertion: maximum participation in economic life is key to overcoming disadvantage. Above all, Fiona stresses the need for prospective leaders to hold a clear sense of purpose.

A leader takes people where they want to go. A great leader takes people where they don't necessarily want to go, but ought to be.

—Rosalynn Carter

Early influences

My parents were sources of proud inspiration as a child. Even while I was quite young, I could see that my family was different to many others around me. In successive communities where we lived, drugs were commonplace and education wasn't a high priority. So many passed too young. For my parents, however, there were no excuses when it came to education—Dad went to work every day, and Mum escorted us to school. We did not have television but I was a keen reader. It wasn't until I attended high school that I realised that my upbringing in terms of education, housing and income had been at the lowest end compared to other Australians.

At around the age of twelve I recall being inspired by the story of Rosa Parks, a black American civil rights activist whose refusal to give up her bus seat to a white passenger catapulted her to national prominence. This was a precursor to a full-blown civil rights movement in the US. I have personally felt the sting of discrimination, and I regard what I do now not as work, but as my life's passion.

After leaving school I went straight into the workforce, acquiring skills as I went. I moved into management roles, first in the education sector, and then in the aviation industry. I would recommend to anyone to take opportunities to travel; in my case it helped immensely by extending my knowledge of Indigenous communities. I learned some big life lessons through work. One was that there are times when you must leave behind a role you know and take the leap into new, unknown territory. Another lesson concerned sustainable reform. I saw myself as a change maker, but while I drove innovation hard and achieved growth and improvement, when I left these roles, so too did the improvements. At first I thought that my innovations had failed, but on deeper reflection, I realised that I needed to make a more profound impact at policy level that would produce enduring change. A young Noel Pearson (of whom I will say more later) was instrumental in bringing me to this realisation, which led in time to my current role.

About the Cape York Institute

The Cape York Institute is the policy and leadership division of Cape York Partnership, an organisation dedicated to the empowerment of Cape York Indigenous people. The partnership operates a diverse set of entities from schools to commercial and social enterprises.

The Cape York Institute takes the lead in the development of innovative policy reform to transition Indigenous people from passive welfare dependency to engagement with the real economy, and to restore Indigenous responsibility. Its work focuses on policy, research and advocacy to shift conservative approaches to Indigenous affairs (from, I might add, all levels of government). The institute leads and participates in national debates, while keeping solutions to local Cape York issues its core business.

The institute's flagship leadership initiative is the Cape York Leaders Program, which seeks to create, grow and nurture natural leadership qualities in its members—from secondary students through to adults. Scholarships are offered to talented secondary students to attend boarding schools, and to those entering university studies. Adults are also offered scholarships to study leadership and further their qualifications.

In a typical day I may find myself dealing with a range of complex and sometimes sensitive situations. I might have to make decisions regarding a student attending school away from their Cape community for the first time who is facing a crisis as they re-evaluate negative or life-threatening behaviours regarded as 'normal' in the community, or as they acknowledge abuse or trauma that is not spoken of. Then I might make a quick mind shift to converse with some of Australia's greatest Indigenous leaders on national policy. (I am privileged to speak most days with executive chairman Noel Pearson to think through innovative approaches to long-standing challenges.) Then there is the world of 'Indigenous affairs'—a struggle of politics and power that often involves trying to get governments out of our lives so that we can be the architects of our future.

There is much work to be done, and it will require real leaders and real leadership.

Leadership

So what is leadership, and how do you grow into it? There are countless books, endless conferences and courses, and millions of websites and blogs about leadership and how it can be developed.

By all means take in as much of this guidance as you can. But in my opinion you should avoid being too deliberate. You should be careful not to rely on 'experts' advising you how to be a leader, as every leader has a complexity of entwined traits that mark them as someone driven by purpose who can inspire others.

I believe most leaders don't choose to be a leader; instead, leadership chooses them.

Leadership will beckon you when you are doing what you value most, and doing it superlatively well. If you are doing that, sooner or later you will be tapped on the shoulder and set on the path to leadership.

At first you might not even notice the moments that are taking you toward leadership. In my life and career I can recall many small steps on my leadership journey, although I did not see them in that light at the time. I never consciously set out to be a leader, and even after I came to the realisation that I had that capacity within me, it took some time for me to fully acknowledge it.

The importance of purpose

So my first message to you is not to be too deliberate too soon. If you are destined to be a leader, the qualities that will take you there will be inside you. And in my view, your most important inner quality is your sense of purpose.

Listen to the signals that come to you from other people, and from your heart.

When you find your purpose, you will know it because it will resonate deep down. It will be congruent with who you are, and yet it will be bigger than you; big enough to humble and awe you. You will feel that you are in the right place, at the right time, doing the right thing.

It is this feeling that gets you out of bed in the morning, and keeps you going when the going gets tough.

Goals and purpose

It's easy to make the mistake of conflating goals and purpose. They are related, but quite different.

I can best illustrate it with an analogy. Suppose you are the captain of a ship. It is your responsibility to bring your vessel and its crew and passengers safely to their destination. To achieve this you must know exactly where you are and where you are going. Your destination may be far beyond the visible horizon, and your vision may be obscured by waves or storm clouds. Along the way there will be many intermediate goals or tasks to be performed by you and your crew. Your role is to let others get on with the details, so that you can maintain a focus on the purpose: getting safely into harbour.

So if you are thinking about leadership—perhaps not of a ship, but of some public endeavour—then above all else you must have a clear idea about where you are leading people. The journey—the day-to-day routine—is important, but it is only the servant of the purpose. As a leader, your responsibility is to keep that purpose firmly in your mind; to keep hold of the purpose for those you lead, even as they are distracted by immediate challenges. It is only by dint of your deeply held, perfectly understood, and clearly communicated purpose that you can hope to make progress.

Purpose is a deeper matter than goals. Purpose consists of your fundamental drivers fused into a singular resolve. It captures what you think, believe and stand for. It contains your bottom line, your non-negotiables and your determination.

Goals are forged out of purpose. Without purpose, you can't hope to be a leader in public life because your goals will be without the depth and substance required to withstand the forces that could push you off your path.

Our purpose

For me, and for my colleagues at Cape York Partnership, the purpose, ironically, is to make ourselves redundant, to be out of a job. That time will come when the remote Indigenous communities are like any other community in Australia. All the children will be in school; youth will be engaged in meaningful training and further education; adults will be in jobs and looking after the children; elders will be respected. The services that are enjoyed by other Australians will be in place, sustaining community.

Indeed, the nature of Indigenous leadership will change when we get to the destination I have in mind. Indigenous leaders will be able to 'get on with' being leaders in their own lives, families and cultures—without necessarily having to bang their heads against governments. Let me put it another way: once Indigenous people have the same rights, opportunities and responsibilities as other Australians, Indigenous leaders won't have to spend so much time in the corridors of power arguing for politicians to give us a bigger say in our own lives and futures. In the future that I and my colleagues at Cape York Partnership envisage, after we've achieved that equality, Indigenous leaders will be treated as the equal of any other leader at the table—giving our communities a voice in the national conversation, but concentrating our efforts on our people and communities.

This, sadly, is not what is happening now. We are a long way off our collective vision of being redundant. As I have said, there is much work to be done.

Family role models

For me personally—and it would likely be the same for many leaders—my purpose was forged in my childhood and youth. And as I mentioned, it all started with my family.

As a young girl, the communities I lived in were in decline and suffering from what you might call the dead hand of low expectations. Well-intended public policy of the previous decades meant that passive welfare was the norm for Indigenous people. People weren't expected to work, and all that idleness combined with alcohol led to a sharp decline in social norms.

But not in my family. Mum and Dad would have none of this low expectation stuff. Not for themselves and certainly not for their three children. My grandfather would talk to me about his childhood—one full of working hard, living off the sea and land, being self-sufficient, and providing for his family and the extended family. He and everyone else looked out for each other's children, even if that meant telling parents of their children's wrongdoings, in order to keep the children safe.

My parents were also vocal about the social decay around us. I think they knew well the allure of the lives being led outside our front door, and they were terrified that we would start asking ourselves an obvious question: 'Why study and work hard when you can sit around, do nothing and get welfare?'

But they were just as concerned for our extended family and the other people in the community. Dad, in particular, often shared his thoughts on the problems and the solutions. In his own quiet way, he would speak of the root causes as he saw them. While many people in the community and in wider Australia were prone to fully adopt a 'blame the whitefella' position, Dad had a more nuanced view. He didn't ignore the sins of the whitefella, but he had a lot of regard for self-agency; for people to take on the responsibility to help themselves. So, in this way, he appealed to his children on a personal level to strive always to do and be your best—no matter what your circumstance. And he framed the drama around us through the same prism.

As a young girl and young woman, such thinking became ingrained in my outlook and my personal politics. Perhaps better put, it became what I believed in. It is at my core.

A young Noel Pearson

In the 1990s I was exposed to the thinking of a young Noel Pearson. What struck me was how ready Noel was to listen and learn. He was a prodigious reader. He would meet and work with the elders (traditional leaders) who were exasperated and saddened by the rapid decline in their communities. He would say little but listen intently as the elders talked about their concerns for their communities. Then he would articulate these concerns to wider audiences. By common consent he was the spokesman, because he could articulate their concerns better than anyone.

Noel Pearson's challenges to Indigenous people to stand up and take responsibility for themselves found fertile ground in my mind. He spoke of the very things that Mum and Dad had impressed upon me.

Over time, these sentiments developed into the Cape York Agenda, a blueprint for the advancement of Cape York Indigenous people that grew out of those early discussions between elders and leaders. In turn the agenda gave birth to the Cape York Welfare Reform program. Its uniqueness was, and still is, in the fact that elders, traditional leaders and our Indigenous-led institutions designed, and are implementing, the reforms.

At the heart of the agenda is a simple assertion: maximum participation in economic life is key to overcoming disadvantage. My purpose is to see all Indigenous people on Cape York, and beyond, participating fully in economic life.

Another way this purpose is expressed is that we want Indigenous people on Cape York to be able to choose lives that they have reason to value. In many ways, that is the better statement. It allows space for the cultural dimension while ensuring economic participation: the best of both worlds.

My personal purpose is to be part of the effort that will see this greater purpose become reality. It guides me every day and I judge everything I do through that lens. To my mind, it is what makes me a leader.

What does all this mean for you?

Perhaps then we could say that to be a leader, you have to craft your own agenda. You might be thinking to enter politics. If so, you should carefully think through what matters to you and use that to create your own agenda. Then, through whatever means, set about crafting goals that will give expression to that purpose.

But the purpose should be the priority for three very important reasons.

First, being a leader involves inspiring people to come with you. In my experience, people don't follow a leader based on goals. They come on board around the purpose. More accurately, they come on board around a well-articulated purpose. They will be attracted to a purpose that fits with their beliefs and thoughts. To lead people, your purpose needs to be sophisticated, fully developed, and, at its core, solid.

All things change, but a purpose is not something to change with the wind. Consistency, I have observed, is the key capital of leadership. Like any capital, you need to spend it wisely and so making changes to your core purpose is not something to be done lightly. That's why you should spend a lot of your time thinking about your purpose, and rather less time worrying about being a leader.

Your purpose will be your guide.

Second, no matter what you set out to do, you will be criticised. In our work at the institute we face constant and often very coordinated opposition. I regularly receive criticism and I am, as all leaders need to be, open to hearing about how we can do better. Your conviction over your purpose should not blind you to genuine feedback and suggestions for improvement.

But the criticism the institute receives often goes beyond that, and I don't think we are so unusual in that regard. Sure, the issues we work on at Cape York Partnership are perhaps more contested than others, but all things are contested. In our work, criticism that comes from people who don't comprehend the level of social breakdown in remote Indigenous towns is often simply and starkly unfair.

No matter what aspect of public policy or politics you are involved in, you will occasionally meet strong opposition. Frankly, some of it will be quite hurtful. Some will, in your eyes, be very unfair. Some criticism will be highly personal. We would all wish for this not to be the case but it is, I have had to conclude, a fact of life—or at least a fact of public life.

Your purpose will be your shield.

Finally, leaving aside the hurtful, the unfair and the personal, you should accept that there will be people, organisations and governments that simply have different views from you and any organisation you lead. And for whatever reason, obstacles will be placed in your path. To return to my earlier metaphor, you may not always be blessed with calm seas and smooth sailing. Endeavouring to keep your boat on a perfectly even keel is futile; your best hope is to chart a steady course through the rough seas.

A sense of purpose will sometimes be the only thing that gets you back on your feet after a hard knock. And there will be knocks. And there will be times when it seems so much easier to walk away. But your purpose will make sure you don't. Steadfastly maintaining your purpose when the going gets tough is, I think, the true hallmark of a leader.

Your purpose will be your strength.

Love, luck and unreasonableness

Andrew Leigh

Andrew Leigh is the federal Labor member for Fraser, in the ACT. Prior to being elected in 2010, he was a professor of economics at the Australian National University. Andrew holds a PhD in public policy from Harvard, and has previously served as associate to High Court Justice Michael Kirby. In 2011, he received the Young Economist Award, a prize given every two years by the Economics Society of Australia to the best Australian economist under 40. His books include *Disconnected* (2010), *Battlers and billionaires: the story of inequality in Australia* (2013) and *The economics of just about everything* (2014). A father of three sons, Andrew lives with his wife Gweneth in Hackett, ACT. His website is www.andrewleigh.com.

In his essay Andrew Leigh relates how he became involved in public life, and advises the young leaders of the future to do what they love, expect good and bad luck, and be a bit unreasonable.

His purpose in writing the essay, he says, is to leave the reader with a sense that a life of service to others is a life well lived. While a few people in public life are daft or mercenary, most public servants and parliamentarians are in fact well-informed people who aim to make the world a better place.

The ideas of economists and political philosophers, both when they are right and when they are wrong, are more powerful than is commonly understood. Indeed the world is ruled by little else.

—John Maynard Keynes

In June 1998, I flew out of Australia to work in London. I had no job to go to and not much in the way of savings to support me, but I knew I wanted to do something related to politics. Tony Blair's government had been elected the previous year, and British Labour was doing exciting things under the rubric of the Third Way. It seemed to be worth taking a chance to secure an interesting opportunity.

In the end, things worked out. I sent about 50 letters to Labour members of parliament, some of whom agreed to meet up for a cup of tea. I spent a few weeks working for the fabulously eccentric Fiona Mactaggart MP, and for Australian expatriate Ross Cranston MP. By Christmas, I was back in Australia, but the experience helped shape me, and I'm glad I took that risk.

For young leaders, there are three pieces of advice I'd offer. Do what you love, recognise that luck will buffet your career, and be a bit unreasonable.

Do what you love

A standard mistake that very bright young people make is to place too much value on money and too little value on time. I remember at school a friend of mine wanted to pursue a career in finance. She didn't think she'd much enjoy studying it and figured the work would be boring, but did think she'd have a great retirement. That's no way for an 18-year-old to be thinking. You'll be glad to hear she's now in a career she loves.

As the cliché goes, if you find a job you love, you'll never work a day in your life. I've been fortunate to do jobs – such as being associate to former High Court Justice Michael Kirby, working as an economics professor at the Australian National University and serving as a member of parliament – that are an untrammelled delight. In this, I know how fortunate I am. For most of human history, hardly anyone had a job they loved. As Hobbes put it, the life of man without the social contract is 'solitary, poor, nasty, brutish and short'. Today, most people in the world work to live, not in a job they love. However, if you can find a job you love, you'll almost certainly be good at it too. Leadership requires that strong sense of commitment and psychological involvement – or in other words, loving all the work the position involves.

Don't expect to know immediately what it is you'll love. If you're choosing courses at TAFE or university, take opportunities to sit in the back row of classes to check them out. Ask advice from plenty of people, and take your time to sift through it. Do work experience and internships – it's striking how much you can learn in just a week in a new workplace. And don't be surprised if you find yourself shifting jobs a bit at the start of your career: job-matching isn't just about employers deciding if they like you, but also about you deciding whether you're a good fit for that career. (Similar advice applies in the romantic realm.)

As you go along, you might find that it helps to have a mentor or two who can keep you on track. The few career and study decisions that I've regretted are mostly those where I didn't take the time to seek more advice from people with grey hair. I don't have just one mentor; rather, I draw heavily on advice from my parents and a handful of senior parliamentary colleagues. They know me, I trust them, and they invariably help me come to the decision that will keep me doing what I love.

Expect some good and bad luck

In his book *Adapt: why success always starts with failure*, Tim Harford tells the extraordinary tale of Italian-born Mario Capecchi, whose mother was taken away to a concentration camp in 1940 when he was three years old. Capecchi's father physically abused him, so he was forced to live as a street urchin from the age of four. At the age of eight he went into hospital, suffering from typhoid. There was little to eat, and he spent a year in conditions that claimed the lives of many orphans.

On his ninth birthday, a woman entered the hospital ward. At first, Capecchi didn't recognise his own mother, because of how much weight she had lost in Dachau. Together, they moved to the United States. There, Capecchi studied genetics at Harvard and applied for a research grant to study whether it was possible to chemically 'knock out' a single gene in a mouse. It was a risky project, but he was successful. In 2007, Mario Capecchi was awarded the Nobel Prize in Medicine.

Capecchi had more bad luck before his tenth birthday than most of us will have in our lives. But he had some good luck too. At Harvard he got to work with the great James Watson, co-discoverer of DNA. Moreover, Capecchi won his US research grant at a time when a UK team were unsuccessful in a similar grant. Luck may not affect you quite as spectacularly, but it will shape your life. The question isn't whether you'll be lucky or unlucky, but how you respond to fortune and misfortune.

The best youth sporting coaches are starting to recognise this. A movement called the 'positive coaching alliance' is grounded in the notion of helping children realise that they control three things: their level of *effort*, whether they *learn* from experiences, and how they respond to *mistakes*. The ELM mantra reminds us that slumps are inevitable, and that the question is how we hard we try, how well we bounce back from adversity, and how successfully we correct our errors.

Luck plays a special role in my own profession of politics. For every person fortunate enough to have served in the federal parliament, there are scores who miss out. Often, those who miss out are at least as capable and hard-working as those who succeed, but simply don't have the good fortune to win party preselection or the general election. Because of this, I don't advise anyone to shape a career with the aim of ending up in parliament. Leaders are found in all walks of life. By all means, bear politics in mind when you're deciding whether to join a political party, what to study and what jobs to apply for. But a career focused solely around the goal of winning a spot in parliament is likely to be a fragile one. Remember rule number one: it's better to do something you love.

As an aside, I also think that Australia is better served by people who enter parliament in their 40s or 50s, having had a substantial career (I fail this test, having been elected at age 38). Politics is an extremely competitive profession, and the risk of entering too young is that one's political career is shaped around power rather than ideas. If you view politics as primarily about beating your opponents rather than building a better Australia, you're unlikely to make as valuable a contribution to the nation. Having a significant career to fall back onto is also an insurance policy against compromise. In the words of economist Max Weber, it allows you to 'live for' politics rather than to 'live off' politics.

Be unreasonable

Playwright George Bernard Shaw could be a bit stuffy at times, but I do love his line: 'The reasonable man adapts himself to the world: the unreasonable one persists in trying to adapt the world to himself. Therefore all progress depends on the unreasonable man.'

Entrepreneurs are almost always a bit unreasonable. So are the best scientists, artists and writers. One of my favourite tales of unreasonableness is that of the West Australian physician Barry Marshall, who was seeking evidence for his theory that a bacterium called *Helicobacter pylori* might be responsible for gastritis. The theory squarely challenged the established medical consensus of the time. To test it, Marshall had a baseline endoscopy carried out, then drank a petri dish of the bacteria. When he began vomiting a week later, the pain would have been partly offset by the happy knowledge that he had proved many in the medical establishment wrong. In 2005, Marshall shared the Nobel Prize for Medicine with his collaborator Robin Warren.

But you don't have to drink bacteria to be unreasonable. Sometimes, innovation can be as straightforward as suggesting a way your workplace could operate better, standing up for a person who is being mistreated, or starting a quiet campaign against a social injustice.

Another way of being usefully unreasonable is to bring an unusual perspective to the conversation. Among my Labor colleagues in federal parliament, I particularly value the contributions of people with backgrounds that are a bit different to the rest. Melissa Parke used to work at the United Nations. Catherine King was a social worker. Mark Dreyfus was a barrister. Julie Owens was a musician. As it happens, Melissa, Catherine, Mark and Julie each entered federal politics in their 40s.

I appreciate the different perspectives that they bring to our conversations about ideas, and it has encouraged me to 'revert to type' as an economist. Fundamentally, I think about issues through the lens of economics, using tools such as cost–benefit analysis, supply and demand modelling, and ignoring sunk costs. Increasingly, I've found that the most valuable contribution I can make to policy debates is from that standpoint. Public policy is formed in the cut and thrust of a range of competing perspectives; my aim is to bring the most informed economic analysis into the mix. The unreasonable nature of my contribution is that policy decisions are not always made from an economic perspective. Being a team player with a quirky well-informed contribution is a bit like cooking – where the meal invariably tastes better than each of the individual ingredients.

Conclusion

A core premise of *So you want to be a leader* is that young Australians are disenchanted with politics. On average, this is certainly true (see my book *Disconnected* for a summary of the statistical data). But as a member of parliament, I also have the privilege to meet a plethora of young people who are idealistic, passionate and purposeful. My purpose in writing this essay is to tell some stories about making a difference, and perhaps to leave the reader with a sense that a life of service to others is a life well lived.

Extremists of the left and right often try to perpetuate a view that political decisions are the result of selfishness or stupidity. 'Elect a smart altruist', the argument goes, 'and all will be well.' While a few people in public life are daft or mercenary, most public servants and parliamentarians are in fact well-informed people who aim to make the world a better place. That doesn't mean you can't make a positive difference too – but don't fall into the trap of thinking that you're the only one in the room with a reasonable argument. If the problem you're worrying about had a simple solution that made everyone better off, chances are that someone would have implemented it already.

When Philip Crisp asked me to write this essay, I jumped at the chance. Working with young people in my own community is one of the most enjoyable parts of being a member of parliament. When I check my diary in the morning and see that I'm speaking at a school, meeting with a group of young people to discuss overseas aid or having a conversation with young sports stars, it always puts a spring in my step. So if you're a young person who's keen to get active in politics, don't be shy about approaching your elected representatives. Chances are that they're as keen to chat with you as you are to speak with them.

Finally, you might reasonably ask: how well have I followed my own three pieces of advice? As I noted above, I've loved all my jobs. I've done my best to recognise the role of Lady Luck in my upswings and downturns. My main mistake is probably that I haven't been quite unreasonable enough. So that's on my to-do list for the years to come.

To the lady in the Lodge

Anya Poukchanski

Anya Poukchanski is a writer who works in various genres. She completed a law degree and a bachelor of economics and social sciences at the University of Sydney, where she was editor of the student paper *Honi Soit* and the magazine *UR* and also student editor of the *Sydney Law Review* and the *Australian Journal of International Law*. Anya's honours thesis about the rise of Vladimir Putin's United Russia Party was awarded the University Medal. Anya has served as an associate to a Federal Court judge and currently works as a solicitor.

Anya Poukchanski's essay is a letter to Australia's second female prime minister. In it, Anya addresses our future leader about her priorities, experiences, values and strategies, and how they relate to her gender. The letter seeks to continue an unfinished national conversation about female leadership, which began under Julia Gillard's stewardship, but was cut abruptly short with her removal. It reflects on what may change with the passing of time, what may stay the same, and how the prime minister's gender could affect the way she exercises the position she holds – whether in five, 10 or 20 years. Does or should a female prime minister govern differently? Does she owe a special allegiance to women, or they to her? What issues will she face with respect to the status of women and, importantly, men? And what does her ascent, with the challenges she faced along the way, tell us about the contentious and imperative goal of equality between the sexes?

We still think of a powerful man as a born leader and a powerful woman as an anomaly.

—Margaret Atwood

Dear Prime Minister

First of all, congratulations! I hope you have your feet up and a shiraz in hand. I'm assuming, for your sake as much as anyone else's, that you've just feted the successful close of a gruelling election campaign, and have a couple of weeks to reflect and react before your reality is blurred into unremitting hyperactivity. The last time around shows this would be better than a backroom elevation to power – and the last time around is likely to be your dogged shadow for a maddening while.

From election hangover day, the media will have been full of commentary and comparison stories. Are you like her? Are you different? Will her legacy infect your leadership and will you suffer her fate? There will have been some stories about your hair and a regurgitated photo of Not the Best Dress You Ever Wore. You are probably not surprised by this. As a woman in politics you will have long ago learned that your femaleness is a badge you wear, while maleness is the skin into which your colleagues are born. So, as Australia's second female prime minister, you are a slightly less fabulous beast than the first, but you are nonetheless a curiosity. Just the second unicorn to wander into the clearing. Everyone naturally wants to know if there are common traits among your species.

Leadership is still a male-tinted picture. I can say that quite safely, writing now for the future. Perhaps after you, for the third or fourth woman to occupy your role, the connotations of leadership will be different. The first sign of this might be that headlines do not count how many women came before her. At present, the belt continues to be notched. The first female prime minister coincided with the first female governor-general, came soon after the first female premiers of New South Wales and Queensland, supported from somewhere in the bureaucratic web by the first female police commissioner. We arranged these people in a constellation and joined the dots. The chart showed progress. But other signs were more telling. There were fewer women in parliament than men; fewer in executive positions and on boards; fewer in highly paid jobs and many fewer in the police and military.

Prime Minister, do not be tempted to see your newly gained position as a finish line. With all due respect, there are many more important markers of equality. Mali, Pakistan and Haiti have all had female prime ministers, and on the UN gender inequality index their rankings are 141, 123 and 127 respectively, out of 186. Not even the laws enshrining equality between men and women should close this issue for you. In your own experience you will have encountered the evidence: studies showing women are still expected to be the primary carers of children and elderly people, that they use more qualifiers and apologies in their speech, that the very tenor of their voices is considered less authoritative. These are among the reasons why they hold fewer leadership positions, why they are paid between 10 and 25 per cent less for performing the same job, and why they are much more likely to live in poverty or decline into it after retirement. Legal equality can help mask de facto discrimination.

Hopefully, your presence at the Lodge will help change the attitudes behind these trends. But it can only be one (albeit prominent) story among many, to which people will only really choose to listen if it has a ring of truth – if they can catch in you, say, a glimpse of their colleague, their sister, their favourite lecturer at university. If you do not resonate with their reality then they can class you merely among that race of strange creatures, powerful women, to which their own kind do not belong, as women in England did under Margaret Thatcher.

So I am writing to you in this very public forum in aid of that cause. I hope that if the challenges you face due to your gender are discussed and addressed with clarity, level-headedness and initiative, not just by you but by those who influence and express the public will, Australia may be permanently steered toward a more stable and constructive way of dealing with gender.

So, please, Prime Minister, do not rest on symbolism. Your trailblazing predecessor must have thought the cheque was cashed when she appointed four female departmental secretaries in one day, because on that day she also demoted the Office of the Status of Women from its ear-accessing post in the Department of the Prime Minister and Cabinet to the Department of Families, Community Services and Indigenous Affairs. A few months later, men with airtime were calling her a witch, and other rhyming variants. Instead, make a practical mark in a cause you may feel you have realised but which still expresses the needs of most women.

What should you do? You would not want me to tell you, even if I were game to give policy advice. There are multiple ways of achieving the same goals. Those goals have not changed, in the mainstream of feminism, since its inception. Promote women's professional achievement. Make institutions more amenable to their participation. Make sure not just the law, but also the culture, of government does all it can to ensure women are treated with respect in the workplace and at home. Make sure your foreign policy, in particular Australia's aid, promotes the basic, non-negotiable values of equality around the world. Listen to women's contributions. Do not act as if there is nothing left to do.

Here is one thing you may not have thought of: you will not change much without including men in this plan. From women in some of society's most powerful posts, such as Professor Anne-Marie Slaughter (former director of policy planning at the US State Department) and Sheryl Sandberg (Facebook's chief operating officer), we hear the same life-learned advice. Having an equal partner at home is the basis for equal achievement in the wider world. A partner who exacts those archaic womanly duties history hung upon us drains a woman of her energy and autonomy. And worse, of course – studies show that men who fixedly play out traditional gender roles are more likely to commit domestic violence.

Gender equality is not a 'women's issue' but a social issue, so you can reject the criticism that you are favouring one half of the population (though as privileged political populations go, that is a high proportion by any leader's measure). It is well known that high levels of women's education, health and workplace participation greatly improve indicators of general health, child mortality and economic growth. Indeed, this is a first principle of our own foreign aid policy, which you have a duty to uphold and fund.

A touchstone of equality is the division of work and family duties, and Australia – unless it has changed much since the time of this writing – still has far to go. Cultural expectations and institutional failures (such as lack of available child care and patchy parental leave) that pressure women to stay home or work less, deny them the liberty of work and the economy of their skills and labours. The conviction that it is a woman's role to care for children, especially young children, is understandably pervasive – the challenge to it arose only in the last 100 years, and forcefully perhaps only in the last 50. Many women themselves feel their urge to bear and nurture children is biologically determined, and the physical facts of maternity would seem to offer support to this proposition.

Nonetheless, research stubbornly refuses to finally confirm these notions. Both men and women show hormonal changes upon the birth of a child that incline them to care for it. Women's greater involvement in the process, beyond the time of breastfeeding, has in modern science been primarily explained by social rather than biological structuring. The idea that children and domesticity is an inherently female role is one that you will frequently encounter in different iterations and, happily, one to which your response can be as close to uncontroversial as politics allows: women may or may not be more interested than men in staying home to raise children – either way, we have to create a situation where all parents have a genuine choice about whether or how to do it.

What is less often recognised, and what lends weight to the argument for establishing a more flexible system, is that the same cultural and institutional pressures can hurt men by cutting them out of meaningful family life, relegating them to work when they may want a substantial role in raising their children. It can also hurt children by denying them the opportunity to build a strong relationship with their father. As James Joyner, a prominent international security analyst, pointed out soon after the death of his wife left him caring for his two young children, the work–life dichotomy is a problem for all of us, not just women.

For this reason, in doing the work of women's empowerment you need not call yourself a feminist. Do not mistake me, that is what you will be. But the slanderous distortion of the term into a disparagement seems likely only to spread, and you would do better to spend your political capital on enacting its values rather than defending its name. The loss of the word is a loss to contemporary society. The historical tradition it invokes is important. Ideas are more distinct when they are named. But the absence of the word need not mean the dissolution of feminist values.

Addressing women of my generation, you will know that many grew up thinking feminists were angry old women of a time gone by. In some ways it is unsurprising that the 1990s saw the term hesitate. Neoliberal thinking, in its emphasis on individualism and rationality and its distrust of collective structures, was our schooling in politics. We were taught that our successes and failures were our own, which made even the latter liberating, because it was in each person's grasp to turn their failures around. Deep, invisible paradigms such as patriarchy jangled like an ageing bogeyman. In addition, we did not want to think of ourselves as victims. Raising the banner of feminism meant acknowledging that there was something to fight against, something which continued to menace us.

It did, of course. Women continued to be sexually harassed and assaulted and discriminated against. But that chimerical legal equality won by previous generations comforted us that basic ideas were no longer in dispute. For most educated people in the West, whether they called themselves feminists or not, it was unthinkable that anyone would take away women's right to vote, to get educated or to work outside the home. This is the only redeeming fact about the demise of the word 'feminism': that it was enabled only by the acceptance of the idea itself. Facts such as that we have few women to vote for, less financial return on our education than men, or do most of the work inside the home, still need the attention of people like you.

Although promoting women's rights serves all of society, and although you need not take up the feminist epithet, do not evade the fact that you are a woman. No one else will. Your predecessor in gender made it a policy, in her first years in office, not to talk publicly about her femaleness. Nevertheless nobody failed to notice it. She was appealed to as a woman almost as much as she was criticised as a woman. It is better to be on the front foot.

Instead, I am going to suggest something you may not like to hear, Prime Minister. It is not that, because you are a woman, your government must understand the needs of women in a more profound way than one with a male at its helm. That belies a central tenet of representative government, which is that our MPs must have the democratic imagination to represent us all, not just the people who voted for them or fit their profile. Anyway, to ask you to understand all women based on your gender would be ridiculous, given that your experience – now that you are Prime Minister – is by definition atypical.

It is, rather, that you have a moral duty to consider women. The basis of the duty is simply that you are best placed to do so. Whether through your own experience or through media attention or lobbying, questions of particular relevance to women will be kept more boldly on your agenda than your male predecessors', and, perhaps in misguided deference to the idea I refuted above, the public is likely to give you more scope to address them. They may say you are 'playing the gender card', but at least they will recognise that that card is peculiarly in your hand. You should not waste this valuable opportunity, whatever you may think of its premise. 'There is a special place in hell for women who do not help other women', said former US Secretary of State Madeleine Albright. I would venture it is not such a special place as to have no rowdy neighbours. I suspect that sharing these women's circle of hell are the wealthy who do not give to the poor, the parents who neglect their children and every person who ever made a pass at their best friend's spouse. It is about supporting those who need you.

You may feel you are paying a high price for giving such support. Media coverage is probably already a concern. You can take some bitter comfort in the knowledge that, no matter what your policies, the tone struck on the air and online would be little different. The media, at least today and with the kind of vicious tenacity that any dog owner would recognise as a long-term hold on the bone, gnaws on women with particular relish. They are classically the object, to be devoured. But they are now also the object to be discussed. Together these criteria mean that the only women met hospitably in the media are both good to look at and placid about being talked about, rather than talking. The others struggle. They get called 'shrill'. The media is hostile to women who demand to be heard and particularly to those who have the nerve to be ugly as they do it.

Angela Merkel, Chancellor of Germany as it led the European Union through economic recession, was mocked for her supposedly awkward attempts to create the feminine image she had previously been criticised for lacking. Hillary Clinton's hair made as many headlines as she did when she ran for president in 2008. Germaine Greer herself delivered a prime-time assessment of Prime Minister Gillard's arse on a TV show meant to engender national discussion. Whether or not she was joking was lost in the general glee. The list could go on. A rather shorter list is the one of giggle grenades lobbed at the looks of male politicians. I think you will agree with me that John Howard's eyebrows were hilarious, and they were perhaps the closest contender in Australia, making it on to the regular costume party dress-up list. But somehow, thinking over the world's gentlemen politicians, I cannot agree that their overall appearance is proportionally more pleasing than that of their female counterparts. It is just that we are used to judging them on substance rather than image.

A big part of the problem is one you are in the wrong industry to solve. A 2007 study confirmed that stories written by female journalists make up only one third of by-lines in Australia's national newspapers. Not one woman currently edits a national weekday newspaper. Yet more than half of all journalists are women. There has been a collective supposition that with the internet's democratisation of expression that we will see this effect reversed. Unless there have been surprising developments, you can see, Prime Minister, that this has not been the case. Sexism moved into the wilds of the internet and, as in most places, made itself comfortable. Not only do women have a small role in many online institutions – Wikipedia, for example, has only 13 per cent female contributors, and Google only 30 per cent female employees – but the abuse and harassment that some men suppress in person comes surging out under the protection of anonymity. Online abuse, trolling and intimidation have become a massive threat to women's participation on the net, prompting new protective laws (yet to be tested properly), boycotts of Twitter, an open letter from the founder of Reddit asking its male users (two-thirds of the total) to please be less sexist, and spirited, sometimes highly entertaining, fights back (such as the hashtag #mencallmethings, which exposes online bullies). The most virulent and baldly misogynistic abuse directed at your female predecessor originated online, and found a nourishing home there. You will likely draw these people's attention in the same way.

Another iteration of sexism which the internet did not create but enthusiastically amplifies is the broad brushstroking of women. This particular cultural tic is based on the understanding I mentioned at the very start of this letter, and it is one which, aptly, is likely to follow you from the start to the end of your career: that women are women, and men are people. When a woman writes (or speaks, or rides a bike, or buys a t-shirt, or goes into space) she does it as a woman. Her femaleness vies for space with the activity, and often wins. So there is women's fiction, written by and for, and there are just books; there is women's history, presumably the history with lady bits, and there is just history; and there is women's (or rather, ladies') golf, and there is just golf.

Hence the most inane question our popular culture has ever generated, in a strong field of contenders: 'What do women want?' I, for one, want a good sushi shop to open near my office. You, if you know what is good for you, probably want an invisibility cloak. But what that question asks, usually of a woman though sometimes, for added gall, of a man, is for one of us to give a single answer on behalf of all women. What turns women on? Do women want families? Do women want careers? What do women want to watch on TV? I hope I am wrong, Prime Minister, but I think some very silly people from both sides of the fence are going to ask you at least some of these questions.

Not only are the questions ready-made, but the answers to questions that were never asked are also given. When, as a woman in the public eye, you say 'I think' or 'I want', what is heard is 'women think' and 'women want'. No wonder Prime Minister Gillard did not want to talk about being a woman – she was trying as hard as she could to be taken on her own terms, rather than carrying the baggage of her entire gender. It did not work. A lot can and has been said about the 'destroying the joint' furore of 2012, but Jane Caro got to the crux. She observed that, in accusing women of 'destroying the joint' by pointing to three female leaders (Christine Nixon, ex-Victorian police commissioner, Clover Moore, lord mayor of Sydney, and Prime Minister Gillard), talkback host Alan Jones 'accepted the all-too-common view that while the failure of male leaders reflects only on themselves, any mistakes on the part of a female leader – whether perceived or actual – reflect on the capability of all women to wield power'.[1] You are defined by your sex, and other women are defined by you.

Your ability to lead is going to be discussed as a function of your femaleness more frequently than you will like. This discussion may be uncomfortable but it will not necessarily always be in negative terms. The traditional view that women were biologically unsuited to lead has inspired the well-meaning but misguided response that perhaps they are naturally better at it. This notion has no scientific credit, and it is a dangerous message, just like any other essentialising one that says there are inherent 'female' attributes. Studies show that male and female cognition is negligibly different on a mechanical level. Yet the suggestion continues to be made that women's style of leadership is different from men's – that it is softer, or more inclusive, or more cooperative, or has some other, supposedly feminine, quality. This may not be entirely off the mark. What remains different between the minds of men and women is the socialisation to which they are exposed. As Simone de Beauvoir so aptly stated, 'One is not born, but rather becomes, a woman.' And part of that process of becoming is being taught that girls are 'nice', girls compromise, girls say yes, and girls care. Those are not bad qualities in a leader, though they may be exhausting or conducive to submission in personal life. In fact, research has confirmed that women's exhibition of these traits in power is precisely a sign of their habitual marginalisation: other minority groups, both men and women, have been shown to exhibit greater willingness to listen, empathise and collaborate when dealing with a dominant power.

Even before your appointment to lead the nation, you will have begun to develop your own style of leadership. It must have served you well, if it has gotten you here. However, it will have to evolve, now that you are the leader of a country rather than just a political party. You will do women a service if you are publicly proud of belonging to their gender, but belonging as any person does to a group in a liberal society: with your individuality intact. Resist others' urges to make you an effigy of women at large, or to project your choices or values onto all women. That is, ultimately, central to the aim of feminism: 'True equality is not making women behave like men, nor is it making us "behave like women", but is about our capacity to choose who we are without social and institutional gendered prejudices.' Eva Cox, one of Australia's preeminent feminist writers, said that, and I have no doubt it is correct.

So, Prime Minister, though parallels are bound to be drawn between you and Julia Gillard, you have no more reason to think them correct than to agree to the similarities you see between yourself and any of your predecessors in the position. Her legacy has no special power over you. The fact that you are a woman does. It should influence the way you do your job – but in substance, not style. You need to pay attention to certain policy areas but your contributions will be born of your own volition, for there are many different answers to any social question – just as there are as many individuals as there are women.

Yours sincerely,
Anya Poukchanski

---

1. Caro, J (ed.), 2013, *Destroying the joint: why women have to change the world*, UQP, Australia, p. ix.

Part 4: KNOWLEDGE

On the shoulders of giants

Peter Acton

Peter Acton has an MA in classics from Oxford, an MBA from Stanford, where he was a Harkness Fellow and an Arjay Miller Scholar, and a PhD in ancient history from Melbourne University. He was a vice-president of the Boston Consulting Group for 13 years. He is a fellow of the Australian Institute of Company Directors and the Australian Institute of Management, and a member of the Peter McCallum Research Advisory Board and of the Industry Advisory Board of the Centre for Cultural Materials Conservation at Melbourne University. Peter's book, *Poiesis: manufacturing in classical Athens*, was published by Oxford University Press in October 2014. He is founding president of Humanities 21, a group whose objective is to bring academics who work in the humanities closer to the community and especially to business.

Peter Acton's essay stresses the value of a broad education and perspective in public life. Events and challenges are never unprecedented and we can learn much about the way to deal with them from traditional disciplines like history, literature and philosophy. History teaches how to recognise patterns, motivations and likely outcomes; literature helps us understand how others think and improves our ability to communicate; and philosophy makes us consider some of the most profound questions mankind has been able to conceive as well as helping us to make and recognise logical arguments. Other benefits of a deep familiarity with these disciplines are the respect it commands from others, the ability to make more interesting conversation on a wide range of topics, and never being bored if you have nothing much to do.

We are like dwarfs sitting on the shoulders of giants. We see more, and things that are more distant, than they did, not because our sight is superior or because we are taller than they, but because they raise us up, and by their great stature add to ours.

—John of Salisbury

It is one of life's sad ironies that, unless you aim to be a famous scientist or doctor (and, let's face it, those are quite rare), being an expert in specific disciplines does not really help you succeed in public life. This is not to say that real world experience is not important – of course it is; and its absence sometimes shows! – but rather, that a broad perspective is more important to success than mastery of any specific field of knowledge. Of course you will need to acquire some professional skills if you are to make a valuable contribution to the public debate; many people believe studying law provides a good grounding for a politician, and everyone should understand basic accounting (which is actually much simpler than universities and business schools want us to believe); actuarial studies have their uses, as do micro-economics and some of the buzzword-laden pretend disciplines like marketing and finance. But to think you can base a successful career in public life on being exceptionally adept in any of these fields is a big mistake. No-one respects you for being especially knowledgeable and, to the extent that those matters inform your daily conversation, you will be considered a crashing bore.

More to the point, this sort of expertise gives you no ability at all to rise above the banality of daily chatter, to see where common perspectives are misguided or limited, or to bring wit and insight to debates that so quickly become sterile and unproductive. The world needs people who think differently. The leaders we admire are the men and women who inspire us with their vision of what we can become. They offer us a special insight into the human condition and help us to rise above the petty problems that bedevil us from day to day. Technical expertise might make you good at carrying out other people's ideas, but true leaders inspire others to carry out their own. To be truly educated in the way a leader needs to be, you must work with truly great ideas. Just as it is important for an aspiring statesman or stateswoman to get some different experiences before entering politics, it is no less important to take advantage of the wonderful fact that those who have gone before us offer marvellous material to work with.

Thinking differently does not mean you need to develop your own answers to every question. This is a challenge beyond even the smartest people; even they are likely to get more things wrong than right if they try to solve every problem from scratch. It is also quite unnecessary because no questions are really new; they have all been confronted before in some form by great minds over many generations. The most powerful ideas come from building on what has gone before. All species pass on their genes and their behaviours but, as far as we can tell, humans are the only ones who can pass on abstract ideas. To try to confront major issues without learning from all the powerful thinking that has already been done is like trying to build an automobile without knowing about the wheel or the internal combustion engine. Your own 140-character diagnostic of the world's problems is unlikely to be much better (or more memorable) than Kim Kardashian's unless it is grounded in some real wisdom. The world has spent many millennia accumulating wisdom. It is dumb not to use it.

Let me give you some examples. It has become a commonplace lament that democracy today is broken. This may be true, although different people seem to mean different things when they say this – often simply that democracy is not working according to their personal preferences. To understand how and why democracy may not be working – or whether it was always doomed as Plato believed it was – there are few better starting points than the study of the French Revolution. Read the great thinkers of the French Enlightenment like Voltaire, Rousseau, Montesquieu and Diderot, whose ideas led up to it. Explore the stimulating disagreement between Fox and Burke about whether it was good or bad. You'll not only be better informed than most of today's political commentators in their comfortable echo chambers; you might actually be in a position to make original suggestions as to what could be done about problems in today's democratic processes.

We can consider a more specific problem (and I select this example at random to illustrate the larger point). One thing that certainly seems broken, in Australia at least, is the relationship between the citizenry and our various police forces. Putting this in the context of why we have a police force in the first place might make for a more informed assessment of what has gone wrong. In ancient Athens when a breach of the peace occurred, our sources' descriptions of the event invariably include the words 'and a crowd came running'. There were two reasons for the crowd to come running: first, in the absence of a police force, it was up to the citizen body to maintain or restore the peace; second, Athens had a well-developed legal system and, whatever the problem was, it would probably result in a court case and a need for witnesses. These are the functions that are now delegated to a police force and this delegation is hard to reconcile with, say, the fact that they always seem too busy to investigate straightforward burglaries or to intervene in cases of domestic violence. On the other hand, the helpful bobby on the corner has been replaced by large teams preparing for a traffic light failure in the city centre, or exploiting a chance of imposing fines for what can often seem to be immeasurably trivial motoring offences. A historical understanding of why police forces were established might help us move from outraged bafflement to identifying constructive solutions.

History is not just a collection of facts about the past, informative though some of them can be. It is a chronicle of how our species emerged from primitive internecine competition for resources and learned to live together. It has not been a smooth journey and it is not over yet. History tells of the adventures, vicissitudes, horrors and disasters that we have made for ourselves along the way. It is not strictly true to say that those who do not learn from history are condemned to repeat it; events seldom repeat themselves exactly, but we can learn to recognise the principles and patterns that have shaped our past. Understanding how things have gone wrong – the underlying dynamics of wars, genocides, revolutions and other man-made disasters – at least improves our chances of avoiding or preventing the same mistakes in future. Greater familiarity with the history of the Middle East would surely have made us more circumspect about joining the invasions of Afghanistan and Iraq. Beyond this, history helps us to see things in perspective. No-one who has studied some of the terrible things our ancestors did to each other can fail to recognise the fragility of our common humanity and the need to work to preserve it; surely this could usefully play a more important role in our discussions on how to manage the world's refugees.

Great literature reinforces this powerful form of empathy. Read Homer's account of how Achilles sulked at the way his boss treated him and was only shaken back into action by the untimely killing of his best friend Patroclus. Go and see King Lear's anguish at the greed and ingratitude of his daughters and his agony at realising that one of them had truly loved him, but that he had misunderstood her. Laugh at the bumbling antics of Don Quixote; tremble at the mental torments of the murderer Raskolnikov in Dostoyevsky's *Crime and punishment*. Feel the haunting emptiness of T S Eliot's *The love song of J Alfred Prufrock*, or the despair in the debtors prison in Dickens' *Little Dorrit* or the dungeons of Hugo's *Les Misérables*, and I defy you to treat your fellow beings with anything but respect. And respecting others is the first step to teaching them to respect you.

Leading well is hard. It means acting with calm conviction and purpose rather than reacting fearfully to the next event that upsets your original plan. You need a clear and considered view on what life is all about. It might not be too much to suggest that anyone aspiring to leadership should have wrestled personally with the greatest question that has ever confronted mankind: why do we exist? This means moving beyond the comfortable tautologies of religion – and, no less importantly, the smug and juvenile name-calling of the modern atheist movement – and applying one's own mind to the terrifying uncertainty posed by the very fact of our presence on earth. You may not resolve it – in fact I bet you won't – but your views on the kind of life we should be leading will be much richer and more inspiring to others when you have tried. Lucretius, St Anselm and Nietzsche would be good places to start. If that seems daunting you could try Jim Holt's new book, *Why does the world exist?*, which summarises the main arguments, ancient and modern, in a very readable way and encourages the sort of intellectual humility that great leaders have always shown and that is sadly lacking in most of today's discussions on this most important subject of all. Recognising that, whatever your beliefs or your achievements, you scarcely matter in the great scheme of things, gives you the calmness and perspective that people look for in a leader.

One of the most valuable benefits of studying the great writers and thinkers of the past is that they knew how to express themselves well. How often do we hear vigorous arguments in which both parties appear to be talking about different subjects and neither side appears to be responding to the other one's points? How often do we listen to lengthy and emotion-laden diatribes consisting of a confused list of propositions that manage to be repetitive, contradictory and irrelevant all at the same time? In contrast, how refreshing it is to hear someone make a case in which their point is simple and clear and evidently supported by all the arguments they bring to bear! And how rare! A great leader needs to know how make a case cogently and powerfully, to know what constitutes evidence and what is special pleading, to rely not on appeals to the emotions (useful though they can sometimes be) but on the integrated and carefully articulated logic of a well-thought-out position. Study the greats that have gone before you and clear argumentation will become second nature. You will also find it much easier to tell when you are being taken for a ride and when someone is deliberately confusing the issue.

This is more important now than ever, when the old certainties are disappearing and we are constantly buffeted by a bewildering array of media with no way of knowing what we can trust. Serious media outlets used to aspire to be seen as 'newspapers of record' that met high journalistic standards and provided the facts in a balanced way. Now it is hard to tell whether seemingly reputable media outlets are any more objective than an anonymous personal blog. No one was very surprised when the *Huffington Post* of 23 May 2012 reported a US survey's conclusion that watchers of Fox News were 'significantly' less informed about current affairs than people who watched no news at all. The left of politics also has its one-eyed reporting platforms. The world needs people who can bring perspective and balance, and it is desperately seeking leaders who can provide them in a way we can all understand.

Aspiring leaders owe it to their followers to be lively and interesting. No-one will die in a ditch for a bore. Nor will they follow you with any conviction if they have to be bullied or cajoled into doing what you want, rather than wanting to do it because they enjoy your company, your ideas and your conversation. Wouldn't it be wonderful if we all looked forward to meetings because we knew people there were going to say interesting things? A great leader is a person people want to have around. Everyone likes to be around people who can talk with knowledge and passion about the great events, people and ideas that have gone before us.

You also need to have fun yourself. Public life is tough and you need forms of relaxation that are admirable (or at least not disgraceful) and absorbing; that will make you a happier, more relaxed –

maybe even a better – person. Perhaps the most compelling reason for studying the world's greatest thinkers and writers is that you owe it to yourself not to miss out. I confess I came late in life to Dante, Milton and Goethe. Like so many others I was deterred by the thought that reading them would be hard work and not worth the effort. I could not have been more wrong. They were not writing for an audience of elitist intellectuals; in fact, if they had been aiming only to impress their clever friends they would never have achieved their status in the human pantheon. They appealed to all levels within their society. The first people to listen to Homer's songs and most of the original audiences of Shakespeare's plays could neither read nor write.

What the great writers have to say is timeless and moving, irrespective of the status, intellect or personal interests of their audience. The greats are 'great' because they are *great*! Make the most of them and they will make the most of you.

Future-taking and future-making for 21st century success

Peter Ellyard

Peter Ellyard FAIM is a futurist, strategist, speaker and author who lives in Melbourne. He is a graduate of Sydney University (BSc Agr) and of Cornell University (MS, PhD). He is currently chairman of the Preferred Futures Institute and the Preferred Futures Group, which he founded in 1991. He is currently establishing the 2050 Institute. Peter's work is directed at assisting nations, corporations, communities and individuals to develop pathways to success in a globalising interdependent 21st century. He is an adjunct professor at the Curtin University Business School.

Peter is a former executive director for the Australian Commission for the Future. He held CEO positions in a number of public sector organisations over 20 years, relating mainly to the environment, industry and technology. He has been a senior consultant to the UN's Environment Programme, Development Programme and Educational, Scientific and Cultural Organization. Peter was a special adviser to the 1992 Earth Summit in the fields of biodiversity and climate change, and contributed to the preparation of the framework conventions in both these areas.

He is also the author of several books including *Ideas for the new millennium* (1998, 2001), *Designing 2050: pathways to sustainable prosperity on spaceship Earth* (2008) and *Destination 2050: concepts bank and toolkit for future-makers* (2013).

In our lives and work there are two things we do all the time that are essential for our future success: we seek to shape the future; and we initiate, nurture and, where necessary, terminate relationships. There are six tools we use to shape the future: leadership, management, planning, design, innovation and learning. Management and leadership play separate roles in this future-shaping toolkit and it is important that we understand this critical difference, as well as how they differently influence how we use the other four future-shaping tools. All of us need to be both resilient future-takers (the effective manager in each of us), and purposeful future-makers (the exemplary leader in each of us).

Do not follow where the path may lead. Go instead where there is no path and leave a trail.

—Ralph Waldo Emerson

If we are to be successful in life and work, we need to embody two capabilities that we seldom have the opportunity to formally learn. The first capability is to shape the future and the second is to initiate, nurture and, where necessary, amicably terminate, relationships. We seldom shape the future alone – most of the time we need the active or implicit support of those with whom we have important relationships. So when we shape the future it is critical that we do not harm our relationships, and ensure there is mutual benefit from working with others. I have therefore sought to develop concept banks and toolkits to help people become the most effective shapers of futures – and managers of relationships – they can be.

We shape the future using six different tools, which I will describe shortly. But to use these tools well we also need to understand both our present situation and the emerging circumstances and trends in which we are going to operate. I will begin by describing some emerging circumstances and trends that will influence everybody's futures.

The planetist future

In 2011, I spoke from the stage at the Golden Plains Music Festival in Meredith, Victoria. My audience was 10,000 educated Generation Yers. I asked them which of these three choices best describes their belief system:

- *tribalism* – giving first allegiance to tribe or group
- *nationalism* – giving first allegiance to nation
- *planetism* – giving first allegiance to our planet.

Almost all of them chose 'planetism'. None had heard the word before but they intuitively knew it described their views. It is just as well they embody planetist values, for if they didn't, they would struggle to create 21st century-relevant lives and career paths. Planetism is based on educated middle-class values and is growing alongside the massive increase of the educated middle class through globalisation. By 2030 there will be 3.2 billion educated middle-class people in Asia alone, and numbers of middle-class people worldwide are increasing by the population of New York City every three months.

Generation Y is much less ideological and less involved in party politics than their parents' generation. However, they are still very active in terms of the causes they support that give political expression to the ideals and values they hold. Tony Blair said in 2000 that just as the 20th century was shaped by ideology, the 21st century would be shaped by ideals. Educated middle-class people believe in small families, self-responsibility and self-improvement, and place a high value on education, intercultural and interreligious respect, gender equality, democracy and sustainability. These are core values of planetism.

How far different societies have progressed on this path depends on the current level of prosperity – the relative size of the middle class, and of the spread and depth of mass education. However, prosperity is growing and more people are being educated and being educated for longer. Even in places like Pakistan and Afghanistan, girls are demanding access to education and are supported by global public opinion in doing so. In the planetist world of 2030, somebody who releases greenhouse gases into the global atmosphere, thereby causing significant collateral damage to others, will be treated as a pariah, just as a smoker in a cafe is treated today. There are other pariahs around as well, the most significant of whom are religious and cultural extremists who want to turn back the clock to an autocratic past and incite conflict over difference. They will create mayhem for a while but their cause will be lost within a generation at the most. Where extremists promote such intolerance and oppression of difference they will face escalating pariah-hood and economic isolation from an increasingly united global public opinion. A recent example of the power of this global public opinion is the decision of Myanmar's military rulers to end autocracy and move towards democracy.

Kenneth Boulding, in his essay 'The economics of the coming spaceship Earth' (1966), advocated that the world needed to be transformed from a 'cowboy economy' to a 'spaceship economy'. In my own work I show how this transformation is well under way. As this proceeds, 10 values are shifting. Emerging planetist values (the values of the spaceship economy or culture) will determine both what people will want to trade in 2030 and beyond, and what will be appropriate and ethical behaviour by individuals, organisations and nations. Values determine what is valued or made valuable; what is valued and becomes valuable in turn shapes market demand and supply. These value shifts are summed up in Table 1.

Table 1: Shifting values

From the cowboy culture – modernism (1960) ...	*... to the spaceship culture – planetism (2020)*
Priority to nation, tribe	Priority to planet
Individualism	Communitarianism
Independence	Interdependence
Autocracy	Democracy
Humanity against nature	Humanity as a part of nature
Unsustainable development, production, consumption, lifestyles	Sustainable development, production, consumption, lifestyles
Patriarchy	Gender equality
Intercultural or interreligious intolerance and hostility	Intercultural or interreligious tolerance and harmony
Conflict resolution through confrontation and combat	Conflict resolution through cooperation and negotiation
Safekeeping through defence	Safekeeping through security

Imagine yourself as a commander of a multicultural and mixed gender spaceship on a journey to a distant planet. What rules would you initiate to ensure that this spaceship arrives safely at its destination? The rules you devise will be similar to planetist values. I describe planetist values as *cosmonaut values* – as distinct from the modernist or *cowboy values* that so completely informed 20th century behaviour. Those who seek to shape the future must recognise the critical role that these planetist values, and particularly interdependence, will play in 21st century society.

The century of interdependence

Interdependence involves two entities voluntarily relinquishing some independence to reap shared benefit from a union. It is based on mutual trust and obligations. Trust, in turn, is based on the perception of honesty, reliability and competence. In the 21st century, interdependence is becoming the cornerstone of all local and global relationships: personal, organisational and political. Women are sometimes said to understand interdependence better than men, which is one reason why emerging 21st century society is increasingly favouring women. In interdependent circumstances we should always seek win-win outcomes – even synergism (2+2=5) – if we wish to successfully shape both personal and public futures in the next decades. Those who still carry modernist values promoting win-lose outcomes and antagonism (2+2=3) will fail in this interdependent world. Individualism involves giving priority to individuals over community when these are in conflict, and communitarianism is its opposite. Communitarianism is really a multilateral version of interdependence.

Mindsets for shaping futures

Imagine a global society that is universally prosperous, sustainable, harmonious, secure and just (just five key words) by the year 2050. I call this vision 'destination 2050'. Excepting some fundamentalists, most of us would aspire for our children and their children to live in such a future. We cannot create a future we do not first imagine. Envisioning in some detail what the world could or should look like is an essential first step for successful future-shaping. The serpent in George Bernard Shaw's *Back to Methuselah* says: 'You see things; and you say, "Why?" But I dream things that never were; and I say, "Why not?"'

When many people set goals, they describe them in terms of eliminating undesirables from the future. They might list reducing poverty, lessening unsustainable practices, reducing conflict, overcoming injustice and defeating organised crime. They see removing undesirables from the future as more practical and realistic than realising the opposite – a desirable – in the future. Solving a problem only delivers a less awful future, not a magnificent one. To realise a magnificent future, one must first visualise it.

There is a big and often unrecognised difference between these two approaches. Reducing poverty does not increase prosperity; ending war does not create peace; ceasing to be ill does not mean one is well; overthrowing autocracy does not produce democracy; overcoming schoolyard bullying does not engender schoolyard kindness; and abating industrial carbon emissions does not guarantee a climate-safe future. When we seek to build a positive future rather than abate a negative future, we generate excitement and stimulate the development of more imaginative and creative approaches to both policy and program development, and to innovation. This distinction goes to the core of the difference between management and leadership.

I describe myself to others as a 'utopian realist' – as someone who imagines inspiring visions and then crafts realistic strategies to realise them. I spent 20 years as a CEO of public sector organisations devising public policy initiatives by doing just this.

There is plenty of evidence that supports Shaw's prescription for shaping the future: grand visions are often realised because they inspire people to stretch themselves. A prime example of this occurred in May 1961. John Kennedy envisioned the United States going to the moon by the end of the decade, something most people thought was impossible because nobody then had a clue about how it might be achieved. The Apollo project became heroic because it inspired humanity to accomplish what previously seemed impossible.

Futurists are a variable lot. Many, like myself, see themselves as optimistic future-makers. We believe we should first visualise a positive and heroic destination and then design and implement a strategy to realise it. There are not enough people who seek to shape the future this way. I believe that the destination 2050 vision, while somewhat utopian, is also eminently realisable – it can also be demonstrated that since about 1970, humanity has already traversed to a midway point on this journey. The flow of events is already proceeding in the right direction. Now, strategic interventions must be taken that advance tipping points and consolidate these promising trends.

Creating market-based approaches for shaping the future

Many think that shaping the future is still principally a task for government. While good public policy and effective governance are still critical for creating better futures, their roles are not as critical as they once were. Laws can stop bad things from happening, but they rarely make good things happen. Governments are now often part of the problem rather than part of the solution – for example, they will often seek to protect the national interest ahead of the planetary interest, and they are probably no more effective outside their own jurisdictions than are many individuals and organisations. As well, as the global market economy continues to grow, command mechanisms driven by government expenditure are becoming less effective. We can now most effectively shape global futures if we change what is traded in global markets. Market-based mechanisms are now both more effective and efficient. An example is putting a worldwide price on carbon to trigger the market to deliver a clean energy future.

Fifty years ago, state and regional governments were where the action was. Then it was national governments. Now, the planet is the action stage of the 21st century. This is one reason why many young people are turning their backs on national politics and governance. It is also why corporate social responsibility is now a more important issue for global corporations. In this market-driven world, it is likely that Steve Jobs has made as big a contribution to global wellbeing as any US president. People outside governments can now contribute hugely to making the future world a better place. Creative visionaries and strategists, innovators and entrepreneurs of all kinds, including social entrepreneurs and, as we all know, artistic celebrities, are people who are now significant shapers of 21st century change. And that group could potentially include all of us.

Innovating the planetist future

The values of planetism will determine what will be in global markets in the coming decades. Seventy per cent plus of these products and services have yet to be invented. So how can we describe these not-yet-invented products or services so that we can first describe and discuss them, and then invent and market them? I use the concepts of *ways* and *wares* to do this:

- *ways* are the new social innovations that change what we *do* in order to achieve an objective: for example, changes to (or new) behaviours, actions, strategies and cultures
- *wares* are the physical innovations that change what we *use* in order to achieve an objective: for example, new designs, products, services and technologies.

Here is an example of ways and wares:

- a water conservation way: shortening your shower from six to three minutes
- a water conservation ware: a new low-volume showerhead.

Together, they enable us to conserve water. Imagine other water conservation ways and wares.

In the coming decades, global markets will be seeking ways and wares to supply emerging planetist markets: for organisational and personal interdependence, democracy, sustainability, gender equality, intercultural and interreligious tolerance and harmony, and security. Each of these is a huge agenda and each of these domains has many subsets of innovations.

We are now recognising that, whether we like it or not, we all share a planetary home and have a shared destiny. This means we must innovate our way to a sustainable future. Sustainability involves causing zero net collateral damage to others and to our planet when we set out to do anything. Some of the ways and wares we must invent to create a sustainable future are ones that will enable us to avoid such net collateral damage to others, and also to live within perpetual solar income and create zero waste. Those who innovate these will do economically well by doing ecological good. There will also be an increasing demand for new ways and wares in health and wellness, education and learning, communications, enjoyment, and for the automation of production, including agriculture and food production.

Generational change and participation in 21st century society

I have already given an example that provides evidence that educated generation Yers are planetists. Many of them tell me it is nice to have at last a word like planetist to describe their thinking and feelings. It is often said that generation X and, even more so, generation Y, are disconnected from politics and that they are uninterested or apathetic about nation and community, and even too self-interested. In fact, they have not shrunk back towards self-interested individualism at all, as some claim. They have actually transferred their concerns to a higher plane – to the wellbeing of our planet – and are working to develop themselves so that they can thrive in a planetary society that will offer greater possibilities and opportunities than have been available to any previous generation. Their schooling has not helped prepare them for this so they are doing it for themselves – they use the social media, the internet and each other to prepare themselves to live in a planetist 21st century.

Generation Yers regard the national interest as less important than the planetary interest. They do not join national political parties that are ideological in character. They are concerned more about global futures than national futures. They prefer to work on issues of specific concern to them and on issues that are significantly intergenerational and global in character, such as abating climate change, improving intercultural and interreligious harmony, promoting democracy and increasing gender equality. And they can do these things and play on a global stage more easily if they work in an international humanitarian NGO, in the media, in a global commercial corporation or as part of an international scientific community, than if they work in state or national government or politics.

Shaping the future

A core aspiration of humanity has always been to be able to predict and shape the future. Over time we have used many different knowledge domains (religion, fictional narratives, myths, rituals, science and history) to do this. We are all interested in shaping our lives for future success and making society a better place for our children and their children to live in. It is noteworthy that conflict is mostly driven by conflicting aspirations for the future and different perspectives on how we might best shape the future.

Most decisions we make are about shaping the future, for example initiating a relationship, buying a house, planning a holiday or making an investment. Many of our conversations involve what decision we should make to shape the future to fulfil our aspirations or to respond to an emerging threat.

We can all learn to become more effective shapers of the future. We shape it through six core tools.

Tools for future-shaping

1. *leadership*: being a purposeful future-maker
2. *management*: being a resilient future-taker
3. *planning*: applying planning skills such as those used in all the planning professions (which include land-use, urban, community, transport, social, financial, industrial and economic planning)
4. *design*: using design skills such as those embedded in design-based professions including engineering, architecture and all forms of design (industrial, systems, fashion and graphic design)
5. *innovation*: developing new means (ways and wares) to do old and current things better, and new things first
6. *learning*: increasing our knowledge and capabilities, changing our mindsets and belief systems in order to become more future-effective, and expanding our capability to seek and take new options and new pathways to the future.

We can most effectively shape the future if we use all six of these tools in combination in an integrated strategy to realise a vision, rather than just rely on one or two of them as most of us do.

Three dialogues for charting life and career paths

One of our first tasks for shaping the future should be to shape our own futures: to create fulfilling and successful life and career paths for ourselves. We can achieve this if we become resilient future-takers-in, and purposeful future-makers of our own lives and careers. In turn, we can accomplish this by the judicious use of insight, foresight and hindsight. To do this, I suggest each person conducts three kinds of dialogue with those who know them best. These people often can see things about us that we do not see ourselves.

Destiny dialogue

Henry Ford said: 'The secret to a successful life is to understand what is one's destiny to do and do it.' This process requires insight. Destiny is different from fate – fate is not under our control, but destiny involves expressing what is inside you to the outside world. Destiny is a combination of two things, your aptitude (what you are good at) and your passion (what you love doing). Many young people consult me about their career plans, what jobs might be present when they are in mid career, and what kind of tertiary education they might undertake. I tell them that it doesn't matter what they study. For most people it will bear little relationship to what they will do when they are 40, for jobs will have changed unrecognisably. Most job categories, products and services that will exist in 25 years time have yet to be invented. In these circumstances, the most effective way to develop your career path is first to look inside yourself and discover your destiny, and then seek to build your career and life path around it.

Then take the next step and try to define your destiny using just two words, an adjective plus a noun: for example, social entrepreneur, innovations broker, intercultural conciliator, security guardian, relationships facilitator, habitat designer, robotics engineer, wellness worker. When you describe yourself to others in this way when they ask what do you do, you will stimulate curiosity and often kindle enlightening conversations. You can also focus your own creative thinking around giving meaning, detail and career path substance to these two words. Following your destiny defines your work; that which you do that gives meaning to your life. Then the challenge is to turn your work into your employment – an activity from which you can earn income. This process can apply equally to charting the future of individuals, organisations, nations, communities and regions.

Destination dialogue

This process requires foresight, in order to chart your future destinations. One can ask, what possibilities and opportunities are emerging that best fit my destiny? And what should be my preferred future or possible future destinations for my life path and career path? The emerging planetist marketplace will provide many new opportunities. I have already shown how its values will inform the ways and wares that will be both sought and developed in the next two generations; we can then build career paths around creating these ways and wares.

Derivation dialogue

This process requires hindsight and involves treasuring and learning from your experiences. There are two elements you bring with you from your past that really matter and are relevant for creating future success:

- *heritage*: the priceless aspects of one's past that should be kept, treasured and nurtured, to ensure that making changes doesn't result in throwing out babies with the bathwater, and
- *baggage*: bad habits and negative attitudes and perceptions accumulated from one's past experiences which, if they are not recognised and jettisoned, prevent one from becoming an effective transformer-of-self for future success.

The leader and manager in each of us

The leader in each of us is a preferred futurist – asking, what should or could the future be? The manager in each of us is a probable futurist – asking, what will the future be? The leader in us imagines, develops and implements a mission-directed strategy to realise this preferred future or possible future. The mission-directed strategy involves both adding desirable elements to the future and removing undesirable elements from it. The manager and leader in each of us differ in a number of other ways; these different and complementary capabilities are outlined in Table 2:

Table 2: Capabilities of managers and leaders

Manager	***Leader***
Responds to change: reactive	Creates and shapes change: proactive
Future-taker, change-taker, path-taker	Future-maker, change-maker, path-maker
Cautious about risk	Careful about risk
Does the thing right	Does the right thing
Guided by fate	Guided by destiny
Controls actions and events	Facilitates actions and events
Works in the organisation	Works on the organisation
Prophet: informed and motivated by understanding and predicting trends, and asking 'Why?'	Visionary: informed and motivated by imagining the future and the future self, and asking 'Why not?'
Probable futurist: asking 'What will the future be like?'	Preferred futurist: asking 'What should the future be like?'
Problem-centred strategist	Mission-directed strategist

To take one pair of these, cautious versus careful: instead of being cautious, one can be careful and bold, perhaps carefully bold. Too many people become cautious when they should be careful.

Imagine that you are on the edge of a minefield. On the other side is paradise. The cautious person would not even take a step forward. The carefully bold person would use his best intelligence, surveillance and vigilance, including through utilising and innovating new intelligence, surveillance and vigilance ways and wares, to minimise risk and reach paradise. In an era of economic crisis, most people become more cautious because the focus is on job losses and declining economic opportunity. However, instead of focusing on saving a sunset industry, one can instead establish a sunrise industry. There are, for example, many motor vehicle manufacturing facilities at the end of their productive lives that could be transformed into robotics manufacturing facilities. The work skill sets required are very similar and, in an ageing society, with the growing automation of mining, manufacturing, transport, health, energy and agriculture, and for creating new ways and wares of enjoyment, future possibilities for robotics are only limited by one's imagination.

The heart of leadership

Leaders imagine (or envision) the future with the right cerebral brain and strategise with the left cerebral brain. However, good leaders also engage the heart as well as the mind, for good leaders use emotional intelligence to inspire and motivate others. People are most willing to accept change, or to transform themselves, when they are emotionally engaged and inspired by leadership. This is particularly so when they are connected to the emotional pairs of hope and fear, and love and hate. Some leaders use the two negative motivators, fear and hate, to drive and engender change. This might be effective in the short term but often leads to disaster. Most of us have also known some inspiring leaders who use hope and love as motivators. Martin Luther King, Jr and Nelson Mandela come to mind as exemplars.

There are six emotions or feelings that are central to effective leadership. Men are usually good at the first three, the ones that are regarded as natural masculine qualities. Women are usually good at the second three, which are regarded as natural feminine qualities. This differentiation into male and female qualities has been described by Karl Jung as animus and anima respectively, and is also distinguished as yang and yin respectively by Taoists.

Qualities of a good leader

- *confident*: has self-belief without hubris (masculine, animus, yang)
- *courageous*: goes where others dare not, overcoming self-interested opposition (masculine, animus, yang)
- *committed*: does what must be done; is assertive not aggressive (masculine, animus, yang)
- *considerate*: listens and responds to the opinions and vi–ews of others (feminine, anima, yin)
- *courteous*: shows respect in conversation and collaboration (feminine, anima, yin)
- *compassionate*: responds with empathy to victims and the disadvantaged (feminine, anima, yin).

Outstanding leaders like Nelson Mandela are strong in all six of these. Many men, however, need to grow their anima, their yin. And many women need to develop the corresponding masculine part of themselves – their animus and yang. Imagine ways and wares to achieve this.

Conclusion

All futurists seek to provide us with tools that enable us to better understand the future, and to become more future-ready. We can be future-ready in either a reactive or proactive way. Reactive future-ready people will become resilient future-takers when they fear that their future self might be disabled or disadvantaged by predicted scenarios and trends. Some futurists, and I am one of these, also aim to provide tools to help us to become proactive future-ready people, to use vision to animate the purposeful future-maker in us to realise an enabled or advantaged future self. We have too much reactive futurism (management-of-self) and not enough proactive futurism (leadership-of-self) in our lives, and this imbalance has always concerned me. We can use our future-taking and future-making capabilities in a communitarian as well as an individual way, so that we can to shape the future of our families, communities, organisations, nations and planet.

Our future is being fashioned by values in two ways. First, our collective values are shaping global markets and ethics, determining what will become available to us as products and services, and what will be future approved or disapproved behaviours. Second, our individual values shape our own aspirations and ethics. We are all being changed by the emerging paradigm of planetism that is spreading through the human family as we all become more prosperous and more educated. Planetist values are those that are required for humanity to achieve universal prosperity, harmony, sustainability, security and justice on our shared planet. Billions of people are now embodying planetist values and living by planetist ethics as they begin to recognise that they cohabit a 21st century global village.

As our world becomes more communitarian and interdependent, it is becoming harder for people to ignore the needs of others or act selfishly, particularly when these actions cause collateral damage to them. Our interdependent society is very productive but is also very vulnerable to oppressive autocrats or cultural or religious extremists who seek to threaten or wreck it. Global pariah-hood awaits those who take this route. On the positive side is the sight of a Bill Gates or his like as philanthropist, a celebrity acting altruistically, or a corporation needing to show it is socially responsible. This behaviour is the new norm – in the changing world, we will increasingly need to demonstrate good planetary citizenship. Over the next two decades, humanity will innovate the ways and wares to enable it to thrive in this emerging 21st century society. All of us, irrespective of our chosen career paths, can both contribute to and benefit from this extraordinary social transformation of human society. We will do this best, however, if we consciously embody within each of us both the resilient future-taker and the purposeful future-maker.

Seven misunderstandings about elections

Malcolm Mackerras

Malcolm Mackerras AO is visiting fellow at the Australian Catholic University's Canberra campus. From 1974 to 2010 he taught both Australian and US politics at the Royal Military College Duntroon and the Australian Defence Force Academy. For some five decades he has been described as 'Australia's leading psephologist'.* He has written and contributed extensively to various media on most federal, state and territory elections. He is particularly known for his predictions of electoral outcomes using the Mackerras Pendulum.

On Australia Day 2006, Mackerras was appointed an Officer in the General Division of the order of Australia (AO) 'for service to the community by raising public awareness of and encouraging debate about the political process in Australia and other western democracies, and through commitment to reform and improvement of the electoral system, and to education'.

In his essay Malcolm Mackerras examines some of the language we use to describe Australia's electoral and political systems – Commonwealth and state – and deals with some controversies and misunderstandings arising from that language.

It's not the voting that's democracy, it's the counting.

—Tom Stoppard

The will of the people

The greatest misunderstanding people have about Australia's political systems (federal and state) is that our election results reflect the will of the people. I assert that quite frequently this is not true. In the main, election results in Australia reflect the vagaries of the electoral system operating for the jurisdiction in question.

The best examples of my proposition come from federal general elections for our House of Representatives, where the electoral

---

* Psephology is the systematic study of elections by analysing their results (ed.).

system has remained unchanged for over 90 years. It is based on single-member electoral divisions upon which the system of the full preferential vote operates.

Over that period, the electoral balance between Labor and anti-Labor has been remarkably even. In the 37 general elections since our current system was adopted for the 1919 general election, the division of the nation-wide two-party preferred vote has fallen outside a 60–40 range only once: in 1931 when the Scullin Labor government was defeated and Joe Lyons became our conservative prime minister. In only four other cases (1929, 1943, 1966 and 1975) did the division lie outside the 55–45 range. So in 32 cases the division of the vote has been within 55–45. In 12 cases the party gap has been within the range 51–49, they being the federal general elections of 1937, 1940, 1951, 1954, 1961, 1969, 1980, 1987, 1990, 1998, 2001 and 2010. In six cases the winning party in seats scored fewer two-party preferred votes than the losing party. The cases were 1940, 1954, 1961, 1969, 1990 and 1998.

Of course, one does need to accept the outcome as reflecting the decisive public will in some cases. It was the will of the people in 1931 that Scullin be rejected and Lyons elevated. It was the will of the people in 1966 that Arthur Calwell be rejected and, along with his rejection, there was a rejection of the proposition that there be an immediate withdrawal of Australia's troops in Vietnam. It was the will of the people that Gough Whitlam be accepted in 1972 but rejected in 1975.

However, consider this. When John Howard sought a second term for his government in 1998 he won a good majority of seats in the House of Representatives on a two-party preferred vote that was 51 per cent Labor and 49 per cent Liberal–National. So the interpretation of the result was that Howard had won a great victory – because seats are all that count. Yet the Rudd–Gillard–Rudd government in 2010 was able to win a second term with a majority of the two-party preferred vote (admittedly only 50.1 per cent) but Gillard was seen to be a failure. The simple reality, therefore, was that in neither case was there a will of the people. In both cases the result reflected the vagaries of the electoral system. To the extent that there is a 'will of the people', I say it is reflected in the two-party preferred vote.

None of the above is intended as a criticism of our systems, which are as fair as one could expect – nothing is ever perfect. I often tell a personal story in this regard. In my semi-retirement, I am a volunteer guide at Old Parliament House. During the period when Julia Gillard was prime minister, when I took the visitors into the chamber of the House of Representatives I pointed to a chair and said:

> Fifty years ago Bob Menzies sat in that chair as prime minister. However, he sat in that chair purely because of the operation of our unique electoral system. Under any other system he would surely have lost the 1961 election. Now I could take you up the hill to the new Parliament House and I could point out the chair where Julia Gillard sits as prime minister today. And I could say her sitting in that chair is purely the consequence of our unique electoral system. Under any other system she would surely have lost the 2010 election.

The various aspects of the vagaries of the federal electoral system include the drawing of the maps for federal electoral divisions, the distribution of preferences, the 'donkey vote' and the placement of names on the ballot paper. In addition, there is the timing of elections which, by and large, favours the existing prime minister.

The system whereby we elect our House of Representatives is unique to Australia. The system of single-member electoral divisions combined with compulsory voting, and the full preferential voting* operates only for our House of Representatives, for the South Australian House of Assembly and for the legislative assemblies in Victoria, Western Australia and the Northern Territory. Nowhere else! My reason for naming Menzies and Gillard was that they were leaders of the opposite parties; Liberal and Labor respectively. In other words, the electoral system is fair but the party system has changed over the half-century in question. In the same way that in 1958, 1961 and 1963 the preference votes of the then anti-communist Democratic Labor Party kept Menzies in power, in 2007 and 2010 the preference votes of the Greens gave office to the Rudd–Gillard–Rudd government.

The remarks made above apply in general terms to the states

* Under a *full* preferential voting system, voters must place a 1 in the box beside their preferred candidate, then number *all* remaining boxes on the ballot paper in order of preference (ed.).

also. Clearly it was the will of the people to reject Labor in New South Wales in 2011 and in Queensland in 2012. However, most state elections are close in terms of votes, so we can say that the result is the consequence of the vagaries of the electoral system rather than any will of the people.

The mandate from the people

The second greatest misunderstanding observers have relates to the question of a mandate. A political leader wins an election, becomes prime minister (or premier) and then claims to have been instructed by the people to implement a policy. Usually this requires legislation, and if there is an upper house in which the government lacks a majority, arguments arise about the mandate for a proposed policy to be implemented.

Claiming a mandate is not always a problem. In Queensland, for example, the fact that the parliament only has one chamber means that the government can claim a mandate and no-one can do anything about it. A similar circumstance can arise federally. For example, in December 1975 Malcolm Fraser led the Coalition into government and won good majorities in both houses. However, such a case is rare. Federal political leaders taking their party from the opposition benches into government have faced various issues in claiming a mandate, which I will discuss below.

The first case is that of Robert Menzies in December 1949. He won a good majority in the House of Representatives but lacked a Senate majority. Consequently he had problems with his argument that he had a mandate for his legislative program. He solved the problem by double dissolving in March 1951. At the general election in April 1951 he won good majorities in both houses so his mandate claim succeeded in full.

The interesting question is why Menzies was so uniquely successful in this regard. Essentially it was because he had won in excess of 50 per cent of the vote in 1949 for both the House of Representatives and the Senate. He had also won a majority of the Senate seats contested in 1949. His lack of a Senate majority was due to the system of rotation of senators and because the electoral system in 1946 was different from that of 1949. The system had been changed by Labor in 1948 and Menzies was able to sell the line that the change was an act of deliberate rigging by Labor to ensure a Labor

Senate majority post 1949, regardless of how badly the party was defeated.

The second case is that of Gough Whitlam in December 1972. He won a workable majority in the House of Representatives, but there was no Senate election that year. Consequently the conservatives continued with a Senate majority, which they used to deny that Whitlam had any kind of mandate at all. In April 1974 Whitlam brought on a double dissolution. Unfortunately for him, however, the general election for all members of both houses in May 1974 gave him a majority in the House but not in the Senate. He had only a partial success in exercising his mandate at the joint sitting of August 1974. In essence it can be said that Whitlam's claim to a mandate failed.

The third case is that of Bob Hawke in March 1983. He had no problem in the short term. Although he lacked a Senate majority, the balance of power there was held by the Democrats who displayed goodwill towards Hawke and his government. As things turned out, there was a double dissolution in 1987, so Hawke gave up the option (exercised by Menzies in 1951 and Whitlam in 1974) of double dissolving in his first term. However, the 1987 double dissolution (the most recent we have had) did not give him the expected mandate for the Australia Card Bill.

The fourth case is that of John Howard in March 1996. In the period before the new senators took their seats in July of that year, there was a fierce debate about his mandate claims. However, the problem was soon solved by the defection of Labor Senator Malcolm Colston (Queensland), who took the position of deputy president of the Senate from August. The votes of Colston and Brian Harradine (independent, Tasmania) enabled Howard to make good his claims for a mandate.

The fifth case is that of Kevin Rudd in November 2007. He began lucky. He claimed a mandate to repeal Work Choices, John Howard's favourite reform, implemented in Howard's fourth term when he enjoyed an actual majority in the Senate. The Liberals and Nationals, having evidently lost their conviction over Work Choices, allowed the Senate to pass the repeal legislation (known as the Fair Work Act).

However, events soon turned against Rudd. The legislation to introduce his Carbon Pollution Reduction Scheme (for which he claimed a mandate) ran into severe trouble in the Senate. There were 11 cognate bills in the reduction scheme package, and the Senate created a double dissolution 'trigger' when these were rejected on Wednesday 2 December 2009. There was a climate conference at Copenhagen later in the month from which Rudd returned depressed. He lost his nerve, proved wrong various pundits (of whom I was one) who confidently predicted a double dissolution in January 2010, and finished up dropping the whole subject. It was left to his successor, Julia Gillard, to revive the subject but she was never able to claim a mandate for her Clean Energy Future legislation, which passed both houses in the second half of 2011.

Since the last federal election there has been much argument about the mandate claimed by the Coalition government, led by Tony Abbott. Here my view is that the Prime Minister had every right to present legislation to repeal the Clean Energy Future laws, commonly known as 'the carbon tax' and as 'carbon pricing'. He also had every right to present legislation to repeal the Minerals Resource Rent Tax. However, he had no right to demand that other members of the parliament must vote for what they think is bad policy. Every one of the 55 Labor members of the House of Representatives has a personal mandate from his or her electorate to defend the achievements of the Rudd–Gillard–Rudd government. Moreover, at the September 2013 election the Coalition received only 45.6 per cent of the primary vote for the House of Representatives and only a miserable 37.7 per cent of the Senate vote.

Australia's 'elected' prime minister

Media commentators love to refer to the 'elected' prime minister and the 'elected' premier. Consequently it is not surprising that ordinary people should think in such terms. I am different. To me an 'elected' prime minister is that leader of the opposition who takes his party out of opposition and onto the Treasury benches, courtesy of victory at a general election. I have named some cases above – Joe Lyons in 1931, Bob Menzies in 1949, Gough Whitlam in 1972, Malcolm Fraser in 1975, Bob Hawke in 1983, John Howard in 1996, Kevin Rudd in 2007 and Tony Abbott in 2013. However, when I say such a thing people ask me why I do not consider Paul Keating to be an 'elected' prime minister nor Anna Bligh an 'elected' premier.

The answer I give is that Keating only ever became prime minister because Hawke was good at winning elections. It was the same with Anna Bligh – she only became premier because Peter Beattie was good at winning elections. In each case rejection followed the elections actually won by Keating and Bligh, in 1993 and 2009 respectively, and these were followed three years later by crushing defeats in 1996 and 2012. My view on this is reinforced by the case of Julia Gillard. In my opinion she won a general election in August 2010. However, few people ever thought of Gillard as an elected prime minister. Consequently when Rudd returned to the prime ministership late in June 2013 many people (including Rudd himself!) described him as the 'elected' prime minister, which he clearly was not at that stage.

In deference to the opinion of others, I am forced to classify Rudd as an elected prime minister but not Gillard. Actually, I think of Gillard as having won four elections. On 24 June 2010 she won party leadership at a Labor caucus meeting. Since the then prime minister, Rudd, chose not to contest she won unopposed. On 21 August 2010 she won a popular general election for the House of Representatives. In two-party preferred votes the result was 50.1 per cent for Labor and 49.9 per cent for Liberal–National. In seats it was 76 for Gillard and 74 against her. However, it was not until 7 September that the result was known when the final pieces of her jigsaw puzzle fell into place. Here I refer to the independents Tony Windsor and Rob Oakeshott, whose decisions were announced on that day. On 27 February 2012 she again won a caucus vote, which was 71 for Gillard and 31 for Rudd. Finally, on 21 March 2013 she again won a caucus vote – unopposed. Unfortunately for her she was not allowed to contest the 2013 general election as prime minister because Rudd resumed his hold on that office on the morning of Thursday 27 June, having won a caucus ballot the previous night by 57 votes to Gillard's 45.

Since Gillard won two of those elections unopposed, I found it worthwhile to find out at the time what the votes might well have been had they actually been taken. On 24 June 2010, the vote would have been 90 for Gillard and 22 for Rudd. On 21 March 2013, the vote would have been 60 for Gillard and 40 for Rudd. Rudd saw both votes as being huge setbacks, so he decided not to advertise them. He did that by allowing Gillard to win unopposed.

Piecing together the four caucus elections, I have the votes for Gillard as 90 in June 2010, 71 in February 2012, 60 in March 2013 and 45 in June 2013. For Rudd, I have it as 22 in June 2010 (as the incumbent prime minister), 31 in February 2012, 40 in March 2013 and 57 in June 2013. This constant attrition is what happened to a three-year prime minister who was never perceived as 'elected', who did all the heavy lifting for the Rudd–Gillard government, and who faced two leaders of the opposition, one internal and one external.

In one respect, this whole idea of an 'elected' prime minister is nonsense. The only electors actually voting for Howard were those enrolled in Bennelong (NSW). The only electors actually voting for Rudd were those enrolled in Griffith (Queensland). The only electors actually voting for Gillard were those enrolled in Lalor (Victoria). The only electors actually voting for Tony Abbott were those enrolled in Warringah (NSW). The only electors actually voting for Anna Bligh were those enrolled in South Brisbane. So this rubbish about the 'elected' prime minister or premier comes in, to my mind, as the third greatest common misunderstanding the Australian people have about the electoral process.

Political infamy

The fourth misunderstanding relates to the concept of political infamy. It is best illustrated by this letter appearing in *The Sydney Morning Herald* on Thursday 6 June 2013:

> There can be no greater act of ill-discipline contributing to the federal Labor Party facing electoral oblivion … than the completely undemocratic and immoral manner in which Julia Gillard became Prime Minister.
>
> Her rise to power stands in infamy alongside the dismissal of the Whitlam government as one of the most shameful episodes in Australian political history.
>
> Moreover, it has locked the party into a moral dilemma, whereby any reinstatement of Kevin Rudd to the prime ministership would signal to the electorate an embarrassing acknowledgement of its own wrongdoing.
>
> The test now is to openly admit these past mistakes before the election. It must begin with Ms Gillard. She must allow her party to have a final vote on the leadership. Depending on the outcome of the vote, it will either morally consolidate her position, or it will

require her to relinquish her office for the far greater good of the party – and the entire nation.

So for Julia Gillard to win four elections was not enough to enable her to contest the 2013 election as prime minister! She must win a fifth! As readers will have gathered, I think this letter is entirely ridiculous. There was nothing undemocratic or immoral about Gillard holding the office of prime minister. It simply told us what we already knew. In Australia, parliamentary parties (federal and state) choose party leaders, and with Labor the body is known as 'the caucus'. It is a sensible system. I say that because fellow parliamentarians have to work with the leader and they are best able to decide who the leader should be. In the case of Gillard, she was not replaced by Rudd because caucus members thought she was doing a bad job. She was replaced because Labor's electoral analysts thought Labor would win significantly more seats under Rudd. Contrary to what the letter asserts, there was no moral dilemma facing Labor's federal politicians in June 2013.

The same goes for the 'infamy alongside the dismissal of the Whitlam government'. In that situation we had a government unable to obtain supply from the parliament, a body that consists of the House of Representatives and the Senate. Although Whitlam still commanded a majority in the House of Representatives, the Senate refused to pass the appropriation bills, thus denying access to public funds. The Australian constitutional head of state at the time, Sir John Kerr, resolved the political crisis by forcing a smooth double dissolution of the parliament. Every member of the House of Representatives and every senator was sent to the people and the result was that the Fraser government won majorities in both houses. That is democracy, not infamy.

My view is that political behaviour cannot be infamy when the constitutional, electoral and political processes are played out according to the rules in place at the time. Some will disagree with me about Julia Gillard, who I admire. Others will disagree with me about Sir John Kerr, who I defend. However, that is my view.

The Australian head of state

Now to the fifth greatest misunderstanding about Australia's political systems. I related above how I am a volunteer guide at Old Parliament House and what I say when we enter the chamber of the

House of Representatives. Actually, the tour starts with the Senate chamber and then crosses to the House of Representatives side via King's Hall where there is a statue of King George V with the year 1927 marked upon it.

When we stop by that statue, I ask the visitors a question: who is Australia's head of state? Overwhelmingly the answer I receive is that the Queen is our head of state. I consider that to be a misunderstanding. The term 'head of state' is nowhere used in the Constitution or in official documents where the Queen is described as 'the sovereign'. When she visits Australia the Queen describes herself as 'your sovereign'.

So my description of the situation is that we (like Canada, New Zealand, Papua New Guinea, Solomon Islands, Jamaica, Barbados and a few other smaller countries) have two heads of state. One of these is the Queen who is the symbolic head of state – hence her head is on our coins, there are paintings of her in our parliament houses, crowns abound in our military and police establishments – and there is the use in legal cases of the term 'the Crown' where the Americans would refer to 'the state'. Our other head of state is the governor-general, technically described in Section 2 of our Constitution as 'Her Majesty's representative in the Commonwealth' but who exercises the entire powers of the Crown within Australia and who is accepted internationally as our head of state. Consequently the governor-general is Australia's constitutional head of state, an appointment that applies also to all the governors of the states. It is they who do the job of head of state within Australia.

Our 'bad record' of constitutional reform

We are continually being told by the great and the good that we have a 'bad record' when it comes to constitutional reform. This is the sixth greatest misunderstanding. I say that because I think we have a good record. The facts are simply stated. There have been 44 proposals placed before the people. Only eight have succeeded.

How important were the eight? My verdict is that the first change (in 1906) was trivial but the other seven were important reforms. In my opinion all the rejected proposals were either bad ideas or were totally and hopelessly unnecessary. So the act of rejection of those proposals means we have a good record.

The position of the states

We are also told by the opinion pollsters that the states are the weak links in the federation. Quite a few politicians (and former politicians) tell us that the federation is dysfunctional. The business community tells us that the present system is costly because of duplication. In my opinion, this is a misunderstanding – the seventh and last in my list. Whenever the Australian people have been asked to change the Constitution and three or more state governments have opposed the change, the result has been rejection of the proposed change.

What this tells us is that opinion poll findings can be misleading. They reflect the kinds of answers people are prepared to give on the spot to questions that are uninvited and about which they have not had time to think. What is important is how people actually vote; not the answers they give to pollsters. For that reason, I think the position of the states is quite guaranteed into the indefinite future.

My final thought about opinion polls, however, is that they sometimes do affect the behaviour of politicians. This was most clearly shown in the Rudd–Gillard contest. Enough ordinary voters told pollsters of their preference for Rudd over Gillard that caucus members put aside their own personal judgement. It was a 'save our seats' exercise dictated by ordinary voters through the polls.

Unintended consequences – advice for politicians and policy analysts

*Frank Milne**

Frank Milne is the Bank of Montreal professor in economics and finance at Queen's University, Ontario, Canada. He received his BEcon (1968) and MEc (1970) from Monash University, and his PhD from the Australian National University in 1975. He has held positions at the University of Rochester, the Australian National University and the Australian Graduate School of Management. He has been a visiting professor at many major economics departments and business schools, including Stanford, Chicago, London Business School, University of Paris, University of Heidelberg and others. He joined Queen's University in 1991, where in July 2000 he was appointed to his current position.

Frank has published many papers in leading economics and finance journals. He wrote *Finance theory and asset pricing* (2002), and is co-author with Edwin Neave of *Current directions in financial regulation* (2005). For many years he has been an adviser and consultant for various branches of the Australian and Canadian governments. He is a regular visitor to the Bank of England. In 2008–09 he was a special adviser at the Bank of Canada.

Far too often, political policy makers are surprised by the consequences of their policy action; a simple policy decision with seemingly obvious consequences can lead to damaging unintended consequences. The careful study of economics reveals the causes of unintended consequences of policy decisions. The economy is not a simple machine that can be adjusted to obtain a certain outcome; it is a subtle social system driven by consumers, producers and investors who can anticipate outcomes and adjust their behaviour accordingly. Any policy maker who does not understand this subtle feedback mechanism will make serious errors. This essay explores some examples of policy errors: for example, US housing policies that encouraged excessive lending; trade policies that wasted resources;

* I am indebted to Peter Boxall, Henry Ergas, Philip Crisp, and Eric and Sylvia Jones for detailed comments on an earlier draft. They are not responsible for any errors or opinions in this version.

and industry regulation that was based on 'rent-seeking'. The essay emphasises the importance of high-quality, accurate policy analysis.

There is only one difference between a bad economist and a good one: the bad economist confines himself to the visible effect; the good economist takes into account both the effect that can be seen and those effects that must be foreseen …

Yet this difference is tremendous; for it almost always happens that when the immediate consequence is favorable, the later consequences are disastrous, and vice versa. Whence it follows that the bad economist pursues a small present good that will be followed by a great evil to come, while the good economist pursues a great good to come, at the risk of a small present evil.

—Frédéric Bastiat

Predicting the consequences of economic and social policy changes is fraught with traps for the unwary. In this paper I will demonstrate, using examples, how policy makers often fail to understand the economic consequences of their interventions. There are three layers of complexity in dealing with policy formation:

1. Members of the public, without professional training in policy-related disciplines, often do not perceive consequences that are readily predicted by professionals. Discussion in the media is often confusing and misleading.
2. Competent policy analysts may be able to anticipate what appears to the public as 'unintended consequences', but still have difficulty with more complex issues. The economy is not a machine, requiring simple adjustments to obtain a certain outcome; it is a subtle social system driven by bureaucracies, consumers, producers and investors who can anticipate outcomes and adjust their behaviour accordingly. Because of this complexity, policy analysts can be unsure of the size of aggregate responses. Often the data are poor, so that careful prediction can only indicate a range of possible outcomes.
3. Applying more sophisticated analysis and careful data collection can reduce the lack of precision, but this complexity is impossible to eliminate altogether.

These three layers of complexity can be illustrated with two examples.

Example 1: Australian commodity exports to China

Australian commodity exports to China were booming until 2008, but prices went into sudden decline as the international crisis intensified because Chinese exports fell, reducing the demand for commodity inputs. The Chinese government faced a decline in its manufacturing sector causing serious economic and social dislocation. What was surprising to many experienced observers was the size of its fiscal stimulus which led to an infrastructure boom from 2009 through 2012. Having observed the stimulus, shrewd Australian policy analysts would have considered the Chinese government's policy options and its political process and alliances, monitored political commentary and attempted to predict the longevity of the infrastructure boom. This would have given more accurate predictions of the strength and longevity of the Australian commodity cycle, its impact on the Australian economy and federal and state tax revenues.

My discussions with international commentators indicated that the Australian government and its policy advisers were far too optimistic about long-run commodity exports to China and the downside risks for commodity exports. This optimism led to large planned increases in mining capacity and mining revenues. But recently, as Chinese demand has declined and commodity prices have fallen from very high levels, we have witnessed the cancellation of several large Australian mining projects. There has been little analysis of this failure of proper risk-management practices in flagging potential downside risks associated with a rapid expansion of mining investment. International commentators have been critical of Australian policy analysis in this area and its lack of professional rigour.

Example 2: taxi licence plates

In this example, I will examine in depth a simple case of a hypothetical policy decision concerning the restriction of the number of taxi licence plates in a city. This example is often used in beginning economics principles texts. Variations of the scenario have occurred in Australian and overseas cities. I will explore its implications, the people who are affected and their lobbying efforts, then analyse the political and economic machinations surrounding the decision and the economic forces that play out over time.

Suppose that taxi owners who employ drivers have to buy a licence plate from an authority in order to provide a service in a given area or city. If the owners successfully lobby for the authority to restrict the number of new licences, the result after many years, especially with increasing population and demand for taxis, would be a dramatic rise in taxi fares, although the drivers would continue to earn only minimum, competitive wages. The reason is simple: the restriction on the availability of taxi services is controlled by the fixed number of plates. The economic rents from restricting the services flow to the owners of the plates, so that the price of the plates reflects the expected present value of the rents. Often regulators are sensitive to the higher fares and impose fare ceilings, particularly for the disabled or disadvantaged. The taxi owners could respond by increasing waiting times for the lower priced taxis, or otherwise rationing their 'availability'.

But this simple story may not end there. Assume that a reforming regulator observes the high prices of taxi fares and long waiting times in the city. There is much public grumbling about the service. Given the high price of plates, the regulator decides to increase the supply by auctioning off more of them, generating extra revenue for the city. The increased number of licences makes their price fall, the taxi service improves and cab fares decline. Existing holders of plates are incensed because the restriction on the supply was imposed long before they bought the plates at inflated prices. They argue that they are only earning a normal return on their investment in the expensive plates.

Shrewd taxi owners could have foreseen attempts to increase plate numbers and tried to lobby at the outset for various legal and contractual devices restricting any attempt to reverse the policy. Once the licensing scheme has been introduced, it creates powerful vested interests to protect their investment through lobbying.

The only beneficiaries of this scheme are those who owned the plates when the original policy, restricting plate numbers, was introduced. They understood the implications and that fuelled their lobbying. The losers were: first, the taxi customers who paid inflated fares over the period when the number of licence plates was restricted; and secondly, the naive new licensees who did not anticipate the deregulation of the supply. If new owners had begun to suspect that sooner or later the supply would be increased, then the value of the plates would have been lower, reflecting the expected impact of decreased rents with increased competition.

A shrewd policy analyst should readily see the possibility of reactions by other vested interests. For example, if drivers were able to form an active union, then they would be able to bargain with the owners to share the monopoly rents generated by the scarcity of plates. The division of the rents would depend upon the strength of the union's bargaining power. If this were achieved, the owners and drivers would lobby jointly to restrict the number of plates, as any increase in supply would decrease the wages of the drivers and the value of the owners' assets. The prevalence of worker–management rhetoric in the media would then obscure the true situation – that the taxi customers would be the victims of the gouging by the owner-driver coalition.

The principal lesson to be drawn here is that once the system is created it is difficult to change.

Political economy

There are many other examples of policy failures that appear to have large, attractive benefits for one sector or group in the economy, and have negligible costs for individual members of the rest of society. This asymmetry, where a few gain a lot and large numbers suffer small individual losses, provides incentives for the gainers to lobby hard, whereas the losers cannot be bothered to make the effort. Much of the lobbying that takes place in our society has this characteristic. Indeed, it happens under governments of both persuasions, although the vested interests may be different. Some economists complain that a policy decision is inefficient, in that the gainers could have compensated the losers and there would have been a surplus. (The surplus is a measure of the loss or inefficiency.) Reflection should reveal that this political compensation mechanism does not occur, because the analysis ignores the political costs of coalition formation with a dispersed group of losers. Even worse, it may be more productive to find one's own rent-seeking scheme to promote, rather than oppose those of others. And so schemes are piled on top of schemes!

A well-functioning political system will try to reduce these lobbying and associated rent-seeking activities, as they are socially wasteful redistribution schemes. But even the most sophisticated society cannot eliminate them any more than an engineer can banish friction. It appears that the more sophisticated the society, the more subtle the rent-seeking machinations of lobbyists and vested interests. The great danger is that left unchecked, lobbying and political rent-seeking can become so entrenched and pervasive that it can lead to lower growth in standards of living or – in the extreme – economic stagnation.

The following is a brief summary of a number of policy failures that have occurred in the United States and Australia. I have chosen the United States because it has a large literature exploring policy failures.

The US airline industry

The post-World War II, highly regulated US airline industry restricted entry, inflated fares and made flying a luxury form of transport. Major beneficiaries were established airlines and airline unions, which shared in the rents generated by competition created by the impediments to regulatory supply. When airlines were deregulated in 1978 under Democratic president Jimmy Carter, the entry of new competitors reduced fares significantly. Existing airlines with high unionised labour costs went bankrupt. As part of the airlines' reorganisation, union power became circumscribed by competition. Since then, airlines have provided cheap, economy class air travel to the great benefit of the general public.

The Australian car and truck industry

The Australian car and truck industry was born in the post-World War II period. Sheltered by very high tariffs and other trade restrictions, it was promoted as an infant industry that would eventually grow up and compete in international markets. Competent policy analysts had long predicted that it would fail because of the crippling costs due to inefficient production runs in a small domestic market. Companies in the United States, Europe and Japan had much larger runs and reaped economies of scale and scope. Many billions of dollars of assistance and elevated prices over decades have not saved a struggling domestic industry. Car industry lobby groups often try to argue that subsidies to the industry are offset by positive externalities to other industries. These arguments seldom hold up after close scrutiny.

The US housing industry

More recently, the US housing market has suffered a major decline in prices. This has caused borrower defaults and a sequence of credit losses for banks, pension funds and other investors, not to mention the personal tragedy suffered by many who have lost their homes and thereby their life savings. The broad reasons for the crisis are now well known, but the details are more complex. We will focus on US government policies that induced the original risky lending policy and led to widespread speculation in the housing market.

The US government provided long-term lending incentives for home ownership, including tax deductible interest payments, indirect subsidies through government-sponsored agencies (Fannie Mae and Freddie Mac), and indirect subsidies to large banks with high credit risks ('too big to fail'). Coupled with the Federal Reserve Board's low interest rates (after the September 11 attacks), the housing industry flourished. Politicians and bureaucrats allowed a shadow banking system to grow rapidly outside the banks' normal prudential supervisory system. The boom was seen to be beneficial in boosting the wealth of a stagnating middle and working class. The housing bubble increased wealth temporarily, but resulted ultimately in a housing crash that dragged house prices back to trend, destroyed home owners' and pension fund wealth, and induced a government bank bailout with increased taxpayer liabilities. The consequent financial crisis increased inequality of income and wealth. The highly levered middle class lost substantially on housing and the long-term unemployed lost many months or years of income. In contrast, there is evidence that the wealthy were better informed and avoided severe losses.

The housing policy interventions were short-run, political fixes that did not address the real causes of the initial income stagnation. That was caused by a number of factors, including the character of technological innovation, inadequate training, an inflated financial system, and the long-term decline of employment in manufacturing in the Western world. What is worse, some policy analysts fear that the causes of the crisis have not been addressed adequately, and a second crisis could occur in the medium term. Given the weakened state of most Western government balance sheets due to slack fiscal policies and demographic factors, the implications are troubling.

The Australian housing market

A similar situation has arisen in Australia, where incentives such as negative gearing and first home buyer grants, coupled with the limited supply of available land for housing (itself a feature of increasingly restrictive zoning laws), have led to very high house prices. A number of economists, myself included, are concerned that high prices could suffer serious falls if there is a major recession triggered by a decline in commodity export revenues. The consequences of high personal debt, coupled with falling house prices, would have potentially serious consequences for the Australian banking system and for federal and state government balance sheets. This is an example of long-term adverse consequences stemming from politically attractive short-term policies. Given the immediate political incentives faced by governments, long-term costs are heavily discounted or even ignored. When the long term eventuates, governments panic.

Popular 'sacred cows'

Another trap for policy analysts is falling for popular 'sacred cows'. Invariably, these emphasise short-term benefits and downplay the long-run costs. They often rely on incomplete or faulty research. The media and vested interests seize on these policies, parading them as simple panaceas for 'major social and economic problems'. Politicians – those that are weak and overly susceptible to pressure from vested interests – can be easy prey. This process of capture, superficial policy analysis and premature implementation is compounded by the frenetic 24-hour news cycle with political spin doctors trying to score cheap debating points over opponents. The consequences are invariably expensive failures.* Let me give an example where all these failings are apparent to the experienced policy analyst.

* See Foster, C 2005, *British Government in Crisis*, Hart Publishing, London for an analysis of the Blair–Brown government's flawed policy process. Ironically the Rudd government imported this process from the outgoing Blair–Brown government. The incoming Labor government had been warned of the UK failings outlined in this book. The consequences are now only too obvious. Liberal governments have had their own sacred cows. The Liberal Country Party government in the 1950s and 1960s encouraged manufacturing using heavy tariffs that drove up domestic prices on some manufactured goods. The Hawke–Keating government reduced tariffs and protection, which reduced consumer prices on cars, textiles and footwear.

For the last two to three decades, governments in the United Kingdom, the United States, Australia and elsewhere have believed that there is an obvious connection between increasing the amount of education obtained by the population and higher economic growth and standards of living. Although education is important for the functioning of a modern society and economy, the scale and allocation of resources between primary, secondary and the various subsections of tertiary education requires careful analysis. As some researchers have observed, there is no obvious correlation (in the relevant ranges) between per capita education expenditure and economic growth rates. Furthermore, the method for determining the allocation of funding is of prime importance. It should be carefully crafted, allowing market incentives to operate on the demand and supply sides. Decentralised mechanisms have long proved superior to centralised, top-down bureaucratic control. Government intervention should focus on clearly identified market failures. This is particularly true in education, which requires subtle matching of types of education to individual ability and demands for training, skills and education. Furthermore, as our economy evolves, education in particular disciplines is a risky investment: the demand for certain types of training can be high in some periods, but then decline markedly within a few years. These cycles can be driven by technological changes, international trade booms and busts, or merely the supply of trained people in an area expanding sufficiently to reduce a tight labour market.* The system should encourage the demanders and suppliers of education to understand these risks fully and to act on them.†

Another trap for the unwary occurs when politicians and the public are presented with tables of rates of return for different types of degrees or training. These tables are based on calculations of the

---

* For example, see the New Zealand study, Mahoney P, Park Z & Smyth R, 2013, *Moving on up: what young people earn after their tertiary education*, Ministry of Education. Note that historical data does not imply that high returns for education in certain disciplines will continue into the future. That requires a careful analysis of future supply and demand characteristics of the particular labour market.

† See Wolf, A, 2009, *An adult approach to further education*, Hobart Papers 168, Institute of Economic Affairs, London for such an approach applied to adult education.

salaries received by graduates in previous decades. Vested interests like to use these tables to justify moving educational funding from a low rate of return discipline to one with a higher rate of return. This analysis is misleading. First, salaries capture much but not all of the returns to education. The deeper understanding of society that comes from studying history or literature may not earn as high a return as an MBA, but it can produce a more subtle mind. Second, past returns are no guarantee of future returns in a discipline. Disciplines come into and out of demand for various economic, political and social reasons. Careful estimates of future returns are more reliable. Third, if a discipline is earning a high return, expanding the number of graduates may rapidly satiate a limited market, driving down the return, so that the eager, new graduates face dismal job prospects.

An additional distortion occurs when vested interests lobby for tougher credentials for a profession or trade. The lobbying for longer and more rigorous training comes only after there are some perceived failures. Vested interests feed the media with horror stories of the inadequacies, which leads to damaging consequences. Increased standards in training raise barriers to entry, restrict the supply of new entrants and drive up the financial rewards for incumbents, who invariably are exempted by 'grandfather' provisions from the more demanding training and standards. Another group that benefits from this lobbying is the associated educational suppliers who see an increase in demand for their services. These credential races are so common that few even reflect on the waste of resources.

Tragically, many of these policy practices have been observed in Australia. Increasingly, federal governments have interfered in the educational system, trying to influence the scale, quality and type of education. There is a perception that 'more' education is the goal. Precisely what this is trying to achieve is not clear. Sometimes the increase in the tertiary education sector is justified by appealing to equity; other times to economic growth, or policy clichés such as 'the knowledge economy'. Far too often, policies are working at cross-purposes. Market incentives are so distorted that unintended consequences abound. For example, Commonwealth funding has been based on the number of tertiary students graduating. This provides clear incentives not to fail students and for institutions to lower quality. Not surprisingly, governments are now worrying about quality, devising complex and costly quality indicators and incentives.

Quality education is very important for the economic and social health of a society – that is self-evident. But when you look closely at education policy and careful empirical research, you become aware that political slogans about education expenditure and reform can be misleading (especially for parents and prospective students) and very socially wasteful.

Conclusion

Using a series of examples, I have illustrated the unintended consequences that can flow from public policy decisions. The examples have been chosen to illustrate a number of dangers that flow from the consequences of ill-conceived or poorly implemented policies. I have outlined the importance of the political process in policy formation. What are the lessons that we can draw from these examples?*

First, policy makers should be very clear about the objective of the policy and study it carefully because social and economic issues are complex. It is only too easy to have an ambiguous objective, or one that addresses an artificial issue promoted by vested interests.

Second, the process of policy implementation is fraught with snares for the unwary. Careful analysis will reveal many of those potential consequences, which require discussion during policy planning. It is better to take longer at this stage to adjust the implementation procedures, rather than to make the adjustments after the policy has been introduced. Consequences that have been ignored can appear after implementation and create the embarrassing impression that the policy makers are incompetent.

Third, policy debates should be open so that serious critics can explore the contents and the implementation procedures. History provides many examples of embarrassing fiascos that an open, honest vetting process would have avoided.

Fourth, honest vetting of policies assumes a cadre of highly professional experts in the relevant areas. It is important that these

* The lessons apply to any organisation. Private companies and non-profit organisations suffer from these all-too-common ailments. For example see, Finkelstein, S, 2003, *Why smart executives fail: and what you can learn from their mistakes*, Penguin Books, London.

professionals be allowed to develop independently in universities, public service departments and think tanks. Indeed, I am continually surprised and delighted by examples where ordinary citizens with relevant knowledge and skills have contributed constructively to policy analysis. Of course, an open system will attract the usual one-issue cranks, but their arguments will not survive careful analysis.

And finally, even detailed policy analysis and implementation can give rise to complex and subtle policy failures. It is crucial that such cases are given forensic treatment by independent experts. The report should be public so that lessons can be learned. Attempts to conceal failure are a sign of weakness in the policy process. Concealment increases the possibility that the failure, or a variation on the failure, will be repeated in the future. Analysts should learn from their mistakes – this is necessary for high quality policy formation and implementation.

Market design for new leaders

Flavio M Menezes

Professor Flavio Menezes is head of the School of Economics, University of Queensland. He was formerly foundation director of the Australian Centre for Regulatory Economics, ANU. Flavio is the author of over 50 journal articles on the economics of auctions, competition and regulatory economics, industrial organisation and market design. He co-authored a well-known textbook, *An introduction to auction theory* (2005), and is regarded as Australia's leading auction expert. He also has considerable consulting experience overseas and in Australia, including on privatisation models for utilities.

Flavio Menezes' chapter deals with designed markets, and explains what new leaders need to know about this relatively recent field. It is written also for those who would seek to exercise influence in public life, and for all those who think about the key issues of our time such as the ageing population, climate change and how to promote the wellbeing of all Australians in an increasingly globalised world.

The paper reviews research and public policy developments in market design. While this may seem a technical and inaccessible topic, Flavio shows that it is crucial to improving the business of government in the 21st century.

You see things; and you say, 'Why?' But I dream things that never were; and I say, 'Why not?'

—George Bernard Shaw

Introduction

I have been asked to write to 'potential new leaders' about market design.

To be fair to the reader, I must disclose my lack of appreciation for much of the academic literature on leadership.* This literature

* Surprisingly, 'leadership' only became a popular word during the twentieth century and a subject of academic study after World War II. See Rost, J, 1993, *Leadership for the twenty-first century*, Praeger, Wesport, CT.

seems to put considerable effort into differentiating leadership from management; yet on another level, the literature suggests that ultimately leadership is related in some fashion to 'good management'.

Be that as it may, this chapter is written not just for leaders and managers, but also for those who aspire to be in a position to influence policy and society; who wish to engage with some of the key issues of our time such as the ageing population, climate change and how to promote the wellbeing of all Australians in an increasingly complex and interconnected world. Finally, it is written for those thinkers who are simply dissatisfied with the current state of public policy in Australia.

The development of public policy has been affected adversely in at least three important ways:

1. The political debate around policy seems to be driven not by considerate and informed public debate but rather by the ability to encapsulate messages into 30-second news grabs.
2. Senior public servants are often perceived, rightly or wrongly, as significantly risk-averse and too close to politicians, given their own career concerns and the fixed-term nature of their appointments.
3. Industry associations are often seen as promoting self-interest and contradictory policies. For example, industry leaders manifest their support for various social welfare programs while at the same time arguing for lower taxes and a reduction in the public deficit.

Yet the message of this chapter is one of hope. The chapter reviews research and public policy development in the area of 'market design'. That term refers to an area of research and practice that is concerned with determining the rules under which market participants interact to achieve some desirable goal. Market design uses techniques and concepts from game theory to develop and test these rules with experiments or field trials to ensure that they elicit the desirable behaviour in practice.

At first sight this might seem technical and remote from reality, but market design has proven crucial to improving the business of government. In Australia, government spending accounts for over 30 per cent of the total value of the goods and services produced, ranging from health services such as pathology tests to jet fighters.

The government also allocates, on behalf of society, licences to explore public resources such as timber, radio frequency for mobile telephony and oil, gas and minerals. Market design can assist in the efficient allocation of resources owned by society and ensure that we receive fair value for them. For example, it can help ensure that a licence to explore for oil and gas is allocated to the party with the highest-value use for it, generating revenue for society as well. Market design can also be used to solve complex problems that emerge in a variety of areas – from energy conservation to reduction of health risks. For example, it allows the development of rules to match organ donors to organ recipients so as to provide the most compatible match.*

Developments in market design offer an opportunity to promote a 'better business of government' agenda. The rigour involved in market design allows special interests to be exposed, as it is possible to investigate the potential impact of particular rules on outcomes and to determine possible winners and losers. The objective of this chapter is to impart some knowledge of market design to those aspiring to influence policy outcomes in Australia. As the examples in this chapter illustrate, the possibilities are numerous and the potential beneficial impact on people's lives can be substantial. My account of this field will, I hope, provide those who develop public policy, and those politicians who have a job of selling public policy to the public at large, with success stories that are sufficiently cogent to hold the public attention – for more than 30 seconds! The success stories are also an important part of recognising those creative, senior public servants who have shown the breadth of vision to promote innovative policy solutions.

The chapter is organised in two main parts. First, I provide a brief history of market design and some real-life examples, in cases where monetary payments have been used as the basis to allocate goods and services. Second, I review a very large experiment in Brazil where markets were created to avoid electricity rationing in 2001. The choice of this example is not inconsequential; it illustrates that such an approach to public policy can be successful even

* Alvin Roth was awarded the 2012 Nobel Prize for developing methods to match doctors with hospitals, school pupils with schools, and organ donors with patients. See http://www.nobelprize.org/nobel_prizes/economic-sciences/laureates/2012/roth-facts.html.

in developing countries with weaker institutions. I will then provide some concluding comments, highlighting one new area where market design principles might usefully be applied.

Market design: theory and practice

In this section I explore some of the theoretical developments over the last 40 years that led to the emergence of the field of market design. This new field has had a substantive impact on policy, especially after the highly successful auctions of the mobile telephony licences in the mid 1990s in the United States. The auctions replaced an inefficient allocation system where licences were allocated to applicants via a lottery and subsequently sold for large windfalls. The auctions raised substantial amount of revenue for the US government and the model was adopted worldwide, including in Australia.

Market design as a field emerged somewhat separately from game theory. However, game theory has provided the foundations for analysing the non-cooperative behaviour that underpins market design.

Non-cooperative game theory, auction theory and mechanism design

Game theory is the study of the interaction among self-interested agents. Here our focus is on the analysis of equilibrium behaviour (that is, where the strategic behaviour of individuals induces a situation or outcome in which economic forces are balanced) in non-cooperative games. To be more precise, we refer to theories about the way we expect individuals to behave in strategic situations when their interests are in conflict. Key contributions in this area include those from John C Harsanyi, John F Nash Jr* and Reinhard Selten, who were jointly awarded the 1994 Nobel Prize in economics 'for their pioneering analysis of equilibria in the theory of non-cooperative games'.

The starting point is the definition of a 'Nash equilibrium' in which it is assumed that each player will choose the strategy (or action) that maximises his net gains, taking into account the strategies of all other players. The Nash equilibrium is the outcome that results when all players are choosing their preferred strategies, know-

* John Nash was the subject of the 2001 film *A Beautiful Mind*, starring Russell Crowe.

ing that everyone else is also choosing their preferred strategies, and no player finds it profitable to deviate from their strategies while the other players keep theirs unchanged.

To illustrate, let us consider the well-known 'prisoner's dilemma' game. This has numerous applications to social planning, although it is beyond the scope of this chapter to examine them all. The story goes along the following lines.

The prisoner's dilemma

Two individuals have jointly committed a crime. They are both arrested and put in solitary confinement. The police don't have enough evidence to convict the pair for the crime they committed but are confident that they can convict both of them to a lesser charge that attracts a one-year jail sentence. The standard sentence for the actual crime is three years. Simultaneously, the police offer each prisoner an opportunity to testify against his partner in exchange for lenience and serving no time in jail while the partner, who stays silent, will get three years in prison on the main charge. However, if prisoners testify against each other, both will be sentenced to two years in jail.

This game can be represented in a matrix form that includes the outcomes of the possible actions by the two prisoners (let us call them Al and Biff).

Table 1: Outcomes of possible actions by Al and Biff

	Biff stays silent	Biff confesses
Al stays silent	(−1,−1)	(−3,0)
Al confesses	(0,−3)	(−2,−2)

Numbers in parentheses represent the sentences of Al and Biff, respectively, for the various possibilities. I have added a minus sign to the numbers to remind the reader that these are punishments not prizes and so a player will prefer, for example, −1 to −3 or 0 to −1.

What is the Nash equilibrium of this game? Let's look at it from Al's perspective. If Biff stays silent, it would be better for Al to confess and go free rather than stay silent (in which case he would serve one year of imprisonment). If Biff confesses, again, choosing to confess would yield Al a better outcome (a shorter term of imprisonment) than staying silent. Clearly, no matter what Biff chooses, Al is better off confessing. As Biff faces the same problem with Al, he too is better off confessing. That is, the Nash equilibrium of the game is for both prisoners to confess and serve two years in jail although they would be better off if they both had remained silent. To understand why the option (stay silent, stay silent) is not a Nash equilibrium, just note that if Al stays silent, Biff would be better off deviating from remaining silent and confessing. By doing so he would go free rather than serving a year in jail.

To sum up, the Nash equilibrium concept is predicated on the idea that players choose actions or strategies that are best for them assuming that their opponents will do the same. This apparently simple but powerful idea has been used extensively in economics and was generalised by Harsanyi* for games with incomplete information (that is, where there is uncertainty about how bidders value an object for sale or about the costs of potential suppliers who wish to participate in a government tender) and by Selten for games where players move sequentially rather than simultaneously.

One can readily understand how games of incomplete information are related to market design. Consider a seller (the government) who wants to allocate a public resource but does not know how potential buyers value the resources. Efficiency requires that the resource be allocated to the buyer who places the highest value on it. Harsanyi's notion of a Nash equilibrium for the case of incomplete information (called a 'Bayesian Nash equilibrium') provides the tools to analyse the behaviour of the seller and buyers and to predict equilibrium. As in a Nash equilibrium, under a Bayesian Nash equilibrium players choose the best action assuming that other players will do the same. The key difference is that their actions are contingent on the information they have (or their types – such as the values that bidders place on the object for sale in the case of an auction), which is not known to the seller.

In this instance, the allocation mechanism somehow induces buyers to reveal (directly or indirectly) their values for the object for sale. It turns out that in any auction, bidders with higher values for the object bid higher;† the resource is allocated to the highest

* who, incidentally, started his academic career at the University of Queensland

† While intuitive, this is not always the case. See, for example, McAdams, D, 2002, *Bidding Lower with higher values in multi-object auctions*, Working Paper #4249-02, MIT Sloan, Cambridge.

valued bidder. The rub is that different auction formats will result in strategic bidders following different strategies, which might have consequences for the revenue raised by the seller.

Bill Vickrey* proposed a mechanism that can lead buyers to reveal their true valuations. Under a second-price sealed-bid auction (now known as a 'Vickrey auction'), bidders simultaneously submit sealed bids to the seller, and the bidder with the highest bid wins the auction but pays the second highest bid. It can be shown that buyers in a Vickrey auction bid their true valuations. For those who wish to understand why this is so I have set out the detailed reasoning in the box.

Vickrey auctions

There is incentive for bidders to bid their true values in a Vickrey auction. To understand this, consider a bidder who bids a for the object he values at v, and denote by $\hat{a}$ the highest bid among other bidders. Here we apply the concept of Nash equilibrium to see that the bidder has no incentive to deviate from bidding his true value $a = v$. Since all other bids remain the same when this bidder changes his bid, such deviation only matters if it changes his win or loss outcome. Bidding higher than his true value, i.e., $a > v$, affects the outcome only if $a > \hat{a} > v$. (Otherwise if $\hat{a} > a$, he always loses or if $\hat{a} < v$, he always wins and pays $\hat{a}$.) In this case, the bidder wins but has to pay $\hat{a}$, which is more than his true value. Bidding lower than his true value, i.e., $a < v$, affects the outcome only if $a < \hat{a} < v$ (otherwise if $\hat{a} > v$, he always loses or $\hat{a} < v$, he always wins and pays $\hat{a}$). In this case the bidder loses, when it is possible to win with non-negative payoff by raising the bid just above $\hat{a}$.

As the game is symmetric, the same argument applies for all other bidders. Therefore, we have shown that no player has an incentive to deviate from bidding his or her true valuation, which is the Nash equilibrium of this auction game.

Although there are sound reasons why Vickrey auctions as described above are not used in practice,† there is a substantial body of literature that aims to implement Vickrey's ideas through

* Vickrey was awarded the 1996 Nobel Prize in economics for his pioneering work on auctions, but sadly passed away three days.

† For example, bidders might be concerned that the seller can exploit this information (that is, the values revealed in this auction) in future auctions by setting a higher reserve price.

dynamic auctions where bidders have an opportunity to revise their bids. Indeed, auction theory is a specialised field of research* and its insights have been extensively used around the world since at least the 1990s, by governments in allocating public resources and buying goods and services, and also by the private sector.

Auction theory is also closely linked to the field of mechanism design, and can be seen as a particular case of it. Much of economic theory, including part of auction theory, is devoted to understanding existing economic institutions and markets to explain or predict equilibrium outcome. Mechanism design aims to reverse the direction of this process. It begins by identifying desired outcomes and asks whether mechanisms (institutions, markets) could be designed to achieve the desired outcomes. Outcomes could include the provision of a public good (such as public education or defence) or the allocation of public resources (that is, who is awarded the resource and the associated payments).

The field of mechanism design has its origins in the work of Leo Hurwicz in the 1960s. He shared the 2007 Nobel Prize in economics with Roger Myerson and Eric Maskin. The connection between mechanism design and auction design is evident in a number of ways. For example, the Vickrey-Clarke-Groves mechanism to finance a public good in the presence of externalities† charges each individual the harm they cause to other bidders, and ensures that the optimal strategy for a bidder is to bid their true valuations of the objects. It is a generalisation of a Vickrey auction for multiple items. Another example includes the work of Roger Myerson (with David Baron) on how to regulate a monopolist, such as an electricity distributor, when costs are unknown. The same principles were applied by Myerson to characterise the optimal auction – the auction that maximises the expected revenue of the seller. These two problems are connected because the seller in an auction is also a monopolist who faces buyers and does not know the values that buyers assign to the object for sale.

As we will see next, when the allocation of public resources is

* See, for example, Menezes, F & Monteiro, P, 2008, *An introduction to auction theory*, Oxford University Press, Oxford.

† This refers to a situation where one's consumption of a good impacts on other people's consumption.

concerned, economic efficiency is often more important than revenue maximisation. However, efficient auctions can raise significant amounts of revenue for the government.

From theory to practice: auctions as a public policy tool

Auctions have emerged as the preferred approach to the allocation of publicly owned resources, including radiofrequency spectrum, electricity, timber, and oil and gas exploration licences. The reason for the emergence of auctions is their ability to allocate resources to parties who have the highest value for them.

Auctions are superior to the commonly used mechanism known as a 'beauty contest'. Under that allocation methodology, the government specifies criteria and invites private firms to demonstrate their ability to meet them. Working to define the correct criteria and make accurate evaluations places a costly compliance burden on the government and creates opportunities for favouritism and corruption. To see this, consider the example where instead of selecting on the basis of the highest monetary bid, a mineral exploration or production licence is allocated exclusively on the manner in which a miner treats Indigenous communities and remediates the environment after extracting the minerals. A key issue is how to evaluate competing proposals – after all, these are essentially promises of actions that will be taken after the event and in some instances decades from now, so judgement has to be exercised. There is a risk that the winner of the beauty contest is not the most efficient party but rather the party that is best at writing proposals.

In contrast, a well-designed auction allocates the licence to the party that is more efficient at extracting the resources and raises more funds to compensate Indigenous communities and mitigate adverse impacts on the environment as defined in the licence requirements. The auction monetises these objectives, which otherwise would be evaluated qualitatively. The government can then use the proceeds of the auction to fund environmental mitigation and to compensate Indigenous communities. Selecting an appropriate reserve price ensures that if the auction cannot raise enough resources to provide compensation for Indigenous communities and to care for the environment, then the licence will not be allocated.

Moreover, unlike beauty contests, well-designed auctions can raise substantial revenue for government. For example, the government has raised over $2 billion in the recent sale of the spectrum of frequency that was released from the switch from analog to digital TV, which will be used for the provision of 4G mobile services.

The revenue raised in the 4G auction can be seen as capturing economic rents that might not be captured by our company tax regime (which is designed to tax accounting profits), as the 4G revenue includes both a normal return to investment and also economic profits (rents). Economic rents are returns in excess of the normal return and are usually either firm- or location-specific. In the former, they emerge, for example, because of a particular technology, know-how or entrepreneurship skills. In the latter, they are associated with the business's location in Australia, such as in the case of mineral resources or oligopolistic industries. Given the direct and indirect costs of taxation,* an auction can be seen as a more efficient form of taxation as, given its lump sum nature, it does not distort investment behaviour.† This was an important reason for the recent decision of the Australian government to use cash bidding for oil and gas exploration licences in mature areas.

In addition to allocating public resources efficiently, and being an effective mechanism for taxing economic rents, auctions can also be used to solve complex problems. For example, consider the market for electricity where supply and demand need to be balanced continuously and on time. Australia is one of the few countries that have a market for establishing the wholesale price of electricity in

* Direct costs include not only the administrative costs of collecting the tax but also compliance costs. Indirect costs are what economists refer to as the deadweight losses associated with taxation; taxes distort economic behaviour and such distortion entails a cost, as society is deprived of the economic benefits of the activity suppressed by taxation. Typically the indirect costs are substantially larger than the direct costs of taxation.

† This is a basic result in the economics of taxation. To understand this, consider the decision whether or not to invest $100 in additional extraction capacity and for simplicity consider only equity investment. Suppose the required rate of return is 10 per cent (this is the opportunity cost of capital) and the corporate tax rate is 33.3 per cent, then if this project returns only $10, it would not go ahead because of the tax. Indeed, the project has to generate at least $15 (to cover the tax of $5 and meet the required rate of return of $10) for the firm to undertake it. In contrast, in the case of an auction, the auction licence fee would have already been paid and, therefore, would be a sunk cost and should not affect the investment decision to be made.

real time. Electricity generators submit bids (schedules specifying how much they are willing to supply at various prices), which are added. An equilibrium price is found at the point where the aggregate supply schedules meet the system demand. All bids below that price are successful and all bids above that price are unsuccessful.

As another example, take Victoria's BushTender, an auction-based approach that was trialled in two Victorian regions in order to allocate funds to biodiversity conservation.* The approach involved the use of a simple auction mechanism to determine payments that farmers in Victoria were willing to receive to undertake certain environmental actions such as protecting the habitats of certain species, weeding or fencing particular areas. The process can be summarised as follows: landholders within the trial areas registered an expression of interest and were subsequently contacted to arrange a property visit, during which a field officer assessed the quality and significance of the native vegetation on the site and discussed management options with the landholder. A BBI (biodiversity benefits index) for each site was calculated. Landholders then identified the actions they proposed to undertake on the site, and together with the field officer prepared a management plan as the basis of their bid. Successful bids were all those bids that were better value for money per unit of biodiversity benefit.

This auction offered large cost savings to the government in comparison to a hypothetical fixed price scheme, where the agency would pay each successful landholder the same price (the price of the marginal offer). Specifically, for the same budget of around $400,000, a one-price auction would give approximately 25 per cent less biodiversity than a discriminative price auction. Expressed in another way, a budget of approximately $2.7 million (almost seven times more than the actual budget) would be required for the one-price auction to get the same level of biodiversity as the discriminative price auction. Direct benefits from the bush auctions consist of the efficiency gains in information revelation, cost minimisation and contract specification. Indirect efficiency gains include more flexibility in other policy decisions such as offsets for infrastructure

* See, for example, Stoneham, G, Chaudri, V, Ha, A & Strappazon, L, 2003, 'Auctions for conservation contracts: an empirical examination of Victoria's BushTender trial', *Australian Journal of Agricultural and Resource Economics*, 47(4): 477–500

development, and providing education to landholders at least in terms of the attitudes towards conservation.

Tenders, the flip side of auctions, are used by governments around the world to buy goods and services, varying from complex weapon systems to roads and health services. Different from an ordinary auction where buyers compete to obtain a good, a service or a licence by making bids, a tender involves sellers competing to obtain business from the buyer. The most common application of tenders is for e-procurement of 'standard goods', a strategy used to reduce spending as part of strategic sourcing. With this type of 'reverse auction', the objective of cost minimisation becomes the low-hanging fruit without causing any distortion to the market. Saving is achieved through increased competition and productive efficiency from economies of scale and scope. Not only are costs minimised, but a range of potential non-price benefits can also be realised, including decreased transaction costs, increased transparency, less bureaucracy and faster acquisition processes. The World Bank (2003) estimates that government e-procurement contributes to efficiency gains of a reduction of 10 to 20 per cent in prices due to increased competitiveness, and a 50 to 80 per cent fall in transaction costs.

An example of these dynamic reverse auctions is the tender process for the supply of blood products in the UK National Health Service. Tenders may either be open or restricted, which is to say companies must be invited to submit a tender. Moreover, potential suppliers must submit additional information regarding their technical, economic and financial capacity. The process serves several objectives ranging from efficient price and quantity to technical competence of the suppliers, high level of delivery performance and lower risk. The saving from this process was estimated to be from £18 to £48 million across England alone.

I hope to have convinced the reader by now that auction mechanisms can contribute considerable efficiency gains to society and ought to be part of the repertoire of approaches used by modern governments in allocating resources and procuring goods and services. However, not all efficient markets need to involve an auction. Other types of market design can serve well in some specific circumstances. In the next section, we investigate a very large market design in Brazil.

A market to avoid electricity rationing in Brazil

Around 2000, Brazil was producing roughly 90 per cent of its electricity from hydroelectric sources. Confronting a severe drought, in May 2001 the Brazilian government implemented a program requiring an average 20 per cent reduction in electricity consumption for the country. The program assigned end users a consumption entitlement (quota) based on about 75 to 80 per cent of average past consumption. Careful design included allowing for changed circumstances and a public information campaign.

Up to their consumption entitlement, consumers paid the regulated price. However, under-consumption was rewarded with cash payments and over-consumption penalised. For residential consumers, the penalty varied from 50 per cent to 200 per cent of the regulated price, whereas for industrial consumers the penalty was linked to the cost of generating electricity in such a constrained environment (approximately US $300 MWh). For the benefit of the reader, average wholesale electricity prices in Australia at that time ranged from $37 MWh in New South Wales to $56 MWh in South Australia.

Consumers were allowed to trade entitlements. Smaller users traded with the retailer or distributor, whereas there was a market for trading entitlements for larger users. This meant that firms that were not efficient users of electricity could sell their entitlements to more efficient firms and use the proceeds of the sale as compensation for reducing production, or shut down.

The program was an unqualified success. There was not a single blackout or brownout. The program achieved over 20 per cent reduction in consumption over eight months, almost country wide. Estimates suggest that at least 1–1.5 per cent of the GDP was saved vis-à-vis the impact that rolling, unplanned blackouts would have had in the economy. Within a year, enough rain had fallen to repeal most of the policy, which by then had been extremely successful in avoiding electricity rationing and mitigating adverse impacts on economic growth.

This example also illustrates how market design works by providing incentives for individuals to change their behaviour, and how small behavioural changes can have large and beneficial impacts. In particular, a survey was undertaken to document the choice of energy-saving strategy chosen by consumers.[1] The result of the survey is revealing of the power of incentives in changing behaviour. The most common action taken was essentially costless but potentially accounted for a significant reduction in consumption; it consisted simply of turning off lights! This is an illustration of how small adjustments in each margin – that is, consumers make small adjustment in their behaviour by watching less TV, switching off lights more often, etc. – as a response to price changes, can lead to big reductions in electricity consumption. The five most popular actions taken by consumers were:

1. switching off lights
2. replacing light bulbs
3. less time watching TV
4. less ironing
5. turning off freezer.

Average individual consumption of electricity was reduced to 1994 levels. Energy efficiency became a part of the decision making process to buy appliances and whitegoods, changing from being mentioned by 8 per cent of consumers before the crisis to 58 per cent of consumers after the crisis.

Concluding comments

There are yet other areas in which market design might be applied to good effect. Consider obesity and the associated health problems faced by more than four million Australians. The dollar value of the burden of the disease (netting out the financial costs of $8.2 billion borne by individuals) has been estimated at $49.9 billion per annum.[2] Most of this money is spent in addressing the adverse impact of obesity on people's lives rather than on reducing or preventing obesity.

Rather than this, how about putting a contract out for tender that will make payments based on outcomes such as a reduction in obesity or the onset of diabetes in particular geographic areas or for a defined population (such as over 50s)?* Through a social impact bond, investors would finance particular interventions (for example, lifestyle change programs) delivered by reputable service providers. Investors would be paid by the public sector on the basis

* I urge the reader to examine the website www.socialfinance.org.uk/work/sibs before coming to a premature conclusion that I have lost my marbles.

of improved social outcomes (for example, reduced incidence of obesity in the population); no improvement would mean no payment. This can be approached as a market design problem – from defining what is to be tendered, the tender rules and the schedule of payments to, importantly, some of the micro rules such as what happens under default and rules to minimise gaming of the system. Such designed markets can provide an innovative way to attract new investment and new solutions that may bring substantial benefits to individuals and communities.

Market design has emerged as a key approach in achieving better public policy outcomes in a variety of settings. In particular, it allows policy makers to tailor a mechanism such as an auction to the particular circumstances and thereby achieve their aims. As illustrated, auctions enable resources to be allocated to those who place the highest value on them as well as raising substantial revenue for the government. Auctions, along with other forms of market design, can be used to solve complex problems that emerge in a variety of areas from energy conservation to environmental protection. Market design has successfully been implemented even in developing countries where institutions are less strong.

It is important that the benefits of market design are considered by potential new leaders, who are in a position to influence policy and society. Propagation of these ideas could lead to an improved government agenda, whereby well-designed markets could utilise competitive forces to enable the best use of public resources. As a result, efficiency gains and a fair return for society could be achieved along with increased transparency, maintenance of quality, sustainable industry, corruption mitigation and minimisation of costs.

---

1. Maurer, L, 2012, *Brazil 2002: Sensible Rationing to Alleviate Prolonged Electricity Shortfall*, http://www.iea.org/media/workshops/2012/savingelectricity/Brazil2002.pdf.
2. Access Economics 2008, *The growing cost of obesity in 2008: three years on*, www.diabetesaustralia.com.au/en/Resources/Reports/National/The-growing-cost-of-obesity-in-2008-three-years-on.

Some problems of politics and knowledge

Jeremy Shearmur

Jeremy Shearmur was reader in philosophy in the School of Philosophy at the Australian National University until his recent retirement. He has wide academic interests, especially in social philosophy and in critical rationalism. Jeremy was educated at the London School of Economics, where he worked with Karl Popper. He taught philosophy at Edinburgh, Political Theory at Manchester and the ANU, and was also Director of Studies of the Centre for Policy Studies (London), and Research Associate Professor at George Mason University.

Jeremy's publications include: *The political thought of Karl Popper* (1996) and *Hayek and after* (1996). He was co-editor of Karl Popper's *After the open society* (2008). Jeremy is currently working on a new volume: *Living with markets.*

Jeremy Shearmur's essay contrasts contemporary politics and public service with Plato's *Republic*, in which the 'good society' was one where the rulers were philosophers, or the philosophers rulers; these 'guardians' would live a secluded life, would not be permitted to hold private wealth and would determine how a society should be run. While these notions might seem quaint and remote, some traces of them remain in our society, and they may be inhibiting progress.

Jeremy argues that Australia has a reputation for innovation and, in general, for performing in many fields well above its weight. It is a country full of ingenious and interesting (if sometimes awkward) people who, between us, know an incredible amount. If the country is to prosper and to work well, it needs to make use of the knowledge of all of us. A key message that needs to be taken on board by our leaders is that they are not Platonic guardians who know everything, and whose task is simply to regulate the rest of us ever more firmly. Rather, they – and also, crucially, our public servants – are just like the rest of us, and are just as fallible. We need to take the social division of knowledge seriously, learn from anyone who can correct us where we have got things wrong and, above all, give people space to make use of their own specialised knowledge, in order to innovate and thus really show that Australia can be a clever country.

'I learnt from Popper that we never know what we are talking about, and I learnt from Hayek that we never know what we are doing.'
—WW Bartley III

Introduction

In his *Republic*, Plato depicts a good society as one in which some people – the guardians or philosophers – have knowledge, while others have mere opinions. In this good society, the rulers would be philosophers, or the philosophers rulers. Their ideas about how a society should be run would be imposed on everyone else, by a kind of police-cum-army. Such an idea is odd, not least to those who have had anything to do with philosophers. However, not only has this view had a resonance through the history of political thought, but aspects of the High Court and of the senior public service in Australia might be looked at as in some ways being in this tradition: decisions of the highest courts (on constitutional and regular legal issues) play a key social role and are not subject to any direct form of democratic accountability, while the detailed content of most legislation is the work of the public service (in interaction with senior politicians and lobbyists), and to all intents and purposes is simply imposed on the rest of us.

Plato's ideas have had their critics. Karl Popper, in *The open society and its enemies,*[1] stressed the fallibility of human knowledge – including that of would-be guardians. He also argued that while not all of us may be able to initiate policy ideas, we are all in a position to criticise them (by virtue of the fact that we would know best how they might affect us and those close to us, and how they would relate to the situations in which we live and work).

Popper's friend, the economist Friedrich Hayek, explored problems with the socialist ideal of running an advanced industrial society without making use of market mechanisms, and was led to some other interesting issues about knowledge. To appreciate his views, one needs to start with a theme raised in the work of Adam Smith concerning the division of labour. Rather than individuals undertaking entire operations themselves, or acting as jacks-of-all-trades, there are huge gains to productivity when people specialise in smaller tasks – provided these coordinate with one another. But how does this coordination take place? In a workshop or a factory, it could be organised by the management, but the coordinated division of labour also takes place in society more generally – and these days, increasingly, across the world. Smith's insight was that such activity is coordinated by means of people and companies acting – under a suitable legal system – in response to the prices of goods and services. These prices, in a rough-and-ready way, sum up the consequences of other individuals' decisions, and if people are guided by prices they are, in broad terms, directed to act in ways that meet the preferences of other people, as expressed in their purchases – people who, in a large society, they cannot know individually. Market prices convey information to us about people's tastes and preferences, and do so in such a way that we are provided with a cash incentive to respond to those prices and thus to people's needs.

In a short article, 'I, pencil',[2] Leonard Read argued that, in a society of any complexity, making anything depends on a huge number of activities, the details of which are known to no-one. Even a lead pencil involves the putting together of wood, graphite, rubber, paint, a metal rubber-holder, and so on. Yet the production of each of these things involves the work of many individuals, and behind each of them are other people, undertaking specialised activities that make their activities possible. The lumberjack depends on the forester, but also on those who make chainsaws – and on miners and metal workers who extract and process the steel from which the saws are made, those who produce oil for chainsaws, and so on. But all these people will typically have no idea what the final products of their activities will be. Everything works on the basis of price.

Hayek also placed emphasis on the importance of other social mechanisms, typically undesigned, that serve to coordinate our various actions (from language, to various social conventions, roles and traditions, to the law). We may thus look at a large-scale society – and, indeed, at the world – as consisting of a multitude of people and organisations who each have their own particular knowledge, which might be of use to others. The knowledge may be positive, or able to serve the important function of correcting ideas that people currently take for granted. But how can such knowledge be made accessible to others? And how can such knowledge at the individual and group level interrelate with such (fallible) expert knowledge as we also have? In what follows, I shall discuss some of these matters in the context of organisations, and also in the context of politics and the public service.

The use of knowledge in organisations

Hayek was concerned with agents who had the freedom to do what they wished, provided that it was within the law. But clearly, one consequence of being employed is that we submit ourselves to what, in other contexts, would be seen as a kind of tyranny. The employee is, on a day-to-day basis, told what to do, and in many cases how to do it. Certain freedoms remain: those with sufficient nerve, and who know that their services are sufficiently valued, may attempt to negotiate rather than simply obey orders. And within common-law based systems, you can simply walk away from your employment. Even if there were a contract on the basis of which you had undertaken to perform the specific service in question, the legal remedy against you would typically be in terms of your having to pay compensation, rather than your being compelled to undertake the service in question.

However, the issues to which I have referred in the introduction do not go away. Those in the most senior positions may have certain kinds of knowledge that is not available to those in other positions in the organisation; for example, about kinds of problems and constraints that the organisation faces. In addition, those in positions of seniority are (or at least should be in principle) accountable for what the outcomes are and can, as a result, reasonably require that specific problems be addressed, and that specific things be produced – and in specific ways.

At the same time, their own knowledge is fallible. They may simply have mistaken beliefs about things, and thus be working on the basis of false assumptions. As well as this, the issue of the social division of information, to which I have referred above, does not go away in the context of a firm. There may be specific things that are required for a company to be profitable or compliant with the law that will not be known by individuals in lower positions in the organisation. But at the same time, those individuals will typically know what is required in order for some job to be undertaken effectively, and thus what will and will not work, better than do those who are running the organisation. This is not to say that those in lower positions are infallible or that they may not usefully learn from what is being done elsewhere: all kinds of traditional practices may be inefficient or in other ways problematic, and doing things more effectively may require that all of us be open to making perhaps even dramatic changes to how we are proceeding. At the same time, those who are familiar with particular tasks or problems are likely to know a lot about them that those in more senior positions don't – and, indeed, typically can't know.

What I have suggested above indicates certain limitations on the knowledge of those in positions of responsibility in organisations. There is also another side to all this. All kinds of knowledge are scattered within an organisation, on a disaggregated basis, which it would be to the advantage of the organisation to use.* A key problem for those in managerial positions is how to find ways in which they can get people to contribute knowledge that they hold, such that it can be made use of. There are several different issues here.

At a purely technical level, there is the problem of how to get access to specialised knowledge that may be 'tacit' in its character (in the sense of not being something that people normally have in a form that can be readily articulated). Here, we may consider three different approaches that might be taken.

The first of these is the adoption of markets internally within companies or organisations. This would amount to making use of mechanisms just like those used outside the organisation. Different parts of an organisation would have to purchase goods and services internally, and this would allow people situated in other parts of the firm to make use of their particular knowledge and skills in making a response. This method is, in fact, used in some large corporations. It has the advantage that it forces departments to price the value to them of the use *in situ* of a particular employee or their time – thus avoiding the misuse of resources that can occur if someone who has a particular skill is used for low-value tasks or is simply seconded

* Except for a situation, say, where there is simply a conveyor belt, into which everyone has to contribute a particular mechanical task. But even in these settings issues relating to the use of disaggregated knowledge may emerge, as interestingly demonstrated in the management novel The goal, which reveals through a storyline some principles of operations management. See Goldratt, E & Cox, J, 1984, *The goal: a process of ongoing improvement*, North River Press, Great Barrington, MA.

from one area to another without proper consideration of the value of what they were doing originally.

The second approach has been explored in certain of the 'knowledge management' literature. I am here concerned with the more 'touchy-feely' end of this approach (as opposed to data mining). Ernst and Young noted the fact that, when people undertook various assignments, they developed particular problem-solving techniques, and also acquired various kinds of local knowledge (such as how certain things are done in Hong Kong, or in a particular Australian university). People might happen to exchange information about these things at the coffee machine, or among a group of smokers outside the building. All this, however, is obviously a hit-and-miss affair, as other people who could benefit from specific information might never know that there was someone in their organisation who had it. Ernst and Young hit on the idea of: (a) systematically debriefing people when they returned from operations, and (b) placing the lessons learnt onto a natural language database, which was then accessible to others in the organisation. (Indeed, for a while they made this available to clients, for a fee, offering them access to it which was mediated by an employee.)*

The third approach is finding ways to get people to explicate expert tacit knowledge, which can then be captured in software or hardware. A famous case of this relates to a Japanese manufacturer of bread-making machines who sent people to watch – with permission – just what actions a Paris-trained pastry chef in a top Japanese hotel performed when making bread. These were tracked and subsequently simulated by their bread-making machine. This third case opens up some interesting problems, for clearly what may be 'captured' in such a case, is, in fact, valuable human capital; something that, until it is so captured, might enable an employee to earn a premium rate for their services. But while the skilled chef is not likely to be replaced by a machine, in many cases in the workplace there is a real risk that people who participate in such processes might find that their skill becomes devalued. Various kinds of computer-aided design have replaced some classes of designers – in the sense that

* For one account of this, see Marshall Electronic Commerce Program, 1998, The evolution of Ernie—the online business consultant, www.usc.edu/schools/business/atisp/ec/Ernie/Ernie.pdf.

what were once skilled tasks can now be undertaken by people who do not have specialised skills.

A different kind of issue relates to problems posed by the fallibility of knowledge in an organisational setting. The key problem here is that there is a tension between authority and responsibility, and learning. All knowledge is fallible, and this includes everybody, however senior they might be. On this score, it is important that everybody's ideas, including those of the most senior people, be open to criticism and amendment, not least because if senior managers get things wrong the results might be catastrophic. The difficulty is that senior managers typically have two other roles that may be in tension with this: on the one side, it will be up to them to take key decisions, and they also are likely to have to take responsibility for overall outcomes. It is worth bearing in mind here that there is a difference between an open society – in the sense of one in which criticism can be voiced – and a democracy. It is striking that Immanuel Kant, in his essay 'What is Enlightenment?', called for openness of criticism, but did so in a setting in which key decisions were taken by a ruler, rather than democratically. This would suggest a model that might be used in organisations.

In *The structure of scientific revolutions*, Thomas Kuhn discussed the way in which scientific activity typically takes place within a framework of assumptions – about what the main problems are, the way in which they should be approached, and the sort of ideas that should be used in tackling them. Such ideas, however, change from time to time – and, while Kuhn was ambiguous about this, we can surely hope that changes in such frameworks might constitute improvements. All this, it seems to me, points to a general problem. Clearly, we can typically cooperate most easily, and communicate particularly well, with people who share a framework with us. At the same time, we can reasonably expect that there may be benefits to improving the framework within which we are working. Yet changing the system within which people are working can disrupt how people are working, lead to all kinds of damaging uncertainty, and slow down all kinds of things that, earlier, were done easily. The key problem that this poses is how best to combine a shared framework and the improvement of that framework.

There is also the issue of people's interests (and their ability and willingness to innovate). The attempt to capture knowledge held within an organisation may, in some cases, pose real conflicts of interests, for if someone's income depended on their control over particular pieces of human capital, they would understandably resist moves to make this generally available within the organisation in ways that would harm their interests. Employers may well say: but anything that our employees do or even think is ours – they signed an agreement to this effect! But this does not solve the problem, not least, because there are limits to the degree to which even the most vigilant of employers can control their employees' thoughts, and because there are all kinds of things that employees can do, within the terms of their employment contracts, to make it difficult for their employers to treat them unfairly. What is needed here is for people who hold such knowledge to be offered a good deal, such that they will willingly cooperate with their employers.

These issues become easier when the knowledge that employees can contribute is less one-off human capital than an ability to generate a stream of innovation. They may then not be at all concerned about making available a single idea to the company, because they know that their value consists of their capacity to generate a stream of such ideas. However, two things here are significant. First, employees need to get appropriate rewards for innovation. Again, the company might well insist that it owns anything its employees produce while they are employees. But if it does this, it might hit a problem. For if, say, an employee were asked to resolve a specific problem, the employee might well be able to see the additional potential of ideas that they first come up with (something that might well not be understood by their employer), and if they were not to be rewarded on the basis of these, they might put such ideas to one side, and come up, instead, with a less innovative solution to the problem – moving off, in due course, to develop their own ideas, independently, in different fields, and to their own benefit.

Second, there are many examples of creativity going along with behaviour that is somewhat eccentric. For example, Dillwyn Knox, who played an important role in breaking of Enigma at Bletchley Park, used to work on difficult problems in a hot bath, which was located in one of the offices there; I have heard many examples of eccentric behaviour on the part of highly creative people in the early days of the Australian National University. Clearly, there may be reasons to impose certain kinds of controls – for example, if there is a shift from a male-only setting, to one in which men and women work together. But it should be clear to anyone, on reflection, that there are tensions between creativity and tight bureaucratic accountability. While, to be sure, it is important that resources are not wasted or diverted to private consumption, the idea that people who are working creatively on problems should be able to behave like public servants, or to give an account in advance of what, in detail, they will be doing, is half-witted. It is no accident that companies like Google and Microsoft have adapted various features of the former practices of universities in order to foster creative interchange between their employees. It is ironic that, at just the same time, universities themselves have been reshaped by people who seem not to understand any of this to look more like hierarchical branches of the public service.

What about politics?

By this point, you might have wondered: but just what does all this have to do with politics and government? The answer is that just the same kind of problem occurs in these spheres, but politicians and the public service seem increasingly to operate as if they were unaware that this was the case.

Politicians and public servants are fallible. They may have misdiagnosed the problems that we face, and they seldom invite criticism of their proposed solutions. They may respond to criticism – well, they have public consultations. But these typically invite the public to respond to problems without explaining properly to them what assumptions are being made and what the constraints upon solutions are. Unless politicians explain the problems and constraints and what their favoured solutions are, and then ask for criticism and alternative suggestions, even criticism may be pointless. It may be the case that the best solution is flawed, but that if there is no better alternative, the ideas which were initially advanced, and were criticised, are the best ones to go for.

For those taking decisions, it is important to understand that what might be called a Euclidian or Cartesian view of knowledge is incorrect. What does this mean? Just because something seems clear, obvious or undeniable to us, does not mean that it is true. Our ideas have all kinds of consequences that we can't even imagine, and that we can't discover just by thinking about them. Accordingly, just because we agree on something now, this does not mean that we should not revise it when its problematic consequences become apparent. The procedure, say, of devising a 'mission statement' that is taken to bind us in the future, is just silly: if an organisation is to operate successfully, such ideas must be open to change and revision as problems are discovered. This is something that will happen routinely in business, where there is constant feedback in terms of the profitability of different ventures. Non-commercial organisations have also, in recent years, adopted all kinds of fads in the name of learning from the private sector. I have suggested[3] that what they really need is to devise ways in which they can submit their operations to feedback – in terms not only of whether or not they are accomplishing their goals, but also of whether and how their goals should be revised – in a manner that simulates (but in a manner appropriate to the sector in which they are operating) the kind of feedback that business receives from information about its profitability.

It is also important that arguments made to government and the public service be made as far as possible in the public forum. There may, clearly, be cases in which a business makes points to government, the disclosure of which would be commercially damaging, or in which individuals raise issues that may be problematic for the privacy of themselves or others. But if arguments are advanced in secret, it may be very difficult to tell the difference between a telling argument and special pleading. More generally, it is worth noting that in the current Australian system, the substance of government business is the work of the public service and the most senior politicians, and that it faces little effective political scrutiny. Given that even the very best people are fallible, and that it is by no means obvious that our politicians and public servants represent the best minds in Australia, it would seem important to look quite radically at ways of opening up all governmental decision making to critical scrutiny. Currently, as ministers do not even pretend to be accountable for what their departments do, it would seem important to consider ways in which the assumptions and ideas that guide the public service might be opened up to serious critical scrutiny of a constructive and responsible character. When I have made this point to people who are knowledgeable about such matters, attempts have been made to reassure me that such criticism and scrutiny takes place within the public service (and, implicitly, within the elite with whom they engage). But this seems to me exactly the problem: that the scrutiny is closed and undertaken only by insiders, rather than open.

Politicians also need to take seriously the fact that pertinent knowledge is disaggregated right through society. In part, this may include knowledge of what is wrong with their own proposals – knowledge in which they should be interested. In part, it is knowledge about how things are best done. This is important to consider, for the following reason. Government and the public service clearly may become aware of problems that are not known to the rest of us. In addition, they may have to take specific decisions in the face of them – for example, by adopting one particular proposal, or set of conventions, rather than another. It is important, when they do this, that they minimise the extent to which they end up telling other people what to do. It may be claimed that they need to tell other people what to do in order to address a specific problem. But, first, this claim should, itself, be open to critical scrutiny. Second, if the problem is real, then it is perfectly reasonable to require that measures must be put in place to avoid it, and examples might be given as to how this could be done (in case people don't know how to do it). But the public service are a small number of people, and the degree to which they – or the sources that they consult – can be informed about the myriad of things that take place in Australia, is severely limited. Thus we may find that we are told what to do by people who it is often perfectly clear have no idea whatever as to what the best way to do things is, in the areas that they are regulating.

It is also worth bearing in mind the advantages of making use, not of regulations, but of law, and, indeed, of law that develops through the common law system. Such a system can respond to particular cases as they arise. In addition, it gives people general rules with which they need to comply, making use of their own knowledge, rather than attempting to tell them, in detail, what to do.

Australia has a reputation for innovation and, in general, for performing in many fields well above its weight. It is a country that is full of ingenious and interesting (if sometimes awkward) people, who, between us, know an incredible amount. If the country is to prosper and to work well, it needs to make use of everyone's knowledge. In my view, a key message that needs to be taken on board by our leaders is that they are not Platonic guardians who know everything, and whose task is simply to regulate the rest of us ever more firmly. Rather, they – and also, crucially, our public servants – are just like the rest of us, and are just as fallible. What we really need, in all organisations and above all in government, is to take the issue of the social division of knowledge seriously, to learn from anyone who can correct us where we have got things wrong, and to give people space to make use of their own specialised knowledge, in order to innovate and thus to really show that Australia can be a clever country.

---

1. Popper, K, 1945, *The open society and its enemies*, Routledge & Kegan Paul, London.
2. Read, L, 1958, 'I, pencil: my family tree as told to Leonard E. Read', *The Freeman*, December, http://en.wikisource.org/wiki/I,_Pencil.
3. Shearmur, J, 2000, 'The Use of Knowledge in Organizations', *Knowledge, Technology, & Policy*, Fall, 13(3), pp. 30–48.

Australia's unresolved war crimes challenge

Tim McCormack

Tim McCormack is professor of law, Melbourne Law School, adjunct professor of law, the University of Tasmania and special adviser on international humanitarian law to the prosecutor of the International Criminal Court in The Hague. He was an international observer during phase two of the Turkel Commission of Enquiry into Israel's Processes for Investigation of Alleged War Crimes (Jerusalem, 2011–13). He served as an expert law of war adviser to Major Michael Mori for the defence of David Hicks before the US Military Commission (Guantanamo Bay, 2003–07) and as amicus curiae on international law issues for the trial of the former Serbian President, Slobodan Milosevic (The Hague, 2002–06).

Tim was the foundation director of the Asia Pacific Centre for Military Law (2001–10) and foundation Australian Red Cross Professor of International Humanitarian Law (1996–2010) – both at the Melbourne Law School.

Despite allegations of there being war criminals among many ethnic communities immigrating to Australia from situations of protracted and violent armed conflict, successive Australian governments of both political persuasions have refused to allocate resources to a proactive investigative process that may lead to criminal prosecutions in Australia. There are many practical reasons to explain the aversion to such a policy, but those practicalities did not stop the Hawke government taking a bold initiative in 1987 to establish the Special Investigations Unit (SIU) within the Commonwealth Attorney-General's Department. On the basis of SIU investigations, the Commonwealth director of public prosecutions initiated criminal proceedings against three individuals in South Australia in the early 1990s. None of those proceedings resulted in a conviction and, ever since, attempts to encourage subsequent governments to recommit to a similar policy have failed. The author argues for a renewed proactive policy decision, while acknowledging the counter-arguments. In doing so he draws out the complexity of choices that one may be called upon to make in political life.

Laws can embody standards; governments can enforce laws – but the final task is not a task for government. It is a task for each and every one of us. Every time we turn our heads the other way when we see the law flouted – when we tolerate what we know to be wrong – when we close our eyes and ears to the corrupt because we are too busy, or too frightened – when we fail to speak up and speak out – we strike a blow against freedom and decency and justice.

—Robert F Kennedy

War criminals among us?

Australia's multicultural experiment has been remarkably successful. Wave after wave of migrants from overseas have made their home here. We enthusiastically embrace food, music and culture and we readily tolerate linguistic and religious diversity from all over the world. I consider myself fortunate to live in the inner Melbourne suburb of Brunswick in close physical proximity to Sydney Road, and I revel in its many manifestations of ethnic diversity – Greek, Italian, Lebanese, Egyptian, Cypriot, Turkish, Sub-Saharan African, Indian, Chinese, Japanese, Vietnamese, Thai – in restaurants, cafes, bars, clubs, supermarkets, grocers, shops. Within a radius of not more than three kilometres from my home, there are places of spiritual worship for Buddhists, Muslims and Christians of many denominations – Russian, Serbian and Greek Orthodox, Roman Catholic, Maronite, Coptic and Protestant of many types – and people are free to choose to worship or not as they see fit. Sydney Road and its environs may well be more ethnically diverse than many other parts of our nation, but for me it represents all that is positive about the way in which Australia has consistently accepted migrants from other countries.

Despite murmurings of latent racism in Australia, we have been mercifully free of the sort of inter-ethnic conflict that has so wracked other nations. However, if you scratch the surface of any ethnic community from a situation of protracted conflict (and there are many such communities – from Africa; the Middle East; Central and Eastern Europe; Central, South and South-East Asia; the Pacific; Latin America) you soon discover allegations that some within the communities are responsible for war crimes, crimes against humanity or genocide, and yet are enjoying their new lives in Australia with apparent impunity for past atrocities.

Imagine the East Timorese father of two young soccer-mad boys who, like so many other parents around the country, drives his kids to training twice a week at the local junior soccer club and sees the coach of one of the other club teams taking training of his squad. The coach is also from East Timor, and the soccer dad knows that the coach was a member of one of the pro-integrationist militia responsible for destroying the East Timorese village of the soccer dad's sister and her family. The sister was raped and her family murdered in front of her eyes and she is a shadow of her former self. Every time the soccer dad sees the coach, he wonders whether it was the coach himself who wrecked his sister's life. He sees the coach laughing with his players and wonders why he should be allowed to enjoy a comfortable life in Australia without ever being held accountable for his past wrongs.

Or imagine the Chilean woman who buys her meat from the local Spanish-speaking Argentinean butcher because he prepares her family's favourite spiced sausages and because his meat is always fresh and of good quality. But every few weeks she finds herself in the same butcher's shop as a former member of General Pinochet's secret military police who was part of a death squad that brutalised the woman's extended family because they were supporters of the ousted Allende regime. The woman hears the other customer speaking politely to the butcher, asking him about his family, and she has to walk out of the shop and come back later because she feels sick to her core at the hypocrisy of his humanity.

These scenarios are, of course, fictional, but indicative of compounded trauma experienced by many newer Australians on an all too regular basis.

Consider some extensions to the hypotheticals for a moment. What if you happened to be the local member of parliament and some within your electorate raised allegations similar to those above? Imagine that you have a sizeable ethnic community within your electorate and members of that community are pleading with you not to remain indifferent to the allegations of war criminals among the community. What actions might you be willing to take in support of your local electorate? What if the allegations are against otherwise respected leaders within the community? What if the group agitating for action is seen as a 'splinter' group within the community – a divisive influence on otherwise harmonious community relations? At what point do pragmatic issues cloud or dilute what might otherwise appear to be clear-cut issues of principle?

Arguments for and against inaction

One common and entirely understandable response to this dilemma is to argue that the Australian multicultural experiment has been successful, at least in substantial part, precisely because ethnic communities from conflict situations have left their conflicts in their countries of origin and have not transported them to Australia. During the 1990s and the shocking conflicts in the Balkans, for example, the Australian Serb, Croat, Bosnian Muslim, Kosovar Albanian and Macedonian communities worked hard to avoid an eruption of inter-ethnic violence here. Australian citizens of one or other ethnic descent travelled back to the Balkans and participated in the fighting with their ethnic group but inter-ethnic tension here was suppressed. There have been moments of significant tension – for instance at the Australian Tennis Open and in some of the soccer matches involving teams established and maintained by particular ethnic communities. The establishment of the A-League was, in part, driven by a desire to dismantle the traditional ethnic community-based soccer allegiances, and that initiative seems to have been successful, with the focus of allegiance, support and recruitment shifting from ethnic identity to physical location and strong team building.

But a counter argument can also be mounted. Successive Australian governments of either political persuasion have consistently supported initiatives for global justice on the basis that some atrocities are so egregious, so repugnant to any notion of human decency, that to allow them to go unchallenged is not only unpalatable but also unacceptably unprincipled. Why would we support the establishment and ongoing work of international criminal courts and tribunals but refuse to pursue the prosecution of war criminals before Australian courts?

Australian experience of war crimes trials – 1940s and 1990s

In the immediate aftermath of World War II, Australia seconded Justice Sir William Webb, formerly of the Supreme Court of Queensland and then of the High Court, to preside over the Tokyo War Crimes Trial, because of our national commitment to accountability through law for wartime atrocity. The Tokyo Tribunal was the Pacific equivalent of the Nuremberg Tribunal for senior Nazi leaders in Europe. Both the Tokyo and the Nuremberg Tribunals were established by the victorious Allied Powers to try the most senior political, military and business leaders from the defeated Axis powers. While the Tokyo Trial was being conducted against 28 senior Japanese military and political leaders (excluding the Emperor himself, much to Webb's and the Australian government's disgust), thousands of so-called 'subsidiary' trials were conducted by various Allied nations against lower-ranking German and Japanese military personnel. In our case, Australian military courts established pursuant to the *War Crimes Act* 1945 conducted 300 trials of more than 820 Japanese for war crimes perpetrated against Australian and other Allied prisoners of war as well as against local civilian populations. Three trials were conducted in Darwin and the rest in New Guinea (190 trials in Rabaul and 35 on Manus Island), Borneo, Singapore and Hong Kong. This extensive war crimes trial experience is still little known in Australia, and yet it continued until 1951 – significantly later than all other Allied trials. Ultimately, both the United States and the United Kingdom pressured Canberra to discontinue the trials because both Washington and London considered that the time for criminal accountability had passed and that it was more important to begin rebuilding relationships with Germany and with Japan.

Australia's trials of Japanese were largely for atrocities perpetrated against Australian prisoners of war. The next Australian experience of war crimes trials involved atrocities perpetrated overseas against non-Australian victims. In 1986, Mark Aarons, then an ABC investigative journalist, produced a radio program entitled *Nazis in Australia*, exposing the presence of hundreds of former Nazis who had migrated after the war. Aarons explained that some of the former Nazis had arrived in Australia by concealing their wartime involvement, but that others had been actively recruited by the Australian Security Intelligence Organisation (ASIO) for their expertise in intelligence gathering against the Soviet Union. For Australia, as for other Western nations with the onset of the Cold War, anti-communism was a higher priority than anti-fascism.

Aarons' exposé resulted in a Commonwealth Commission of

Enquiry headed by Andrew Menzies QC. The Menzies Report confirmed the allegations, identified hundreds of suspected Nazi war criminals in Australia and recommended both the establishment of a special task force to investigate the allegations and the enactment of legislation to enable the prosecution of Nazi war crimes. The Hawke government adopted the recommendations, established the Special Investigations Unit within the Commonwealth Attorney-General's Department and amended the War Crimes Act extending jurisdiction for Australian courts over war crimes committed in Europe between 1939 and 1945. Even though the atrocities under consideration were perpetrated externally to Australia by non-Australians against non-Australian victims, Prime Minister Bob Hawke and deputy Prime Minister and Attorney-General Lionel Bowen were both unwilling to allow Australia to become a 'safe haven' for Nazi war criminals. Speaking on the draft legislation, Lionel Bowen said:

> [W]here there is evidence of serious war crimes being committed during World War II and there being no punishment of the offenders, the Government has a duty statement [sic] to ensure that justice is done, no matter how long since the events in question have passed. Accordingly, the War Crimes Amendment Bill 1987 is designed to ensure that any serious criminal activities committed in the course of World War II, the commission of which is established beyond a reasonable doubt, by persons who are now residents or citizens of Australia, will not go unpunished. … [T]he basic scheme contained in the Bill for the prosecution of persons alleged to have committed war crimes during World War II involves selecting the most serious criminal acts encompassed within international law relating to war crimes and making them triable in our criminal courts in accordance with the normal rules, procedures and standards applying to our criminal trials. The Government believes that this approach provides the most comprehensive and efficacious answer yet devised anywhere in the world to the difficulties of prosecuting alleged war criminals in a jurisdiction other than that of the place where the alleged crimes were committed.

After years of complex investigative work in Australia and overseas, the Special Investigations Unit transferred files on four suspects to the Commonwealth Director of Public Prosecutions (DPP) recommending that the DPP lay charges. The DPP initiated criminal proceedings against three accused: Ivan Polyukhovich, Mikolay Berezowski and Heinrich Wagner. The cases against Berezowski and Wagner both terminated at committal stage (insufficient evidence to warrant a trial in the case of Berezowski and withdrawal of charges on the grounds of the ill-health of the accused in the case of Wagner), and only the case against Polyukhovich actually went to trial. Before the trial commenced, Polyukhovich's lawyers challenged the constitutional validity of the amended War Crimes Act in the High Court. One of Polyukhovich's arguments was that the legislation offended the presumption against retrospective criminal law. The majority of the High Court disagreed and distinguished retrospective criminalisation of conduct not criminal at the time it was committed (which is prohibited) from the granting of retrospective jurisdiction to Australian courts over conduct unquestionably criminal at the time it was committed (which is permitted). The amended War Crimes Act fell into the permitted category because the conduct had to have constituted a violation of: (1) international law at the time it was committed; and also (2) Australian domestic criminal law at the time it was committed if hypothetically the conduct had been committed in Australia.

The trial against Polyukhovich proceeded and despite the accused's unsuccessful suicide attempt during the proceedings, the trial was completed and the jury returned a not guilty verdict. Almost 50 years after the alleged atrocities, the prosecution was unable to adduce sufficient admissible evidence to prove the case against the accused. The government's reaction to the failure to secure a single conviction was to close down the SIU and to terminate any further efforts to investigate and prosecute former Nazis in Australia.

A limited reactive approach

In the years since, successive Australian governments have refused to take a proactive approach to alleged war criminals in Australia. Instead, action has only been taken reactively in two limited sets of circumstances.

The first involves applicants for refugee status. Article 1F(a) of the 1951 UN Refugees Convention, replicated in s. 36(2C)(a)(i) of Australia's *Migration Act 1958*, denies the protection of the convention to those for whom 'there are serious reasons for considering that' they have 'committed a crime against peace, a war crime or a crime against humanity'. In the course of interviews by officials of the Department of Immigration and Border Protection to determine whether or not the applicant faces a well-founded fear of persecution if returned to their country of origin, from time to time the applicant describes their involvement in a particular organisation or arm of government that leads the administrative decision maker to the view that Article 1F applies and that the applicant is not entitled to refugee status. Sometimes the applicant appeals the decision. Most appeals against refugee status decisions are heard by the Refugee Review Tribunal but, by quirk of legislation, appeals against adverse Article 1F findings are heard by the Administrative Appeals Tribunal. In most years there are at least one or two AAT decisions on Article 1F appeal cases.

The Article 1F exclusion process is certainly not an exhaustive mechanism for identifying those who should not be welcomed in Australia. Some individuals responsible for atrocities are caught by this process and deported but many are not. Administrative decision makers from the Department of Immigration and Border Protection are not criminal investigators and, even if they had such skills, this process only ever deals with applicants for refugee status and not those arriving in Australia under other migration categories.

The second reactive mechanism is in response to extradition requests from other countries. Australia has only received three requests for extradition in relation to alleged war crimes, crimes against humanity or genocide. None of the three individuals involved have actually been extradited.

In the first of the three cases, Konrad Kalejs was the subject of an extradition request from Latvia in 2000. The Latvian authorities alleged that Kalejs had been a senior figure in the infamous Arajs Kommando and responsible for World War II atrocities against the Latvian Jewish community. Kalejs had migrated to Australia in 1950 and subsequently acquired citizenship but had later lived overseas. He had already been deported from the United States and from Canada and had also been threatened with deportation from the United Kingdom – all in relation to his World War II activities. A Melbourne magistrate found that Kalejs could be extradited to Latvia but, in late 2001, while his legal representatives were appealing that decision, Kalejs died and proceedings against him were terminated.

More recently, Charles Zentai was the subject of an extradition request from Hungary in 2005 in relation to an alleged murder of a Jewish man in Budapest 1944. A Perth magistrate found that Zentai could be extradited but his lawyers appealed the decision. The High Court of Australia decided in 2012 that Zentai could not be extradited because the alleged offence – the war crime of murder – was not a criminal offence in Hungary in 1944 even though 'ordinary' murder clearly was a crime at the time. Zentai's extradition was avoided on the basis of a technicality. Had Hungary requested extradition for the domestic crime of murder and not for the war crime of murder, the extradition could have proceeded.

Many would consider the High Court decision nonsensical. Why should it matter what specific type of murder Hungary requested extradition for? It is a requirement of Australia's *Extradition Act* 1988 that the alleged offence that is the subject of the extradition request constitute a serious 'offence against the law of the [requesting] country', and the High Court chose to interpret that requirement narrowly. Given that Zentai is now 93 years of age,* it is highly unlikely that any new extradition proceedings will be initiated against him.

The third request was for the extradition of Dragan Vasiljkovic (aka Daniel Snedden) by Croatian authorities in 2006. Vasiljkovic is an Australian citizen of ethnic Serb descent who travelled back to the Balkans and allegedly led a Serb paramilitary group in the conflict with Croatian forces in and around the Knin region of Croatia. He has also been involved in a protracted court battle to challenge his extradition. Vasiljkovic lost a High Court appeal against extradition in 2010 and the minister for justice, with final discretion in the matter, determined in November 2012 that Vasiljkovic would be extradited. Shortly before going to press,† an appeal against the Minister's decision was rejected by the Full Federal Court, and it was not known whether his lawyers will seek leave to appeal to the High Court.

* As at 1 January 2015.

† This was the situation as at 1 January 2015 (ed.)

Australia's reluctance to conduct trials

None of Australia's responses to these instances are satisfactory. The notion that the Australian government only acts in response to specific information gleaned from an interview to determine eligibility for refugee status or that it only acts in response to a specific request for extradition (especially given that there have only been three such requests in 13 years) is problematic.

The case of Dragan Vasiljkovic is particularly enlightening. In the cases of Konrad Kalejs and of Charles Zentai, it can at least be argued that neither was an Australian citizen at the time of the alleged offence. Both of them immigrated to Australia after the conclusion of World War II and were subsequently wanted by their countries of origin for alleged war-time atrocities. The same cannot be said for Dragan Vasiljkovic. He was an Australia citizen who travelled from this country back to the Balkans and contributed to the war effort in Croatia. How could successive Australian governments of both political persuasions not take more seriously the importance of trying Vasiljkovic here? If the Australian authorities will not try an Australian citizen for alleged international crimes perpetrated in a foreign country, what possible hope is there that they might be prepared to try a foreign national for similar alleged offences?

I am convinced that there is more to the Australian reluctance to conduct contemporary war crimes trials than simply the 'don't bring the conflict to Australia' argument outlined above. After the disappointments of the 1990s, the prevailing view seems to be that Australian investigations and trials of alleged war crimes perpetrated overseas are expensive, complicated and of limited national benefit. Surely the more appropriate physical location for war crimes trials is in the country where the crimes were perpetrated. Quite apart from the logistical issues of accessing crimes sites, securing forensic evidence, identifying witnesses and obtaining relevant documentary material, the victims of atrocity should be able to follow trial proceedings and see that justice is being done. These are all compelling arguments. But not every country where atrocities are perpetrated is willing or in a position to request extradition of those allegedly responsible – particularly where the relevant government is either itself the alleged perpetrator of the atrocities or has ceased to function effectively. The country where the crime(s) occurred may be incapable of guaranteeing a fair trial or of conducting trial proceedings transparently and with guaranteed security for trial personnel – for judges, prosecutors, defence lawyers and the accused themselves. If the country where the crimes occurred is always the best physical location for trials, why does the international community need an International Criminal Court in The Hague?

But the combination of expense, complications and limited national benefit, strengthened by the view that we risk stoking inter-communal ethnic tensions here by undertaking war crimes trials against one side or the other, produces a potent aversion to trials. Once the Australian government committed resources to the investigation of alleged war criminals in our midst, where would the process ever end? Every time a new wave of immigrants arrives in Australia from a situation of protracted armed conflict there will be some among that community allegedly responsible for atrocities in the country of origin. So the numbers grow and the scale, the sheer magnitude, of the task becomes increasingly overwhelming. Who wants to tackle that sort of problem? Whenever an individual was charged with alleged offences the criticism would be intense: Why him and not these others? Why someone from that party to the conflict when we all know that this other party was engaged in far more routine atrocities? This is not justice – this is a politically motivated witch-hunt singling out individuals from just one side of a complex and protracted conflict! Add to the mix of arguments against initiating trials the additional reality that there are no electoral votes in pursuing Australian war crimes trials (in an era of hyper-political sensitivity to electoral concerns), and the orthodoxy of the status quo appears virtually unassailable.

The pragmatics of a multi-faceted argument against Australian trials may be overwhelming but they are not the entire story – there are also important counter-issues of principle. My refusal to accept the inevitability of the status quo is about the sort of Australia I want to live in and the sort of nation with which I want to identify. My preference is that these issues are discussed and debated publicly, even if the majority of Australians disagree with the position I advocate here. It is inherent in an informed civic dialogue that others will disagree with the position one takes and it is a distinct possibility that challenging orthodoxy fails to produce policy change. I accept that possibility, but I find the lack of informed discussion disappointing, and I wonder whether or not the orthodoxy prevails because it represents an easier 'line of least resistance' rather than a reasoned policy preference.

From those who prefer not to try foreign war crimes in Australia, I would want to know why victims of overseas atrocities should be forced to observe the perpetrators of those atrocities living freely among us. Why should Australia be satisfied with a global reputation for inaction in the face of recurrent allegations of war crimes? Canada, for example, has taken a far more proactive stance in the face of similar allegations. The Canadians have a national investigative authority that follows through on allegations of international crimes perpetrated overseas by some who have come to live in Canada. In recent years the Canadians have tried Rwandan nationals as well as some who have come to Canada from the Balkans. The Canadian experience has demonstrated that the concept of war crimes trials is feasible and beneficial.

It seems to me that there is a certain level of hypocrisy in unwavering Australian support for global criminal justice in multilateral forums unmatched by any willingness to proactively investigate allegations of war crimes at home – to assert in New York or The Hague that some crimes are so egregious as to constitute an affront to all of humanity but then, in the absence of an extradition request, to conveniently ignore allegations of similar crimes against a person living comfortably in Glenorchy, in Newtown or in West Torrens.

Several like-minded colleagues and I have met with successive Australian Commonwealth attorneys-general for several years now to push the case for proaction and for political commitment to investigation and trial here. Two principal concerns are raised on a recurrent basis. The first involves the prohibition on retrospective criminalisation of conduct that was not unlawful at the time of its conduct. Our consistent response is to cite the High Court decision in *Polyukhovich v. The Commonwealth*. To the extent that any new legislation might be necessary to cover gaps in Australia's existing war crimes law, we already have an important High Court precedent in support of constitutional validity where the relevant conduct was a crime at international law at the time it was perpetrated and would have constituted a crime under Australian law had it been perpetrated here. The second recurrent concern is to know what our major Commonwealth partners – the United Kingdom, Canada and New Zealand – have already done in relation to the same issue.

Again, we have assured the attorneys that all three other nations have enacted legislation granting their respective courts jurisdiction retrospectively over offences that unquestionably constituted violations of international law at the time the acts were committed. One recent attorney went so far as to concede that he was 'almost persuaded' of the merits of Australian proaction to investigate allegations of foreign war crimes.

The stumbling block is not some legal impediment to a more proactive stance. The real issue is the combination of practical challenges and political pragmatics identified earlier. Imagine this time that you are not just a local member with a particularly aggrieved constituency but that you are also the Commonwealth – a member of cabinet with real political influence over this particular issue that falls squarely within your portfolio. How hard would you push in response to a visit from a delegation of concerned individuals keen to see policy change on this issue? Would you be willing to argue the case for a change of policy in cabinet despite the fact that some of your colleagues will not agree with you and will see the initiative as a waste of scarce resources they would much rather see allocated to their own portfolios? What if the president of the foreign country in question is due to make a state visit to Australia next month, and action is deemed likely to introduce a sour note at a sensitive time in the development of the bilateral relationship? Would you be able to summon the energy to confront criticism and outright hostility that will inevitably follow – including, perhaps, from influential circles among traditional supporters of your own political party? How would you feel when having taken a principled, just decision you are nevertheless accused of taking sides, and your motives are misrepresented? Would it simply be easier to take a more convenient, less provocative, route to avoid trouble?

Conclusion

Perhaps I am naive and overly idealistic but I yearn for the kind of political leadership that commits to policy because it is right to do so and because it is in Australia's national interest. That can and does happen from time to time: gun control and the disability insurance scheme are just two examples from opposite sides of the political divide.

I would prefer more and not less of that.

Critical policy challenges for Australia

Mark Butler

Mark Butler was elected to federal parliament in 2007 representing the electorate of Port Adelaide. His career in parliament has so far included: Parliamentary Secretary for Health; Minister for Mental Health and Ageing; Minister for Social Inclusion; Minister assisting the Prime Minister on Mental Health Reform; Minister for Housing and Homelessness; Minister for Climate Change, Environment, Heritage and Water. Since the 2013 federal election he has been the Shadow Minister for the Environment, Climate Change and Water.

Before entering parliament, Mark worked for 15 years in the Liquor Hospitality and Miscellaneous Union (LHMU), including 11 years as state secretary, and was awarded the Centenary Medal in 2003 for services to trade unionism. In 1997, Mark was elected president of the Australian Labor Party (ALP) in South Australia, and has been a member of the ALP National Executive and National Executive Committee since 2000. He has also served as a member of several government and private sector boards including the South Australian Social Inclusion Board and the South Australian Tourism Commission.

Mark holds a first-class honours law degree, an arts degree and a masters degree in international relations. He lives in the western suburbs of Adelaide with his wife and two children, and is a keen supporter of the AFL team Port Power.

The best political leaders are able not just to deal with daily functions of the job but to lift their gaze to focus on long-term, strategic challenges. Australia faces two such challenges.

First, the ageing of the baby boomer generation significantly affects the age dependency ratio (the number of working-age Australians [15–64 years] relative to the number over 65) and carries obvious revenue and spending implications that have been a concern of treasurers on both sides of politics. But we should resist the temptation to characterise ageing as a problem or a burden to be borne. Older Australians are volunteering, studying, travelling and trying new things as never before. We should rediscover our cultural respect for age, and recognise the contribution older people are making in building the society we enjoy.

Second, climate change – due largely to the release of greenhouse gases into the atmosphere through the burning of fossil fuels – is already having significant effects on Australia, affecting, for example, the Great Barrier Reef and many communities along the Murray–Darling Basin. Ultimately, this is a global policy challenge. Recent developments in China and the United States – the two biggest emitters – offer hope that in the next few years critical progress will be made in establishing a global commitment to avoiding the most dangerous levels of climate change.

To err is human, to forgive divine.

—Alexander Pope

Exercising leadership in any field is a privilege and a great responsibility. Each generation of leaders faces a new range of challenges and has a different set of tools at its disposal, but the fundamental elements of good leadership essentially stay the same from generation to generation. This is especially the case for national political leadership.

Political leadership is both a vocation and a calling. It's a vocation in that, like other jobs, it has a set of daily functions and responsibilities to manage. And it's a calling in that it also requires you to lift your gaze from those daily tasks and focus on longer-term strategic challenges. The best political leaders are able to juggle these two facets of the job, especially during periods of transition for the nation.

Every so often, our society experiences a seismic shift that shakes our political, economic and social foundations and profoundly changes the nation. In the mid 1940s, a young generation scarred by the deprivation of the Great Depression and the horrors of World War II demanded a new social compact that would guarantee them a fair share of the nation's wealth. This led to a raft of new social service programs. Twenty-five years later their children demanded a social dividend from the post-war prosperity, leading to a profound shift in how we viewed gender, race, sexuality and relationships.

The early part of the 21st century presents a number of challenges and opportunities on a similar scale. In many ways, Australia is well-positioned to continue as one of the most liveable countries on the face of the earth. We are a wealthy nation in our 22nd consecutive year of recession-free economic growth – a record never before achieved by a major advanced economy. We enjoy a tolerant, multicultural society, with cities that are consistently rated as the world's most liveable, and some of the most spectacular rural and regional areas anywhere. We are situated in the region that will drive the 21st century more than any other – and, like the rest of the world, we continue to reap the benefits of the ever-expanding Information and Communications Technology (ICT) revolution.

Political leadership in coming decades in Australia will, however, be significantly framed by two great transitions in our society – ageing and climate change.

Ageing

To ageing first! The ageing of our society is obviously a slower phenomenon than other historical transitions – but its impact will be pervasive, profound and enduring, to paraphrase the United Nations. The average age of a community is affected by birth rates and immigration, but the major driver of an increase in the median age for most societies has been longer life expectancy.

Thomas Hobbes famously described human life in the absence of civil society as 'solitary, poor, nasty, brutish and short'. And such has been the lot of man and woman since the day we crawled out of the cave. But in the developed world at least, that all changed last century.

One hundred years ago, the average Australian died in their mid to late 50s. Premature death was largely caused by infectious diseases like tuberculosis, influenza, hookworm and others that are nowadays largely unknown in Australia. Public health measures to control the spread of disease and the discovery of antibiotics brought these rates down dramatically. In the post-war decades, premature death was caused more by an increase in circulatory disease, reflecting the fact that in the 1950s and 1960s fully three-quarters of Australian men were daily smokers. Again, public health programs (to quit smoking) and new medicines brought these death rates down dramatically – by three-quarters for males and two-thirds for females since the 1960s.

This outstanding public health policy and medical research has added around 25 years to average life expectancy – something the

World Health Organization describes as 'one of humanity's greatest triumphs'. In and of itself, however, this only partly explains what's happening in Australian society. The game changer for Australia and many other nations is the ageing of the baby boomer generation. This generation was born in the two decades following World War II when the total fertility rate peaked at 3.5 children per woman in 1961 (almost twice their current level of 1.88 children per woman). The oldest of the baby boomers turned 65 in 2011. Prior to 2011, about 40–50,000 Australians turned 65 each year. From 2011 onwards, that number will be in the order of 120–140,000 each year, an increase of around 200 per cent. Over the years to 2050, the share of Australia's population over the age of 65 will climb from 13 per cent to 23 per cent – or, in absolute numbers, from three million to nine million.

The most significant policy challenge that flows from this phenomenon is known as the age dependency ratio – the number of working-age Australians (15–64 years) relative to the number over 65. That ratio declined from 7.5 in 1970 to 5 in 2010, and is likely to reach as low as 2.5 in 2050.

Under both treasurers Peter Costello and Wayne Swan, the Commonwealth Treasury has assessed the obvious revenue and spending implications of this shift in the age dependency ratio, in regular Intergenerational Reports (IGRs), projecting to 2050. Commonwealth spending on older Australians largely falls into the areas of the age pension, aged care and healthcare, the last obviously covering the whole population but increasing rapidly after age 65. The IGR projects that spending in these areas to 2050 will increase from around 7.5 per cent of gross domestic product (GDP) to over 12.5 per cent – an increase of about $75 billion per year in today's dollars. And this will occur at the same time we see a shrinking of the taxpayer base.

These changes will pose a profound challenge to Australia's capacity to maintain overall living standards – as well as to our common views about intergenerational equity. Fortunately, Australia is better placed than many other nations to deal with this, thanks to the introduction of a universal superannuation system more than 20 years ago. But we have also had to examine some expanded scope for seniors to make contributions to the cost of their aged care where they have the capacity to do so.

This demographic shift will shape federal budgets for decades to come. Achieving a sustainable budget position while delivering strong social services will require deep strategic thinking and a number of tough decisions by future political leaders.

But it will also be important that political leaders (and others in the community) resist the temptation to characterise the ageing of our population as simply a question of budget maths. As the Minister for Ageing for three years, I regularly came across people (especially in the media) who characterised ageing as a problem, a burden, or even something we should 'fix'. It's important that political leaders promote the many positive consequences for our community that flow from Australians living longer.

For the individual, living longer allows you to live a third life that was unimaginable for most of human history. After the busiest years of their life at work and raising families are behind them, older Australians are volunteering, studying, travelling and trying new things like never before. Australian business is now starting to realise that a large, relatively wealthy and healthy generation in retirement is a hugely attractive customer and client base. More broadly, though, Australian society has much to gain from tapping into the wisdom and experience of its seniors. In some ways, this will require a shift in mindset to rediscover our cultural respect for age – to recognise the contribution older Australians made in building the society we now enjoy, rather than too often signalling that they are regarded more as a burden.

People interested in helping frame Australia's economic and social policy in the future must get their heads around the complex challenges and opportunities associated with ageing. That will engage the day-to-day management skills of those leaders as well as their capacity for long-term strategic thinking.

Climate change

Similar challenges and opportunities flow from climate change. There is no area of public policy in Australia that is more complex or controversial. The science is enormously detailed and the range of policy responses extremely challenging. While most obviously an environmental issue, climate change will also dramatically challenge our economic and social policy settings. But perhaps the most pressing challenge is to reach a common level of understanding about what, if anything, is actually happening to the climate. In Australia, this has been especially difficult in recent years. As a former Minister for Climate Change, I should be transparent and state early that I accept the overwhelming view of climate scientists, 97 per cent of them according to the US National Aeronautics and Space Administration (NASA), that the earth is warming due in large part to the release of greenhouse gases into the atmosphere through our burning of fossil fuels and changes in land use.

When I began reading about climate change 10–15 years ago, the discussion about its actual impact tended to focus decades into the future. In more recent times, we've come to understand that we are already seeing the impact across the world.

Australia is still recovering from the end of the worst drought in 100 years, a drought that ended a few years ago but whose effects are still felt by so many communities along the Murray–Darling Basin. Average temperatures in Australia are about 0.9 degrees warmer than a century ago. The calendar year 2013 was the hottest calendar year on record here in Australia. Our Bureau of Meteorology (BOM) had to add a new colour to their weather chart, the colour purple, to indicate temperatures over 50 degrees Celsius. And globally, NASA tells us that 13 of the hottest years on record have occurred since 2000. Extreme weather events, as the scientists have predicted for years, are becoming more frequent and more intense. A few years ago, Australia experienced devastating fires across the country, but particularly in Victoria which, again, led the authorities to introduce a new level of fire warning beyond extreme because the conditions in Victoria were beyond anything they'd seen before.

In recent years we've had flooding much more regularly and more intensely than the historical average. In Queensland, particularly, we have had many more cyclonic events in recent years. Those cyclonic events have had the most direct and obvious consequences for communities living along the Queensland coast as well as on the Great Barrier Reef. The latest reef report card shows that the Great Barrier Reef is in a state of very serious distress, mainly because of decades of agricultural run-off and increased nitrogen loads that particularly cause the rapacious crown-of-thorns starfish to spawn. But the last few years of regular cyclonic activity and flooding, which lead to more sediment load being pushed onto the reef, have placed the reef in a very precarious position. The reef is also suffering from coral bleaching through the acidification of our oceans caused by the additional carbon dioxide in the atmosphere.

As well as this, the World Meteorological Organization has told us that ocean levels are rising now about twice as fast as they did on average across the 20th century. This is leading to far more significant storm surges inundating areas that have never been subject to flooding events before, most spectacularly seen in 2012 with the superstorm Sandy flooding New York's subways.

President Obama in his 2013 State of the Union address put it far better than I could when he said:

> Now, it's true that no single event makes a trend, but the fact is the 12 hottest years on record have all come in the last 15. Heatwaves, droughts, wildfires, floods – all are now more frequent and more intense. We can choose to believe that superstorm Sandy and the most severe drought in decades and the worst wildfires that some states have ever seen were all just a freak coincidence. Or we can choose to believe in the overwhelming judgement of science and act before it's too late.

It is generally accepted that strong and sensible action on climate change must be taken in concert with the rest of the world. Ultimately, this is a global environmental challenge. Equally, it's important that action taken in Australia places our industries in the strongest possible position to meet future challenges and opportunities.

On both counts, it's critical that we understand what the world's two biggest polluters and most important economies – the United States and China – intend to do in this area. In both countries, a significant shift in favour of decisive action is underway. What's been happening in China particularly gives me hope about the next phase of international climate negotiations.

In mid 2013, a comprehensive suite of policies was released by the Chinese leadership. The centrepiece of the new Chinese policies is a cap on energy emissions of about 400 billion tonnes of coal equivalent by 2015. What is perhaps more widely known is the Chinese leadership's decision to pilot seven emissions trading schemes, the first of which started in July 2013 in Shenzhen, a very significant economic centre with a population of about 10 million.

Overall these seven pilot emissions trading schemes will cover a population of more than 200 million people.

The Chinese leadership also recognised the need for a robust renewable energy effort to complement emissions trading schemes. A decade ago, China was not a significant player in renewable energy, except for hydro power. But the Chinese have made vast progress in wind and solar power over the last few years, working to a renewable energy target of 15 per cent by 2020. In 2012 China spent about US$67 billion on renewable energy projects, making it already the biggest renewables investor in the world by quite a significant margin. All of this – the idea of capping emissions in an economy that continues to grow at about 7 or 8 per cent per annum, moving to emissions trading schemes in areas that cover more than 200 million people, and a very significant push on renewable energy – constitutes nothing short of a seismic shift in what is now both the largest emitter of carbon dioxide pollution by quite a significant distance and a country that accounts for fully two-thirds of all of the growth since 2000 in global carbon dioxide emissions.

After years of gridlock on this question in the United States Congress, in 2013 President Obama also decided to enact a range of measures, particularly regulating the energy sector's emissions, to deliver on a commitment to reduce their emissions by 17 per cent on 2005 levels by 2020. And a number of US states, most notably California, the ninth largest economy in the world in its own right, have introduced an emissions trading scheme.

These actions by China and the United States follow the European Union, which has had an emissions trading scheme and strong renewable energy policies in place for a considerable time now. With that strong international foundation, the next few years will be critical in establishing a detailed global commitment to avoiding the most dangerous levels of climate change.

In Australia, I'm convinced that we too should put in place a model based on an emissions trading scheme and strong policies to support the growth of clean and renewable energy sources. An emissions trading scheme sets a legally binding limit on the amount of carbon pollution produced every year and then lets business work out the cheapest and most effective way to operate within that limit. A strong renewables policy requires a suite of approaches, centred around a renewable energy target (RET), which drives the electricity market in the direction of clean energy.

The politics of climate change in this country have been as hotly contested as anywhere in the world. It is hard to see that changing in the near future. But Australia's long-term national interest requires action today; and achieving a consensus to make that investment in our future demands strong political leadership.

In his essay for this book, Greg Rudd complains that major political parties have spent considerable resources seeking to implement inherently contradictory policies on climate change and that the parliament is not well equipped to work though these big debates to achieve a national consensus. While Mr Rudd's observations seem superficially attractive, the reality of our politics is that the really big discussions in Australia are often settled only after a long debate between the major parties.

This is what happened with the introduction of Medicare over a period of 20 years. At the end of that debate (essentially the 1993 election), it was understood that the community had decided to accept universal health insurance as part of our social fabric. The same argument could be made for the entrenching of the GST into our federal tax system, albeit over a shorter timeframe.

As messy as these processes might appear, it is sometimes only through an extended debate of the type we've seen around climate change that the nation eventually reaches a considered position about the issue.

I am convinced that the stars are aligning in a way they haven't for a very long time at a global level for the next phase of climate change negotiations to be ambitious and positive.

It is critical that Australia take to that negotiating table a credible climate change policy that reflects our responsibility to future generations of Australians, and our global responsibility as a rich country that emits a lot of carbon pollution to make serious change to the way in which we operate.

Conclusion

These two policy areas present complex and enduring challenges for Australia's future leaders, particularly in the political and policy-making arena. They require close attention to the daily management of the nation's economy and social services, as well as clear articulation of how Australia can continue to prosper in a period of such significant transition. The political leaders who are able to achieve this balance will have served their nation well.

About the author

Philip Crisp is a copyright and IT lawyer based in Canberra. He was a systems analyst on early legal information retrieval systems, then a copyright policy adviser, and eventually joined the Australian Government Solicitor where he became Special Counsel – Commercial. He developed a number of IT- and IP-related legal solutions for Commonwealth agencies. He also designed a copyright trading system, AEShareNet, under which around 30,000 registered training materials were accessible at much reduced transaction costs. His IP manual was, for about seven years, the most comprehensive source of guidance on Commonwealth IP management.

On retirement Philip had arguably done more than anyone to shape the way the Commonwealth manages its copyright.

Philip enjoys philosophy, carpentry, recreational mathematics, family history research, and occasional satirical writing for children in his extended family.